One Little Orchid
Mata Hari: A Marginal Voice

ONE LITTLE ORCHID

MATA HARI: A MARGINAL VOICE

SANUSRI BHATTACHARYA

Westphalia Press
An Imprint of the Policy Studies Organization
Washington, DC
2016

ONE LITTLE ORCHID | MATA HARI: A MARGINAL VOICE
All Rights Reserved © 2016 by Policy Studies Organization

Westphalia Press
An imprint of Policy Studies Organization
1527 New Hampshire Ave., NW
Washington, D.C. 20036
info@ipsonet.org

ISBN-10: 1-63391-430-5
ISBN-13: 978-1-63391-430-8

Cover and interior design by Jeffrey Barnes
jbarnesbook.design

Daniel Gutierrez-Sandoval, Executive Director
PSO and Westphalia Press

Updated material and comments on this edition
can be found at the Westphalia Press website:
www.westphaliapress.org

To my mother who endured in silence

Preface

It is apparently quite strange for someone having studied Philosophy for so long to take up a subject of historical importance; but being an amateur historian I have dared to venture into the realm primarily due to two reasons—my interest in spy stories and Mata Hari's claim to be an Indian. Therefore, this book should not be taken as a historical documentation. However, the most important reason probably lies in an incident of my adolescent days, which I would love to share with my readers. I remember one night in the early 1970s, when I had gone to see a local tent theater called *Vietnam* with my mother. The play had pertinently depicted the role of spies in the Vietnam War. While walking back home on that moonlit night with her, she told me about Mata Hari. I have lost my mother nearly 30 years back, and Mata Hari had somehow slipped out of my mind. In 2010 I had an opportunity to visit Holland. While searching the internet for some details about the country before my visit I stumbled on her name, and thus Mata Hari resurfaced in my life.

When I started reading her biography I curiously came across not only the story of an ambitious courtesan and a famous demimondaine of the early previous century, but the era that had actually been very important to the narrative. Colonialism had been playing a significant role in cultural exchange worldwide. European industrialization, the new feminist waves, misogyny, and the bourgeois beliefs of the day—all had played respective roles in her life story. I was amazed to notice many similarities between the European and Indian societies of that time, similarities in the social values, in the way women were treated by men, and also how religious racism engulfed human mind. For me Mata Hari's life is primarily a story of male domination, of women's oppression under the then patriarchal culture and in a thoroughly hypocrite bourgeois society, and her struggle to get freedom from enchainment. Her dancing had only been an expression of her emancipation. There is no dearth of Indian women of that time who had experienced similar plights. I have found some verses in the more than two millennia old *Manusmriti* or the

Code of Manu having striking parity with the Code of Napoleon, especially those in relation to women's social conduct, which had influenced the whole of European society during the nineteenth century and after years. For example, *Manusmriti* (9.3) says—"Her father protects her in childhood, her husband protects her in youth, and her sons protect her in old age; woman is never fit for independence." Napoleon believed that disorder would reign entirely in society if women came out of the state of dependency where they ought to remain. He also strongly believed that women are nothing but machines for producing children and that women's proper role in the society was being a wife. Similarly, *Manusmriti* (9.96) says that women are created to become mothers.

Victorian morality, that had its base in the Napoleonic Code, had equally affected the colonized Indian society. Like Napoleon most Indian men prefer to be acquainted with womanly woman and not with a sort of owl who would sit and talk serious matters with them. The social prejudice against Mata Hari is identical to that of any bold, assertive, and independent woman of that time in India. And strangely even today, mostly in suburban and rural India, women's ideal place in the society is still considered to be inside the house, ideal behavior unquestionable obedience to the social patriarchal norms, their ideal destiny marriage and child bearing. Women have perpetually been expected to be feeble, dependent, and to lack grey matter. The "two-sphere" social model is equally dominant in the Indian society as it had been in Europe. So, while reading about Mata Hari I could very well understand the ordeal that she had to go through and also her struggle to get out of it. She had been convicted as an enemy spy and was killed as a measure to purge the society of evil. It was due to the war situation in France that she had been thus eliminated. If there happened to be no war, even then she would have been the target of the French society that had taken much interest in her at her prime time. She had been a perfect example of "give the dog a bad name and hang him." France had deliberately done that to her. But why? I have tried to look for a reasonable answer to this question in the following chapters.

Mata Hari's life has intrigued many through the past century, and there is no dearth of her biographies to research from; but my chief constraint has been my lack of knowledge of French, German, and other European languages apart from English. Therefore, I had to base my study only on the English biographies. I would like to take this opportunity to thank all the authors who have toiled diligently to put together all the nuances of her life, especially Sam Waagenaar and Pat Shipman, through the eyes of whom I have first seen the "little orchid" Mata Hari. I have tried to travel through that epoch in order to collect every possible bit related to her story, and have enjoyed the journey immensely. I thank the UK government for declassifying important documents (1999) related to her case. I have benefited significantly from the uploaded information in the website during this work. I thank The Mata Hari Foundation of the Fries Museum (Leeuwarden), Bibliothèque nationale de France (Paris), Getty Images Media India Private Limited, and Alamy Images India for giving me the printing right of some of their copyright images for this book. Images have carefully been chosen that would enable the readers to have a clear idea about Mata Hari and her time. I thank my teacher Dr. Shefali Moitra from the core of my heart for her invaluable advices and her patience with me. I also mention my friend Dr. Ratna Munshi with gratitude for all her support.

It is however not the least easy to pick up the pen and assemble word after word in an effort to look for a long lost episode in history. Moreover, since anti-propaganda has built a wall of perception which is hard to demolish. But still I have tried to rebuild the story bit by bit, which mirrors the then society that had long been buried in our memory. I accept responsibility of all inaccuracies in this work.

West Bengal (India), 2016   Sanusri Bhattacharya

Contents

Preface..vii

Introduction: A Sketch of Life...xiii

Chapter 1: The Socio-Cultural Canvas of the Fateful Drama..................1

Chapter 2: The Persona—Margarethe/Mata Hari, Adam Zelle, and Rudolf MacLeod..33

Chapter 3: Why Paris?..71

Chapter 4: The Socio-Political Scenario in Europe.............................111

Chapter 5: The Scapegoat..141

Chapter 6: Miscarriage Of Justice...189

Conclusion: *Mata Hari Syndrome* Revisited.....................................241

Appendix A: Timeline of Margarethe/Mata Hari's Life.....................251

Appendix B: List of Mata Hari's Mistakes throughout Her Life.........255

Appendix C: Sketchy List of Mata Hari's Lovers and Patrons............261

Select Bibliography...263

Image Acknowledgements..275

Index...277

About the Author..289

Introduction
A Sketch of Life

In the summer of 1914, everything had suddenly started changing in Europe. On June 28, Austrian Archduke Francis Ferdinand was killed in Sarajevo along with his wife. Gavrio Prinzip, an 18-year-old student member of the Serbian Black Hand group, had shot them from close range. The fatal attack killed both in full view of a cheering and triumphal crowd. The horrible assassination had led to the July Crisis, eventually inflicting bitter battles involving almost all the countries of the world—either for the Triple Entente and against the Central powers or *vice versa*. Austria–Hungary's invasion of Serbia had been well planned, and the First World War had begun. As in any other war, common citizens of the combatant countries became the worst sufferers. The landscape in Europe had started changing rapidly due to the offenses in the following years from both sides. The Great War had started casting its impact on the world—nature, environment, people, economy, and culture—nothing had been spared. Fritz Stern wrote about the war: "The first calamity of the twentieth century, the Great War, from which all other calamities sprang." Regarding the impact of the war Christopher Clark wrote that the war had unleashed the demons of political disorder, extremism, and cruelty that disfigured the twentieth century. He added: "The conflict ... mobilized 65 million troops, claimed three empires, 20 million military and civilian deaths, and 21 million wounded."[1] Comparing with the war of 1870 John H. Cox wrote in the *New York Tribune* (August 23, 1914): "The war of forty-four years ago was child's play compared with the war at the present time."[2] Magnitude of devastation of the First World War has clearly been reflected through these comments, and the common people's plight therefore is not difficult to imagine.

The only person who could continue unperturbed by all of that was Mata

---

1 Christopher Clark, *The Sleepwalkers: How Europe Went to War in 1914*, 1.
2 John H. Cox, "Alsace Blighted by War Horrors," *New York Tribune*; August 23, 1914, 2.

Hari, the famous dancer and infamous woman of that era—infamous because inspite of being a woman she loved freedom, had challenged the male world by denying to adhere to the rules that had been set forth by the privileged sex, and because she had been arrested and executed by the French for being a notorious enemy spy during the First World War. There is no doubt about her being famous as a dancer, whether trained or not, but as regards to her being an infamous spy there is ample scope for re-evaluation. Pretty much has been written about whether she had actually been a spy or not, some concluding that she was indeed an enemy spy working for Germany having instrumented much harm to France and the people in wartime, including collective assassination (Thomas Coulson, Edouard Massard, George Ladoux, and others) in the Battle of Somme in 1916, and some of her biographers have defended her even with documentary proof claiming that she had never been a spy (Sam Waagenaar, Pat Shipman, Bernard Newman, Julia Wheelwright, and others). I personally prefer to side with the latter group, as I certainly find the former's allegations unfounded by reason and guided almost entirely by hearsay and prejudice. Even the juries and the judge of the military court, who had virtually been blind against her, had preferred to rely on unfounded sources while passing the judgment of her guilt, and of awarding death penalty to Mata Hari. The prosecution did not care to support her execution by conclusive evidence, which had been a glaring injustice as justice can never be delivered on the basis of insufficient evidence.

I wonder why—why did the French do injustice to her? It cannot arguably be true that they had been inexperienced or incompetent in their job. It becomes all the more hard even to imagine that all of them had lost their heads while dealing with the case of a once famous demimondaine. Therefore, for me the biggest question happens to be—why did the situation move to that extreme for her? It could undoubtedly be asserted that Mata Hari's court-martial and the subsequent death sentence was a grave miscarriage of justice on the part of France. But one becomes compelled to wonder what did go wrong for her? Alfred Dreyfus, arrested for treason and espionage in 1894 by the French army, had been lucky to have had stalwarts like Bernard Lazare, Émile Zola, and all the eminent republicans by his side to defend and eventually to save him from the firing squad by all means; but despite having enumerable lovers and acquaintances at the highest ranks of the society, Mata Hari had found no one to stand by her at the time of her deepest distress. Feminist movements had already been in the wake in France from the previous century, and eminent personalities like Dr. Madeleine Pelletier, Marguerite Durand, Natalie Clifford Barney, Nelly Roussel, and a few others had been working in the field to make the private as well as the public space more suited for women by defending equal rights for them in all the aspects of social life. Why did they not try to motivate the press in order to generate a public debate regarding her case? Was it only because she was being tried in a military court? Alfred Dreyfus, for that matter, had also been tried in a similar way, but that did not prevent the French media and the people in general to take sides firmly. France, and particularly Paris, had been the center stage for remarkable feminist movements of the Marquis de Condorcet, Etta Palm d'Aelders, Olympe de Gouges, and others since the eighteenth century, who had professed equal rights for women. Published in 1791 there had already been *The Declaration of the Rights of Women and the Female Citizen* in France, which gave equal rights to all the citizens—men and women alike. Moreover, Mata Hari was not even a French citizen since she had hailed from The Netherlands. Did she not have the right to fair trial?

Hence, the "why" question really haunts. Was it so that Mata Hari had been the only so-called spy apparently working for Germany? Certainly not. Did the French identify, capture, and punish those for whom she was accused of spying? Definitely not. During wartime it had been absolutely proper for the French to have suspected her as an enemy spy and even to have prosecuted her, but could the death sentence be justified by any means? Was there enough evidence to prove her guilty of enemy espionage beyond any doubt? Many of her biographers have detailed on the issue, and even after a century one is prompted to believe that virtually no justice, rather some kind of injustice had been delivered to her in the form of capital punishment, which took her life in the cold and foggy morning of October 15, 1917.

Search for the truth claims for looking back into her life from the early days—the backdrop of the colorful and sparkling existence that had been her own creation, which she enjoyed to the hilt, is primarily important, because that could help one to determine the persona of Mata Hari, which is especially significant to analyze her fate. She was born on August 7, 1876, as Margarethe Geertruida Zelle, the eldest child of a successful hatter, Adam Zelle, of the small town of Leeuwarden in northern

Holland. Her mother Antje Johannes van der Meulen was as usual a very gentle lady from an unprivileged and humble background, who loved to remain busy with her household chores perfectly suited to the traditional model of femininity in a bourgeois family of that era. Not much is known about her, only that she was born in Friesland at a place named Franeker in 1842 to Johannes Henderikus van der Meulen and Sjoukje Ymes Faber, and had married Adam Zelle in 1873. She had a choice for cultivated qualities, and Margarethe must have thus had it in her blood. Antje's diary of poetries[3] had remained with Margarethe for much long, even after her marriage with Rudolf MacLeod. However, besides owning a considerably big and fashionable hat shop Adam had also made successful investments in the oil industry, which gave him enough affluence to develop a great ego—he preferred to be called a "Baron," which shows his feudal mindset as well. His family had increased with the increase of his wealth—Antje gave birth to three boys (some of Margarethe's biographers wrote four)—Johannes Hendriks was born on November 26, 1878—2 years and a few months younger to Margarethe, (though unconfirmed, some said Antje gave birth to another boy called Jacob, who was born in 1880 and lived unto his mature age, had been married to Antje Brouwer, his son became a pastor in Leeuwarden), and the twins Arie Anne and Cornelis Coenraad, born on September 9, 1881—5 years younger to her.

Margarethe on the *bokkenwaagen* presented to her by Adam on August 7, 1882. (The Mata Hari Foundation, Fries Museum, Leeuwarden)

---

3   Russell Warren Howe wrote that it contained love poems written to her husband (Adam); *Mata Hari, The True Story*, 18; though according to Sam Waagenaar, Antje copied mostly religious poems in her diary, with the exception of one love poem; *The Murder of Mata Hari, 1964*, 21. I presume Waagenaar had been right.

A SKETCH OF LIFE

Adam Zelle had a good physique—he was tall and handsome. When King William III of The Netherlands had visited Leeuwarden in 1873 Adam was selected for the Mounted Guard of Honor as he had been a good rider, and in one of his rare paintings he was seen on a horse back in full uniform—Adam had got it painted by A. Martin,[4] the famous Dutch painter of his time, which had obviously decorated the Zelle's interior for quite some time. He was so conceited that later he had handed over the painting to the Fries Museum in Leeuwarden, because he must have thought that it had been a piece of artwork worth for preservation. From the very beginning that painting had hung in front of little Margarethe's eyes, and she had always admired the smart and handsome man (her father) in uniform. The love for uniform all through her life might have had the root in that painting of Adam. He had enough money to keep his family well and to afford good upbringing for his children. Especially for his gorgeously charming darling Margarethe who was sent to Miss Buys' school nearby on the Hofplein, where she had learnt impeccable manner, classic music, beautiful and elegant handwriting, along with French and other subjects. Due to such an exquisite upbringing she might have developed a liking for music and dance.

As the first child Margarethe had been pampered to all extremes by her father, who had presented her a goat-driven carriage on her sixth birthday. Goat carriages had been a common sight in many European homes—lower and upper classes alike—which were mainly used to carry children, but also to carry various household goods like milk, water, vegetables, etc. Those lightweight carriages had been a favorite with the European children in the nineteenth and the early twentieth centuries. When chubby-cheeked and gorgeously-dressed cute little Margarethe drove in that splendid carriage everyone in her town stared at the spectacular sight with awe. She was fondly called "an orchid among buttercups" by Adam, who often gifted her with expensive colorful dresses. Even at a much later date her friends from the school she went to recalled her charming looks and her wonderful fashionable dresses she had always been seen in. Margarethe was admired for all that and she enjoyed the attention very much. She was proud to be a daddy's girl and must have been thankful to her father for all that he had provided her. In January 1883, as Adam was earning well from his oil shares, and to satisfy his inflated ego, he had decided to take a beautiful bigger house at 28 Groote Kerkstraat

---

4 Waagenaar, *op. cit.*, 1964, 17.

in Leeuwarden. He was quite extravagant in his lifestyle and had been drawn to the "paraphernalia of gentility."[5] He loved to show off his wealth and status to the aristocrat community of the small town of Leeuwarden. The treatment Margarethe had received from Adam might have developed her passion for opulence, which she had pursued all through her life. Never did she tire from seeking luxury, not even in difficult times.

The Freudian theory of femininity seems to be pertinent to explore her psyche. Johannes had been born when Margarethe was just a 2 year plus toddler. According to psychoanalytical theories it is the defining stage in the development of gender and sexual identity for a woman. Seeing her brother with a penis, which she did not have and hence felt castrated, she might have developed a kind of penis envy, which had persisted into her adult life in the form of an unfettered attraction for men. I would like to link this to her "father fixation" as well, derived from a sort of Electra-complex,[6] due to which she had developed a nostalgic longing for man's love from a very young age. Little Margarethe had certainly developed this kind of attachment toward Adam as he was very good looking and used to pamper his daughter completely to her delight. With her father she felt like a princess, and it is quite normal that she would like to feel the same always. She had learnt from her father to think of herself as someone very special, and all through her life she wanted to "live like a butterfly under the sun"—free from all duties and responsibilities, free from all bondage and servitude.

Margarethe as a teenager
(The Mata Hari Foundation, Fries Museum, Leeuwarden)

---

5   Patricia Branca, *Silent Sisterhood*, 6.
6   Sigmund Freud, *On Sexuality*, 108; Jill Scott, *Electra after Freud: Myth and Culture*, 8; Sharon Heller, *Freud A to Z*, 94.

However, the contentment in Adam's life had not been long lasting. His failure of right speculations in the share market had resulted in his bankruptcy on February 18, 1889, and he had to declare his inability to pay off his loans. Due to his financial conditions he had to give up the big house, and leaving behind his poverty stricken family in Leeuwarden he had to go to The Hague in search of a better living. Margarethe was an adolescent teenager at that time, who had been forced into severe financial hardship as no longer did her father bring expensive gifts for her, no beautiful new dresses anymore, and a cheaper house to live in near the railway station and the cattle market on the Willemskade with her mother and three brothers. The children had been admitted to the Cammingha State School there, which matched in no way with Miss Buys' aristocratic school. Like Adam, Margarethe too loved to show off, but the newly developed untoward circumstances had prevented her from doing so. She was a pampered teenager with an extravagant taste, and therefore had genuinely been unhappy with the consequences, for which she had only blamed her father. After more than a year later, Adam had returned to Leeuwarden, but could not reconcile with Antje. By the end of that summer they had opted for a legal separation, which was granted in September 1890. Freed by law Adam had moved on to Amsterdam, and had started living with another woman immediately. Antje could not bear the shame and poverty, which took its toll upon her health, and on May 10, 1891, she had died (presumably of tuberculosis) leaving the four children to their own destiny. Adam was still not in a position to take care of them together, and hence Margarethe was sent to Sneek (a small town 17 miles south of Leeuwarden) to live with her uncle Vissers' family, Johannes was sent to Antje's paternal family in Franeker, (since Antje's father Johannes Hendrikus van der Meulen had died in 1881, young Johannes must have been taken to the care of her brother Yme van der Meulen) and the twins, who were not even 10 years old at that time, had been taken to live with Adam in Amsterdam. Margarethe was literally outraged with the arrangement. She had desperately wanted to live with her father, and the Royal City of Amsterdam was far more attractive to her than Sneek. A strong sense of disgust had seized her. The thought of avenging her betrayal must have occurred in her subconscious mind at that young age.

In Sneek at the Vissers', Margarethe did not find any reason to behave like an angel, which had infuriated the hosts for obvious reasons. Leiden had been a place of many educational experiments from the middle of the nineteenth century and was known as the "City of Books." In 1892, she was sent to a boarding school at Leiden for Kindergarten training, so that she could become a teacher in future. By that time Margarethe was 15 and knew pretty well that her character traits did not match to those of a dedicated motherly teacher, and she might also have detested the idea that other people would be controlling her destiny. She was seen getting involved in a scandalous encounter with the Director of Kindergarten Training and headmaster of the school Herr Wybrandus Haanstra, an accomplished teacher and reformist in the field of girl's education (inspired by Friedrich Fröebel he had developed a special learning method—the Leyden method—for the pre-primary children) who had been a respectable elderly man of 51, and Margarethe only 16 then. Varied versions of the incident are available—Margarethe herself had initiated the shameful sexual encounter with the headmaster, who had blamed and disgraced her for the mishap, and then had rusticated her from the school (1893) fearing more scandals.[7] Another version has speculated that the headmaster had actually fallen in love with the extremely attractive teenager and had exploited her sexually.[8] She was then shamed for having loose morale and had been expelled from the school.

The second version is hard to be believed, because such attitude could rarely be expected from an accomplished elderly man, especially when he had been respected for his work as a headmaster for quite long (he was appointed as the Director in 1882) of the Kindergarten Training School for girls. So, if the former version had been true, then it might be logically presumed that Margarethe had staged the scandalous drama not out of lust, but actually to get rid of the meaningless exercise of getting trained as a teacher, and also to get relieved from the Visser's household where she did not want to return. Whatever the fact might have been, as it appears that, by that time she had already learnt to use her feminine charm to get things done in her favor. As a naïve teenager she might have thought that out of sheer shame the Vissers would send her back to her father in Amsterdam, but things did not turn out to be the way she wanted to. She was instead sent to live with Pieter W. Taconis, husband of Geetruida Zelle, who was the younger sister of Adam,[9] in The Hague.

---

7   Pat Shipman, *Femme Fatale*, 11.
8   Waagenaar, *op. cit.*, 1964, 22; Julie Wheelwright, *The Fatal Lover*, 10.
9   *Netherland's Patriciaat*; (from the official website of Centraal Bureau voor Genealogie).

A SKETCH OF LIFE

This had been the actual turning point in Margarethe's life. By then she was almost 17 years of age, and had ultimately realized that Adam would not take her along to stay with him ever again. So she would need to do something on her own to fulfill her dreams of opulence and comfort, which she had been deprived of by her father. From the core of her heart she had believed that she was indeed a princess and it was her right to be so. Therefore, if her father refused to provide her that status, she could look for a husband who would. Margarethe had failed to realize the actuality of life or she might have never wanted to. She had developed wrong self-esteem, for which she was not to be blamed though; but it had reflected her immature and impulsive nature, due to which she even had to suffer wrongful death. Margarethe had actually lived four lives—Greeta, the "little orchid;" Griet, Rudolf MacLeod's wife; Mata Hari, the larger than life identity designed by her; and Marina, Vadime de Massloff's beloved sweetheart—and as we would see that all were linked together in an invisible intimate bond—the former life always became the foundation of the latter, and at the end Marina came heavy on all the rest.

Mata Hari's personality might be regarded as narcissistic in nature. Significantly, narcissism is usually considered as a disorder, although many psychologists have pointed it out to be a significant stage in the development of human mind. Havelock Ellis, who had coined the term "narcissism" in 1898, used it to refer to some kind of sexual perversion that he thought was characterized by considering the self as a sexual object. In 1899, Paul Nacke, in the same vein, wrote: "Narcissism" is a term "to denote the attitude of a person who treats his own body in the same way in which the body of a sexual object is ordinarily treated ..."[10] Sigmund Freud has dealt with the concept in great detail in his psychoanalytical theories, from which what might be gathered with regard to Mata Hari is her passion for self-preoccupation. Narcissism or self-love has been focused upon in the field of psychoanalysis and has been defined and technically analyzed variously by many psychologists. The Diagnostic and Statistical Manual of Mental Disorders (DSM-III) described narcissism as possessing "grandiose sense of self-importance." According to the noted American psychoanalyst Theodore Issac Rubin, "The narcissist becomes his own world and believes the whole world in him."[11] This version indicates a narcissist to be extremely self-cen-

---

10 Sigmund Freud, "On Narcissism: An Introduction," *On Metapsychology*, 61.
11 Alexander Lowen, *Narcissism: Denial of the True Self*, 6.

tered. Theodore Millon has presented the following five characteristic trends for a narcissist—(i) inflated self-image, manifested through egoist, haughty, and arrogant behavior; (ii) interpersonal exploitativeness, manifested through indulgent behavior and expectation of special favors; (iii) cognitive expansiveness, manifested through exhibiting immature fantasies and undisciplined imagination; (iv) insouciant temperament, manifested through nonchalance and buoyantly optimistic behavior; and (v) deficient social conscience, manifested through flouting conventional rules of shared social living.[12] The well-known American psychologist Otto Friedmann Kernberg however defined narcissism as the libidinal investment of the self. He has significantly noted that a narcissist manifests "great need to be admired, a shallow emotional life, an exploitative and sometime parasitic relationship with others."[13] He pointed out that to find out the root of narcissistic traits in one's personality, it is necessary to delve deep into the early childhood of that person, because the child's "fusion of ideal self, ideal object and actual self-images" are "a defense against an intolerable reality in the interpersonal realm."[14] A quick look into Mata Hari's adolescent days may have an answer from Kernberg's view.

Margarethe's father had deserted them after his bankruptcy and his eventual legal separation with her mother for another woman had led to her mother's untimely death. The family was totally disintegrated resulting in unwanted bumps and turns in Margarethe's life. Longing for her father's love, care, and comfort went in vain, as if Adam had forgotten his dear "little orchid" completely. It had surely been an "intolerable reality" in her personal life at a very young age. Therefore, as a defense against the intolerable mental agony, it is most likely that her ideal self, ideal object, and actual self-images had been merged together resulting in her narcissistic character traits. For Kernberg, narcissistic personality disorder is a defense of an adult, who, as a child, was left emotionally hungry by the mother, due to which the child felt unloved. So, as the only refuge he or she would choose "some valued aspect of the self as the only defense available."[15] Margarethe's mother became seriously ill immediately after

---

12 Theodore Millon, "Narcissistic Personality," *Encyclopedia of Psychology* (Vol. 2), Raymond J. Corsini, ed. 417.
13 Ibid., 417.
14 Otto Friedmann Kernberg, *Borderline Conditions and Pathological Narcissism*, 231.
15 J. Lachkar, *The Narcissistic/Borderline Couple: A Psychoanalytic Perspective on*

A SKETCH OF LIFE

Adam's bankruptcy and eventually had died within 2 years never being able to cope with the series of inappropriate happenings in her life. Adam did not take the responsibility of Antje's treatment, nor of the requirements (emotional and material) of Margarethe, who had deep attachment with him. She was deprived of the parental love and care that she had yearned for. Therefore, it is quite comprehensible that the only refuge she could possibly choose as a defense was self-love. When she was no more special for anyone else, she had to be special for herself. Adam had pampered her with luxury, and thus she might have equated luxury with fatherly love, care, and security. As had been evident later in her life, she always enjoyed men's love and attraction for her, more specifically of those in uniform, and an affluent life full of all material provisions. It must have certainly been rooted in her childhood mental state of unresolved helplessness.

Marriage advertisement of March 11, 1895
Het Nieuw van den Dag, The Netherlands (Internet archive, no known copyright)

Announcement of marriage on July 11, 1895
Algemeen Handelsblad, Amsterdam (Internet archive, no known copyright)

Marital Treatment, 9.

After reaching The Hague at her uncle Mr. Taconis' house (1893), Margarethe had realized that it was not what she had dreamt her life to be. Hopping from one relative's house to another was quite boring and tiring for her. She wanted to live a life of her own. As she was not ready to take up a job to support herself, which had absolutely been on line with the middle-class societal custom of her time, she had thought of marriage as the only option. In her imagination, only marriage could give her the security and opulence she had been looking for. So, it is not hard to assume that the decision for marriage had primarily been her economic compulsion. Later she had revealed to a journalist, "I married to become happier."[16] It was quite normal for a girl of 17 to think that way. The Hague had been a coastal spa city where soldiers and officers in uniform used to throng during their holidays, and for Margarethe the sight had been exceedingly attractive. Meeting Rudolf Macleod (then 39 years old) for the first time (he came in his uniform) on March 24, 1895, through a matrimonial advertisement (March 11, 1895) and courting him for a couple of months before getting married to him on July 11, 1895, had been like a fairy tale for Margarethe. Rudolf had provided her with every luxury she had dreamt of, and their courtship had exceeded all social norms to being intimately physical as well. At 18 she had been very beautiful and highly attractive by all measures, and for a middle-aged officer who had spent nearly 18 years in the Dutch East Indies serving in the Colonial Army (Rudolf went there in 1877 at the age of 21), Margarethe's attraction and accessibility had been irresistible. Rudolf had appreciated her sexual confidence as well, which stands evidence to the fact that she did not have any social or moral scruples. With Rudolf, Margarethe had seemed to be on top of the world ever since Adam had left her. She was fatally attracted to the man in uniform who was almost 21 years' senior to her. Did Margarethe consciously try to find the shadow of her father in Rudolf?

---

16 Wheelwright, *op. cit.*, 10.

A SKETCH OF LIFE

Rudolf and Margarethe after the wedding
(The Mata Hari Foundation, Fries Museum, Leeuwarden)

Pat Shipman presented Margarethe's possible mental state quite vividly—"If she were to create in her mind a man who would restore her golden past, he would be an older man, a handsome man in uniform, like her father on his horse in the painting that hung in their house in Leeuwarden. He would be a man who would treat her like a princess. She was consciously looking for such a man, because she was seeking to re-create her father's magical love during her childhood ..."[17] I agree with Shipman on her comments in this regard, but I presume Margarethe had not been doing anything consciously as the psychoanalysts would also agree to. It must have been her subconscious mental state which had prompted her to go for such a choice. After all she had yearned for her father's love and care for much long. Had Rudolf not showered her with expensive gifts and luxurious niceties, she might presumably have backed out. Margarethe had been too naïve to foresee what fate she was embracing so dearly. If only she did not lose her head during the courtship she might have realized that Rudolf enjoyed female company very much and had been known among his colleagues for being a womanizer, which might have even affected his health. It was not uncommon among the army ranks in the Dutch colonies, or for that matter for any colonial people, to have native women as their sexual partners in their colonies. Margarethe had been too young to even have any idea about all these menaces, and worst, she did not even have a guardian to warn her of the

---

17 Shipman, *op. cit.*, 12.

consequences.

Rudolf was on leave from January 1894, and as his health had been deteriorating steadily he had started for The Netherlands for proper cure in June. He had been suffering from acute diabetes and severe joint pains due to rheumatism. His illness was so severe that on the day he was to take the ship from the Dutch East Indies he actually had to be carried on a stretcher to board the ship. Back in Holland for nearly a year and even after getting engaged to Margarethe, he had often suffered recurring spells of unbearable rheumatic pain, and therefore could not go out to meet her on those occasions. Shipman raised the question whether Rudolf was physically suited to marry by then. She speculated that he might have been affected by syphilis, and might not have been cured completely only after a year of treatment. Syphilis had been a common disease among the army men and planters who lived without their families for long periods in the Indies. It is well known that Rudolf was a womanizer who enjoyed physical company of the native women in the Indies before he had known Margarethe; moreover, as a custom, he had kept nyais (housekeepers and companions) in his living quarter to take care of his material and sexual needs. Although syphilis had been part of the Columbian Exchange, it had in fact been transmitted from the New World to the Old World, and had been carried over to the East Indies particularly by the Europeans. It is however not at all absurd that Rudolf might also have been infected. Shipman wrote: "Circumstantial evidence suggests strongly that he had suffered from syphilis, and this scenario would explain much that has remained mysterious about the married life of Margarethe."[18] The circumstantial evidences collected by her are—(i) Rudolf's medical problems; (ii) his unfaithfulness; (iii) the letter of Margarethe written to her father on August 3, 1901;[19] and (iv) the peculiar circumstances of his infant son Norman's death. The symptoms of syphilis closely correspond to those that Rudolf had been suffering from—diabetes and rheumatic pain. In an article titled "Syphilis in its Relation to Diabetes" (*The Journal of Nervous and Mental Disease*, July 1892, Vol. 17 (7), 521-524), Edward D. Fisher had speculated that only in the third stage of syphilis does diabetes occur. So it could be asserted that Rudolf was affected by the disease and had been suffering for quite a long time, and therefore had urgently needed leave to get back to Holland for proper cure.

---

18   Ibid., 32.
19   Ibid., 125.

A SKETCH OF LIFE

Whatever might have happened Margarethe had indeed been infected, which is known through her letters to Adam from the Dutch East Indies. Norman, the first child of Margarethe and Rudolf, was born on January 30, 1897, nearly a year and a half after their marriage. By that time Rudolf's leave had been extended twice—in March 1896, for reasons relating to his health, and in September the same year due to Margarethe's pregnancy. So, it is evident that Rudolf was not fully cured even after a year of their engagement in March 1895. Therefore, it would not be wrong to conclude that Norman might have had congenital syphilis of some kind. Shipman surmised that Norman had died not directly suffering from the disease, but from the poisonous overdose of mercury while getting treated for syphilis.[20] It could be true even for Non (the girl), who was born on May 2, 1898, after nearly 3 years of their marriage and 15 months after birth of the first child. She too had died untimely in her early 20s. Not much light has been shed regarding her death on August 10, 1919, at the age of 21, besides merely being known that she had died in sleep of cerebral hemorrhage. Charles Robert Drysdale's statement about the nature of syphilis is fairly significant in this regard. He said, "Persons with inherited syphilis do not seem to reach old age, and probably die of some disease of liver or kidneys in middle age."[21] Therefore, it could be presumed that both the children had suffered from congenital syphilis.

However, Rudolf had reached Java with his wife and the little son in June 1897, and in May 1899, the MacLeods were in Medan. Late in June 1899, both the children had fallen seriously ill. While the girl had survived (despite being only 13 months old), the poor boy was betrayed by his luck. Norman had died very early on June 28, 1899, and the story about Norman's death had circled around the children being poisoned for revenge—either because Rudolf had abused a native soldier who was in love with their maid and therefore she took revenge by poisoning the children; or because Rudolf's sexual advances towards the maid had enraged her native lover who had poisoned the children for revenge.[22] Nearly all the biographers of Margarethe, including her father, and even the Dutch colonial people residing in the Dutch–Indies at that time, had believed the story. Whatever might have happened, the body essentially required a post mortem to determine the genuine cause of the kid's death. Rudolf

---

20   Ibid., 103–106.
21   Charles R. Drysdale, *The Nature and Treatment of Syphilis*, 126.
22   Pat Shipman extensively argued against such possibility; *op. cit*., 99–103.

did not permit an autopsy, which provides ample scope for suspicion—did he know the precise cause of Norman's death and was desperate to suppress fact to prevent an inquiry? A proper inquiry could have revealed that he had married while still having the symptoms of syphilis, and thus had infected the children. Shipman has pointed out that their symptoms of high fever, frequent vomiting, etc did match mercury poisoning,[23] an element used in those days for the treatment of syphilis.

Could then the story of revenge have been invented by Rudolf himself in connivance with the Dutch doctor, who had been treating the children, in order to shift the blame on the helpless native maid? The revenge story was never verified and the Dutch press in the East Indies did not publish anything other than merely reporting the little boy's unfortunate death. But Rudolf had subsequently been demoted from his position and was transferred back to East Java, which was somewhat unusual in the Dutch colonial system. Did it result from serious suspicion against Rudolf regarding the toddler's death at the upper ranks of the Dutch army? Never was it known who had been the lover of the maid, and what treatment did they get for such kind of a grave destructive behavior involving death of the little child of a colonial army personnel. Had the revenge story been true it would have implied severe punishment of the perpetrators, but nothing of that sort had ever been recorded in the government documents of the Dutch East Indies. Rudolf at times had even blamed Margarethe for having contracted syphilis from some other men and having passed it on to the children at their birth, which could have never been true. Unlike Rudolf she did not show signs of promiscuity during her marriage.

There could have been another angle to Norman's death. In 1898 Rudolf had been promoted to the post of Garrison Commander, and was posted in Medan, the biggest port and capital town of Sumatra, which had predominantly been under Muslim rule. He had arrived in the city sometime in March 1899, and took the charges immediately. Due to his disgusting and thoroughly oppressive behavior towards the local plantation labors he was greatly hated by them. Margarethe had joined him with the two little children in the insistence of Rudolf. In no time she had realized that the social atmosphere was not conducive for the Dutch people residing in the city. The local ethnic groups of the Aceh and Batak people of Northern Sumatra had not been happy with the colonial people,

---

23 Ibid., 103–112.

because their presence had affected the natives' spice business badly, and therefore were considered to be intruders into the natives' own land. The Bataks were very aggressive and had also been known for their ritual cannibalism.[24] Both the groups had resisted foreign intrusion indulging in guerrilla warfare (Jihad for them), which involved high levels of atrocities against the Dutch colonials.[25] The latter had declared war against the Aceh Sultanate in the end of March 1873. It is known in history as the Aceh (Atjeh) War, which had continued for an amazing four decades. It was in 1898 that the Dutch colonial people had caused death to nearly 3,000 native Acehs, including women and children, in a counter-insurgency move. So, when Margarethe went to live in Medan in May 1899, the situation was still not favorable for the resident Dutch families, and there had been a persistent need to be vigilant all the time against any fatal attack on them. It is in Medan that Norman had died in the wee hours of June 28, 1899. In that case the story of poisoning the children could very well be true, but for a different reason. Still, Rudolf's refusal to allow an autopsy on Norman's body would remain a mystery.

Nevertheless, Rudolf and Margrethe's conjugal life had started to ruin right after their honeymoon. They had been to the fashionable spa city of Wiesbaden in Germany after the wedding, which was especially known for Mother Buchanan's Bath House and other hot springs (23 in total at that time), and with its pleasing meadows and splendid architecture had been a luxurious destination of the international tourists. There are ample reasons to suspect that as Rudolf still had not been fully cured of syphilis while he married Margarethe, he had chosen Wiesbaden for honeymoon, because the mineral waters there had been known to be useful cure for almost all skin ailments and also for rheumatism.[26] They could however never know the sweetness of an ideal union. There was no dignity and respect in their union—it had been a union of convenience on both sides. I would like to borrow a few words from G. W. Burnap, a Unitarian clergyman of the early nineteenth century, to describe the situation. "No sooner" he wrote: "... her bridal attire transformed into mourning, and her blushes changed into tears."[27] Rudolf had a habit for luxury

---

24 Khoon Choy Lee, *A Fragile Nation*, 269.
25 Julia Keay, *The Spy Who Never Was*, 22.
26 Anonymous, 1832, *A Guide through Wiesbaden and its Environs*, 21–23; (Pamphlet printed for H. W. Ritter).
27 Burnap, George Washington; *The Sphere and Duties of Woman*, 64.

including heavy drinking. As he was on leave during their wedding, he was not being paid full salary; and due to his heavy expenditure during the courtship and honeymoon, he also had loans to repay. Moreover, he had started seeing other women within merely 2 weeks of returning from honeymoon. Having a bourgeois mindset he might have thought that he had the license to do whatever he liked to. He had been promiscuous and did insist his wife to give company to his money lenders in order to evade repayment of loans. On Margarethe's own account their marriage had deteriorated mainly due to the following reasons:[28]

1. Lack of enough money to support her luxury.

2. Rudolf did not approve her flirtatious nature.

3. Rudolf was much older to her and therefore had been jealous of her young male friends who admired her beauty and attractiveness.

4. Due to her individualistic temperament she was not fit to be a good housewife.

The letters written by Rudolf on various occasions to his younger sister Louise Frida had revealed his disgust about Margarethe. His attitude towards his wife had been explicit through the choice of phrases like "a stinking wretch," "blood-sucker," "beastly depraved scoundrel,"[29] etc. What had actually been communicated by Rudolf could be stated in the following way—Margarethe had failed to be a "true woman." Qualities of a "true woman" included modesty, purity, religiosity, submissiveness, domesticity, and complete dependence and devotion to the husband and family. "With them she was promised happiness and power,"[30] said Barbara Welter, the noted feminist historian. Social invisibility had been the most notable feature of a "true woman," as they were happy within their social and familial boundaries. She was supposed to be a "womanly woman," a true wife, which Margarethe had never been. She had enjoyed dictating her own terms, and to fulfill her desires she was ready even to step onto the forbidden pastures. She was not born to be "The Angel in the House" (Coventry Patmore, 1854). This disposition in Margarethe

---

28 Shipman, *op. cit.*, 52.
29 Waagenaar, *op. cit.*, 1964, 40.
30 Barbara Welter, "The Cult of True Womanhood: 1820-1860," Lucy Maddox, ed., *Locating American Studies*, 44; Helen Tierney, ed., *Women's Studies Encyclopedia* (Vol.1), 321.

infuriated Rudolf because he had expected her to be an infinitely submissive wife, who would be merely a beautiful ornament to the MacLeods' household. He was not ready in any way to admit any value of his wife other than adornment, and had hated her strength of expression. So, for Rudolf, whatever Margarethe did could only be wrong, and all her decisions were entirely inaccurate. Rudolf did not trust her under any circumstance and had desperately wanted to get rid of her, especially after Norman's death, for which he had always blamed her for being a negligent mother.

Margarethe did not get married to have a family or to rear Rudolf's children. All of what she had in mind while planning for her wedding was to live in freedom and affluence, and to have a husband who would provide that. She had been extremely unhappy with the constant struggle she had to face after her mother's death and wanted to have a pair of imaginary wings to fly high. Did she ever realize the commitments and responsibilities of marriage, and what it meant to have a family? This accusing question has always been pointed toward Margarethe, as if family happiness had been her sole responsibility. In the same vein I would like to pose the same question for Rudolf. Did he ever bother to play the role of a perfect husband with her? The Dutch Law of Persons defines marriage as the union of man and woman, entered into for the purpose of begetting children, and for mutual assistance through life.[31] Did Rudolf truly comply with the latter part of the law? Did he at all have any intention to assist Margarethe through life? Margarethe was even less than half his age. Moreover, she was a motherless teenager when he married her. Did he not have the duty to lovingly initiate her to the duties and responsibilities of a wife? People who knew the couple in the Dutch East Indies had admired Margarethe as an excellent host and as a beautiful well-behaved lady. Only if she had a well-behaved, affectionate, composed and sensible husband she might have become a responsible wife as well. G. W. Burnap wrote: "If there be on both sides good sense and generous feeling, as well as true affection, nothing will seem hard ..."[32] Both Rudolf and Margarethe had lacked all these essential qualities which could make their marriage successful. The marriage had been one which went totally haywire due to misunderstandings at various levels, mostly because they did not want to be considerate enough to understand each other—both

---

31 J. W. Wessels, *History of the Roman-Dutch Law*, 429.
32 Burnap, *op. cit.*, 65.

had entered the nuptial contract with their own cultural and personal hangovers about the institution, which was a gross mistake, and therefore both were equally responsible. The then European society had been mostly following the Napoleonic Civil Code, which professed subjugation of women by prescribing marriage, family, and children to be their only concern—the roles as wife and mother being supremely important. I would like to assert that the life and death of Margarethe (a.k.a. Mata Hari) had been determined by the male-dominated culture of her time, which held women liable for every social wrong. She was expected to practice the art of suffering in silence, which she had refused to comply with.

Rudolf could bear no more of the Dutch colonial life and particularly the arduous tropical conditions in Indonesia that had instilled a dull unpleasantness in him. Norman's death might have evoked a sense of guilt in him which he could not evade. He missed his dear son too bitterly, and with his failing health he could not continue with his service any longer. In October 1900, he had been released with a pension by the Dutch authority. Margarethe also was no more interested to carry on with Rudolf and with the marriage any longer, and therefore in March 1902, they had decided to return to Holland. On August 27 she had filed for legal separation before the Amsterdam Tribunal on the ground of cruelty and torture, which was granted in 3 days. Margarethe was quite aware that separation from Rudolf would deny her the social rank and standing along with the economic security and comfort that she had enjoyed so far, still she had been desperate to get rid of the monstrous man. She had denied her natural destiny to sculpt a new identity for herself. As a mother she could not overcome the grief of her son's death. Erika Ostrovsky wrote: "She felt as if one half of her body had been ripped away."[33] She had desperately wanted the custody of Non (little over 4 years in 1902) which was granted by the court, but Rudolf had taken the daughter away as he refused to provide anything that could make his wife happy. As he was terribly disgusted with his wife, he grabbed every little chance to humiliate her, both in private and in public. Denouncing her responsibilities he had even published announcements in a leading newspaper in Amsterdam warning all people not to supply Margarethe with cash and goods. It was a measure taken by him to malign his wife publicly, which had left his once dear Griet with no other option whatsoever.

---

33   Erika Ostrovsky, *Eye of Dawn*, 51.

Margarethe knew that she had to start life afresh. She was lonely—terribly lonely—not a single soul to support, no care, no love, not even a single word of solace—she had felt completely alienated. She had then started her journey to find her own identity, to create her own destiny. Margarethe loved herself, she dreamt big, and had been audacious enough to claim her right to be treated as a woman. If these were her weaknesses in a fundamentally bourgeois society, she was prepared to change them into her strengths. She only had a gorgeous physique to start with and was determined to exploit it for a dignified living. Her body was her exclusive asset that could become her fortune. She had no other means—no choice left (committing suicide could never have been an option to her as she was not an escapist in any way and loved life too dearly). It had finally marked the end of Margarethe, and then onward her sojourn to create the dream persona of Mata Hari began. At the turn of the century Paris had been a happening city and could have been the only destination for her. In the Spring of 1903, she began with trying her luck there in a circus (Molier Circus) as a rider, did modeling for some painters, tried her hand as a trainer in a riding school, and had taken up part-time prostitution as well (after separation from Rudolf she had been in part-time prostitution for a while in the Van Woostraat, which was known as the red-light area in Amsterdam); but nothing worked out the way she had expected to. Without the support of her husband, without the support of her society, without a family to fall back on, and above all without any money, she had stepped out for the new journey all by herself. It had become her obligation to prove her worth—to Rudolf and his family, especially to his orthodox sister Tante Frida, whom she had held responsible for her disastrous marriage, and to the rest of the merciless world.

The owner of the circus in Paris where Margarethe had started working was Ernst Molier, who had advised her to take up dancing as her career. That piece of advice had created history—it had created Mata Hari ("The Eye of Dawn" in Javanese). It had been during the Belle Époque in France, and Paris was bustling with new artists, poets, musicians, dancers, and others with their novel art forms. Moreover, the Universal Exposition in Paris, held in 1900, had showcased an Oriental theme leaving its Oriental fervor on the French populace. She had started dancing in early 1905 with private performances in the romantic city of Paris, through which she could prove her worth as an extremely attractive dancer with a whole new style of dance—the sacred Hindu temple dance. Being an Indian I have vivid knowledge of what that is like, and therefore can refute her claims of authenticity, because whatever she performed might have had some affinity with the dances from Java and not from India. She bared herself under the garb of divine servitude, and people simply applauded her artistic display. Paris had already seen other nude performers at the music halls and at Moulin Rouge, but nothing even closer to what Lady MacLeod had been exhibiting in the evenings. She could read the pulse of the Parisian society and its hypocritical bourgeoisie sentiment rightly, and knew that her shows must be cloaked with decency of culture. It had worked for her. She could hit the jackpot through her debut performance at Mrs. Kireevsky's house sometime in early February, 1905. News reporters did not leave the opportunity to enhance sale of their papers. Marcel Lami, correspondent of the *Courrier Francis*, wrote: "… her profane dance is a prayer, her passion is a prayer."[34]

At her debut performance she was noticed by Émile Étienne Guimet, the wealthy collector of classical artifacts from Egypt, Asia, and other regions of the Near East and Far East. He had displayed his collections in a museum in Paris, which had also housed a magnificent Oriental collection. In order to promote his collection, Guimet had invited Margarethe, then known as Mrs. Lady MacLeod, to perform at the library of his museum on March 13 and 14, 1905. A new name became necessary for her public debut, as her Scottish (Rudolf's family originally hailed from Scotland) name was unsuitable for depicting authentic Oriental dance, and thus "Mata Hari" was born. She had mesmerized the audience by dancing before the eleventh century South Indian statue of Natarāja provided from Guimet's collection. The invitees had been enthralled to see her slow and voluptuous movements. Shipman wrote: "Her dances were thrilling, daring, and exotic, and hence were praised by all—even by the newspaper reporters."[35] A new star was shining bright on the horizon (she was conferred the title "A Star of Dance" in 1908 by one of her wealthy admirers). Margarethe Geertruida Zelle, alias Mrs. Lady MacLeod, had found her true identity—Mata Hari. She had achieved her dream never to part with again and thus had chosen her own destiny.

---

34 Keay, *op. cit.*, 37.
35 Shipman, *op. cit.*, 152.

A SKETCH OF LIFE

Artist's impression of Mata Hari in 1905
(The Mata Hari Foundation, Fries Museum, Leeuwarden)

The newly born Mata Hari became an instant craze in Paris. Whatever she did and uttered had started being reported in the leading newspapers—her dining with elite people, living in magnificent hotels, her majestic lifestyle—every bit had intrigued the masses. A Dutch cigarette manufacturer printed her picture on the cigarette tins in the hope to sell well and so did a manufacturer of beauty soap. In the span of only a couple of months Mata Hari became an icon in France. Soon she had started receiving invitations to perform in Madrid, Milan, Berlin, Venice, London, Nice, Monte Carlo, St Petersburg, and other places of class. She had then felt the need to create a mystery around her because the image of a battered woman could definitely not match her newly created iconic image, and therefore she had started telling imaginary stories to the newspaper reporters fictionalizing her past. She was smart enough to create stories that would authenticate her allegiance to her Oriental dance form. So, in the self-concocted stories for her admirers she had been born in Jaffna Pattanam (Ceylon, renamed Sri Lanka) to a Brahmin father. Her mother had been a temple dancer (devadāsi), who died after giving birth to her. She had grown up amidst the glorious culture witnessing and learning temple dance from authentic sources. As a teenager she had been offered to Siva, the Hindu Lord of destruction, who is also the source of all creation. She must have known about the devadāsi system of India from the travelogues of Europeans who had lived and worked in India and Ceylon; presumably from the Dutch writings of Jacob Gotfried Haafner, who had confessed about being infatuated by a devadāsi of Tamil origin, and had elaborated on the Indian devadāsis in his popular book *Travels in a Palanquin* (1808)[36], and had also written about his travels in Ceylon (*Travels on Foot through the Island of Ceylon*, 1821). Moreover, some real Indian devadāsis had adorned European stages (especially in Paris and London) from the early nineteenth century[37]. Louis Jacolliot, the colonial barrister and judge who had worked in India for several years, contributed to the popularity of the devadāsis in France through his travel document written in French (1877)[38]. So, it would not be wrong to assume that Mata Hari and the Parisians both were familiar with the traditional Indian temple dancers and must have been adequately curious about them. She must have posed some sort of continuity to the Indian temple dancers on the Parisian stage. Her fictitious stories had been so well configured that no one dared to raise any suspicion. Her tanned complexion, black hair and dark eyes endorsed her fabrication, though this fanciful self-mystification had proved to be fatal later in her life.

Chance, or for that matter fate, had played a significant role in all the four lives that Margarethe had lived. On various occasions destiny had been playing a wicked game with her. Being born as the only daughter of a rich businessman, her mother's death at a much early date, being sent to The Hague to live with her orthodox uncle's family, sending a photograph along with her reply to Rudolf's matrimonial advertisement, meeting Émile Guimet at a private performance in Paris, her instant fame—all had been destined for her. As her fame rocketed through countries so did the number of her admirers. It was an era when having mistress had been considered to be a status symbol, and who else than Mata Hari could be more suitable? She had been gorgeous, intelligent, well mannered, a polyglot, and had an elegant lifestyle. She was a *femme galante* in the truest sense. She was gifted with the talent to impress people belonging to the higher strata of the society with much ease; and that is precisely what she

---

36 Martin Clayton and Bennett Zon, eds., *Music and Orientalism in the British Empire, 1780s–1940s*, 47.

37 Ibid., 55–61.

38 Ibid., 67.

liked about herself; she basked in her own glory. Every city she conquered had gifted her with many lovers, who were ready to spend a fortune for her. Men and dance had become the dual source of her sustenance. She stayed lavishly in expensive hotels and villas, was assisted by servants and maids, had enjoyed delicious platters for luncheons and dinners, bought the latest fashionable clothing from the renowned dress makers, collected jewelry and shoes at her own fancy, and rode the best breed of horses. At last she could achieve what she had always wanted to, could make her dreams come true, and could enjoy life in her own terms to her own satisfaction. She became a princess once again, for her lovers and her admirers. Everyone who came to watch her performances or read about her in the newspapers and magazines wanted to be her lover—wanted to be special to her, though only a few had been fortunate. The fortunate ones, with a few exceptions, most significantly had been in uniform. Least did she realize that her passion for uniform would turn into her death trap within a span of merely 10 years.

Rudolf could not have been happy with the success of the incorrigibly evil, dishonorable, fallen woman, a captive of her own sensuous passions, he had known two years back. The sexual confidence that he had appreciated and enjoyed during his courtship days had eventually been the cause for hatred towards his estranged wife. And as he was prepared to marry again (his second wife Elisabetha Martina Christina van der Mast was 28 years his junior), he had appealed to the court of law in Amsterdam for a divorce. The ground for his appeal was Margarethe's infidelity and malicious desertion. To be sure Rudolf did not forget to collect and attach a nude photograph of Mata Hari along with his divorce petition, which had been clicked by a renowned photographer (some of the well-known photographers of her time were Leopold Reutlinger, Professor Edward Stebbing, Jean Agélou, and Lucien Walery) in Paris after her success on stage. One of her photographs had tied the knot with him, and to end the relationship he had resorted to another. However, initially Margarethe did not want a divorce as the legal separation had been serving her purpose quite well, but due to fear of a scandal which could have become a scorn for her career as well as for her daughter's reputation she had decided not to contest. Mata Hari knew that adultery had always been a justified ground for divorce, and she could prove her innocence in no way. The divorce was granted in the Amsterdam court on April 26, 1906. Rudolf had married for the second time on November 22, 1907, and again for the third time in 1917, but Mata Hari never married again. The bitter experience of her marriage with Rudolf had drained her courage to opt for the nuptial bond one more time. She was sufficiently happy with her life as Mata Hari, and could never love anyone more than herself (save once at the mature age of 40). Her journey had continued through Europe as "Mata Hari" for 10 more years. She had started her career with what she called the Hindu temple dances and had carefully created opportunities on stage to show her spectacular nudity to captivate her audience. She was not a trained dancer and might have guessed that it was the only way to conquer the game. By no means could she afford to lose.

But France was not in a mood to allow that for long, as the French censors had been shadowing the bourgeoisie ideology and had worked to uplift the café-concerts and music halls in the view to shape the society with moral citizens. Government-appointed moral police frequented the theaters and music halls to find any deviant, who were arrested and imprisoned for 15 days as per the existing law. In order to pursue her career, Mata Hari had to abide by the current norms of the country, and thus she was seen in full clothes at her latter public performances. It was somewhat good for her as well, because she had already been aging and had feared that her erotic appeals might have feigned. As she had many wealthy lovers it was no more necessary for her to perform for a living. She performed at various benefit events during that time, and private garden parties as well including some at her villa in Neuilly-sur-Seine. She had also performed (1912) with the orchestration of the Indian Sufi mystic Hazrat Inayat Khan. During that time Inayat Khan had been traveling in America and Europe with the mission to spread Sufism in the west, and in 1912 had settled in Paris. She had once performed in a dance recital in Neuilly at the famous salon of Natalie Clifford Barney, the renowned feminist, where she had spectacularly rode nude on a white horse into the garden as Lady Godiva.[39] On December 13, 1913, she had assisted music critic Paul Oliver by demonstrating for his lecture at the University of Annals in Paris on the subject of Indian, Javanese, and Japanese temple dances. It is quite amazing because she had no formal training in any dance form, but still was fortunate enough to have a chance to impress the academia of Paris. Her superb reputation as a dancer enabled her earnings to swell, but no amount of wealth was sufficient for her as she had been ridiculously self-indulgent and extravagant in her ways, and

39   Joan Schenkar, *Truly Wilde*, 144.

although she earned much she would soon have huge loans. Some of the newspaper reports suggested that she was the highest paid dancer of her time, and she had no dearth of wealthy lovers who had been supporting her lavishly in every way; still she always needed more. Her self-image as if had solely rested on her capacity to buy.

Mata Hari's success nevertheless had generated many enemies, and she was condemned as a "vicious man eater"—a man-devouring woman who ruined men financially; truly, because to keep her in good humor, her patrons and lovers had to spend a fortune. She flaunted her grandeur publicly and had no qualms to show off that she was too expensive, still men wanted her as their mistress because she had truly been the paragon of male fantasy. She certainly did not barge into any man's life, but that did not prevent her rivals from maligning her. The wives felt threatened by her irresistible fatal attraction that engulfed their husbands, and the husbands felt intrigued by her gallant personality. She had stepped into the male world and had uncovered their fantasy, which they had been carefully suppressing under the garb of civility. With Rudolf Margarethe had a deep feeling of rejection, which, as the proud demimondaine Mata Hari, she wanted to avenge by choosing lovers particularly in uniform, who would joyfully be willing to become dead broke for her. She had been exceptionally confident of her seductive prowess and ignored all criticisms with grace. She had no more been a daughter, a wife, or a mother, and therefore did not need to have any semblance of social decency. She had become the shadow of Ūrvashi, the infinitely charming celestial nymph, of the Indian Vedic mythology. She felt liberated as men could no more enchain her; on the contrary, it was she who enslaved them by enkindling their lust and by satisfying their savage instincts. After all she had been able to subjugate the male world, no matter what Rudolf and his widowed sister had thought of her.

As Mata Hari traveled to many countries with her dance contracts, she had the opportunity to have foreign lovers. While in Berlin in 1906, she had been the mistress of Herr Alfred Kiepert, a lieutenant in the 2nd Company of the 11th Westphalian Hussars Regiment, Crefeld Garrison, from the Imperial German Army. They were often seen dining together in expensive restaurants and other public places, and with him she had also attended the Imperial Army Manoeuvres at Javer-Streigan in Silesia from September 9 to 12, 1906. As any sort of display in uniform fascinated her, she obviously had enjoyed the event very much. Mata Hari never had the faintest idea that her presence at the show with Kiepert would be used as evidence against her later in her life. She however had soon realized that her performances were losing attraction among the Parisian audience, and inspite of being an untrained dancer she had tried to explore new dance styles. She had an insatiable urge to remain attractive forever, and therefore in 1907 had traveled to Egypt to learn something new. During that time she might have been in the company of Kiepert for a few months. Some of the newspapers had reported—"She has renounced Shiva and his cult ... she has adopted Berlin and speaks German without the slightest Oriental accent ... she hopes to settle on the banks of the Spree."[40] Waagenaar said that it had been reported as part of a message sent from the Italian intelligence service to Paris, which he had found to be spurious. However, after her return from Egypt Mata Hari had parted with her rich lover Kiepert, and he had to part with a share of his wealth as her farewell gift; although, at a later date, she had a chance to revive the relationship for a short while. In 1914 Mata Hari had returned to Berlin with a 6 month dance contract at the Metropol Theater, and a wish to create a new Egyptian Ballet with the help of Egyptologist Professor Johann Adolf Erman (Émile Guimet's old friend), director of the Egyptian department at the Royal Museum in Berlin. Her performance at the Metropol had been scheduled to start in September. She had to stay in Berlin for a couple of months and had been the mistress of Constant Bazet, a banker in Berlin, but still she had renewed her relationship with Herr Kiepert, inspite of knowing about his beautiful and jealous wife. Mata Hari had been, in a sense, unknowingly inviting trouble for herself, as their intimacy was no more secret to Kiepert's wife, and in order to get rid of the menacing woman she had surely tried out some tricks.

Thus, briefly elucidating Margarethe's life, I would now like to embark on the climax of her career, i.e., the issue of her alleged enemy espionage and execution by the French government. It was quite customary for a demimondaine to have a lover and also to venture out with other men at the same time. So, at the end of July 1914, and early in August, Mata Hari was seen dining with Herr Griebel, the Chief of Police in Berlin, who had been acquainted to her earlier. Fate had again played the nemesis. Later, during her trial, her association with the German police chief became

---
40   Ostrovsky, *op. cit.*, 79; Waagenaar, *op. cit.*, 1964, 132.

A SKETCH OF LIFE

very important to her prosecutors. On August 3, 1914, when the expansive grape vines in the European fields were almost ready for harvest, Germany had declared war against Russia and France. Britain had joined its allies. The theater halls had closed immediately, and Mata Hari had to get out of Germany violating the dance contract. Certain things had happened quickly at the outbreak of war, which she did not like—while her agent had held back her money, the costumer, who was supposed to be paid by her after the performances, had wrongfully confiscated her valuable furs and jewelry due to nonpayment of his charges, and because she was a resident of France her bank account had also been freezed in Germany. In a hurry she had initially planned to go back to Paris through Switzerland, but because of some technical trouble at the border regarding her passport and permit she could not. Ultimately, after a couple of days, she had landed in Amsterdam with the help of a Dutchman. The political upheaval had disgusted Mata Hari not because she was worried about the consequences of a devastating war, but because her movement and enjoyment both had been restricted by the war.

However, all had been going well for Mata Hari even after the war began. She had Baron Edouard Willem van der Capellen, a colonel in the Dutch Cavalry (Hussar Regiment), as her lover in The Hague who had been taking good care of all her needs, and a dedicated and caring maid Antje Lintjens, an unwed mother, who had been meticulously looking after her domestic chores. With the help from her lover she had rented a house in the picturesque locale of The Hague at Nieuwe Uitleg and had started to renovate it. On August 11, 1915, she was registered as a resident of The Hague at the Vital Statistics Office of Holland. Nothing should have gone wrong for her. The war was supposed to end in a short time, but lingered on unexpectedly. As she always loved to be in the limelight, she could not stay idle during the war. She continued with some sporadic performances in Holland,[41] although it was not at all necessary for her survival. Fate once again had pushed her into grave trouble and due to the war it had been the fatal one. After nearly a year of the start of the Great War she was contacted by Karl Kroemer, the German Consul in Amsterdam, with the proposal of spying for Germany. In late 1914, he might have spotted her at some of her performances in Holland,[42] and might have thought of

---

41 Waagenaar, *op. cit.* 1964, 126.
42 There are varied opinions regarding their first meeting. Waagenaar said that Mata Hari had been introduced to Kroemer in January 1915 by one of her acquaintances;

the opportunity to explore the possibility as he had been a member of the German intelligence service for a long time (which was being commanded by Walter Nicolai, head of the German intelligence service, during the war) and was in charge of recruiting spies for his country. Kroemer might have thought that Mata Hari could become a local small-time recruit to serve as an informer. She was not in a position even to realize the outcome of that fatal communication. A series of naïve decisions taken at the wrong time had pushed her into the death trap. Britain, France, and even Germany had accomplished their own political interests by entrapping her. Fate did not extend any support to her either, and ultimately she became a scapegoat in the hands of the French army during the First World War.

While being free from any inhibition whatsoever and prepared to inquire with an open mind I had started reading about Mata Hari, I found many hidden layers that had interacted together against her at varied levels—religious, social, psychological, and albeit political. Right from the religio-social bias of anti-Semitism and anti-feminism, pressure of the divergent views of the conservative and republican France, her story had a dimension for revenge as well, and it had ultimately been the adverse political situation of wartime France which had culminated in her execution. I have tried to organize the chapters accordingly. In the first chapter I would like to discuss the socio-cultural background of the European society, especially of Britain and France, in the late nineteenth century and at the turn of the new century, as it appears to bear much importance in the study of Mata Hari's fateful life. The society and culture of her birthplace, her schooling, influence of the Napoleonic Code on the society and its values, anti-Semitism and anti-feminism in the French bourgeois society, emergence of the New Woman against the True Woman, her success as an Oriental dancer, espionitis (collective fear of disguised enemies[43]) that had grabbed Europe during the turn of the century, and social turbulences during the Great War in Europe—all seems to be quite pertinent to her predicament. In the second chapter I propose to elaborate on the persona of Margarethe and Rudolf, which would be significant to interpret their relationship in the unfortunate marriage and also the end of it.

---

ibid., 237; although according to Julia Keay he had met her at a dinner party in May 1916; *op. cit.*, 112; Eva Horn opined that they had met at a reception in Den Haag (The Hague); *The Secret War*, 183.

43 Horn, *op. cit.*, 169.

In this chapter, I would also like to reflect on Adam Zelle in an effort to understand Mata Hari more vividly. In the third chapter I would like to take up Paris during the Belle Époque as the backdrop of the entire narrative, and to discuss why Margarethe had chosen Paris to start her new life. This chapter would also include some detail about her contemporary danseuses and their individual dance styles as compared to that of Mata Hari. In the fourth chapter I would discuss the socio-political scenario in Europe that had led to the army mutiny in France during the war. Issues like the Dreyfus Affair and the execution of Edith Cavell and others who had suffered in the hands of Germany would pertinently be discussed in this chapter. In the fifth chapter I would discuss about the grave miscarriage of justice and her being a scapegoat of France during the Great War, and also her activities during that time. In the sixth chapter I would discuss about the role of anti-propaganda, her pre-trial and trial, the accusations against her along with her defense, and her execution—all the issues would be taken up for discussion in this chapter. Since nothing after October 15, 1917, apart from her infamy as a notorious spy, is relevant to this effort, in the concluding chapter I propose to make an effort towards a paradigm shift regarding the universal negative judgment of Mata Hari's role in the war as the *Mata Hari Syndrome*. I propose to add three appendices to this biography, in the first of which I would provide a timeline of her life spanning from her birth to her execution, in the second I would provide a list of her mistakes committed throughout her life, avoidance of which could have surely changed her life story, and in the third I would try to enlist names of her lovers as far as possible.

However, whatever had happened has made Mata Hari immortal in time, and beyond the French imaginations, a heroine forever. She may not have deserved all that—Margarethe may not have deserved to become Mata Hari, and Mata Hari certainly did not deserve to die at the execution ground. I suppose she has become immortal because she had been wronged, because she had suffered injustice. Had she been a prototype of "The Angel in the House" she would have been lost in the crowd, and no one would ever be interested in her story. I strongly believe that she is remembered because she was a heretic. I would nevertheless like to borrow a few lines from "Return into Time" penned by the famous Austrian writer and poet Karl Kraus,[44] although in a varied circumstance, and would also like to imagine that these lines had been uttered by Mata Hari at

---

44 W. R. Everdell, *The First Moderns*, 13.

some point in time—

"My watch is turned backward

Never is what's past over for me

And I stand differently in time.

Whatever future I may reach

And whatever I grasp for the first time

Becomes for me the past."

In October 2017, after a century of her execution, The Netherlands would certainly commemorate her sacrifice with much enthusiasm and glamour, and in the other corner of the globe, in the country she spoke of so dearly for being born in, i.e., in India, no one would even care to discuss her. The story of innocent "little orchid" Margarethe and her miserably fateful end truly pained me, and this is an effort on my part to pay her a humble tribute on the occasion of her death centenary.

Chapter 1
The Socio-Cultural Canvas of the Fateful Drama

Margarethe was born in Leeuwarden during the last quarter of the nineteenth century (1876). Leeuwarden was the capital city of Friesland in the northwestern region of The Netherlands, which had been witnessing development of a secular culture. Although a predominantly bourgeois society, the country had been undergoing novel experiences of vertical pluralism or "pillarization" (*Verzuiling*) since the second half of the nineteenth century. It has been described as a structural phenomenon, "… a way in which religion or denominations organized themselves, even within those institutional spheres which are not primarily connected to religion."[1] It had been segregation of public life and a way to handle religious diversity within society. Pillarization had been a kind of modernization of the Dutch society through the emergence of socio-political formations along religious and ideological lines. The renowned Dutch sociologist J. P. Kruijt has identified the most important motives behind the phenomenon as—emancipation, protection, social control, conflict regulation, and response to modernization.[2] In The Netherlands there had been four pillars—Catholics, Protestants, Socialists, and Liberals. However, as a capital town, Leeuwarden had been quite a flourishing region brimming with wealthy residents. The area is geographically surrounded by water of the Wadden Sea, but that did not restrict its extensive commerce. Local people traded effectively giving them enough wealth to maintain a prosperous living status. The traditional costume used by the women of Leeuwarden, complete with heavy gold ornaments and a helmet-like unique head dress (*Oorijzer*) made of gold and decorated with a forehead ornament, had very much reflected the prosperity of the region. Jewelers, silversmiths, and goldsmiths had been quite famous in Leeuwarden for centuries. It was due to the wealthy people around that Adam's hat shop had been doing good business, and he might have nurtured the desire of

---
1   Jacob A. Belzen, ed., *Psychohistory in Psychology of Religion*, 211.
2   Belzen, *Towards Cultural Psychology of Religion*, 220.

being noticed and acclaimed by them. His expensive lifestyle and novel gifts to little Margarethe would surely support the state of his mind. It is most likely that Margarethe's mother, as the wife of a wealthy businessman who loved to be called a "Baron" and had believed himself to have belonged to the aristocrat circle, had also used an *Oorijzer*; and I presume that Margarethe's love for jewelry might have been inspired by her childhood images of the aristocrat ladies of Leeuwarden.

 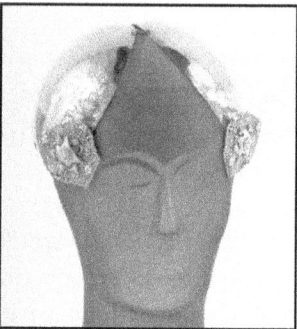

A mannequin displayed in the gold headgear of Friesland (*Oorijzer*); Internet archive, no known copyright

However, as the daughter of a successful businessman she was sent to Miss Buys' school—the best private school in the town. Girl's education during the nineteenth century had been at the preliminary stage and therefore did not develop any individual character. There had mainly been three types of schools in The Netherlands—the French schools or the elementary schools, the Higher Burgher Schools (HBS), or the secondary schools which offered modern curriculum of various science subjects including mathematics and economics, along with foreign languages for the boys in order to prepare them for some position in the industrial society. Therefore, these schools had not been considered to be fit for the girls, although a few of them did in fact attend HBS before 1867. Finally, there had been the Latin schools, which were exclusively for boys, where they were prepared for university. Although girls received education on various subjects like history, geography, hygiene, arts and crafts, etc at the elementary level, the French schools for girls had essentially taught French language, which was in vogue those days, and had also taught embroidery. The pivotal concept of girls' education had been guided by their gender-specific role for future motherhood. It is not particularly known whether the elementary schools for the girls in The Netherlands had any system to evaluate the students through examinations, or if so then how Margarethe had fared in the examinations at Miss Buys' school, although, as Waagenaar wrote: "she had continued her studies at the high school for girls on the Groote Houtstraat."[3] Not much is known about her schools, like when those had been established, how many teachers were appointed, how many students were admitted every year, what had been the school timing, or whether any sort of sports and games had been taught to the girls or not, etc. Waagenaar wrote that Miss Buys' school admitted girls from the socially established middle-class and upper middle-class families of Leeuwarden. It is also not known what kind of relationship Margarethe had shared with the teachers. She was different from all others in her own way, and according to one of her classmates who had written the following lines for her at a young age—"Amidst a thousand dandelions, one shining orchid stands."[4]

None of these things however had attracted little Margarethe. School, for her, had primarily been a place where, unlike others, she could show off her remarkably beautiful and flamboyant dresses to her peers and admirers, and also could brandish her other prized possessions gifted by her father. Her bold and beautiful cursive handwriting was albeit admired by one and all in her school, as is evident from some of her friends' statements at a much later date. Writing couplets for the friends and exchanging them had been a common game among young girls in those days, and Margarethe had indulged in it quite frequently. Some of her friends had even carefully preserved few of her couplets gifted to them during their schooldays. Waagenaar wrote about one of her friends Mrs. Ybeltje Kerkhof-Hoogslag, who had actually presented him with one of the poems penned by Margarethe at the age of 12, while they had still been studying in Miss Buys' school.[5] Although, according to them, she had a flair for languages and music, she was never known to be meritorious or even studious for that matter. That was not something expected from a girl of her age either, as it was not the call of the time. Girls had ideally been prepared for domesticity and motherhood in the European society as they were expected only to become the helpmates of their husbands; and even if middle-class or upper middle-class women required to work for a respectable living it had necessarily to be about teaching

---

3 Waagenaar, *op. cit.*, 1964, 19.
4 Ibid., 20.
5 Ibid., 19.

in Kindergarten schools, which had become popular due to Friedrich Fröebel's model of child education. It had been due to this reason that the Vissers at Sneek had sent Margarethe to a teacher training school to prepare her as a future Kindergarten teacher.

There had plausibly been another angle to this choice of job by women, which might be mentioned pertinently. In the Dutch society, men had discouraged women to work outside the home on a regular basis, because that implied compromising with child care and domestic chores, which had been the sole responsibility of women, especially of married women. Moreover, men were worried about morals of women who would be free from their control at workplace for at least a considerable time of the day. It was a common social understanding that without any surveillance women might go astray. Close proximity assured control over the wife, lack of which had been cause for suspicion regarding her sexual promiscuity. Betty A. DeBerg aptly wrote: "Women's morality was important to men also because it eased the doubts men had about their own sexuality... Since men could not really be manly and preach sexual restraint, it fell to the women to be the guardians of decency. A man worried about controlling his sexual drives could place that burden on women and feel safer from the sin always lurking in him."[6] Therefore, for a woman, participation in the economic and productive world outside the private domain was seen as mark of a drastic shift from virtuous womanhood. Woman had been considered morally superior only within the boundaries of her domestic sphere. The cultural prejudice was nothing new to the European homes, and because women's position had been subordinated even by the law, they had no other option than to endure. Teaching in a Kindergarten school meant dealing with small children who required motherly care, and hence was seen as an extension of their ideal role of motherhood which, men had significantly thought, women could perform with comfort. The only other profession for respectable middle-class women was nursing, as it had involved their service as care givers. Florence Nightingale had made efforts to establish nursing training schools in England quarter of a century before and had shown to the Europeans that it was a noble profession which involved all the feminine aptitudes of compassion, sacrifice, and devotion. As nursing required women to provide motherly care to the sick, it had been taken as an extension of women's ideal role that was approved by the society. Teaching

---

6   Betty A. DeBerg, *Ungodly Women*, 21.

and nursing had thus been considered to be the two most feminine jobs suited for middle-class respectable women in Europe. Russell Warren Howe speculated that the two occupations open to women at that time were domestic service and teaching.[7] In my opinion domestic service had not been a choice for the middle-class women who had opted to take up work for a living, although it might have been a choice for women of the underprivileged classes. There were however other fields where women had been working during that era, which included factory work of various kinds, although it had not been quite popular.

However, Margarethe was born and brought up in a simple or nuclear family, consisting of both of her parents and her three brothers. It had been the usual family structure of her home town as elsewhere in the northwestern region of Europe in those days. As the eldest child she did get complete attention of her parents, at least till birth of the second child, and had always been pampered in all possible ways by her wealthy egoist father till his bankruptcy in February 1889. Margarethe was only twelve years and a half at that time. After her mother's death (May 1891) the family had crumbled right away as Adam had never set up any alternative support system for his family. Not much is known about his extended family and his relationship with them, although he had three sisters, all of whom were married and had been well settled, and both his parents had died before his wife's death. If however the children had been born in a joint family they still would have had some elderly member in the family to back them up in the absence of their mother and in that case the family could have been held together. I strongly believe that moving out from home as an adolescent after her mother's early demise had been detrimental to Margarethe in every way, because it had started off a trail of unfortunate occurrences which she was neither prepared to face, nor was she capable to handle. All of a sudden, as if, Adam had thrown away his "little orchid" into the deep waters of hard reality. From the cozy nook of her sweet home she had abruptly been put into the agonizing realm of the odious world. She was therefore bound to get lost in the hazardous web of life.

Margarethe had seen her mother's dedication for the family and the children and had also witnessed her sufferings and eventual death caused by Adam's apathy after his bankruptcy. Like numerous other Dutch women

---

7   Howe, *op. cit.*, 18.

of her time Antje van der Meulen must have followed the "Marriage Bible" of Jacob Cats (*Houwelyck*), which was published in 1625, and had been extremely popular in the then Dutch society. It had preached the duties of women at all the six stages of their life (maiden, sweetheart, bride, housewife, mother, widow), stressing on their duties of domesticity and child rearing in marriage. Deeply shaken by her mother's premature death Margarethe might have thought that adhering to the traditional model of womanhood was simply futile and was not really necessary for her. She had certainly not been born to suffer or to vegetate like a slave as her mother did. She knew she loved the adventures of life and all the enjoyment it offered. After all she had Adam's blood in her veins, and since early childhood had been deeply impressed by his love for sophistication and grandeur. She must have thought why would only men have all the right to enjoy! As in all other western countries during the middle of the nineteenth century, in The Netherlands too, feminism had started to spread wings as women had traditionally been denied the right to higher education, right to equal opportunity and equal pay for work, right to property and possession, right to guardianship, and above all, their voting right. In 1878, Aletta Henriette Jacobs had been the first European lady from The Netherlands to have completed the medical degree. In order to fight for women's rights, in 1888, women's weekly magazine *The Women* was started by Wilhelmina Drucker (a.k.a. Gipsy), a First Wave feminist in Amsterdam, followed by the Free Women's Association (VVV). Her Association had been the first organized league in The Netherlands to have raised women's issues strongly and had voiced for the relief of women's stupid, insensible, ridiculous, and unreasonable household duties. Was Margarethe aware of the revolutionary feminist currents of the late nineteenth century in The Netherlands, or as such in Europe? Did she ever get an opportunity to go through the Dutch translation (1870) of *The Subjection of Women* penned by John Stuart Mill, where he had aptly described woman as "the actual 'bond-servant' of her husband"?[8] If given a choice she might have rebelled for the novel idea of equal right to enjoyment, which none of the feminists of her time would have dared to. Margarethe had never cared for right to equal education, equal wage, and not even for the voting right. Feminism had never been her forte.

After Antje's death, Adam had compelled his teenage daughter to leave the family for good, while she had longed to be with him in Amsterdam.

---

8   J. S. Mill, *The Subjection of Women*, 55.

As an adolescent teenager to feel awfully insecure without her mother was quite normal for Margarethe, and separated from her brothers she was even abandoned by her father. She had been sent alone to her uncle's house, which had infuriated her as she felt terribly alienated, but she was helpless. She could only blame Adam for everything that had happened to them. At the age of only 13, she had realized that her life would become miserable in the company of her orthodox relatives, because her idea of happiness differed vastly from what they had planned for her. Margarethe had felt the need to take life in her own stride. However, I wonder whether she had ever pondered about the following what–if scenario—what would have happened if instead of the twins Adam had taken her along with him to Amsterdam. Under any circumstance his second wife would surely not support Margarethe's extravagant lifestyle, and after his bankruptcy Adam would in no way continue to pamper his darling daughter as he had always done before. In that case also she would have blamed Adam for all unhappiness that would befall her. The only thing Adam would then have done according to the social customs was to get her married to a groom of his choice. Would she be happy ever after in that case? Was she prepared to accept all domestic responsibilities customary for a wife in the male-dominated bourgeois society that she had been a part of? I suppose the answers to these questions would surely be in the negative, because she had hated the idea of being a domestic slave to the husband. She could have never lived in anonymity like the millions of European wives of her time. Margarethe was inclined to challenge masculine identity of the society from the very start, and therefore might not have been suited for the customary role of a wife and mother. Hence, the first phase of Margarethe's life was bound to end there, and so it did, although by then she had started to show one of the dangerous traits of her personality—strength and assertiveness—in a thoroughly bourgeois society where women had been liberated neither socially nor legally. Therefore, she was denied the social space that she had claimed for.

My efforts at a socio-cultural post-mortem of Margarethe's life and her tragic end necessitates digging into the socio-cultural past of the European society, especially of The Netherlands, France, and England, during the second half of the nineteenth and early twentieth centuries, because that had been the center stage of her narrative. The *Napoleonic Civil Code* in France and in The Netherlands, and the Victorian sentiment in England, had cast overwhelming impact through the length and breadth of the populace. Napoleon, the proud creator of the *Civil Code*, was exceptionally inspired by the laws of ancient Rome (Justinian Code) while compiling it, which had been implemented in France in 1805, and in The Netherlands in 1811. Although his *Code* had undergone certain modifications in The Netherlands in 1838, it had continued to influence the society for more than a 100 years. The *Civil Code* had manifested a double standard regarding the laws prescribed for man and woman, for example, in cases of adultery, property rights, rights over children, etc. In continuation of the traditional patriarchal ideals of that era the *Code* had confined women to the private sphere and had characterized them with the feminine qualities of beauty, charm, and seductiveness. Popular belief had been that women were never guided by reason and therefore lacked the essential aptitudes to participate in the public sphere. According to Napoleon, women were "chattels" of men, and hence, their obligations were complete dependence on and submission to their husbands and family.[9] In his opinion nothing could have been more important for a woman other than marrying and producing children, because she was in essence her husband's personal property. Due to the husband's marital power, he had the right to rule his wife and was considered to be the sovereign lord of his house. Woman was expected by the society and bound by law to be obedient to her husband all through her life. J. S. Mill wrote: "... no slave is a slave to the same lengths, and in so full a sense of the word, as a wife is."[10] Thus, women had been considered to be the "second sex" who were undoubtedly stationed inferior to men by all means, and it was quite normal for men to have control over them—could be the father, brother, husband, or even the aged sons. Women who had not been under such control were looked down upon as fallen, were not respected because they posed a challenge to the gender-role defined by the society, and in most cases had become social outcasts.

The same had also been true in Victorian England. Victorian values had included strict set of moral standards reflected particularly through sexual restraint and rigid social control. The Queen believed that because God had created men and women separately, they should be different in all ways and continue to remain in their own positions—man being the master and woman the subject. Respectability had been an important social construct both for men and women. Marriage and motherhood

---

9 June K. Burton, *Napoleon and the Woman Question*, 6.
10 Mill, *op. cit.*, 57.

held the central position in the notion of ideal womanhood. Family bore all features of the bourgeois society, where women were expected to be sacrificing, caring, and devoted. Nothing was more respectable for a wife than bearing and rearing children. Bram Dijkstra explained this position of women as that of "household nuns."[11] Woman was expected to be so passionless, pure, and spiritual that she almost would not have a body. The perfect "household nun" should support her husband spiritually, and protect him from all kinds of moral pitfalls; and this service could only be possible if she was morally perfect. Therefore, her place had to be inside home, which was considered to be unpolluted by sin. DeBerg wrote: "Men needed a refuge entirely free from the trials and uncertainties of the world of business and politics."[12] And it had been the wife's task to provide him the safe haven after every tiring day. Men compensated women by naming her "queen of the home," thus making them joyous and content with the position. The French *Civil Code* of Napoleon surely had a deep influence on Queen Victoria. J. C. Herold suggested, "It was with him, not with Queen Victoria, that Victorian morality originated."[13]

This particular value system of the then society had been extremely important in the trial and execution of Mata Hari. It has been evident from the various writings of her biographers that she was convicted not for what she had done, but certainly for what she had been. Rosie White wrote: "Her real story is a morality tale of a different kind, as it maps the changing roles of women in modern Europe. In this sense, she may be a feminist fore-runner …"[14] White furthermore added: "Mata Hari fed into projections, fears and anxieties regarding women and modernity that emerged in the late nineteenth century." The conservative people who had been powerful, especially the Catholics, somehow had despised her for what she was and had seen her life as that of a heretic—as deviation from the traditional female position in the society. A Protestant by belief, Mata Hari had never shown any sort of ardent religious behavior. Her character traits could never have come anywhere closer to that of a "household nun." Therefore, she could obviously be targeted for her lifestyle by those who believed that being a woman she should have been confined to the private realm of domestic life; instead, she had shunned

---

11   Bram Dijkstra, *Idols of Perversity*, 3.
12   DeBerg, *op. cit.*, 20.
13   J. C. Herold, *The Age of Napoleon*, 149.
14   Rosie White, *Violent Femmes: Women as Spies in Popular Culture*, 34.

her family to enjoy life in horribly unacceptable ways displaying depraved morality. For them she had definitely been setting a bad precedence in the society as she became an icon of carnality in her time. She in fact had been too visible in a male-dominated society, which did not even permit any legal status to women living apart from men. She had always been more active than was socially assigned to respectable women of the then society. Rosie White was of the opinion that, "This active role marks her out as not 'proper', not 'feminine'; in her wifely behavior as in her subsequent career, she exceeded the bounds of her gender, class, and race."[15]

During the turn of the century, Europe had been witnessing many changes. The first wave of feminism had already flourished by that time and women became more vocal regarding their social and legal rights. Women suffrage movements had been uprising as they had claimed to establish their own identity and dignity. It had given birth to the notion of "New Woman" (coined in England and used by Sarah Grand in her essay "The New Aspect of the Woman Question," published in *North American Review*, Vol. 158, No. 448, March 1894, 271), who had rebelled against man's control over her and had wanted to live life on her own terms defying all illogical orthodox norms of domesticity. The New Woman had aspired to step beyond the limit of motherhood and to create a new identity in the public sphere by taking up jobs that had traditionally been meant for men. She had vouched for equal opportunity of the sexes and had claimed respect not as man's slave or helpmate, but as a human being. She had realized the value of economic independence, as it entailed all kinds of freedom. Only because woman had no other way than to depend on man for her living that man took advantage of her situation to enslave and ridicule her. New Woman had vowed to stop exploitation by the dominating sex, who had traditionally considered themselves to be superior in every way, as they had the control over productive paid service. Men, through ages, had considered women to be particularly suitable only for unpaid domestic work and therefore they were assigned merely with reproduction. For them the ideal woman had to be domestic goddess who would take care of his every mundane need. But in order to become self-sustaining in all possible ways, New Woman was keen to exchange unpaid work for paid work. Productive work had been her chief goal, and she had wanted to shed the burden of reproduction, which only enchained and disadvantaged her. The image of a

---
15 Ibid., 36.

domestic goddess no more fascinated her. The New Woman had hence been depicted by the conservative society as a menace that had directly challenged the Victorian concept of femininity in Britain. Most of the literary and art works of that era had been misogynic in nature, although exceptions existed. Henrik Ibsen's *A Doll's House* was staged in London in 1889, which had presented the protagonist Nora as a rebel. She had questioned the customary marriage rules and did quit at the end. Ibsen's play had strongly inspired the ideal of women's self-development and had boosted the spirit of feminism in Europe.

France was no exception as the new wave had rapidly broken on its shores as well. During the dawn of the new century (1900), the French society had continued to be sharply divided into two spheres—the private or the domestic, and the public sphere. The former had been the place demarcated for women, while the latter was characterized by masculinity which had strictly belonged to men. Debora L. Silverman wrote: "the *Femme Nouvelle* inverted traditional sexual roles and threatened the essential divisions ordering bourgeoisie life: public from private, work from family, production from reproduction."[16] Even in the New Republic women had not been treated as free citizens, they did not have the liberty to enjoy life, nor did they have the right to take decisions on their own. The principles of liberty, equality and fraternity, on which the new Third Republic had been founded, had appeared to be out of their reach. Woman was still paid less for a specific work compared to her male counterpart. Husband enjoyed the position of being head of the family having absolute social and legal rights over the person and property of his wife, and because woman was considered to be dependent minor, her earnings belonged to him. The New Republic could not bring any change to woman's position in the society as love, submissiveness, and obedience to her husband had still remained the absolute measure of femininity. In April 1901, the National Council of French Women had been founded to promote women's rights, which was headed by Madame Isabelle Bogelot, a French philanthropist and women's rights activist, and was led by her assistants like the author and journalist Avril de Sainte Croix and philanthropist Sarah Monod. Majority of the members had been Protestant by religion, as the Catholic women philanthropists had accepted the patriarchal social order and had refrained from participation. The Council arranged frequent meetings to bring up issues like women suffrage, extremely biased and anti-feminist

---

16   Debora L. Silverman, *Art Nouveau in Fin-de-Siècle France*, 63.

legal code which had been designed to ban women from public life, women employment, equal wage, equal education, etc. The new wave of feminism in France, which had challenged gender stereotype, had exposed the crisis of male identity and the manner in which it threatened women empowerment in a highly bourgeois society. The Conservatives and Catholic citizens had feared that the feminist trend would soon destroy France by destroying the family structure of the society.

It is quite obvious that men would not encourage such "unconfined femininity"[17] of the New Woman, as she had induced unfounded fear in them—fear of losing control over half of the population and fear of becoming insecure in the private domain by losing sovereignty. It might also have been the fear of getting avenged for the wrong they were doing for very long in the domestic space. Men had firmly believed that if women stepped beyond the private sphere they would immediately get involved in immoral sexual acts and their newfound freedom would certainly provoke them to stray from their domestic duties. They had started believing that if the New Woman was not restrained then the entire social structure along with its moral order would eventually collapse. Therefore, the New Woman had been portrayed as disoriented "wild woman"[18] (Mrs. Eliza Lynn Linton, 1891), who opposed marriage and sought absolute freedom for sexual license and unparalleled power—social, legal, and political. "Mistress of herself, the wild woman as a social insurgent preaches the lesson of liberty broadened into lawlessness and license." Mrs. Linton gave a list of womanly virtues, like patience, self-sacrifice, tenderness, quietness, modesty, etc,[19] which the New Woman lacked. Mona Caird wrote: "The logic is stern: either a woman is a "modest violet, blooming unseen," unquestioning, uncomplaining, a patient producer of children, regardless of all costs to herself ... or a rude masculine creature ... an adventuress ..."[20] However unreal it had been, Linton's depiction implied that the New Woman was a pervert, who had despised family, had considered fidelity as bondage, and thus had ridiculed the basic foundation of society. She was identified with the bloomers and the bicycle. Since

---

17 White, *op. cit.*, 36.
18 Eliza Lynn Linton, "The Wild Woman as Social Insurgents," *The Rebel of the Family*, D.T. Meem, ed., 417.
19 Linton, *The Girl of the Period* (Vol II), 1883, 117.
20 Mona Caird, *The Morality of Marriage and other Essays on the Status and Destiny of Women*, 161.

New Woman was seen as a threat to the cult of domestic angels, contemporary magazines, journals, and pamphlets published cartoons and articles despising such practice. All of that had been meant to humiliate women in every possible way, but it had only expressed the inmost wrath and insecurity of men. A few anti-feminist women had also joined their league due to their Catholic background and allegiance. Kevin Passmore wrote: "Catholic women also embraced anti-feminism, for female access to the professions implied that women and men were the same, and thus undermined Catholic women's claim to moralize the male world as mothers."[21]

Here I would like to make a note of the trend of anti-Semitism that had been prevalent in many European societies through centuries, Britain and France not being exceptions. In the New Republic anti-Semitism was being used as a means by the Conservatives to secure the hierarchical society and its institutions, especially the army and the church. During the end of the nineteenth century, Alfred Dreyfus had been a victim of that discriminatory trend in France. He was convicted of treason and espionage in 1894, on the charges of informing the German Embassy in Paris about French military secrets. It had been a much debated classic case of miscarriage of justice. His most sensational trial and subsequent conviction had greatly been affected due to his Jewish descent. Bernard Lazare, a Jewish journalist who stood firmly by Dreyfus after his arrest, wrote: "... because he was a Jew he was arrested. Because he was a Jew he was convicted. Because he was a Jew the voices of justice and of truth could not be heard in his favor."[22] It had been presumed that the Panama Crisis in 1892, and the subsequent anti-Semite propaganda in the leading newspapers of France, especially in Edouard Adolphe Drumont's paper *La Libre Parole* (Free Speech), had strongly influenced the consequences of the Dreyfus case.[23] Drumont was a renowned French journalist and a strong defender of the Catholic ideals, who had founded the Anti-Semitic League of France because of his deep rooted belief in anti-Semitic ideals and principles. Piers Paul Read wrote: "He was ... shy and self-effacing, a closed personality, set in his ways, very old-fashioned, rather eccentric,

---

21 Kevin Passmore, *The Right in France*, 103.
22 Quoted in Robert Michael, *A History of Catholic Antisemitism: The Dark Side of the Church*, 132.
23 Leon Poliakov, *The History of Anti-Semitism: Suicidal Europe, 1870-1933*, (Vol. 4), 47.

excessively introspective, contemplative, scholarly—'a kind of secular monk.'"[24] In fact the Dreyfus Affair had triggered a bitter political and judicial scandal in France, but although he had been acquitted of all charges in 1906, the trend of anti-Semitism did not cease to continue. It was too deeply rooted to have stopped with a single incident, and there had been no dearth of anti-Semitic literature during the Belle Époque, as hundreds and thousands of titles and pamphlets were published in France during that time. "The Jew" was depicted as "the other" and therefore alien to the true nationalist France. Dreyfus had been a victim of the social stigma.

The international body of anti-Semites had their head quarters in Paris, and the French journalist and author Louis Veuillot, as the leader of French Catholicism, had significant contribution toward the movement. Father Emmanuel d'Alzon's Assumptionist paper *La Croix* had been the most widely circulated Roman Catholic publication in France, which propagated anti-Semitism as a principle. Drumont's book *Jewish France* (1886) and the subsequent articles in his *La Libre Parole* had revived the anti-Semitic sentiment in France to a great extent. After the crash of the Union Generale bank in 1882, blame had been put entirely on the Jews, as the conservative French Catholics of France were afraid of losing their influence in every matter—educational, social, economical, and political. That financial disaster might have led to the monumental success of Drumont's *Jewish France*. He was highly prejudiced against the Jews and blamed them for every disaster France had been facing—be it social, political, or economical. He wrote: "France was a conquered nation and was ruled by an alien minority, the Jews." His book was so popular in France that it had been reprinted many times (200 prints in 25 years), even after the Dreyfus case had terminated. He had once said that his only merit was the commitment to print what everyone had been thinking. Drumont had depicted the Jews in a repulsive way as "Semites, mercantile, greedy, scheming, devious ..."[25] who had inherently been spies, traitors, criminals, and carriers of diseases.[26] The negative propaganda had farfetched implications and even instigated anti-Jewish riots in France at the end of the nineteenth century. In 1901, a notable anti-Semitic congress was held in Paris, which had elected Drumont as an honorary president. The two chief slogans of the congress had been—"Down with the Jews," and

---

24 Piers Paul Read, *The Dreyfus Affair*, 33.
25 Quoted in Poliakov, *op. cit.*, 41.
26 William Brustein, *Roots of Hate: Anti-Semitism in Europe before the Holocaust*, 119.

"France for the French." But Drumont had not been a loner in this league as he was joined by stalwarts like Auguste-Maurice Barres, Jules Soury, and others. Even Britain, Germany, and Italy had a strong current of anti-Semitism. *Civilta Cattolica*, the Jesuit bi-monthly magazine published in Italy, had been printing articles lambasting the Jews, which undoubtedly amounted to anti-Jewish militancy.

During the end of the nineteenth century, observed Robert Michael, "more than one-third of the officers graduated from the French military academy at Saint-Cyr had studied in religious institutions, profoundly influenced by the Jesuits and the Assumptionists, leading anti-Semitic Catholic orders of the period ... Many members of the General Staff were faithful readers of *La Croix* and Drumont's popular *La Libre Parole*." Then again he said, "Dreyfus was accused and convicted primarily because he was a Jew. France needed a scapegoat for her serious social, economical, financial, and political problems, and for most French Catholics, the Jews were the perfect scapegoats; they were France's Cains, Judases, Shylocks, and Wandering Jews."[27] I find strange similarity between the fate of Alfred Dreyfus and that of Mata Hari, although they had been destined to face varied ends. The Protestants were seen by the French Catholics as ardent sympathizers of the Jews, and according to her passport Margarethe Zelle had been a Protestant. Due to her considerably dark complexion, dark hair, and black eyes she was mistaken to be a Jew, although due to the same reasons she had been mistaken to be a dancer of Indian origin. That which gave her fame and had once been her asset had become a burden for her in the end. Moreover, due to her lifestyle she was seen as a deviant woman who had defied the traditional female role of passivity, and due to her inclination for a luxurious and lustful life she was despised by the conservative Catholics of France. For them Jewish women by nature were coquettish and profane. Therefore, when Thomas Coulson, a British intelligence officer who had been working in France, wrote *Mata Hari, Courtesan and Spy*, he did not hesitate to mention her as a Jew. He wrote: "... an amber-tinted body which she inherited, not from her Hindu parents, but from Jewish progenitors." Elsewhere he said, "Her nearest approach to oriental ancestry was a strain of Jewish blood through her father's descent."[28] Coulson had been inspired by Emile Massard's *Women Spies in Paris: The Truth about Mata Hari*, where Massard had

---

27 Michael, *op. cit.*, 131.
28 Major Thomas Coulson, *Mata Hari: Courtesan and Spy*, 14–17.

put forward the idea that Mata Hari was "of Jewish origin, converted to Protestanism." Even though she had never stepped on its soil, some newspapers and magazines in America had published articles referring to her Jewish-Protestant origin. Although nothing related to her religion had ever been discussed during her trial and conviction, I presume, like Dreyfus, Mata Hari too had been a scapegoat of France, her case being related to the First World War. It appears that finding a scapegoat to sail over severe crises might have been a trusted practice in France.

But how did Margarethe become Mata Hari, the iconic demimondaine of the early twentieth century Europe? She had a vivid vision about what she aspired for (luxury, appreciation, attention, and love—everything that she missed after Adam had deserted her and also in her marriage with Rudolf), although she might never have contemplated making it immensely big for herself. Many factors had played important roles in her making, the most significant had been Paris of the Belle Époque. Starting in the last decade of the nineteenth century and spanning till the beginning of the First World War, it had been an era of optimism and opulence particularly in France. Science, technology, arts, and literature had flourished as never before, and so did fashion and popular culture in the form of light entertainment, which had been appreciated widely. Many public theaters and operas had been established to hold music and dance performances by upcoming singers and dancers of varied styles. Salon music and dance, cancan dance, ballet, and the cabaret had been particularly of roaring craze. Prominent dancers like Loie Fuller (America—1862), Caroline la belle Otero (Spain—1868), Liane de Pougy (France—1869), Émilienne d'Alençon (France—1869), Sarah Brown (France—1869), Maud de Allan (Canada—1873), Cléo de Mérode (Paris—1875), Carlotta Zambelli (Italy—1875), Isadora Duncan (America—1877), Ida Rubenstein (Russia—1885), and many others had stormed the stage during the last quarter of the nineteenth century in Paris. Otero, de Pougy, and d'Alençon had together been known as the "*Les Grandes Trios*" of the Belle Époque. Each one of the demimondaines or the "*Grandes Horizontales*" had appeared with some new dancing styles, but the common feature among all had been their exceptional beauty. To make it a success for herself, Mata Hari had to compete with all those gigantic stage personalities.

It becomes quite evident from the newspaper reporting of that time how

Mata Hari had composed her performances and how she had enchanted the audience by her charm. It was not at all relevant whether she had been a trained dancer or not, people were simply mesmerized to see what she presented on the evenings before a selected audience. Those who were not so privileged remained content with the gossips and pictures published in newspapers and magazines. After the successful performance of "*The Dream*" at the Olympia Theater in Paris in the month of August 1905, she had earned 10,000 francs in an evening for the first time. There was no dearth of reviewers who had been enchanted by her graceful performances and had used carefully chosen words to express their obsession with her. She had actually based her choreography on the dances of Central Java, as she had lived in Malang for some time and had been familiar with their dancing styles. The *Prambanan* Temple in Central Java (west of Malang) is a cluster of three temples dedicated to the Hindu Trinity—Lord Siva, Vishnu, and Brahmā, the biggest one at the central position being dedicated to Lord Siva. It had been built in the ninth century AD by Lokpāla, a Hindu king of the Sanjaya Dynasty. Some of the traditional dance forms of that region are the sacred Javanese Serimpi court dance, the Surabaya dance, Bedhaya dance, the Ronggeng dance of seduction, etc. All the styles comprise of slow and graceful movements of the dancers while they unfold some mythological storyline. As a westerner Margarethe had seen for the first time something absolutely different from her known genres and must have been effectively impressed by these styles while in the East Indies. During her days in Holland, before her wedding, she probably had known about ballet dance, which require rigorous training and meticulous discipline for the performers to execute its impeccably uniform style. She did not like the dance form because nothing related to rigidity and discipline had ever appealed to Margarethe (although later in her life as Mata Hari she had tried to learn ballet at one point of time). She believed in complete freedom of expression. Therefore, shadowing the Javanese dance styles could have been her first choice when she got a chance to perform in Paris, although she did not meticulously follow any particular style distinctive to that country. She had created the magic on her own. After seeing the Cambodian dance performances of Cléo de Mérode at the Paris World Exposition in 1900, the Parisians might have been delighted to see something more exotic from Mata Hari, something that had transcended all imaginations.

Mata Hari however had never worn bloomers, nor did she ride a bicycle symbolic of the New Woman, but she was very fond of horse riding, which, at her time, had been considered to be a sign of aristocracy. Although she was ambitious, idealistic, worldly wise, and adventurous—the qualities attributed to the New Woman—she had never belonged to the cult of New Woman in the truest sense of the phrase, but unfortunately had got bracketed by the orthodox people for her ways—because she had separated from her husband and lived independently on her own terms, because she had willfully defied the social role of suffering in silence that had been assigned to her as a woman—the role of a domestic goddess—of a perfect wife and mother. Instead of becoming a perfect "household nun," she had become a goddess of sensuality. Mata Hari had never claimed to be a New Woman, nor did she wish to step into the man's productive sphere and compete with them. She rather had aspired to become the goddess of male fantasy (like Ūrvashi—the Vedic nymph) and rule over their erotic passions.[29] Men could only be her subjects and never her competitors. She was too happy to have been an independent woman devoid of any family ties, living in comfort and opulence that she had always aspired for, and for having considerable number of patrons and admirers for her sustenance. Although she never had thought of becoming a courtesan, destiny had drawn her to that profession. After all, Mata Hari might have thought, she was not an insignificant street prostitute. Her sense of pride would have prevented her by all means to settle for so little. As a courtesan she had been engaged in "relatively exclusive exchanges of artistic graces, elevated conversation, and sexual favors with male patrons ..."[30] She had undoubtedly been highly accomplished in that particular art, at least more than any of her contemporaries.

As a courtesan Mata Hari had been free to choose her patrons, could effortlessly combine both pleasure and leisure, and was admired and respected by the society at the same time. So, it could at the least be asserted that she had become a respectable and reputable lady on her own caliber. Through her lived experiences she had known very well that no matter how much respect for the family one might have, it was virtually a torture to be wife of an inconsiderate husband. If Rudolf had the right to abuse her only because she had to depend on him for her living,

---

29 Mata Hari perfectly suited the description of "spoilt woman" as depicted by Linton; *The Girl of the Period* (Vol I), 321.

30 M. Feldman, and Bonnie Gordon, eds. *The Courtesan's Arts: Cross Cultural Perspectives*, 5.

then did she not have the right at least to live with respect? In no way would she have accepted the social equation of bondage and respect. She had therefore decided to put an end to her torment by getting separated from him. Rudolf did not even honor the court order granting alimony to Margarethe. That is where her life as wife of Rudolf was to end, and Griet had been lost forever. She had to suppress the mother in her as well, as Rudolf was not ready to part with baby Non. Although Margarethe had a court order in her favor regarding the custody of Non, but she had decided not to challenge Rudolf. By then she had realized that the course of her life was going to take a sharp turn and having Non with her could have certainly been an impediment. She must have felt awfully bad for that, and later in her life had made quite a few futile attempts to bring Non back.[31] Even if she had much grudges against Rudolf, Non was truly innocent, and as the mother she had genuinely missed her daughter very much. Coulson quoted Paul Frantz-Namur, the French painter who had painted two of Mata Hari's portraits, where he had said, "The most striking thing about her was the astonishing fact that ... (she) rarely lost the expression of inmost sadness ... I cannot recall that I ever saw Mata Hari smile."[32] Margarethe's innermost self must have suffered unconsoled pain for losing both of her children—Norman and Non. She must have remembered how she had felt on the death of her mother—how lonely, forsaken, and insecure she became. Knowing Rudolf as an alcoholic and a womanizer she must have been worried about Non's wellbeing and about her future in the custody of a stepmother (Rudolf was going to marry soon after their divorce in 1906). But she was helpless—the opportunity to become Mata Hari had been irresistible, and nothing could have compelled her to retreat. While Margarethe as the mother lost, Mata Hari had won.

However, while Ibsen's *A Doll's House* was effecting considerable social discord in Edwardian England, a new genre of literature had emerged, which strongly affected the political consequences of Europe—the invasion novels and the spy novels of early twentieth century, which had belonged to the literature of patriotism. Between 1901 and 1914 an estimated 300 spy stories had been published only in England. Thomas Boghardt wrote: "The ascent of scare literature occurred parallel with the restructuring of British society and Britain's relative decline *vis-à-vis* the great

---

31 Waagenaar, *Mata Hari: A Biography*, 1965, 91, 120–122.
32 Quoted in Coulson, *op. cit.*, 44.

powers."[33] Even before that a few novels had been written in English, which dealt with the plot of a possible German invasion of England. It might have been inspired by the victory of Germany in the Franco-Prussian War of 1870–1871. The first of its kind had been *The Battle of Dorking* authored by George T. Chesney in 1871. The next notable novel in that genre was William Tuffnell Le Queux's *The Great War in England in 1897*, which had been published in 1894. The plot became instantly popular in England and had inspired more similar novels, not only in England but in other European countries as well. Later, probably inspired by the Kruger Telegram of Kaiser William II in 1896 regarding the Second Boer War,[34] more spy novels had appeared. In 1896, William Le Queux wrote his path breaking fiction *A Secret Service*, and in 1898, E. Philips Oppenheim had published *Mysterious Mr. Sabin*, which also intrigued the English readers. Edwardian England had witnessed a boom in that genre of literature. *How the Germans Took London* had been authored in 1900 by T. W. Offin, in which the storyline revolved around the Boer War. Erskine Childers wrote *The Riddle of the Sands* in 1903, which had been the trend setter in the genre of spy novels. It had sparked a series of novels and stories with similar themes published in England, France, and Germany, setting forth the well-known phenomenon of spy-fever or espionitis. The plots of the English novels had usually been dealing with German spies living in England with the goal to obtain information in order to sabotage the British Empire. A few other novels that were published in 1906 had been *The Shock of Battle* (Patrick Vaux), *The North Sea Bubble* (Ernest Oldmeadow), *The Enemy in Our Midst* (Walter Wood), and *Writing on the Wall* (General Staff—pseud.).

The most successful among all had been Le Queux's remarkable novel *The Invasion of 1910: With a Full Account of the Siege of London*, which was published in 1906. It had been a classic depiction of Germano-phobia, where the author had reflected on his own experiences to make his

---

33 Thomas Boghardt, *Spies of the Kaiser*, 4.
34 On January 3, 1896, Kaiser William II of Germany had signed a telegram with the following words congratulating for the victory against Britain, which was dispatched to President Paul Kruger of the Boer Republic of Transvaal—"I express my sincere congratulations that you and your people, without appealing to friendly powers for help, by dint of your own vigor, have been able to restore the peace against the armed hordes that invaded your country as disturbers of the peace, and to preserve the independence of the country against outside attacks." The dispatch had triggered a long-term anti-German sentiment among the British people.

fictions absolutely realistic. His *Spies of the Kaiser: Plotting the Downfall of England* was published in 1909, which had great impact on the readers and almost had made every other person a suspect of enemy espionage. He had been a great sympathizer of the British Empire and had particularly written against Germany. As he had been the war correspondent of the *Daily Mail*, most of his espionage novels were serialized in that paper. His fantastic stories had been laden with the flavor of patriotism and were presented so convincingly that the readers found truth in each of his words, and in no time the circulation of the paper had increased significantly. Le Queux's binary purpose had been to alert the British citizens about the danger of a possible German invasion, and to make profit out of the fear psychosis that was generated among them. *The Invasion of 1910* was made into film in 1914 named *If England Were Invaded*,[35] which had successfully cast deep impact on the society and had heightened public hatred against Germany in Britain. His wartime novel *The German Spy* was published in September 1914, in which he claimed that he in fact had known the protagonist who actually lived in London. In early 1915 he wrote *German Spies in England*, which had a record sell and only in 18 days it had gone through 6 editions. It had been one of his most remarkable works in which he had persistently claimed that every corner of England was virtually flooded with German spies. His presentations used to be so vivid and realistic that the insecure common people in general readily believed him. Le Queux had also popularized his spy theme through lecturing in many places in England.[36] Mention of *When William Came: A Story of London under the Hohenzollerus*, authored by Hector Hugh Munro in 1913, would be pertinent, because it had significantly predicted the First World War and had enkindled Germanophobia by elaborating on the presence of an army of sleeping German spies in England. There had been no dearth of literature on the subject that had continued to influence people throughout the war years.

The spy novels, a few films made on those stories in the years prior to the First World War, and the effectual spy-mania or espionitis are particularly noteworthy in the case of Mata Hari's conviction and execution. Le Queux's novels had created much public tumult as the *Daily Mail* had reported that thousands of German undercover agents and spies had been residing in England in the guise of waiters, barbers, help-maids, nannies,

---

35   B. F. Woods, *Neutral Grounds*, 36.
36   Panikos Panayi, *Enemy in our Midst*, 160–162.

nurses, governesses, washers, and in all other possible occupations. It had actually been the idea of Wilhelm J. Carl E. Stieber, who was the most trusted master spy of Otto von Bismark. His brilliance in the field had awarded him with many prestigious accolades, and he had served as the director of the Prussian military police after the Revolutions of 1848. He had also investigated against Karl Marx in 1850. I would pertinently like to quote from a book written by an "Ex-Intelligence Officer," who might plausibly have been Le Queux himself, but had tactfully ascribed it to Stieber. The author wrote: "... Stieber recognized that such a system as he proposed to establish in France prior to the war of 1870 could be rendered more effective if women were employed in conjunction with men. Thus, he requested that there might be sent from Prussia to France a certain number of domestic servants, governesses, women-workers, and others who might, by gaining access to the family life of the French people, pass on to the fixed agents information which might be useful. Further, he requisitioned the services of a smaller number of attractive-looking girls who were to be placed out as barmaids, and in similar positions, where they could incite men to talk a little too freely for the benefit of the Grosser General Stab of Berlin ..."[37] The *Daily Express,* the *Daily Mirror,* the *Herald,* and some of the others had also joined the league through publishing articles, caricatures, and pamphlets on the issue. People had no means to verify the stories, and most of the time did not even feel the need to. The *Globe* had also contributed significantly in this regard during the early days of the war. The usual method followed was to mention letters from the readers, and in one of the most controversial letters, which had allegedly been written by a German, the writer had declared: "England is thoroughly and since long time studied by our German compatriots living here."[38]

However, the British parliament had to take up the issue immediately for discussion because it had caused great impact on the British society and had requested Sir James Edward Edmonds to promptly prepare a report on it. He was a highly accomplished officer and head of the Secret Service section of the Directorate of Military Operations (MO5) from 1907, and had been greatly influenced by the anti-German spy novels of his friend Le Queux.[39] So he had promptly consulted Le Queux, whose

---

37 Ex-Intelligence Officer, *The German Spy System from Within,* 105.
38 Ibid., 154.
39 Wesley K. Wark, *Spy Fiction, Spy Films and Real Intelligence,* 57; Oliver S. Buckton, *Espionage in British Fiction and Film since 1900,* 32.

Spies of the Kaiser was being serialized in D. C. Thompson's paper *The Weekly News*. To sensitize both the novel and the issue, the weekly paper had published an advertisement with the headlines—"Foreign Spies in Britain—£10 Given for Information—Have You Seen a Spy?" Many incidents of spy-hunting took place as an immediate response to it, while most of them had been falsely implicated by the over-enthusiast patriots of Britain. Inspired by the spy novels and caricatures published in the papers and magazines, the general public had collected inaccurate and even false intelligence to prove their patriotism. Thus, many innocent lives had been lost in The Tower of London and on the streets of England in the pre-war years. No one had felt the necessity even to prove the victim's guilt before killing them on the basis of mere suspicion of enemy espionage.

At the same time, innumerable letters had reached Le Queux from the readers, which had promptly been sent by him to Sir Edmonds, who in turn used those civilian feedbacks as evidences to prepare his report. He came up with a detailed report comprised mainly of non-existent German spies and persuaded the British parliament's Committee of Imperial Defense to set up a Secret Service Bureau in order to assure its citizens of support and security in case of any attack by the enemies. Based on his inept and amateurish report, the Secret Service Bureau was established in England in 1910.[40] R. B. Haldane, the then secretary of state for war, had also played a significant role in setting up the bureau. It had comprised of two sections—a Foreign Section (MI6) and a Home Section (MI5). While MI5 took care to protect Britain from all kinds of security threats to her citizens and was concerned with internal security issues, MI6 had been responsible for combating overseas security threats and was concerned with foreign intelligence. Greatly influenced by the powerful and realistic spy novels of that time, it was taken for granted from the very beginning that Germany had in fact been planning to seize England, and had already spread its spy network not only in Britain, but also in other European countries. Therefore, it can be posited most certainly that the novels had played a significant role in aggravating the Anglo-German tensions, which took the form of collective paranoia in due course.

Consequently England had started spreading its own undercover agent network all around Europe—France, The Netherlands, Belgium, Spain,

---

40 Christopher Andrew, *Defend the Realm*, 13-14.

and even in Germany. Richard B. Tinsley, a manager at a steamship company in Rotterdam (Holland), had initially been recruited in the Secret Intelligence Service by the local British consul-general Ernest Maxse. Later, in 1915, he had been working for Mansfield Smith-Cumming, the head of MI6, while his team was codenamed T-Service. During that time the British had three intelligence organizations working covertly— Cecil Aylmer Cameron had his organization (code-named EVELYN) at Folkestone (CF), Ernest Wallinger in London (WL), and the T-Service in The Netherlands. In The Netherlands alone Smith-Cumming had a team of 250 agents who had mostly been appointed on casual basis.[41] Moreover, in order to collect authentic intelligence materials, Smith-Cumming himself travelled in disguise many times in and around Germany. Britain had also established an elaborate train-watching network in Holland and Belgium in order to keep watch on the movements of enemy troops and ammunitions. France did not lag behind. Along with the Belgian intelligence authority, the French had set up the largest Allied network in the German occupied territory which was code-named "The White Lady."[42] It had a strength of 1,200 people as train watchers who had been observing the movements of trains carrying German troops and provided almost 75 percent of intelligence to France during wartime. Germany also had important clandestine network in the European countries, especially in The Netherlands, Belgium, and Spain. Karl Kroemer was one of the important contacts of Doctor Elsbeth Fräulein Schragmüller (a.k.a. Fräulein Doktor), head of the Antwerp post from early 1915, and had been responsible for appointing secret agents in The Netherlands for Germany. The Doctor, an accomplished lecturer in civic education, had already established an elaborate network of secret agents for her country in Belgium.

Mata Hari certainly did not know anything about these networks, but Tinsley surely did. On February 3, 1916, barely a couple of weeks after Mata Hari had returned to Holland from her first wartime trip to Paris, he had filed a report against her suspecting her of receiving 15,000 francs from the German Embassy in Amsterdam through an agent named Hans Sagace.[43] So, it is quite evident that she had been under surveillance for very long, might have been since her return to Holland from Berlin at

---

41   Keith Jeffery, *MI6: The History of the Secret Intelligence Service, 1909–1949*, 68.
42   Jeffery T. Richelson, *A Century of Spies*, 23.
43   Shipman, *op. cit.*, 192.

the outbreak of the war.[44] During the early days of the war Mata Hari was back in Amsterdam (August 16, 1914), and as mentioned earlier, she had been performing irregularly on stage. However, with her growing age and diminishing glamour, she had failed to mesmerize the Dutch audience, although Kroemer had been quite impressed by her—not as a dancer, but certainly as a possible secret agent for his country—and sometime later came up to her as his usual recruitment strategy with an offer to spy for Germany in return of money. He had offered her a hefty sum of 20,000 francs for the first assignment. Her job would have three stages—the first being perfectly on the line with what she loved to do and had been doing since long—while taking advantage of her fame as a demimondaine she was supposed to get access into the intimate circles of the influential people in France; at the second stage, she was supposed to collect any information significant for Germany that would be spoken by them at a careless intimate moment; and at the last stage, she would pass on those secrets to Kroemer in Amsterdam. Nothing of it had seemed difficult to Mata Hari, and moreover she had perennially been in need of lot of money. Her ace style of undressing on the stage had diminished with her growing age, and she was very much worried about her acceptance in fully covered body. She knew it full well that people had flocked only to see her nude body, and as she had nothing to attract them anymore, she must look for other sources to survive. Kroemer's offer at that juncture had seemed to be quite promising to her. She must have thought if doing merely that much could fetch her some more money then there was no harm in accepting his offer.

Moreover, since the amount offered by Kroemer could reimburse the loss for her expensive furs and jewelry taken away in Germany at the outbreak of war, she had reasons to accept the lucrative offer eagerly. Mata Hari was infinitely confident about her talents as a cosmopolitan adventuress, and knowing nothing about the tricks of espionage had guessed immediately that she would succeed in that field as well. Again and again she had been the victim of her ill fate, and during the war it was going to be fatal for her. Tinsley might presumably have spotted her somewhere with Kroemer in Amsterdam and must have passed on the information to the British secret service in London. Major Cameron and Lieutenant O'Caffrey of the

---

44 Many of the MI5 secret files related to WWI had been declassified in 1999, which revealed that Mata Hari was actually being watched by the British intelligence agents for almost two years.

British Secret Intelligence Service had also been in Holland to oversee the spy networks. So, it is quite evident that Mata Hari had been suspected from the very beginning by the British government for her German connections. Tinsley supposedly was the key person who had acted to prevent Mata Hari from entering Britain in May 1916, during her second wartime visit to Paris. But even before that she had been "most unsatisfactory" to the British intelligence apparently due to the reasons that she had been in Germany at the outbreak of the war and had exhibited lack of morality by becoming a nude dancer. Something that once gave her colossal success had later become her encumbrance. At the outbreak of the war, in order to stop inflow of enemy spies into Britain, the British government had started to maintain a register with the names and details of all aliens over the age of 16 (Register of Aliens at the London office of MI5). Mata Hari's file had been marked as "secret" in the book (dated December 9, 1915). It might therefore be speculated that her chance meeting with Kroemer had taken place sometime in the autumn of 1915, and not in May 1916, as had been claimed by her during her interrogation. Nevertheless, meeting Kroemer had significantly been the turning point in Mata Hari's life, due to which she was stigmatized as an enemy spy for the first time.

I would now embark on portraying the society in France during the war because it had been the center stage of the entire drama regarding Mata Hari's execution/judicial murder. France had been reeling under the generalized threat of Germany after the defeat in the Franco-Prussian War of 1870–1871, because it had lost the province of Alsace-Lorraine to Germany in the war. The angst had aggravated during the end of the nineteenth century due to widespread spyscare that had engulfed the French society, very much like the British. Margaret Darrow wrote: "... spy stories remained more integral to France's response to the war than to that of the other combatant countries. In the decades before 1914, spy stories were popular in France, as they were in England and Germany; but in France they were touted as more than adventure tales."[45] The prolific writer and well-known journalist Léon Daudet had published his novel *Avant-guerre* in 1913, which became extremely popular with the story of Jewish betrayal of France in the next war. As stated earlier, William Stieber had been the master spy of Otto von Bismark, and the key person behind both the victories of Germany in 1866 and 1871. Many fabricated stories had been making the rounds in France accusing

---

45 Margaret H. Darrow, *French Women and the First World War*, 269.

him for having employed enumerable secret agents throughout France who were disguised as priests, farmers, maids, school teachers, nurses, washers, governesses, travelers, waiters, and factory workers. Germany had already violated the neutrality of Belgium (August 4, 1914) in an attempt to proceed toward northern France. It had cast grave impact on the society and especially on the Deuxième Bureau (Second Bureau of the French General Staff), the external military intelligence agency of France, as the citizens had generally believed that German agents would sabotage the country in every possible way at an opportune moment. Press had played a significant role in aggravating the espionitis by fabricated identification of various "spy-nests" in the country. French cartoonists had also joined the league by contributing provocative and derogatory cartoons against the enemy[46] that were published in the popular magazines. E. Demm quoted one of such cartoons published in the French weekly *La Baïonnette* during the war, which is in the form of a dialogue between a French husband and his wife. The wife says to the husband: "Can you imagine, our German nanny—that was General von Kluck!" to which her husband replies: "Shocking! Imagine that, I deceived you with her!"[47]

In such milieu of spy-mania in 1915, Léon Daudet had formed the League for Supporting War (*Ligue pour la Guerre d'Appui*), a group with hypersensitive nationalism, the concern of which had included "parasite catching." Julia Keay wrote: "Any unusual activity, unscheduled visit, or unguarded conversation, indeed any behavior that seemed remotely suspicious, they instantly reported to the authorities."[48] Such behavior could have been applied to the anti-militarists and defeatists as well, but in effect the league had targeted only those who spied against France or had been suspected to be a national enemy. The French government had also encouraged the League's activities, because the War Minister Alexandre Millerand personally wanted to alert the French citizens against enemy espionage. He had launched an anti-espionage slogan in that effect—"Shut up! Beware! Enemy ears are listening"—which became popular instantly. The slogan, virtually a form of warning, had been widely published over the whole city of Paris by printing on slips of paper and sticking on the

---

46 Tonie Holt and Valmai Holt, *Till the Boys Come Home*, Plate no. 274, 137.
47 Eberhard Demm, "The Battle of the Cartoonists: German, French and English Caricatures in World War I," *France and Germany in an Age of Crisis, 1900-1960*, Haim Shamir, ed., 139.
48 Keay, *op. cit.*, 94.

street walls, window panes, on trams, on the hoardings, and even in the underground. Darrow wrote: "French public opinion identified the archetypal spy who was to blame for all that threatened France within a few days of the declaration of war ... the Lady in the Hat stands out ... everyone believed in the Lady in the Hat. Elegant, seductive, apparently rich, possibly foreign, she was mysterious, and evasive ..."[49] Under such difficult circumstance, Mata Hari had arrived in war-ridden Paris in December 1915, and soon was noticed by the women of the League. She was not unknown to the Parisians, and therefore came immediately under the scanner due to her extravagant habits. When the whole of Europe, especially France, was suffering from the devastation of the war, she had been keenly pursuing her passions. Her card had got the inevitable stamp at the immigration office—"To be watched." With growing feminist activism in France during the Belle Époque and emergence of the New Woman, Mata Hari had obtained fame as a dancer in Paris. Significantly, French Law on the Separation of the Churches and the State had been passed in December 1905, marking triumph of the Republicans. Still it is true that women's position in the society did not change much as the Republicans had failed to shed orthodox beliefs regarding women. It could therefore be supposed that the legend of Mata Hari being a German spy during the First World War could have been an extension to the legend of William Stieber, because the blame game was never to end.

However, when war broke out on August 4, 1914, it had been accompanied by all the menaces one could think of, not only at the war front, but equally at the home front—psychological anguish due to separation from the dear ones, scarcity of food, especially of essentials like bread, meat, milk and milk products, egg, fresh vegetables, etc; scarcity of conveyance like tram, bus, taxi, etc; scarcity of domestic fuel and electricity, price hike, closure of markets and public amenities as a result of curfew, lay-off from work—everything had been in jeopardy. People were being deprived of the minimum basic necessities. Like Germany and Britain, France had also been badly hit on the civilian front by the war. Keay quoted Vera Brittain (*Testament of Youth*) on this issue: "France was the scene of titanic, illimitable death, and for this very reason it had become the heart of the fiercest living ever known to any generation."[50] The capital city of Paris had also been hit by the unending flow of passing troops and soldiers on

---

49 Darrow, *op. cit.*, 269.
50 Keay, *op. cit.*, 120.

leave. Scarcity of food had led the French government to publish pamphlets requesting the civilians to consume less food, bread, and meat in particular, and thus to save the soldiers at the war front. Food rationing had been implemented to ensure that no one starved, but the amount of food provided weekly per head at the government controlled shops was so meager that people could hardly survive on it. Milk had been provided only to the children and the ailing. Most of the bakeries had been closed due to non-availability of wheat, and bread for the civilians was being made from a combination of wheat, rice, rye, and maize. The awful taste compelled the civilians to remain satisfied with eating potatoes for months together. Along with food and material shortages there had been constant fear of death due to long-range enemy shelling and aerial bombardments. Every house was grief stricken, although expression of grief had strictly been prohibited. A cheerful social atmosphere had to be imposed by the government in order to enkindle the morale of the brave fighters at the Front and to boost up the national mood during the war. Almost all the houses were inhabited only by the female members, as the men above 16 had all been sent to the war. Women had to take up various jobs for earning in order to maintain their families. They had started working in banks, post offices, businesses, markets, railways, bakeries, hospitals, Red Cross, and in other places including becoming street cleaners, newspaper vendors, ticket-collectors, barbers, and had been employed in every other possible field which was occupied so far by men. Most of the women had become "godmothers" to the soldiers, sending good wishes, gifts, and letters at the Front. Sometimes the soldiers spent their leave at the godmother's house in order to recuperate from war fatigue. The social ambience of France had been filled only with the sentiments of battle, and the overall situation had become strained.

The condition became so unbearable that hundreds and thousands of civilians had thronged the railway stations and the subways in Paris in desperation to get out of the city as early as they could. The French government had made a call particularly to the women to contribute in their own feminine ways to the war effort. Darrow however wrote: "The mobilization scene depicted war as separating the genders—men to the front, women to the rear—but war ... did not solely involve men ... it required women to wait, to weep, and to be worthy."[51] Women were expected to perform patriotic self-sacrifice. Three of the favored ways in which

---
51   Darrow, *op. cit.*, 98.

women could contribute had been (i) acting as war godmothers (*marraine de guerre*) to the soldiers at the Front in order to support them emotionally and morally; (ii) volunteering as nurses at the war hospitals to take care of the wounded, thereby providing great psychological support to the soldiers in time of war; and (iii) organizing charities for the benefit of the soldiers and families of those who had died in the war. Women of France had answered the call with a patriotic fervor by contributing to the warring nation in every possible manner. Even the society women and renowned stars of the stage had participated actively by taking up menial tasks at the hospitals and by caring for the wounded.[52] Every city and every village had been affected by the war as every family had sent their dear ones to the Front. Each day there was news either of soldiers' death at the war front or of their being severely wounded; hence, civilian mood in France persistently remained somber.

What was Mata Hari's contribution to France, the country she had loved to call her home, in the time of such grave national crisis? She had been at the war front, not by virtue of her dignified suffering, but due to her idiotic self-centered enjoyment. While women had been expected to stay back in their private space, to suffer from anxiety for the fate of their loved ones who had left for the Front, and to carefully guard the family sentiments, Mata Hari was still busy with herself in Paris, chasing her own selfish goals—seeking to meet her lovers, keeping company with wealthy people, continuing with her usual life striving to dance in some of the renowned music halls in Paris (which had reopened during the war), and also pursuing her wanderlust. No sign of patriotism, no manifestation of solidarity, and no voluntary service had been offered by her to the nation in need. She did not even offer to be a "godmother" to the soldiers who had been fighting tirelessly at the Front. She instead had thought that she was genuinely serving the nation in her own special way by providing sexual companionship to the holidaying soldiers, who earnestly needed to be cheered up in the trying time of war, thereby providing moral support to them. Unfortunately for her no one else had comprehended her mindset, and she was seen as a sexually depraved woman who had been slaughtering the soldiers' morale, and thereby contributing alarmingly toward the spread of the most dreaded venereal diseases among them.

High-ranking people in the French government had firmly believed that

---
52 Gail Braybon, ed., *Evidence, History and the Great War*, 146.

the soldiers could never win the war if their morale weakened. Mata Hari, as always, had been unaware of such complications and was happily performing her wartime role of a prostitute. However, as she did not perform her feminine role of "the social glue that kept the family and society together," she was considered one of those who "were potential sexual miscreants ... who posed the greatest danger to social order."[53] But why had she been doing anything of that sort at the time of war? Mata Hari did not have any contract for dancing in Paris during the war (not that she had needed one to survive), and as a matter of expediency might have thought of doing some good to herself by earning through prostitution thereby serving the country as well in her own limited manner. But she was bound to be identified as an enemy of France, hence an agent of Germany, appointed especially to distract the dedicated soldiers and in effect to destroy the nation. By that time the French government had already been alerted by its British counterpart about Mata Hari's German connections (through a circular of the British Aliens Registry office dated February 22, 1916). Thus, no matter whether such derivation had been well founded or not, Mata Hari was destined to become the victim; and it would not be wrong to state that in a way it had been her own choice.

---

53   Ibid., 119.

Chapter 2
The Persona

Mata Hari was different from all the others in her profession—as a person and also as a performer. It seems pointless to say this because it is essentially true for everyone—no one is identical to anyone. But in her case it has a varied connotation due to her unique personality. Contrary to all propagandist wrong notions about her (like, she needed only sex and money), she had basically been an insecure lonely soul, in search of a true soul-mate all through her life. At an age when she had genuinely needed sympathetic parental care to support her social and emotional development, she was left alone. Her being abandoned by her father at a very young age, her parents' divorce and subsequently her mother's death, and then being separated from her brothers, had obviously been traumatic for a child of fourteen. She had been left alone among interfering relatives who had tried to impose their conservative decisions on her in order to make her a womanly woman, which she could not accept. She adored strong men like her father, who were well positioned in the society and had considerable command over wealth and the other state of affairs; and therefore, men in uniform had always attracted her. She felt secure and comfortable in their company, and having quite a few of them as lovers had meant a lot for her. Her fascination for the uniform had been reflected in one of her own photographs where she is seen in a uniform in her familiar proud look. It had been one extremely significant aspect of her persona that had made and had also destroyed her. However, according to Pat Shipman, the most significant thing about Mata Hari is that she loved men and did not love truth.[1] I think it is plausibly not that she ran away from truth, but in fact "truth" had always been different for her. She seemed to have been living in another world, where she could conveniently create truth according to her own fanciful ideas. "Truth" for her had not been what the real state of affairs was, rather had been that what had worked for her purpose. And at the end, during the Great War, such kind of fancy had miserably boomeranged against her.

---

1   Pat Shipman, *op. cit.*, 1.

ONE LITTLE ORCHID

Mata Hari photographed in a uniform
(The Mata Hari Foundation, Fries Museum, Leeuwarden)

To comprehend Mata Hari's plight, it becomes essential to understand the person that Margarethe had actually been, most importantly her characteristic mold. All through her life she had acted not according to the demands of the situations she had been in, but according to her own readings of the situations guided by her obvious emotional overtone. Due to this trend she had responded to every state of affair in a ridiculously naïve manner, although she thought that she was adequately intelligent. It had been her signature behavior pattern, and therefore could be the starting point of the journey toward an interpretation of her life and personality. It has already been noted earlier that her personality could be characterized as narcissistic in nature (all of the narcissistic character trends described by Theodore Millon typically fit her), and due to obvious reasons it could be presumed that her family culture might have contributed much to the self-centered and fun-loving temperament of her persona. Modern psychologists have linked parental over-praise and over-valuation to narcissistic traits in the children.[2] This fits well with father Adam's treatment of his "little orchid." She was pampered to such extent that she had not even been trained in the household chores as per the social norms for middle-class girls of that time. Due to this reason she had never liked to do housekeeping, nor did she bother to learn it ever.

---

2   Eddie Brummelman, Brad J. Bushman, and others, eds. "Origins of Narcissism in Children," in *Proceedings of the National Academy of Sciences*, 112 (12): 3659-3662.

She had strongly felt that she was not meant for menial work. Once she had confided to Gerrit Hendrik Priem, a lawyer and journalist who wrote a pamphlet titled *The Naked Truth about Mata Hari* in reply to her fabricated biography penned by her father: "... this calm life of little household duties, kitchen-glittering and living-room-glory is boring."[3] However, going by the Freudian model of personality it could well be asserted that her life had mostly been controlled by the self-indulgent nature of her *id*, although it would be wrong to conclude that she was completely devoid of moral reasoning as guided by the *superego*. The strong internal drive that motivated her all through her life had been the life instinct *Eros* (sexual in nature according to Freud) or the libido, as opposed to the death instinct *Thanatos* (aggressive in nature). This guiding force had prompted her to find an escape for every negative situation she had been in, the trail of which had begun right after her mother's death.

Margarethe was born in a bourgeois family that had clung to the traditional orthodox values of society. It had implied on one hand adhering to the contemporary misogynic norms, and on the other, endorsing male chauvinistic dictates of the society, which had justified the double standard of supporting male atrocities in the private domain while condemning women's claim for dignity. The Zelle family had perfectly fitted into that model. Margarethe had seen her mother's sacrifices for a man who had been awfully dishonest with her. She had also observed the embarrassingly pitiful looks and whispering gossips of the neighbors after her father's bankruptcy—her mother's severe illness due to shame and poverty, her father's utter neglect toward his wife and the family (Adam did not even arrange for treatment of Antje while she had been unwell), the disgraceful divorce in a society that did not approve of such act, his taking a mistress while abandoning the little ones to fend for themselves, and also his nonchalance toward their sufferings, her mother's intense anxiety for the wellbeing of the children, and ultimately her succumbing to the unfortunate circumstances at the age of 49. Every bit of it had shaken Margarethe from the core of her existence. Antje's feeling of insecurity might have been transmitted to Margarethe at a very young age. It has already been mentioned that as the proud daughter of a wealthy businessman she could never even envisage the misfortune that had suddenly befallen them. While as a child she drove her *bokkenwaagen* (goat carriage) in the town and wore extraordinarily beautiful clothes to the school, she had proudly

---

3   Shipman, *op. cit.*, 171.

noticed the gaze of all who looked at her in amaze and had felt elated to imagine that they were jealous of her. But when every precious thing had been unexpectedly stripped off her, she had certainly felt ashamed and humiliated to face them. Margarethe felt belittled and betrayed by her father.

Her father had betrayed her terribly in return of all the love that she had showered on him. She was only 14 by then, and as a young teenager might have vowed to avenge every wrong done to her mother and also to her by her father and by the society. Margarethe might have thought that they had been direly punished for none of their faults. Most of her biographers have mentioned that on the day her mother had died she was heard on the piano by the neighbors. It had been her own special way to grieve for her mother. It is truly impossible for a young girl, who had thought of herself to be the princess of her wealthy father, even to imagine that her healthy and hard-working mother would die so early. She must have expected that her father would surely take care of her and her brothers after her mother's death, but she was hopelessly disappointed as Adam had already made other plans. When he decided to sent her away from the rest of the family, she had felt incredibly bad, and must have bitterly regretted loss of her mother's love and care. Margarethe's love and attachment toward her mother is evident through her preserving the poetry copy of her mother for very long. Ever since she had been quite assertive in her ways—self-confident, self-assured, and strong, although was as naïve as a child. She must have promised to regain her inflated self-esteem by regaining wealth and luxury by all means, and must also have promised not to sacrifice her life and enjoyment in future for the sake of her own husband and family. Did she also vow never to love men truly and thenceforth only to subjugate and use them to fulfill her own ends? These disturbing thoughts must have occurred in her mind quite often even at a mature age—after her marriage to Rudolf and also after becoming successful as a dancer.

Margarethe's relatives had much negative opinions about her. They knew her as a spoilt teenage girl with extravagant habits, an incorrigible headstrong brat who had been exceptionally stubborn, and limitlessly rigid. She did not even have traditional good looks to attract any man for marriage, as she had been unusually tall (5 feet and 10 inches), dark complexioned, and was short of heavy bosom.[4] It could well be supposed that the Vissers must have passed taunting remarks regarding her ways

---

4   Ibid., 9.

and looks at the time she had been staying with them in Sneek. She had been overtly emotional in both the cognitive and motivational spheres and had never taken an insult passively. Like any headstrong teenager she must have taken the insults as a challenge, and later was found looking for a groom on her own. She was 18 and must have meticulously been going through the matrimonial advertisements published in the local newspapers. As mentioned earlier, she had responded to the one placed by Rudolf's friend (J. T. Z. De Balbian Verster) on his behalf by attaching one of her charming photographs, thereby not leaving the first opportunity to impress Rudolf and his family elders, in order to ensure her wedding with him. On the day of their first meeting Rudolf came in his full uniform. Julia Keay wrote: "... his twirling moustaches, gold-braided uniform and tales of oriental derring-do, was the very image of the dashing hero Margarethe had always known would one day come and sweep her off her feet."[5] She was mesmerized at his first sight in uniform and due to various reasons had been quite happy with Rudolf's decision to marry her—first, she could disprove her relatives' ridiculous assessments about her; second, she could show her father that inspite of his betrayal and his efforts to ruin her she could successfully mend her life on her own; and third, she could fulfill her dreams with Rudolf, as he had kept her in luxury from the time she first met him. Margarethe loved fun and excitement, which Rudolf had provided amply. Moreover, he was a man in uniform who had supposedly been ready to spend a fortune for her. She was overjoyed—what else could she have desired in life? She had felt like a princess again, of a man who she naively believed had loved her more than anything else.

Shipman wrote: "Their attraction was sexual, mutual, and very strong."[6] True, it had been mere "attraction," and surely not "love," from both sides.[7] Her charm and sexual confidence had attracted Rudolf, his money and uniform had attracted Margarethe. She had thanked her fate for having been so kind by showering all happiness on her. Her letters to Rudolf during the courtship reveal her mind very clearly, which had been filled

---

5   Julia Keay, *op.cit.*, 6.
6   Shipman, *op. cit.*, 44.
7   Sam Waagenaar wrote: "... John was in love ..." *op. cit.*, 1964, 29. I do not endorse his speculation simply due to the reasons that (i) Rudolf (a.k.a. John) had been calculating his benefits from his marriage to a Dutch lady, and (ii) he had been promiscuous soon after the wedding. This surely is contrary to one's behavior when s/he is truly in love.

with narcissistic flavor—she signed those with the words "your future little wife," "with a delicious kiss from your very loving wife," etc. Emotion had overpowered her always and reason took a back seat every time. Her inimical naivety and perennial tendency of impulsive reaction resulted in impatience and desperation, and she had relied upon Rudolf so blindly that without even consulting any elderly and experienced member of her own family she got married to him within a short time. Her naïve and childish ways had been expressed in enumerable instances throughout her life. For example, before her wedding she had told Rudolf that both her parents were dead, not knowing that as she was underage for a legal marriage her father's consent would be necessary. Later her shameful lie was revealed to Rudolf. Margarethe had neither consulted nor had she informed Adam about their courtship and her decision to marry Rudolf. It could very well have been that she had deliberately avoided seeking for an advice from her near ones, because she was afraid that in case of their disapproval she might have to abandon the relationship along with the luxury that Rudolf had been providing her before marriage. It is also plausible that after Adam had deserted them Margarethe could never trust anyone in her family. Moreover, her experience with her uncles and aunts had not been such that she could rely on them regarding such a delicate matter. It is quite intriguing that a young girl of only 18 did not have anyone in her family whom she could confide in. It is also surprising that she did not have any close friend to share her feelings with. However, least did she realize that marrying Rudolf was going to be the first grave mistake of her life.

Rudolf MacLeod was very close to his younger sister Louise Jeanne (Frida) Wolsink (married to Lammert Wolsink of Zelhem in August 1881, who had been a notary by profession) and had been staying in Amsterdam with her and her two daughters (the elder—Jenny and the younger—Jeanne Brienen) during his leave in 1895. So, after returning from honeymoon he had continued to stay there along with Margarethe. The decision might also have been linked to the financial condition of Rudolf which had started to deteriorate after the expensive courtship, spectacular wedding, and the extravagant honeymoon. Louise, a.k.a. Tante (Aunt) Frida, was a widow (Mr. Wolsink died in 1888), and had been enough experienced to judge Margarethe's temperament apparently by seeing her before the wedding. She was not the least impressed by her charming appearance, and had warned her brother Rudolf not to marry that girl; but Rudolf was too excited with the wedding and did not pay heed to her advice. Therefore, it could be presumed that, Frida might not have been affectionate to Margarethe, and hence their relationship would obviously not have been cordial. Being born in a bourgeois family Frida had learnt to respect and uphold orthodox values, and had expected an ever-submissive, docile, and passive woman as the wife of her beloved elder brother, but Margarethe had never cared to fulfill her expectations. She knew that she was not born to become a domesticated housewife, and so, inspite of Frida's much censorious and condemnatory remarks, she had refused to be tamed. The more Frida forced Margarethe to learn domestic work, the more she retaliated. Obedience had never been her forte. Shipman wrote: "Griet knew nothing about housekeeping and was hardly inclined to frugality."[8] From the very beginning Margarethe had shown striking signs of her inadequacy to become a true housewife, i.e., the angel of the house, and had hated to live with her relentlessly censorious sister-in-law. She had grown up with her loving father, her silent mother, and her three younger brothers. Never had she been censored for anything in her own family, and therefore was comfortable only with indulgence. She was still a teenager, confident of her gorgeous looks and winning presence, and to escape the persistent nagging of Frida had naively hoped for Rudolf's leave to end. She must have thought that as the wife of a colonel she would be happy to live in an exclusive bungalow with native servants doing the menial household chores for her in the distant land of Dutch East Indies, rather than to live on in Amsterdam and suffer with the awful galling lady and her irritating daughters "who are dirty characters."[9] Margarethe could never get along well with them. However, she was not wrong about the colonial life in the Indies. Frances Gouda quoted Cornelia Hendrika (Cor) Razoux Schultz-Metzer, the first woman to have been appointed to the Assembly of the Dutch East Indies in 1935, who wrote: "… daily life in the Indies did not pose serious challenges to most Dutch wives, because servants were the ones to buy food, prepare meals, clean, tend to the garden, and watch over fair-skinned Dutch children as eagle-eyed, if indulgent, nannies."[10]

Margarethe could not bear Frida any further, and in April 1896 (after eight months of marriage), had compelled Rudolf to move out of her

---

8 Shipman, *op. cit.,* 51.
9 Ibid., 130.
10 Frances Gouda, *Dutch Culture Overseas,* 158.

apartment. Rudolf had arranged for a small rented accommodation, which was not very far from Frida's house, enabling her to pay frequent visits to Margarethe and to continue with her censorious criticisms against her. As noted earlier, right after their honeymoon Rudolf had started to visit other women, to drink heavily, and to spend sparingly. Money had become a grinding issue as he was short of money due to his loans, his extravagant courtship with Margarethe, followed by the expenses incurred for the wedding and the luxurious honeymoon in Wiesbaden, and therefore was in no mood to spend unnecessarily on his wife (his "loving" Griet) anymore. Still her chief irritability had concerned Tante Frida's relentless nagging regarding her true womanhood and the compulsory responsibilities of marriage. As motherhood had been the most significant role of women in the then society, Frida must have pursued her to bear child soon after her marriage (as she herself had done—Frida's first child was born barely after 10 months of her marriage), in order to compel her to fulfill her duty as a responsible wife. Margarethe and Rudolf had been enjoying passionate physical relationship before they were married,[11] and must have adopted contraceptive[12] methods as she did not become pregnant during courtship, and had regularly written to Rudolf about her normal monthly cycle. They must have continued with the practice even after the wedding, but within a year she became pregnant (possibly after shifting to the rented house), although she was not a woman of motherly dispositions. So, it seems plausible that, Margarethe might have submitted to the perpetual pursuance of elderly Frida regarding childbirth, and might not have been happy with her pregnancy because it had hindered her normal life in many ways. Moreover, because she had married Rudolf to live a passionate life in opulence, she was not yet prepared for accepting herself as a mother. Motherhood had not been her marital priority. In some sense, therefore, she might have rebelled against the prevalent social norms. Still when Norman was born in January 1897, she took him in her arms affectionately and had cared for him sincerely. Like a truly protective mother she had nurtured her newborn son. She had fed him, bathed him, and watched him with awe when he would blissfully smile at her. The little bundle of joy had been like a living doll in her arms. Both Rudolf and Tante Frida must have been very happy with the turn of the events, and because she had fulfilled their wish for a baby, but it had only

---

11 Waagenaar, *op. cit.*, 1964, 30–31.
12 Russell Howe speculated that contraceptives were virtually unknown at that time; *op. cit.*, 23; but this is contrary to my findings on the issue.

been a temporary phase in Margarethe's life.

With the 3 month old Norman Margarethe had left with Rudolf for the Indies on May 1, 1897. The ocean-liner S. S. *Prinses Amelia* moved along the Mediterranean through the Suez to sail through the Indian Ocean to Batavia in Java, making brief stops at the scheduled ports. It had been her first sea journey, and although she became ill on the 5 week long tiring voyage, it had been a dream journey for her to her dreamland—thousands of miles away from Tante Frida and her relentless criticisms, far away from her intolerant uncles and aunts, and also away from her selfish father, into a new environ of colonial people. As the wife of a colonel and a would-be Major she had expected to enjoy her high social status. Waagenaar wrote: "The departure found Margarethe in a buoyant mood, for this trip was an adventure. She was on her way to a new country, was going to meet new people, and there was the lure of the tropics to be looked forward to."[13] As her marriage had already started to suffer and as she was betrayed of the promises made by Rudolf before the wedding, Margarethe had looked forward to her life in the Indies with much expectation—social freedom being her priority. She had always wanted to "live like a butterfly under the sun," and imagining Java as a place full of splendid colors, warmth, and spectacular lush green vegetation, she had hoped for her (childish) wish to come true. She was leaving behind the comforts of her homeland to embrace a different social and natural environ, but still she did not bother at all.

On board the ship while Rudolf had occupied himself for most of the time writing letters, reading books, chatting with the co-passengers, drinking, or simply taking rest, staring endlessly at the sea Margarethe had been fantasizing all day about the strange new world that she was going to be in. On June 7, they had landed at the Tandjong Priok harbor in North Batavia, a comparatively new one built to accommodate bigger steamers and cargo/passenger ships, and then might have taken the newly built railroad to Willem I Railway Station for reaching Ambarawa. Shipman however wrote that they had taken a more tiring journey: "The MacLeod family had boarded the S. S. *Spleeman* to travel from Batavia to Semarang and then went on horseback and oxcart to Ambarawa."[14] Soon she found her dreamland to be more beautiful than she had ever imagined it to be.

---

13   Waagenaar, *op. cit.*, 1964, 33.
14   Shipman, *op. cit.*, 60.

Rudolf had been posted to the 8th Battalion at the Willem I military fort in the plantation town of Ambarawa near Semarang, which was surrounded by green mountains. For Margarethe the new world was more attractive than "staid, dull, carefully controlled Holland."[15] She was delighted because in Java she could hope to shed her old life and the old orthodox rules that had suffocated her. She had desperately hoped to move out of the gnawing emptiness of her life in Holland, to get a new identity that would not be sullied by the nagging sister-in-law, and would rid her of the rancor toward Frida. At the core of her heart she was still a silly childish girl, who had evidently been living on an ivory tower of her naïve imaginations and fantasies about her own existence, no one being an essential part of it; and for her Rudolf was the ladder necessary only to get to the top of that tower of imaginations.

Margarethe's self-centered narcissism had been reflected in her behavior all through her life. Keay wrote: "From being the cherished only daughter of an indulgent father she had … become the adored and cosseted wife of a successful soldier."[16] She knew not to give, but only to have—everything that gave her pleasure. She had been so fun loving that even her bonding with her son had not been guided by the duties and responsibilities of motherhood, but like a child attached to her doll. As all the household routine work was taken care of by the native maid servant (*babu*), including all the responsibilities of the child, she was free to be on her own having ample scope to explore the locality and to enjoy nature at her own will.[17] Everything outside the boundaries of their house enchanted her. In Java, at that time, they had been living in Tumpang,[18] a suburb approximately 10 miles east of Malang. Malang, a city in the eastern part of Java, was inhabited by many Europeans, and quite obviously offered pleasures according to their choice. Accessibility to Malang gave Margarethe more freedom, and in a sense she had been enjoying her indolence reading books and fashion magazines, watching local customs and rituals, attending native dance and music recitals, touring nearby ancient Hindu and Buddhist temples, wandering through the woods and walking barefoot through the untamed grass with her long black hair loosely tied in a knot or kept unbound with gloriously fragrant local blossoms carefully

---

15   Ibid., 59.
16   Keay, *op. cit.*, 10.
17   Ibid., 15–16.
18   A beautiful description of the town is penned by Shipman, *op. cit.*, 68.

twined, checking on the latest arrivals of European fashionable clothes and jewelry in the local Dutch stores,[19] spending quality social time with the European community, presenting her sparkling persona at the dinner parties and receptions, making some embroidery designs on table cloths or cushion covers, playing her favorite tunes on the piano, learning Malay words and to drape *Kebaya* and *Sarong* from her maids, and doing everything that she enjoyed. It is however not known whether she had learnt to cook any Javanese cuisine or to make traditional Indonesian batik textile printing from her maids. It might be presumed that because she did not have patience with anything, she might not have tried her hand in any of those crafts.

Every bit of it had perfectly suited her temperament, the only spoilsport being Rudolf and his perennially angry mood. He seemed to have been carrying on the legacy of his sister Frida by furthering her ritualistic duty to censor Margarethe in every possible way. While young Margarethe was proud of her attractive looks, middle-aged Rudolf was evidently jealous and suspicious of her. Her grace and sobriety added to her attraction, and Rudolf certainly loathed that. The more he ridiculed her for her unwifely misconduct and irresponsible behavior, the more she became adamant and defying. Inspite of her positive attitude the marriage had started deteriorating rapidly because she did not find any reason either for mending her ways or for Rudolf's anger, and therefore could not figure out the means to salvage it. However, people who knew Margarethe in the Indies had the impression that she was "a young woman of best intentions,"[20] although according to Shipman "she was seen as a morally dangerous, selfish, and frivolous woman who enjoyed clothes and jewels."[21] In her opinion such general impression about Margarethe might have been caused by her dark skin complexion, black eyes, and dark hair, which was fairly uncommon among the Dutch women, rather had been quite common in

---

19 Margarethe might have been affected with Compulsive Buying Disorder (CBD), which could have been an effort to compensate her loneliness, or could have been developed due to her disturbed adolescence. She might have wanted to replicate her father's care and affection through buying enormously for herself, often going beyond her capacity. It might also have been that since she had a feeling of loss after losing her mother and subsequently being left by her father, she wanted to possess more to feel assured. It might have been an identity-construction measure in her case.
20 Quoted in Waagenaar, *op. cit.*,1964, 33.
21 Shipman, *op. cit.*, 68.

Java among people of half-caste with mixed blood. As racism had been a crucial social construct in the Dutch East Indies, she was subjected to spiteful remarks and scornful looks from the proud European women, who, inspite of her impeccable command of the language, never believed that Rudolf had actually married a Dutch lady. It might therefore be speculated that as a newcomer to the place she had not been readily accepted by the European community already living there, and it might have taken considerable time for her to establish herself among them. Margarethe had faced similar reactions from the Europeans in Medan as well, but she had ignored the social complications and had handled the situations with her characteristic youthful charm and smartness.

1898 had been very significant to Margarethe in many ways. Soon after arriving in Java, Margarethe became pregnant with her second child, and gave birth to a girl on May 2 in Tumpang. Rudolf had named her Jeanne Louise after his dear sister Louise Frida, but had fondly called her Nonnie or Non in short. It is evident from the pictures of the children that Norman looked exactly like Margarethe, and the baby girl resembled Rudolf more. She was happy with two children, or might have plausibly been fed up with the difficulties of childbirth, and so had never heeded to Rudolf's and Frida's wish for another child in the family. She must have thought that she was over with her wifely duty of giving birth to Rudolf's children and was therefore free to pursue her own interests. In fact, in March 1902, in a letter written from the Indies to Madame A. Goodvriend, a cousin of Rudolf who was sympathetic to her, she had expressed her mind on the issue. Rudolf had already retired from his job by then, they had been living in the remote village Sindanglaja, and the marriage was in complete jeopardy. So Margarethe was determined not to have more children and therefore had practically laid down two conditions—first, Rudolf must change, and second, she must get her rightful place in the MacLeod family.[22] Only after that, she had said, she would think about the matter. She was more than sure that none of those were going to happen. However, the first condition evidently expresses Margarethe's discontent about Rudolf's passion for womanizing, his habit of miserly living (could have been because he did not approve her unwarranted lavish spending), and of bitterly bullying her at every moment, while the second implies that she had not been accepted and loved in the MacLeod family, although they had approved the marriage before.

22   Ibid., 131–132.

Rudolf's family must have known about her unconventional and uncompromising ways from Frida and Rudolf, and because they were comfortable with the traditional social values, they had presumably developed strong dislike toward Margarethe. Due to the same reasons she had been disliked by her own relatives as well. She failed to understand what was so terribly wrong in being unconventional or in yearning to be an individualistic person that she had always been.

The next most significant incident that had overwhelmed her that year was her taking part in a musical play in Java. In September Margarethe had debuted in the lead role as the crowning Queen Wilhelmina in the musical play *The Crusaders*, staged on the occasion of her formal ascension to the throne in The Netherlands (September 6, 1898) and had considerably impressed the audience. She was possibly chosen for the role due to her young age, her charming appearance, and graceful presence, and surely not due to the official rank of Rudolf. It was her first independent triumph that had given her attention, applause, and acclaim as a performer. Rudolf had bought her expensive dresses for the occasion in which she looked stunningly beautiful. Shipman wrote: "She drew every man's eye and lustful admiration, every woman's envy."[23] For the first time she had tasted the sweetness of success, unmatched to any pleasure she had ever experienced before. No amount of money could have bought fame and admiration for her. It meant much to her as she had got enough reason and scope to nurture her inflated ego. Margarethe might have thought that through her performance she could prove her true worth even to Rudolf and did not care for what he actually thought of her. She had proudly observed that none of the officer's wives were as beautiful and as talented as she was. She felt that Rudolf should be proud of her, should stop abusing her for her inefficiency as a housewife, and should also stop treating her as any other common woman. He should realize that his wife was special. And what about Tante Frida? Rudolf must have informed his ridiculously orthodox sister about her grand performance and all the applause and attention that she had obtained. Margarethe had tried to imagine what could have been her reaction. Could she have appreciated her talent? She might have thought with conceit that she was far beyond Frida's capacity ever to fathom, and had grinned, let her be happy with her meticulously followed domestic rules—but Margarethe knew that she had been carved out to become something else—someone

---
23 Ibid., 70.

more important than a virtuous, docile, and obedient housewife. She once again felt content with her talent and had felt extremely proud for not confining herself within the limits of domesticity. Margarethe had been flying high in her imaginations about her own potential and had sincerely wanted to pursue her newfound talent in some way. She must have also realized that Java was not the proper place to pursue her talent, and therefore she must return very soon to her own country some day.

In December 1898, Rudolf was posted to Medan in northern Sumatra, a beautiful city near the Strait of Malacca, with a promotion as the garrison commander at Fort Van Den Bosch. Medan had been dubbed as the "Paris of Sumatra" by the Dutch colonial people because of its impeccable appearance and aesthetic layout. It had been an occasion to rejoice for Margarethe due to at least two reasons—first and foremost, because she could enjoy her exalted position as the wife of one of the most highly placed officers in Sumatra; and second, she could enjoy her life thoroughly as Rudolf would be away from home. At least, for some time, he would not be able to ridicule her by seeking explanation for every bit that she did. She was surely relived to think that, although temporarily, she could escape his perennially humiliating remarks for her. Margarethe as usual had immediately started dreaming about her imaginary freedom and about how she would relish her liberty in the absence of Rudolf—she thought that as the garrison commander Rudolf would surely get a salary hike, which meant more money for her, which had also implied that she would then be able to buy some of the latest fashionable new arrivals from Europe at the local dress stores and also some new jewelry of her own choice. Freedom for her, during her colonial days, did not mean taking sexual favors from young men. Even in the absence of Rudolf she had only wanted to impress the young army officials, highly positioned civil servants, and planters in Malang by dressing wonderfully for the dinner parties at the local club. It could have been because he had always suspected her of promiscuity and had never bought her elegant fashionable dresses.

Margarethe's eyes glittered with the prospect of heightened admiration she could foresee for her. She had been so engrossed in her imaginary world of freedom that she failed to contemplate that under any circumstance Rudolf would not leave her alone with the children back in Tumpang and would certainly make some arrangement to control her even in his absence. She could never look beyond her narcissistic bounds and never really liked walking on the beaten track. Eventually she had been left under the custody of the van Rheede at their house for 2 months after Rudolf had left for Medan in March 1899, and contrary to her extravagant expectations she had to manage with a worn out *Sarong* and a *Kebaya* for her daily-wear as Rudolf did not send any money to her so that she could at the least contribute for her daily expenses at the van Rheedes' or could buy even an ordinary European dress. He did not heed to her repeated requests for money which might have been due to the fact that as he was alone in Medan he had been spending more on drinking, gambling, and women. Margarethe became so desperate with the embarrassing situation that in order to return the insult to him and compel him to send fund immediately she had sent a message to Rudolf begging for money through the sister of Mrs. van Rheede who lived in Medan at that time. She knew for sure that it would work, because it would be too embarrassing for a garrison commander to get exposed about the fact that he had left his wife and two little children with some other family without any money. Margarethe had never been a silent sufferer and was clever enough to get things done in her own way. Rudolf had to submit.

Mrs. van Rheede had been fairly sympathetic to Margarethe and accordingly thought that she was intelligent, charming, and nice, although a little bit frivolous. In her opinion Margarethe had suffered "from being married with a much older man, who was extremely jealous and who did not guide her along, but on the contrary was in some way her enemy."[24] It is evident from Margarethe's letters written to her father and step-mother from the Indies that she had literally been living with an enemy. Wheelwright wrote: "... her greatest crime was her refusal to live up to his rigid expectations."[25] She had realized with dismay that she did not marry a human being, but virtually was wedded to an entire social package of the bourgeoisie system in the form of Rudolf. Margarethe was fed up with his suspicion, his jealousy, and hatred for her and had expressed to Mrs. van Rheede her wish to die so that she would not have to return to that heartless and inconsiderate bundle of flesh and bone. She became so indifferent that she wrote sparingly to Rudolf while he had been in Medan, and did not even feel like sharing with him her opinions about their life in Malang at the van Rheedes. She did not even write to Rudolf

---

24 Quoted in Shipman, *op. cit.*, 82.
25 Julie Wheelwright, *op. cit.*, 10.

about the children, although she knew that their wellbeing had been his great concern. She knew that they both belonged to the opposite mental poles and did not want to make futile attempts any further to make him understand her feelings and emotions. Margarethe had been obsessed with fashion and luxury, and her thoughts had always revolved around it. She was also careless with her expenses and impractically expected that Rudolf would go on providing her whenever she needed money.

Rudolf hated all that she lived for. In a letter to her from Medan he wrote: "You are too limited, too stupid and superficial to ever write an interesting letter, you can speak only of beautiful dresses, of hair-dos and other banalities, for outside of this nothing interests you and everything is strange."[26] He had realized that it was necessary to bring Margarethe and the children to Medan very soon as he could no more bear the anxiety of staying apart from the little ones. He virtually did not trust her with the children. So, in the month of May, the family had started for Medan. Margarethe was so hopelessly incorrigible that while travelling to Medan she was seen shopping for dresses and gloves in Surabaya, a place where the passengers had to stop briefly en route to Medan. The only thought that had preoccupied her was that she must look extraordinarily good when she would be arriving at the new place and would be meeting new people. She would not leave a single chance to reach out for compliments. How did Rudolf overlook such relentless passion in her before the wedding? Margarethe was stuck in a loveless marriage. It might have been true for many women of that time, as it is true even today. But for Margarethe it had been different, because like others she was not ready to accept any of the torturous humiliations of her husband and had retaliated every time. Although she never joined the league for women's liberation, she in fact had been a staunch believer of individual freedom; and therefore, in a sense, she had been way ahead of her time.

In order to understand Margarethe's persona an incident in Medan is worth a mention—the family had arrived on May 26, 1899, a hot summer day in the tropical region, and had stayed briefly in the newly built majestic architectural splendor—Hotel de Boer—on the Town Hall Road. It had been a huge colonial structure built in the middle of a lush green field by the side of the Deli River and was situated in the heart of the city, which offered every possible comfort to the European boarders (in those

---

26 Shipman, *op. cit.*, 84.

days it was an all-white hotel with mosquito-free rooms). It had been a temporary arrangement for the MacLeods and soon they had moved into a magnificent house at an aristocrat locale. As Rudolf was a garrison commander, he had rented a house for his family according to his rank and social status. Margarethe was extremely happy with the arrangement. It has already been mentioned earlier, as was usual in her case, soon after her arrival in Medan she was openly insulted by the European wives of other army officers for her non-European dark complexion and her Oriental appearance. Margarethe had been brooding over it and as she was not to take the insult passively, she had looked for an opportune moment to return the humiliation. On May 31 Rudolf had hosted a party on the occasion of the farewell of the preceding garrison commander General Reisz.[27] She loved extravagant social life, and parties being an integral part of it, she was immensely happy with the chance to play the host. It had been a dream come true moment in her life, because in the new city as the hostess for the first time she could show off her grace and charm in the presence of the noble guests comprising of army officers and rich planters from various European countries who had been living in the "Gold Land" of Medan, and also because she could use the event to satisfy her perpetual need to be admired. Rudolf had ordered fashionable dresses for her from Amsterdam for the occasion.[28] She made no effort to hide her conceit as the wife of a highly placed military officer and dressed exquisitely she had insisted on maintaining the order of rank while welcoming the guests. She refused to move up to the older officers' wives to greet them as they arrived as guests for the occasion, and stood elegantly by the side of Rudolf making them realize that they were subordinate to her. Rudolf was enraged by her unbecoming behavior as a hostess because it could directly affect his reputation as a high-ranking officer, but she didn't care at all and was happy because in her opinion they had received what they deserved.

However, inspite of the children being at risk from attacks of malaria,

---

27 Waagenaar mentioned his name as General Beisz, *op. cit.*, 1964, 38.

28 Ibid., 37, reported to him much later by Rudolf's third wife. I presume this had been a wishful fabrication by her. Rudolf had been extremely angry with his wife during his stay in Medan before the family had joined him, and had also been in constant anguish regarding health of the children. Given the situation is becomes obvious that he would not have ordered a dress from Amsterdam to be worn by Margarethe on a future occasion. The fabulous dress could therefore have been bought at a local European store in Medan after the party was arranged.

typhoid, dysentery, cholera, and other terrible life-risking diseases, Rudolf had insisted on having them with him in Medan; and only after a month of the family joining him Norman died. Death of the toddler had affected Margarethe as badly as it had affected Rudolf, but her expression of grief did not match with him. While Rudolf had cut a lock of Norman's hair to preserve it, had saved the page of the calendar with the dates of his death and burial, and would break into tears at the slightest mention of his dear Norman, Margarethe had become exceptionally calm and quiet after the incident. Keay wrote: "… she could not confront her anguish. Like a white-hot branding iron or a rabid dog it was something to be kept at a safe distance, to be locked up far away where it would have no more power to hurt."[29] She did not speak of Norman even once. A month later in a letter to her father and step-mother she wrote: "The passing of my dear Norman has taken everything out of me."[30] She wanted to leave Java immediately. It is needless to mention that no two people would be identical in their feelings and expressions, but Rudolf had started blaming the bereaved mother of utter insensibility and negligence for the death of his son who had supposedly been poisoned. It has already been known that he did not trust Margarethe with the children and because he had to leave them behind in Tumpang with her he always worried about their wellbeing. It is true that Margarethe had depended wholly on the native *babus* as caregivers to the children and did not feel the necessity to scrutinize them in any way. She had been much closer to the native servants than the other European employers and had no reason to suspect them regarding the babies. She was happy with the arrangement and it was the same for every European household in the Dutch East Indies. No untoward incident involving the *babus* had ever been reported as they were unequivocally careful toward the children. She had been kind and friendly toward the servants and therefore they felt at home with her. How could she suspect them who had been so caring and affectionate to her children?

Margarethe did not understand how the question of negligence on her part could occur regarding Norman's death. Is it not a crime to falsely accuse the bereft mother for causing death of her child? Yes, she was careless, was not dutiful, and had been preoccupied with herself, but could she ever kill her son? I would like to borrow a few words from

---
29   Keay, *op. cit.*, 24.
30   Shipman, *op. cit.*, 97.

Maria Deraismes here, the nineteenth century women's right activist, who wrote: "... this mother who has carried the little creature for nine months in her womb ... who has formed it of her own flesh and blood ... who has merged her life with its life ... who has fed it with her own milk ... this mother must passively stand by and submit to the acts and deed of the father."[31] Rudolf's discontent with Margarethe was being venomously expressed in every opportune moment, and the death of his dear son had not been an exception. He always complained that she did not adhere to a single family value; that while he had to work hard to keep the family she virtually did nothing and lived without concerning herself with anyone or anything important to the MacLeods; that she was a useless creature doing nothing except dressing herself, eating, and sleeping; that she did not have any refinement or education, and was silly, stupid, superficial, and irritating. He had even warned her once that after he remained no more she would have to cry tears of blood for not having done her duty better in her life. At the moment of severe personal grief both Rudolf and Margarethe needed to support each other, but that had not been the case. The couple had never showed signs of being understanding and compassionate to the other and had always been preoccupied with their own preconceived ideas about life and marriage. None of them could transcend the limits of their petty egoistic self and therefore had remained isolated within a conjugal relationship. Rudolf's accusations regarding Norman's death might have affected Margarethe deeply and the scar had remained with her forever.

Some of the numerous tropical insects found in the Indies (Author's collection)

---

31 Ann Tylor Allen, *Feminism and Motherhood in Western Europe, 1890–1970*, 47.

While Rudolf had been wallowing in grief of his deceased son, Margarethe's endeavor to overcome was notable. Soon after Norman's death Rudolf was transferred with a demotion to Banjoe Biroe near Semarang to the Willem I military base. The place, as described by Waagenaar, "... was not a tropical paradise." It was a nearly deserted area which was infested with hundreds and thousands of varied insects, where life offered only depressing monotony. Margarethe was not the one to remain confined indoors and fight crazily with the battalion of unwanted tiny creatures; so she had started going out and socializing, and at some occasion had been introduced by a friend to the Balkstras of Blitar, who owned the Kemloko coffee plantation on the slopes of Mt. Kloet (Kelud) volcano near Malang. She sometimes went to their house for long visits in order to get some solace away from the harrowing emptiness and the unbearable adverse situation at home. She had been choking in the company of Rudolf as he constantly watched and censored her, and abused her on frivolous issues every time they came face to face. On one occasion he did hit her cruelly with his cat-o'-nine-tails because he thought she had used lip paint. He kept all money to himself so that she could not spend on her own; on occasions he did spit on her face in a fit of rage, and to get rid of her he had even wanted to kill her. Margarethe hoped for a divorce from Rudolf, although she had not been serious about it because she worried about her and Non's future. So, the Balkstras' had been a place she could escape to. There she danced in the evenings, dressed elegantly, flirted with men at the plantation, visited nearby ancient temples (especially the *Penataran* temple complex and the *Singasari* temple), went for long walks in the plantations, watched local tent theater or the spectacular stambul plays, and freely chatted on every possible topic for very long with the Balkstra sisters Louise and Laura—Louise was especially very close to Margarethe. For them she was a high-spirited and energetic young woman full of life. In fact, no one who knew her personally ever found her to have been rude or ill behaved, and they had always spoken well of her. Nevertheless, on an occasion, most significantly, Margarethe had told the Balkstra sisters: "I will be celebrated ... or notorious ... I will die eventually on the scaffold."[32] Was it a farsighted prediction about her own fate that afterward became tragically true?

Without the hope for any further promotion Rudolf had retired from his stressful job in October 1900 and went to live in the small picturesque

---

32   Shipman, *op. cit.,* 109.

no-white village named Sindanglaja in south-east of Bogor (Buitenzorg), the oldest European hill station and summer residence of the Governor-General of the Dutch East Indies. As far as one's sight could stretch there had only been lush green fields and forests punctuated by small native huts and a volcanic mountain at the horizon—no European soldier, civil servant, merchant, missionary, or planter would ever catch a glimpse in the isolated village. Margarethe's heart exploded at times like the nearby volcano Mt. Gede, which stood high overlooking the yellow-green paddy fields. Often in extreme frustration due to living with such a brute person she returned the humiliations by accusing Rudolf for giving syphilis to her and the children. In a letter from Sindanglaja in 1901, she wrote to her father that according to the doctors in Batavia he was not even fit to marry. She wrote: "My children caught a disease from their father, the monster, he gave them skin sores! And so have I."[33] Rudolf, on the other hand, obviously believed otherwise. Their relationship deteriorated even further and practically became intolerable to both as they were thoroughly disgusted with the other. Shattering the ambience of the quiet surrounding of the village they shouted at each other at the slightest of provocation and at every moment looked for a ploy to do so.

At times she teased Rudolf by pretending to have affairs with other men, which perturbed him to the extreme (maybe because of his old age) as he believed it to be true and reacted violently by hitting and beating her, by spitting on her face, by threatening to divorce her, or even to kill her. She had done it before as well and might have been doing it repeatedly to expose Rudolf's nature to his colleagues, to get sympathy from all people around, or might have simply been to irritate him even more and, in her own words: "to make his life as unbearable as possible, so that he would take upon himself all the trouble of arranging to leave."[34] She however did not want a divorce because that would imply losing Rudolf's pension and embracing poverty. She had reiterated it in many of her letters written to her father from the Indies expressing her anxiety on the matter. As it is already known that she abhorred the idea of living in misery and poverty, and so her decisions had always been steered by the consideration of opulence. It has also been noted earlier that to meet her ends she had always resorted to telling lies on various occasions. Shipman wrote: "Gretha was not above telling a falsehood when it suited her, and she displayed a keen

---

33 Ibid., 126.
34 Ibid., 124.

sense ... of what stories would advance her cause." So, when returning to Holland became imminent, and she knew that living with Rudolf was no more possible for her, she had theatrically written to her mother-in-law making up a story that as the colonial authority had held back Rudolf's pension, and as she had her passage already paid by his office, she was going to return to Holland without Rudolf; and as none of her parents were alive (a blatant lie, because Adam was still alive in 1901, and was in good health) she had nowhere to go, and therefore wanted to stay with her after returning to the homeland.[35]

Some of Margarethe's biographers have suggested that she had been a congenital liar, the trait being transmitted through the genes from her father. Although she had been a perennial liar, she did not create a make-belief world for her own self. If she had done that then her case would become pathological. But each time she resorted to falsehood her motive was to meet her calculated ends. Lie for her had been a means to some ulterior end, not the end or goal of her life; although it had been one of the causes for her end. She had made it an integral part of her life, even to the extent that she had to pay with her life for that. However, she did not succeed to impress Rudolf's mother at that time as she did not submit to her trick. Margarethe did not hold a good reputation in Rudolf's family because of the reporting that had been made by Frida about her, and also by Rudolf himself, and it was quite normal that none of his family members would believe her. She knew it very well and once wrote to her father and step-mother that Rudolf's family treated her as if she did not exist. Had she not been so impulsive and naïve, and had been more mature, she would have realized before writing all those lies to her mother-in-law that she must have been aware of the trouble between the couple and that she would have immediately smelled foul. Margarethe had also been an opportunist in some sense. She did not have any qualms to write to her mother-in-law that her father was dead, while at the same time she was actually writing to her father to send her money in the Indies. Moreover, despite all the drama she had done with Frida right from the time of her wedding and after despising her from the core of her heart, she went to stay with her before going to Paris after her separation with Rudolf. Similarly, even after getting separated from Rudolf and not shedding the hatred she nurtured against him, she had written nicely to him seeking for pardon and apologizing for calling him names.

---
35 Ibid., 119.

To end the letter she wrote—"with big kisses from Gretha to John." She agreed for reconciliation and had even gone to live with him only due to shortage of money. There are many more instances of her opportunistic behavior, which would be discussed in the proper context. All through her life Margarethe had never thought about the consequences before doing anything, and as we have observed, had passionately followed the dictates of her heart. Although she was adequately smart and clever, she was not prudent, nor was she wise. Her lack of intelligence, awareness, and that of farsightedness had resulted in her wartime tragedy, which inevitably came upon her.

Margarethe had been greatly disturbed when in a fit of rage Rudolf once told her that she had bored him to death. "Her vanity, pride, and fragile sense of self were deeply wounded"[36] wrote Shipman. He had insulted and humiliated her (even publicly) a great many times and had even beaten her badly on many occasions, but nothing matched with his disclosure that he "did not find her sexually attractive anymore." Shipman wrote: "This statement was by far the most hurtful and dreadful thing Rudolf had ever done to her ..." Margarethe's heart bled profusely. Her extreme confidence about her beauty, her good looks, and charm had been questioned by someone who was utterly crude and never had known the value of real beauty. How could an alcoholic brute with a "ruined body" (implying that Rudolf had syphilis), who had a very bad reputation for being a notorious womanizer, have the audacity to say that she had bored him to death? She utterly regretted that she had felt like a princess with that man during their courtship. Although she had realized too bitterly in the 6 years of her marriage that she had drastically been wrong, still she might have had some hope for sympathy, if not admiration, from Rudolf, but it all had ended with that final blow. Margarethe's romantic fantasy about marriage had been finished. She must have pledged to prove to Rudolf that even if he did not admit her charm and sexual allure, she was not finished; she was only 25 and still had the potential to attract and mesmerize the entire men's world by her charismatic persona. After the severe insult she desperately needed to prove herself—Rudolf had crossed all limits. She was intensely obstinate, and once she would decide to take up a course of action, nothing could deter her from doing that. At that juncture the seed of Margarethe's life as Mata Hari had been sown, and consequently the end of her life as Griet had become imminent. The

---

36   Ibid., 127.

marriage, by all means, was virtually over, and Margarethe waited impatiently for a separation. She desperately wanted to flee from the unending confinement in Java and the punishment of living with the monster—Rudolf. Some years later, after she became a famous dancer, she had told to the journalist Gerrit Hendrik Priem that her condition had been worse than that of Dreyfus as a prisoner in the Devils Island.[37] However, she must have thought that Holland could be the only refuge for her. Nearly 6 years back she had looked forward to Java as her refuge, but the situation had taken a drastic turn. At that time she had been trying to get rid of Frida and her orthodox censorship, and then it was Rudolf and his alcoholic abuses. Enough of sacrificing all pleasure for an undeserving man she had thought. She must have resolved to shed all the unnecessary nuisances and to enjoy life on her own terms. If Rudolf's money could serve her purpose then what was the use of enduring so much insult by living with him? With her characteristic optimism she was determined to get out of the mess very soon, although did not know how she could do that. Least did she know that her destiny was going to shower all the blessings on her only within a couple of years.

On March 19, 1902, the MacLeods bade goodbye to the Indies and boarded S. S. *Koningin Wilhelmina* from Batavia (Jakarta) to reach Rotterdam. Margarethe must have said "adieu" from the bottom of her heart, because like the ongoing voyage the return voyage had also been her dream journey toward her freedom and toward her imaginary new identity. On the journey she avoided Rudolf as far as had been possible for her, but often they were heard screaming at the other in public without caring about European civility and Dutch tolerance. Most of the time on the long voyage she had been preoccupied with planning about her and Non's future without Rudolf, because she was most certain of the separation with him once they reached Holland. But Margarethe had been quite courteous not to rush to the civil court in Amsterdam direct from the ship port at Rotterdam and had waited for an opportune moment. Almost after 4 months of their return from Java Non had suddenly fallen sick, and the next day, on August 26, Rudolf took her with him not to return ever again (he might have been instigated by his sister Frida to take the step). Recalling Norman's fate he must have become too scared about Non's illness, and therefore wanted to take her away from Margarethe. It became the precipitating factor for Margarethe to file for the separation.

---

37   Ibid., 124.

On August 27 she had appealed in the court of law bringing a total of 16 charges against Rudolf including adultery, insult, cruelty, physical and mental abuse, heavy alcoholism, suspicion, blaming her for their son's death, and kidnapping her daughter.[38] She had pleaded for the following legal provisions—daughter's custody, permission to live with the Goodvriends (Baroness Sweerts de Landas had been a cousin of Rudolf, whom she called "aunt") in Arnhem without her husband, a monthly alimony of 100 guilders from Rudolf, along with support and items of daily living. As the court had believed that reconciliation between the couple was possible in no way, the separation was granted in 3 days on August 30, 1902, granting her all the provisions she had sought for.

It had been Margarethe's first victory over Rudolf and his family, and she was obviously quite happy with the court's decision. She had only 3 guilders and 50 cents with her at the time of the separation, still she had breathed a sigh of relief after long last and had looked forward with heightened optimism to enjoy her freedom. Non's wellbeing and a decent living became her priority, which could not be possible with Rudolf's 100 guilders. Therefore, with full confidence and determination, she had started looking for a job to support themselves. Ironically she had started looking for a housekeeping job to start with, because she was ready to do anything for her dear Non. She must have thought that she would give Non a respectable upbringing so that the little girl never felt the absence of her father and that she could prove her worth as a mother to Rudolf, to his irritating sister Frida, and to the rest of his family. This surely proves her desperation and her unrelenting nature. She had hoped to earn honestly and pay all her debts respectably, and certainly did not want to cheat anyone. Although Margarethe had not been a dutiful and responsible mother, her love for Non was unquestionable, and therefore she did not want to lose her at any cost; but tragically she could not keep Non with her for long and had to agree to leave her with Rudolf. It must have been a very hard decision for a mother who had unfortunately lost her son not much before. Margarethe had remembered how she was compelled to part with her younger brothers for no fault of hers, and she was again being pushed to the extreme to part with her innocent little daughter. She had never apprehended that separation with the atrocious Rudolf would lead to separation from her dear little Non, but going back to him for Non was also not possible for her anymore. She did not know what to do and

---

38 Ibid., 133–135.

how to cope with her great personal loss.

Margarethe nevertheless always fell in trouble because she had somewhat been impatient regarding everything, jumped to conclusions in haste, and had acted accordingly. Her judgments therefore were almost always wrong. Her basic traits being self-love and queer childish naivety, she was bound to behave in a strange and socially unacceptable manner, and therefore in a society with high bourgeois values she was destined to doom. She had been displaying risk-taking behavior ever since she had adapted herself as Mata Hari. Her life as the dancer and courtesan Mata Hari as well as Marina had been an extension of her basic personality traits—childish, naïve, narcissistic, impulsive, emotive, lonely, fun-loving, immature, egoist, proud, elegant, dazzled, tenacious, unrealistic, maverick, opportunist, clever, unwise, strong, assertive, expressive, extrovert, confident, sensuous, ambitious, unscrupulous—all put together in a fatal combination—fatal, because inspite of being a woman she had the courage to stand against and defy laws of the society that had been implemented by men only in their own interest. This had precisely been Margarethe Zelle's greatest crime. She was so adamant that in a highly bourgeois and misogynic society she had believed in and had the courage to indulge in sexual freedom, for which she had never been forgiven. Had she been born as one of the privileged sex, all that would have been considered as flamboyant qualities appropriate for a bourgeois man of honor. It is quite intriguing then as to what relevance does the million-dollar question whether she had been a notorious spy during the First World War or not have? Knowing her character traits well one can easily deduce that although she might have been a flagrant courtesan, she could never have been even a novice spy. Spies must possess certain characteristic traits to become successful as a secret agent for his/her country—one must be brave, adaptable, hard-working, intelligent, stable, loyal, calculating, devious, deceptive, clandestine, unnoticeable, diplomatic, suspicious, must submit completely to the employer; and also must have the power of observation, social consciousness, self-control, commitment, far-sight, patience, secrecy, etc. Margarethe did not have any of these qualities; although she matched some for which anyone could have been suspected as a spy—e.g., knowledge of many languages, conscious effort for self-mystification, unwarranted income, and wanderlust. But to determine her fate on the basis of her character traits had surely not been appropriate for the French army. Shipman wrote: "She was at heart a shape-shifter who became what those around her wanted her to be."[39] I somehow find Shipman's assessment about Margarethe's personality to be quite strange, and so strongly differ with her because, on the basis of the information about her life collected from Mata Hari's biographers, I have never found her following any other. She had been unique, in all her thoughts and actions, and had always responded to what her heart commanded. She had been too stubborn to become a shape-shifter and to follow what others had wanted her to do or to be. She was too proud to dance to others' tunes, which had undoubtedly been the strength of her character and also her weakness at the same time.

While analyzing Margarethe's character traits I would pertinently like to mention one incredible aspect that must never be overlooked—although she had been an incorrigible liar all through her life, reaping the benefits whenever possible, she had surprisingly refused to lie about her pregnancy right before her execution, inspite of knowing that the lie could definitely save her at the last moment. She must surely have known that the French Criminal Code (Article 27) did not allow killing of a pregnant woman, and an opportunity was offered to her at the suitable moment by her lawyer Edouard Clunet—not to conceive a baby in prison, but to escape the bullets by telling lie about it, but she had refused with a smile. She had decided to embrace the inevitable end gracefully. Did she lose her desperation to live after knowing that even her beloved Vadime had disowned her? She might not have wanted to fiddle with motherhood at the final moments of her life. Margarethe's life had been tainted in many ways, and the French government did not leave a single chance to blacken her further, but in death she wanted to remain immaculate. Whatever had happened to her in the 7 months of her captivity had arguably transformed her into a mature individual, especially after the pronouncement of her death sentence and the consequent incidents. Adam's "little orchid" must have realized at last that she needed to grow up long before. Still, at the early hours of October 15, 1917, when she was called for getting prepared for her final moment, Mata Hari did not forget to look her best in the black Amazonian tailored silk suit, specially made for the occasion, along with her hour-glass corset, a pair of white gloves, and other accessories. This had indeed been her signature trait—even in death she wanted to look good. She refused to be blindfolded during her execution, possibly because also in her death she wanted to have control

---

39   Ibid., 142.

of herself, as she had always done in her life.

However, if Margarethe had been emotive, impulsive, clever, narcissistic, fun-loving, egoist, conceited, proud, snob, opportunist, selfish, irresponsible, undutiful, imprudent, unwary, extravagant, and a perennial liar, the trends had actually been inherited by her from her father Adam. As mentioned earlier, he had a big hat shop, but was such an egoist that he hated to be called a "shopkeeper." He rather preferred to be called a "hatter," enjoyed being called a "baron" (although the locals would sarcastically refer to him in that way), and even believed to be one. Quite often he dramatized facts, which was evident from the biography he had written of his daughter, where he had narrated that Margarethe's childhood was spent in an old aristocratic house in Cammingha and had also proclaimed that her grandmother was Baroness Margarethe van Wijnbergen. None of the information had any factual truth. Although his pretentiousness was noticed and gossiped by the local gentry, he had been nonchalant about that. Appearance was much too important for him, and he used to spend enormously to take care of the family's aristocratic appearance—his expenses included those for extravagant house, more servants, fabulous clothes, and gifts for the children—but he did not save money for the future. So, when Antje became severely ill she died without proper treatment. Adam was also proud of his good looks, he always dressed well, and his narcissism had been exposed through getting his painting in full uniform on horseback made, and keeping it hanging on the wall at a prominent place in the Zelle house. Like an irresponsible and indulgent father he had pampered his daughter, the first child, without even realizing that he was actually spoiling her completely. By doing that he had virtually been flaunting his wealth and status in the aristocratic society and, in a way, had been using Margarethe as his "most becoming accessory."[40]

Contrary to what appeared, it had not been his love for the little child, but only a way of enkindling his narcissistic feeling. As long as it suited his fancy he had been showering his "little orchid" with lovely and costly gifts, giving an impression to the little child that she was meant only for that and she deserved nothing less. Margarethe's lifelong craving for opulence and comfort and also her hyper-ambitious temperament had by all means been genetically loaded through Adam. But when things became difficult for him after his bankruptcy, due to his utter selfishness he had

---

40   Ibid., 5.

simply fled Leeuwarden leaving his loving "little orchid" behind, and did not even think of her social and psychological needs. He had not been dutiful to his family and children. He was not farsighted at all, obviously because of which he had lost his oil shares miserably due to miscalculations and also had to give away his hat shop after his bankruptcy. Adam could not stay back in Leeuwarden because it would have been a blow on his vanity. He could not have continued to live in poverty in the place where he once loved to be called a "baron." He had somewhat abandoned his family after that mishap, but did not mind to get involved in an extramarital relationship with a young lady while his wife Antje had still been alive and was suffering from ill health. He had been so selfish that he did not care about the wellbeing of his children even after his wife's death and went ahead to marry the "other woman" (Susanna Catherina ten Hove) leaving behind the two elder children. He never felt the need to suppress his conceit and had blatantly been exposed in the event of Margarethe and Rudolf's wedding, when he had demanded that they must visit him in a majestic two-horse driven carriage and had also consented to endorse the wedding only if he would be brought to the venue in a grand carriage. At that time he was an ordinary part-time salesman and wanted to impress his neighbors and his buyers in that way showing off his linkage to aristocrat families. Adam had been so conceited that he could never accept his dejected condition and downgraded position as a salesman.

Adam's opportunism had been exposed when, at a later date, after Margarethe became successful as a dancer and got divorced from Rudolf, he wrote a fabricated biography (*The Life of Mata Hari: The Biography of my Daughter, and My Grievances Against Her Former Husband*; Amsterdam, 1906) of his darling daughter only to make some money out of it. In a sense he had actually exploited his daughter's torment to make profit. As Rudolf's family was in every way far better off than Zelle's, Adam might have felt inferior to his son-in-law, which had been expressed through his resent against him. In his daughter's biography he had painted an atrocious picture of Rudolf, which did not wholly match with the person in reality. Mata Hari's opinion about the book on her reveals the truth—she had remarked that the book had actually spoilt her image.[41] Adam did not trust Rudolf, although he knew that perhaps his son-in-law was not wrong as per the bourgeoisie culture of that time. He somehow lacked the will to tolerate and adjust and had by nature been litigious. According to

---

41   Ibid., 170.

Margarethe, he "was always at odds with the whole world." She had told G. H. Priem that, Adam "loves legal wrangling, who lodges a complaint to the Public Prosecutor after the slightest bagatelle, who in the past was at loggerheads with half of the whole of the freemasonry ... who later was at odds with the family and accused every member of the family of unfair intensions ... who always made a mountain out of a molehill ..."[42] It could be due to such mindset that Adam did not keep close contact with his relatives, or *vice versa*. Nevertheless, at a more mature age, after knowing about Margarethe's sorry state with Rudolf, he had genuinely tried to provide moral support to his distressed daughter. It might have been his way of showing solidarity to his daughter whom he had deserted at one time or it could also have been his way of satisfying his sense of inferiority *vis-à-vis* Rudolf by thus feeling superior to him. He had been inconsiderate and careless in all his decisions, and kept accordance with the bourgeoisie culture of his time. Margarethe's carefree and careless lifestyle thus had not been cultivated by her and had been her gift by inheritance.

Margarethe, due to her extreme naivety and inexperience, had been grossly mistaken in assessing Rudolf before her formal engagement to him, and even during the courtship she had only been intrigued by his personality and his indulgent nature. She was overwhelmed by his appearance in uniform and therefore, as most likely of her, had been swept off by her passions while she had closed all doors to her reason. Had she been in her senses she could have noticed Rudolf's bourgeoisie allegiance and extreme pride, with which she was choosing freely to cohabit without assessing the consequences. Rudolf was born (1856) into a migrated Scottish family of proud army gallants, who had cherished and flaunted their achievements through generations. Bernard Newman wrote: "The Leods trace their ancestry back to at least to the twelfth-century Olaf the Black, King of Man and the Isles."[43] His father had retired from the post of infantry captain in the Dutch army, and his uncle Norman MacLeod had once been an adjutant to King Willem III of The Netherlands and had retired as an army General. From the very childhood Rudolf knew that he was going to be an army officer like his predecessors in the MacLeod family and had aspired to become a Lieutenant Colonel some day. He was trained at the military academy at Kampen in Holland from the age of 16, and had graduated in 1877 as a Second Lieutenant at the age of 21. At the

---

42   Ibid., 125.
43   Bernard Newman, *Inquest on Mata Hari*, 47.

military academy he had learnt unconditional obedience to the superiors and had proved to be an exceptionally brilliant cadet. His family might have been proud to see him develop a strong and aggressive temperament suitable for an aspiring army officer. So, he had been quite excited while deciding to join the Dutch Colonial Army in the Indies.

Being adequately strong, he was "cultivated and courageous,"[44] and therefore was ready to take up the challenge of serving in the Royal Dutch Indies Army (KNIL) in the Atjeh War (or Aceh War), known in The Netherlands as the "Glorious War," fought against the natives in the north of Sumatra. Shipman wrote: "Rudolf MacLeod was a hard man—hard-living and hard-drinking, sure of himself, and used to command."[45] He had known much about the colonial life there from the newspapers and also from his uncle and cousins, and had felt drawn toward the country which he knew could offer him laurels. He had fought in Atjeh for 7 long years and had earned the Expedition Cross (Cross for Important Military Operations) for his contribution in the war. Rudolf could satisfy his superiors in the army with his impeccable service, and at the end of 1881 he was promoted to First Lieutenant. But his career had started to suffer right from the time he was transferred from Atjeh (Aceh) in 1884, and a trail of transfers without any promotion had followed. By then he had taken to heavy drinking, gambling, and womanizing—all the social evils that had been rampant among the European population living without families in the Indies. A strong and courageous person by appearance Rudolf must have been very weak at heart and therefore could not resist the temptations. His career suffered stagnation, which could be due to his unreliable behavior, but he had tried his best to overcome the stalemate. He was promoted to the position of Captain in 1892, and was awarded the Officer's Cross, although, by his own consideration, he deserved the Willem's Cross. His superiors however had thought otherwise.

It has already been mentioned that Rudolf had been very close to his sister Louise Frida, who was only a year and a half younger to him. By the time he had returned to Holland on leave due to his health problems she had been widowed with two daughters. Rudolf had missed her wedding because he was actively involved in the Atjeh War at that time (1881) and must have felt awfully bad to know that Mr. Wolsink had died (1888)

---

44 Ibid., 47.
45 Shipman, *op. cit.*, 14.

while he was still in the Indies. The MacLeods had been a close knit family and so they shared a cordial relationship with each other. The only odd person who stood out was Margarethe, because primarily due to her unconventional lifestyle she had never been included in the predominantly orthodox family, and therefore could not become an important part of the MacLeods. The process of alienation had been complete with the legal separation, and because Non had been an inseparable part of the MacLeods, Rudolf could not stand the idea of her staying back with Margarethe after the separation. He undoubtedly loved his children very much and was completely shattered at the loss of his son; but I suppose that it could not have been fatherly attachment per se. I rather presume that he might have harbored a feeling of possessiveness for his children because they were part of the proud MacLeods and so became violent at the slightest possibility of harm to them. Rudolf's almost pathological grief for his deceased son has both a subjective and an objective implication, as it (i) hints at the fact that he knew how much he had been responsible for the toddler's death (by giving him congenital syphilis); (ii) he had continued with his grieving as a shield because he feared a backlash at his professional as well as at the social levels from his seniors in case they came to know about the truth of Norman's death; and (iii) he wanted to make Margarethe feel exceedingly bad for the fact that she had compelled him to go through hell due to death of his son, as he earnestly believed that Norman had died only due to her carelessness. For a strong army officer who had commanded battalions and had participated in bloody battles from quite young age, it was particularly unusual to have grieved in the way he did for his son, all the more because death of European children in the Indies had not been a rare occurrence. I therefore presume, Rudolf had been using Norman's death as a means toward his own ends, both at the professional and personal spheres. This also explains why he could become preoccupied with his promotion within only a few days of Norman's death.[46] Blaming the poor *babu* for the toddler's death might have been an outcome of the deeply set racism in the then Indies society.

Rudolf had never been understanding, compassionate, or supportive to his wife with whom he curiously had a love marriage, although during the brief courtship he had ostensibly expressed all of those trends with the definite motive to impress his fiancée. He had always treated Margarethe

---

46 Ibid., 109.

in the way he had treated his subordinates in the army and the native labors working under him. According to the then misogynic social norms he had considered her to be his subordinate, and likewise had expected unconditional obedience from her. Margarethe must have thought otherwise, and hence, it was not only the issue of money that had been responsible for deterioration of their conjugal relationship. Rudolf was exceptionally arrogant and never missed the pleasure to bully her on every possible opportunity. He was also very excitable and frequently did burst into anger at the slightest provocation from Margarethe. Enumerable instances of their frequent bitter altercations as the result of their matrimonial feud have been cited by her biographers. She had as if been his rival whom he desperately needed to destroy in order to win the game of life. Or it could have been his way to dump his professional frustrations. It might also have been an expression of his fear about losing control of the domestic sphere as he could plausibly have become jittery of Margarethe's imposing and assertive personality. As mentioned earlier, in the then European society a submissive and passive woman was assured of all the security and comfort inside the house, and therefore any woman who defied the social norms was considered to be undeserving—not entitled to the love and care of her husband. Rudolf surely had an abusive personality, frequently expressing spiraling rage to release his "aversive arousal," and must have perhaps enjoyed his state of mind. However, in today's parlance he would have certainly been marked as a psychopath, or even as a criminal, for his torturous ways of treating his wife that included physical and mental abuse of the worst kinds; but in his time he had been spared, because such behavior was neither regarded as a symptom of any mental disorder, nor as a crime; rather it had been the standard pattern of social behavior which the MacLeods had been following meticulously. Wife battering had been considered to be the only remedy for her deviance, because she was seen as a rogue. As Rudolf was born and brought up in a bourgeois family, he had been quite familiar with the bourgeoisie beliefs in misogyny; and in accordance to the social norms of his time he maintained perfect double standard—while he had expected Margarethe to be a perennially passive and submissive wife, he never cared to follow the norms of gentility toward her. While he himself had been susceptible to cajolery, he was especially jealous of her because she was attractive and was admired by the young Europeans in Java. Although he had appreciated her sexual confidence previously, and never hesitated to exchange passionate and sexually explicit letters prior to their marriage, he did not like it anymore, because wives were expected to be household nuns. Her overtly seductive behavior that had attracted him irresistibly before the wedding had afterward become akin to that of a prostitute for him, and therefore, in order to humiliate her he passed cutting remarks at her on every opportune moment.

Rudolf used to complain to Frida continuously through letters (due to some unknown reason he had kept copies of all the letters he wrote to his relatives; or he might have wanted to keep record of the incidents involving Margarethe that had irritated and enraged him, and it could also have been his way of maintaining a daily diary) from the Indies detailing about Margarethe's silly behavior and her unnecessary expenses, calling her bad names in each one of those. He had been a foul mouth not only to Margarethe, but had somewhat lost the habitual decency of a European gentleman and many a time uttered lewd and obnoxious words before other women as well. Due to this reason he was disliked by many aristocrat women who knew him in the Indies. He had been known as a "hot-tempered, coarse-tongued rake,"[47] with no sophistication or sublimity. Long years of struggle in the tropical Dutch Indies might have had some negative impacts on his temperament, but it is also true that he had never possessed any sophistication suitable to the gentility. A few instances of his ridiculous meanness could be cited here—(i) when Margarethe had been ill with typhoid in Java, Rudolf was compelled to buy five bottles of milk every day along with medicines for her. To recuperate from her illness she had to be sent to a hill station at a coffee plantation. He could not accept the financial burden and complained to his cousin through a letter about the expenses he had to incur for her. Shipman wrote: "It is an ugly truth that Rudolf earned roughly 700 to 800 guilders a month and yet begrudged his deathly ill wife a daily expenditure of 1.5 guilders for milk;"[48] (ii) he used to steam-open all the letters written by Margarethe from Java in order to read them before mailing; (iii) on her separation Margarethe had a court order for 100 guilders alimony from Rudolf. He had made a plan to evade the payment and still had the audacity to flout the court order for a reduced amount of alimony; (iv) inspite of getting a decent pension along with having income from other sources Rudolf never paid her a single penny after the separation, and moreover had declared through a newspaper notice not to lend her anything in his name;

---

47   Howe, *op. cit.*, 23.
48   Shipman, *op. cit.*, 114.

(v) he had also made a clever plan to take away baby Non from her mother, who had legally been her custodian. There are so many more instances that it would take much space to enlist all of those, and so I refrain from the exercise; but it becomes absolutely obvious from this that Rudolf was indeed an indecent man who had never truly cared for the norms of civility—neither in his personal nor professional life.

Rudolf's arrogance reflected vividly in his way of living. He had been so careless about his passionate physical relationships with women in the Indies as well as in Holland that he had contracted the immoral disease much before his marriage—syphilis. Still, only after a brief period of treatment in Holland, he had married Margarethe knowingly, which he should not have done. He had been an extremely egoist person and did not care to heed to anyone's advice regarding the matter before taking the decision for marriage. His personal interests had always topped his priority list, to the extreme of even risking the health of his wife and children, although he had never admitted his fault. Shipman referred to Jean Alfred Fournier, the renowned dermatologist and syphilologist of the nineteenth century, in this regard. In his opinion an affected person may decide to marry only after 3 to 4 years of treatment, and when no recurrence would be manifested for more than 1 year. According to him, if a man whose syphilis is still active and is in a dangerous state decides to marry then "the consequences of such mistake are truly disastrous and ruinous, because:

1st: This man may infect his wife …

2nd: the infected couple will engender children that will, inevitably, either die almost as soon as they are conceived, or be born with the father's disease …"[49]

He moreover wrote: "a man with syphilitic antecedents who contracts marriage may become dangerous in marriage in the three following relations: 1st, as husband; 2nd, as father; 3rd, as head of the social community constituted by marriage."[50] So, Fournier said, "When one has the pox, one should cure it; and when by force of care one has rendered it innocuous for others as well as himself, then, having again entered upon a normal

---

49 Alfred Fournier, P. Albert Morrow, Trans., *Syphilis and Marriage*, 5.
50 Ibid., 13.

condition, one has the moral right to aspire to marriage."[51] The question therefore remains whether Rudolf had the moral right not only to marry, but knowing full well that he was infected with that disease, also to enjoy physical intimacy with his would-be bride. He had deliberately been giving the disease to Margarethe who was not suspicious to any extent and had surrendered to his indulgence for physical intimacy before the wedding. I do not subscribe to the view that accuses her of being a sexual pervert and of initiating physical intimacy with Rudolf during courtship, because there is simply no evidence in this regard. On the other hand, it was Rudolf who had the habit of womanizing and a history of indiscriminate physical intimacy, and the onus therefore lies with none other than him. Margarethe, as a young woman of 18, no doubt enjoyed physical intimacy with her future husband, and I suppose that it might have been an added reason for her to marry Rudolf blindly, because premarital sex is known to have a psychologically binding effect on women.

On the question of how is syphilitic contagion transmitted from the husband to the wife, Fournier wrote: "In two ways ... by the close and continual intimacy which results from marriage;" and "syphilis by conception," i.e., even if the husband does not have any manifested symptom of the disease during his wedding, still his wife can receive the disease by conception through placental circulation. This theory was forwarded by Dr. Philippe Ricord and had been supported by many syphilologists including Hutchinson. Rudolf was undergoing treatment for nearly a year, although there is no evidence to show whether he had been completely cured before the wedding or not. But even if it is presumed that he did not have any suspicious manifested symptom while marrying Margarethe, she might have received it by conception—in that case, not from Rudolf, but from the first born child.[52] There had been a controversy regarding this issue as Dr. Max Kassowitz had denied this speculation, and said that the syphilitic poison cannot pass from the maternal into the fetal or from the fetal to the maternal vessels. As I am not an expert on this matter, endorsing Pat Shipman I can only mention some of the experts' views to support my hypothesis of Rudolf being infected with syphilis even during his wedding.

Nevertheless, I somehow feel that Rudolf had also been affected by deeply

---

51 Ibid., 16.
52 Ibid., 21–26.

set anxiety and by inferiority complex. He had joined the Dutch colonial army with much expectation, and had accepted the difficult life of tropical Indies with the dream of achieving a high rank like his uncle Norman MacLeod had. After spending a few years in the army and toiling in the Atjeh War, he was awarded with only a nominal Cross and a routine promotion. He had obviously thought that he deserved more and believed that despite his best services he had been wrongfully deprived. His uncontrolled drinking, gambling, and womanizing speak much of his frustrated mindset. Shipman wrote: "Rudolf was a soldier's soldier. Even on leave, he always wore his uniform and insisted that subordinate soldiers he passes in the street salute him properly."[53] This explains why he had come for his first date with Margarethe in his uniform, although it was very unusual. He was quite tall and had been adequately handsome before his Indies days, but by the time he met Margarethe he had become baldy, and therefore might have lost confidence about his appearance. I speculate that marrying a much younger and gorgeous Margarethe might have been his way of boosting up his morale and having a winning feel. He might also have gladly taken Margarethe to be his prized possession. He might have proudly thought that having a young and beautiful woman like her as his wife would surely elevate his social position among the colonials in the Indies because (i) he had been disliked continually for his heavy drinking and womanizing habits, and (ii) none of his colleagues and friends had wife prettier than Margarethe. One might be fairly tempted to speculate that Rudolf must have tried to compensate his professional frustrations by having Margarethe as his wife. Therefore, when she refused to submit to his bourgeois commands and had been living the way she wanted to he became awfully enraged. He was naturally not ready to accept his failure.

Rudolf might also have been struck with a sense of loss—nothing around him had been going the way he wanted to, and he could not control any of the situations—neither in the private nor in the professional domain. As all egoists do, he had never admitted any of his faults, and had always blamed Margarethe for every wrong that affected the MacLeods badly. Margarethe, on the other hand, later in her life, had been quite courteous to take all the blame for their family discords, and did not shun her responsibility. Rudolf must have been aware of his incapability as a perfect army officer, but could never accept it genuinely from his heart.

---
53 Shipman, *op. cit.*, 35.

Moreover, suffering from syphilis must have instilled a feeling of lowliness in him. The more he became frustrated with himself the more he projected hatred toward Margarethe. In order to overcome his feeling of inferiority he might have resorted to wife battering as a way to feel superior. Interestingly, the causes generally identified by the modern psychologists for wife battering and domestic violence—viz., husband's short temper, infidelity of the abuser, financial constraints, and alcoholism—all had been present in Rudolf's case. As he could not achieve the place he had aspired for in his profession, he might have wanted to have full control over his domestic front. But due to Margarethe's arrogance he could not gratify his desire, and therefore had hated her from the bottom of his heart. Rudolf had decided that she had been instrumental in destroying his self-confidence. For him it was like—if you do not submit to me completely and become my slave, then you are my enemy. As she had never chosen to become anyone's slave, she readily became an enemy. He wanted to shed her from his life by any means, but would not agree to part with his daughter. Non was too young to defy her father's orders, and thus she had not become his rival. Rudolf had been following the bourgeoisie social norms very closely, but Margarethe was not. She had ardently refused to accept the silent role of a domestic angel, and therefore, confrontation between them had become inevitable.

CHAPTER 3
WHY PARIS?

Life in the Indies with Rudolf had become greatly unbearable for Margarethe. Rudolf had overtly been expressing hatred toward his wife and humiliating her in public. Life had become "real hell" for her.[1] She knew that she had to live and enjoy life and did not want to die with such a terrible man in a faraway land. She wanted to return to her homeland, to Amsterdam, where she could live in peace. As noted earlier, Rudolf, in a fit of rage, once had told her that she had bored him to death. It was the ultimate insult for Margarethe. Her self-esteem was hurt beyond redemption. She had seen admiration for her among the young army people and the young planters in Java, and regardless of her being married, many of them had even been romantically attracted toward her. How could a man say that she had only bored him all along? In a letter from Java to her father she wrote: "I am so beautiful; how is it possible that I bore a man …" Her self-respect prompted her to sleep separately from Rudolf. She wrote: "… I prefer to die before he touches me again."[2] What a glaring irony! Their relationship had developed barely a couple of years back chiefly on the basis of physical intimacy, but eventually they loathed even to touch each other. Knowing Rudolf well she had assumed that he must have wanted to have another woman in her stead, and therefore, in order to fulfill his desire, he had been treating her like dirt. Adam could only advice his dear daughter to move out of the brute through a legal separation. For that they needed to return to Holland together. But the idea of living again with her sister-in-law Louise Frida and her daughters while back in Holland repulsed Margarethe. She had moreover presumed that Rudolf's sister would take away his pension because she "subjugates John entirely," and she was sure that Frida would exploit Rudolf in her own interest. She had witnessed how he submitted to all her commands. Margarethe also blamed Frida for all their marital disputes and misfortune, and could never truly forgive her.

---

1   Pat Shipman, *op. cit.,* 124–131.
2   Ibid., 126.

Rudolf had already retired from work sometime back, and on Margarethe's insistence the MacLeods started for good to return to Holland in March 1902. Margarethe was rejoiced because no more was she able to bear isolation in the small village Sindanglaja, where Rudolf was staying with his family after his retirement. Much later in one of her interviews to the journalist and writer Gerrit Hendrik Priem she had expressed: "I wanted to get away, at any price! I wanted to live, I did not want to bury my youth in a grave like Sindanglaja, and I desired to enjoy my life."[3] Europe was absolutely fascinating at the start of the new century. Ostrovsky wrote: "And she was returning, a survivor from death, isolation, slavery, with the wealth of the Orient stored in her mind and her senses like precious contraband."[4] It was quite a long journey of 5 weeks and they must have reached Holland sometime in the end of April. Margarethe's assumption surely came to be true, since while back in Amsterdam Rudolf went to stay with Frida. It could be the only choice for him, because making a separate arrangement for the family would have been more expensive. Margarethe could not be happy with it and only within 2 weeks she had compelled Rudolf to move out. He had many creditors in Holland and was also facing some lawsuits against him. Given the situation his mood could not have been cheerful and Margarethe had to bear the heat. The situation for Margarethe had truly been like out of the frying pan into the fire, and for her it was the limit. As mentioned earlier, she got separated from Rudolf on August 30, 1902. Rudolf had conveniently informed his friends in Holland as well as in the Indies that Margarethe had deserted him.

On the day of their separation Rudolf had published a notice in two local newspapers (*The News of the Day* and the *Arnhem Daily*) in his name saying "Warning! Do not furnish credit or merchandise to Mme. MacLeod, née Zelle, because the undersigned has resigned all responsibility for her."[5] The Goodvriends however did not hesitate to stand firmly by Rudolf, and therefore Margarethe could not stay with them despite the court order. On September 2, only after 2 days of the separation, she had to shift to a boarding house in Amsterdam with her daughter. She had immediately started to look for a job because she wanted a decent upbringing for Non. She must have thought of her own lavish childhood by the courtesy of her

---

3 Ibid., 124.
4 Erika Ostrovsky, *op. cit.*, 57.
5 Shipman, *op. cit.*, 136.

wealthy father's love and care as the ideal mark of a decent upbringing. What Margarethe did not contemplate was Rudolf's bourgeois nature, due to which he was surely going to find some excuse to shed the financial responsibility. On September 10, the day he was to pay Margarethe for the first time, he had pleaded poverty in the court and had somehow convinced the judge to get the amount reduced to 50 guilders a month. However, he had never paid anything to Margarethe and had never cared about the ruling of the court. Quite normally she became frantic by the sudden turn of the events, and as she had desperately wanted to keep Non with her, she feared that she might have to return to Rudolf out of sheer poverty. Margarethe had informed everything to Adam in a letter on September 12 requesting him for some money and wrote: "I will shoot myself rather than return to MacLeod." She had presumed that it could well be Rudolf's trick to take away Non from her. She was not ready to part with her daughter at any cost. Her anxiety was quite justified because at the time of separation Margarethe had only 3 guilders and 50 cents with her, and did not even have warm clothes and shoes for herself or for Non for the forthcoming terrible winter in The Netherlands.

During the close of the century women had started working in various factories, had taken up jobs as teachers, nurses, typists, seamstresses, pharmacists, etc, and were also seen doing small business (like grocery, milk shop, newspaper vending, and others) for a decent living, but due to her knack for extravagance and luxury Margarethe could not choose her profession from any of those. She could not envisage herself as a labor because that would have amounted to belittlement for her. Therefore, even after much effort Margarethe did not get a suitably decent job, and the only option left to her was prostitution. The mounting bills, debt to her lawyer, cost of renting a satisfactory place to live, and spending for day-to-day living was surely becoming a burden for her. By then Rudolf had already started to live with another woman (Elisabetha Martina Christina van der Mast, whom he had married in 1907), and Margarethe knew for sure that he would no more support them in any way. Still, out of sheer helplessness and desperation, she had tried for a last time to get some money from Rudolf, and, as stated before, wrote to him nicely with a note of apology for her behavior to him. It really worked, and not only did she get money from him, Rudolf moreover wanted to take them again to stay with him. Unable to bear the hardship Margarethe had agreed. Only after 2 months of the separation, on November 4, 1902, she had returned to Rudolf with Non, but because both had been disgusted and fed up with each other they could not stay together for long. It had become absolutely evident that no reconciliation was virtually possible between them. It had certainly been a ploy on the part of Rudolf to get back Non from Margarethe, and presumably she had realized by then that she was also not in a position to keep Non with her for long. So she had agreed to leave Non forever with Rudolf, and had moved in with the Taconis' in The Hague. It was ironically the same place where she had been living when she had replied to Rudolf's marriage advertisement in 1895. In 1902, Margarethe was 26 years of age, young, and pleasantly attractive with cultivated qualities. Still she could not find any respectable job for her sustenance due to lack of any specific skill. One of her biographers wrote that she had returned to her father and had joined his hat business for some time,[6] and also did housekeeping to earn some money; but there is no proof in this regard as Adam had discontinued with his hat business after his bankruptcy in 1889, and had been doing some sort of small sales job in Amsterdam after his second marriage. Some wrote that in complete despair she had returned to Tante Frida, who then had advised her to take up modeling for clothes as a mannequin.[7] This could have been true, because she had indeed taken up modeling for some time although not for clothes, but for the painters, in The Hague and subsequently in Paris as well. She might have recalled that in Leeuwarden Adam had modeled for a painter to make his portrait, and therefore, she might have thought of trying out a bit of modeling for painters.

The oldest art academy in The Netherlands is The Royal Academy of Arts, which is situated in The Hague, and while staying with the Taconis' Margarethe probably had started to do some part-time modeling for the painters there. Her condition for sitting as a model was that she would not pose nude, and the painter would paint only her head.[8] However liberal she might have been in her outlook, from the core of her heart she was still a mother and a wife, so she could not shed the social bindings. She had been trying to put a step forward while another was firmly rooted in her past. She must have modeled for some students and art teachers of The Hague school, but some of the renowned painters she had posed for

---

6 Sam Waagenaar, *op. cit.*, 1964, 43.
7 Shipman, *op. cit.*, 142.
8 Bernard Newman, *op. cit.*, 52. He said that Mata Hari had first posed for a painting of Messalina. Quite suggestive!

at various occasions were Piet van der Hem, Paul Franz-Namur, Octave Denis Victor Guillonnet, Monsieur Otto Dix, and Isaac Lazarus Israels—all had been famous in their own fields at that time. However, modeling did not turn out to be a viable profession for Margarethe because it could not provide what she wanted, and the way she had dreamt to fashion her life was far beyond that of a small-time painters' model. She had then thought of taking up acting as an option for a living,[9] because she had previous experience and was confident about her skill in it. As mentioned earlier, in 1898, when Queen Wilhelmina of The Netherlands became 18 years of age, she was formally crowned as the Queen. To celebrate the occasion many festivals were organized at the local and the national levels in The Netherlands. One great Rembrandt exhibition was arranged in Amsterdam, and also a National Exhibition of Women's Labor was organized, where female typists, cigar makers, pharmacists, textile printers, and others had taken part. Queen Wilhelmina had personally gone to see the Exhibition and had expressed her pleasure about the state of affairs. As in the homeland, the occasion was also celebrated with great enthusiasm in the Dutch East Indies.

Margarethe had played the lead role of the Queen in the musical play *The Crusaders,* for which she was appreciated greatly and did get considerable attention of the press.[10] A year later, in a letter from the Indies to her father (December 2, 1899) she had expressed her wish to study theater in Amsterdam after they returned to Holland, which she thought would help her to "become something."[11] Her dream did not materialize, even though, once back in Holland, she had indeed started to learn acting at the Toonel School in Amsterdam.[12] However, for an acting career no other place than Paris could have been the ideal destination. Although when at a later date a journalist in Vienna had asked her why she had chosen Paris to start her career from, her reply was: "I don't know. I thought all women who ran away from their husbands went to Paris."[13] She must have known about some women, mostly dancers and actresses, who had gone to Paris in search of a profession after separation or divorce, because in fact there was no dearth of them, e.g., Anne Marie Chassaigne, a.k.a.

---

9 Shipman, *op. cit.*, 142.
10 Ibid., 70.
11 Ibid., 110.
12 Ostrovsky, *op. cit.*, 65.
13 Ibid., 143; Waagenaar, *op. cit.*, 1964, 41.

Liane de Pougy. Interestingly, Anne Marie too had married at a very young age, had a brute and abusive husband who was a naval officer, from whom she had fled to reach Paris for a living and had started with doing prostitution in the City of Lights. Later she had been trained by the famous courtesan Valtesse de La Bigne and became a renowned courtesan in her own right. Mata Hari might have been significantly inspired by her life story. There had however even been some feminists of that era who had settled in Paris after divorcing their husbands. Most notable mention would be of Cecile Goekoop de Jong van Beek en Donk, whose feminist narrative *Unreadable Novel* was published in 1898 in The Netherlands. The novel became so popular that within 6 months its sale had surpassed a record of 4,000 copies.[14] After getting divorced from her husband Mr. Adriaan Eliza Herman Goekoop in 1899, Cecile went to Paris and settled there for the rest of her life. Her protagonist Hilda van Suylenburg had represented the women who yearned for emancipation. Margarethe must have read the book at some point of time and might have known about the author very well. However, through her innocent reply to the journalist, the reasons for her decision to go to Paris for a living had not been truly revealed.

At the turn of the century (*fin de siècle*) Paris was a happening city, the pleasure capital of Europe, the City of Lights, the paradise for consumers, and the center for celebrations. Richard Harding Davis, the renowned journalist and writer of that time, wrote: "... there is certainly no other capital of the world ... for enjoyment and adventure."[15] Paris became "a city dedicated to pleasure," "a spectacle for mass consumption," and "a vast theater for herself and all the world ..." With her well-planned boulevards, huge buildings, decorative facades, effectively decorated shops, cafés and bars, sparkling river front, and happy crowd, Paris epitomized the founding principles of the New Republic of France—liberty, equality, and fraternity. The underground railway, which had started in 1900 during the World Exposition, took people easily to the other cities in France and enabled them to throng to Paris in comfort and in much less time. The factor of accessibility undoubtedly added to the attraction of the city. During the end of the nineteenth century in Europe, Paris was thriving also in the new art (*Art Nouveau*) of the Belle Époque. From the last decade of the nineteenth century artists, painters, sculptors, architects,

---

14 Jacqueline Bel, and Thomas Vaessensed, eds., *Women's Writing from the Low Countries 1880–2010: An Anthology*, 34.
15 Richard Harding Davis, *About Paris*, 47.

actors, dancers, singers, musicians, technologists, designers (comprising of fashion, furniture, and jewelry)—all filled Paris with the hope to exhibit their talents and to get acclaim. The city had provided them adequate space for the freedom they required to express their art forms. Liberal ideology of the New Republic had allowed free expression of art in every field combining tradition and aesthetics with new technologies. The key feature that made the new art more dramatic was a tendency to combine contradiction, proficiency for ambivalence, and indecision. The sudden explosion regarding liberalization of art produced enormous magic in a short span of time. Cinema had been newly invented in 1895 by the Lumière brothers of France, and Paris saw the first screening of that wonder. To greet and celebrate the beginning of the new century the Paris World Exposition of 1900 (from April 15 to November 12) was organized, which showcased a combination of modern art and tradition from all over the world with the participation of more than 25 countries. Having depicted a modern theme the 1900 Paris World Fair had become the ultimate destination of new consumerism and had created history by counting a total footfall of about 51 million visitors. Paris became the paradise for international tourists due to the grand Exposition, which could only be identified with exuberance and optimism.

The Exposition was held with the theme "Evaluation of a Century"[16] and had the following aims—(i) rebuilding confidence of the French people by showing France as an industrial, technological and cultural power in the modern world; (ii) unity of the French nation; and (iii) support for the Third Republic.[17] It had also aimed to project France as a colonial empire, which was somewhat neglected at the previous Paris World Exposition of 1889, and as Algeria had been the most lucrative French colony, the pavilion for Algeria took the central position on the Trocadéro hill. Exotic Oriental pavilions had also been built, in which French colonies like India and Indochina had exhibited their fineries. Oriental pavilions of some of the other European colonies included those of Persia, Burma, Japan, The Dutch East Indies, Siam, Korea, and China.[18] The Dutch East Indies pavilion had made a true replica of the famous eighth century Buddhist *Candi-Sari* (*candi/tjandi*=temple) embellished with life size sculptures reproduced from the original temple in Java. Great many visitors had

---

16   Bill Marshall, ed., *France and the Americas*, 427.
17   Marieke Bloembergen, *Colonial Spectacles*, 181.
18   R.N.Willcox, *Paris Exposition*, 65–66.

found it to be the most beautiful edifice of the Exhibition. Although many countries from the west like Africa, America, Great Britain, Russia, most of the European countries, and western British colonies had participated in the show, the Oriental exhibits had practically mesmerized the visitors and had triumphed over the west. While the west predominantly exhibited their newly invented technologies at the show impressing visitors with marvels like x-ray photography, incubators, cinema, automobiles, telegraph, the *trottoir roulant rapide* (the fast moving walkway), electric lights (in fact the Vienna Electricity Exhibition of 1883 was faded by the vast use of electricity in the Paris World Exposition 1900—adding to the grandeur the Fairy of Electricity had been spouting multicolored flames into the sky[19]), etc, the Orient presented their cultures. As the genre of entertainment provides great scope to demonstrate cultural wealth it had received prominence at the Exposition. Theater halls that had been staging Oriental dances filled quickly. Loie Fuller was the most noted performer at the Exposition who had combined Oriental dance styles with western cabaret through her presentations. Another noted dancer of the Belle Époque who had captivated the audience with her Oriental dances was the famous ballet dancer Cléo de Mérode of Paris.

I somehow feel that Margarethe's (a.k.a. Mata Hari) career as an Oriental dancer in Europe has certain untold links with Mérode's performances, even though Mata Hari had never expressed it in any way. Born in Paris in 1875 as Cleopatra-Diane de Mérode, she had been gifted with exquisite beauty and grace. She had appeared on stage at the tender age of 7 as a ballet dancer. Mérode had presented Cambodian dances at the 1900 Paris Exposition—"danses javanaises."[20] She knew nothing of the far eastern culture, and therefore had based her choreography on the statues and sculptures of the famous *Angkor Wat* temple, the largest religious monument in the world, by which she had been immensely motivated. The temple reliefs elaborately depict the story of Rāma as per the Khmer tradition. Her costume for the performances was inspired by a film on Cambodian dancers that she had viewed at the Exhibition. Mérode had appeared on stage for the occasion as a "sacred dancer" along with Vietnamese *don ca tai tu* (Southern Opera Singing), Nguyen Tong Trieu's band,[21] which had

---

19 Bloembergen, *op. cit.*, 182.
20 M.D.Garval, *Cléo de Mérode and the Rise of Modern Celebrity Culture*, 130.
21 H. Nguyen, "Movie Depicts *don ca tai tu* Artists in Early 20th Century," *The Saigon Times*, August 2, 2013, Internet archive.

added to the authenticity of her performances. A journalist at that time wrote about her: Cléo "provides a very exact feeling of Cambodia. You'd think you were there."[22] The general impression she could create about the Oriental style through her Cambodian dances was that of delight. A strange charm along with her splendid grace entranced the audience in such a spell that she gave hour-long performances five times a day for which the theater had always been full. She was paid handsomely with 1,500 francs per day (300 francs for each performance of 1 hour duration) during the Exposition. People had craved to see her Cambodian recitals even after the World Fair was over.

Mérode had already been famous after winning the contest for the most beautiful woman on Parisian stage. Inspired by her exemplary beauty, Jean Alexandre J. Falguiere, the renowned sculptor of the nineteenth century, had sculpted her nude statue "The Dancer" in 1896. She had been the most photographed face in Europe by 1895, and was painted by many renowned painters of her time including Giovanni Boldini (1901). Before the turn of the century her pictures were sold as penny postcards, which had been an advertisement strategy of that time to infuse eagerness in the admirers to see the diva in person. So, it had been quite predictable that she would only add to her fame through her Cambodian recitals at the Paris World Fair. Mérode was not above criticism though, and critics wrote about lack of ethnic flavor and local color in her dances. Her face was too white to be believed to have been Cambodian. Still, with her legendary beauty (she was known as the "Beauty Queen" in Europe for her divinely chiseled face) she had been the ace performer from Paris at the Exposition. However, Oriental dance performance was not unique to the 1900 Paris World Exposition. Western audience in Paris had first witnessed Oriental dance at the Paris World Exposition of 1889, when, at the Javanese pavilion, they had seen original Javanese dance by native performers, accompanied by gamelan music of Sari Oneng. The famous French musician Claude Debussy had been so impressed and inspired by the music that he had incorporated some of the ethnic style in his later compositions. He had even written about the sacredness of gamelan music. Rae Beth Gordon mentioned Eugène-Melchior de Vogüé (Maurice Talmeyr, *The School of Trocadéro*, 1900), who wrote that, in the 1889 Paris World Exposition the Javanese dancers hypnotized an adoring Parisian

---

22 Garval, *op. cit.*, 131.

public with their undulating movements that reminded him of a snake.[23] So, it is quite clear that the Parisian audience had already been familiar with Oriental music and the dance styles by the turn of the century and was fairly intrigued by the recitals.

Mention of the Paris World Exposition of 1900 would be incomplete without mentioning about the fashionable clothes worn by the visitors, especially by the women. Women of all ages and from all levels of the society want to be fashionable in the public domain, not because they want to show off their wealth or passion, but because fashion dictates position and status in the society. Being fashionable also means having adequate sense of wearing suitable garment for the right purpose and occasion. Complying with the latest fashion trends moreover implies some kind of belongingness to the society. Most importantly fashion reflects the persona of the individual. Margarethe knew every bit of it too well as she had chosen to become fashionable from her early days, when Adam used to buy her exquisite clothes. During the nineteenth century Paris had been the fashion capital, not only of Europe, but also of the whole western world. During the turn of the century Paris had employed nearly 400,000 workers who made women's clothes exclusively.[24] Women who could afford to buy expensive dresses looked up for the latest fashions launched by renowned brands like the House of Worth, L. Savarre, Mme. Merlot-Larcheveque, Mme. A. Laferrier, Mme. Levillion, and Ernest Rauditz. Numerous fashion magazines in Paris announced arrival of the latest designs in lingerie, chemises, petticoats, corsets, morning gowns, afternoon gowns, evening gowns to lounge, walking gowns, and dresses for every other occasion, and to make the products more attractive even demonstrated with the help of line drawings and photography.[25] A few of the most sought after designers of that era had been Paul Poiret and Mme. Jeanne Paquin of France, Mariano Fortuny of Venice, and Charles Frederick Worth of England who had shifted to Paris and was succeeded by his two sons Jean-Philippe Worth and Gaston Worth. Charles Worth had invented the *Haute Couture* style in fashion and none other than Empress Eugénie had adorned his clientele. Fortuny was so popular that he had a number of celebrity customers devoted to his fashion statement, like Isadora Duncan, Cléo de Mérode, Émilienne d'Alençon, Liane de

---

23 R. B. Gordon, *Dances with Darwin, 1875–1910*, 200.
24 Theodore Zeldin, *A History of French Passions, 1848–1945*, 436.
25 Valerie Steele, *Paris Fashion: A Cultural History*, 104.

Pougy, and others. Mme. Paquin had been a trendsetter in the Parisian fashion world in many ways, and her clientele comprised of European queens, princesses, wives of business tycoons, and courtesans. The World Fair had been an open arena to celebrate the latest fashions in vogue—for both the *Haute Couture* and the Ready-to-wear styles. Changing fashion of the *fin-de-siècle* reflected vividly on the Fair ground. Stylist shoes and fashionable hats were not left behind. Stylish furs were also in vogue among the Parisian society women, and designers like Paul Poiret, Jeanne-Marie Lanvin, and Mme. Jeanne Paquin were mostly popular in fur fashions. Living in the Indies Margarethe could only dream of the Parisian fashion world, and if she could ever lay her hands on any such magazine (like *Le Petit Echo de la Mode*, and others) she would go through the pages with great passion.

All these had been painfully inaccessible to Margarethe. Living in faraway Indies had been a punishment for her, especially because Rudolf had been a strong-headed army officer, who did not even buy nice and elegant clothes for his wife, which might have been, in her own opinion, due to the fact that he was too jealous of her beauty and attraction. She was living in the Dutch East Indies (in Banjoe Biroe near Fort Willem I) at the time of the World Exposition 1900, and had been under medical treatment from the month of March for a severe attack of typhoid. Being advised by the medical officer Dr. Roelfsema, in the third week of May, she was sent to the Kroewoek coffee plantation in the hills near Ulingie to recuperate from her illness.[26] Even though in ill health, Margarethe was relieved by staying away from Rudolf at least for some time, but missed her daughter since she had to leave her back. Margarethe was looked after by the nurses there. The Paris World Fair had been the focus of discussion on many occasions and she enjoyed participating in it. She returned home in good health, but staying again with Rudolf drained her of good humor. The only solace had been getting back to Non. Situation at the MacLeods soon became unbearable due to the frequent fighting of the couple, and during the end of July, in order to bring back composure, Margarethe was sent for 2 days to Semarang to visit friends. Rudolf however had retired from his job on October 2 that year and due to financial reasons had chosen to live in the small remote village Sindanglaja. Although it was a health resort, the place was quite inexpensive. As there were no modern resources available of any kind, Europeans did not prefer to live

---

26   Waagenaar, *op. cit.*, 1964, 39.

there. But to Rudolf it appeared to have been a divine place, because it was cheap, because it was serene, and because no one would be around to witness the frequent quarrels between them. He could do whatever he wanted to do to Margarethe in order to teach her a lesson.

Margarethe nevertheless felt completely isolated in the small village surrounded only with the natural treasure of abundant greenery. She would come to know about the World Fair only through newspapers that reached quite late to her and would regret living in such a remote place—away from life, away from the celebrations, away from the splendor, and enjoyment that was happening in Paris. She simply despised to continue unnecessarily to live on in the Indies, but had been helpless. Like every other episode of the World Fair she must have known about the recitals of Cléo de Mérode through newspaper reporting. Standing in front of the mirror in the seclusion and privacy of her room she might have cherished a dream at the deepest corner of her mind. Did she try out some Javanese dance movements she had been familiar with? In the remote village of Java life was quiet, monotonous, and suffocating for her, nothing in the Indies attracted her any longer—she hated the solitude and had only longed to return to Holland. Margarethe felt like an imprisoned soul in the small village—no one to support her, no friend, and no well-wisher around. She not only had to withstand Rudolf's notoriety, but also had to accommodate with the tropical hazards of deadly vermin and armies of irritating insects that continuously entered their house from nowhere. The situation was deplorable to Margarethe. Rudolf was not in service any more, but still would not return to Holland because he might have thought that with his meager pension and extravagant wife he would not be able to support his family there. He moreover had feared litigation against him in Holland from his creditors. He was however happy with his retired life in the small village, with his alcohol addiction and had also enjoyed leisure with frequent abusive cathartic outbursts on Margarethe. But she hated the idea of staying back in Java and enraging Rudolf had occasionally expressed her wish to visit the World Exposition in Paris. It is therefore quite evident that while she was still living in Java she had been irresistibly attracted to the city of celebrations, the City of Lights, the paradise of consumers, and the ultimate destination of fashion.

However, the separation had left Margarethe homeless. She did not even have any money. Therefore, after some failed attempts for reconciliation with Rudolf and his family, and a bout at prostitution in the Van Woostraat, the infamous red-light area of Amsterdam,[27] in early 1903 she had finally decided to move to Paris for a suitable career. Even though she had wished to pursue a profession in acting and had knocked at the doors of every theatrical agency in Paris, it did not materialize because either she did not know the right people to approach or she had lacked good looks appropriate for the work. She felt dejected. It was as if her fate had turned her down in every endeavor toward dignity. She had tried modeling for painters, but was not paid according to her expectations. Margarethe could see no option other than joining some degraded brothel in her dream city and she hated to embrace the idea. She had dreamt of a pair of imaginary wings to start with, but nothing seemed to be feasible. She was still Rudolf's wife and under the legal bindings to adhere to his wish. He had threatened her to send her to a state institution for incorrigibles if she did not return to Amsterdam without delay. Margarethe had no choice. Russell Howe wrote: "She had not come to Paris originally to conquer the stage but to move up from poverty to luxury, and the obvious route to that was marriage to an affluent and attentive husband."[28] Howe's opinion seems to be somewhat out of place—Margarethe was not in a position to enter into another marriage at that moment as she was not yet divorced to Rudolf, and there is no proof that at that point she had desperately sought shelter in the arms of a new husband for a luxurious living. Rather, like a fighter, she was determined to struggle for her dignity and existence. However, even though Rudolf did not take any of her responsibilities, he was still her "master" according to the society and the law. With a heavy heart she had returned from Paris, but did not leave hope. Rudolf did not allow her to stay with him or with Non, and had immediately exiled her at his cousin Edward's country house in North Brabant (nearly 50 miles south-west of Nijmegen), a district bordering Belgium that had been dominated by the Roman Catholics. There she was compelled to live under the surveillance of his elderly relatives who treated her like a heinous criminal, because inspite of being a respectably married lady she had lost her head and had taken to prostitution. Rudolf's relatives would obviously take his side. There are varied versions of Margarethe's return from Paris and her stay at Rudolf's cousin's house, although I presume Sam Waagenaar and Erika Ostrovsky could be closer to truth, which has been represented here.

---

27 Ostrovsky, *op. cit.*, 65.
28 Russell Warren Howe, *op. cit.*, 44.

Only a week had passed after she returned from Paris, but it seemed to be eternity to Margarethe. She was drained of all patience, and had been in no mood to tolerate confinement and isolation any further. The only way to get rid of the torment she could think of was another trip to Paris. She was determined to go back to Paris—for the last time. No other city attracted her as much. But she was not going to make the mistake of venturing alone again. She remembered Baron Henry Jean-Baptiste Joseph de Marguerie, a wealthy second secretary at the French Legation in Holland, whom she had met sometime after her separation at a reception in The Hague,[29] and had befriended. Learning somehow[30] that he was about to return to Paris Margarethe had expressed her wish to accompany him to her dream destination. Henry de Marguerie was a bachelor and had accepted her proposal with pleasure. She was overjoyed. She could, at the least, start her new journey with support from someone and had pledged not to make any mistake like before. While in Paris, de Marguerie, her first lover after separation from Rudolf, whom she lovingly called "Roberts," had gladly paid all her bills and even had bought her some nice clothes that were urgently needed by her. With a lover by her side and half a franc in her pocket Margarethe had landed in Paris once again in the winter of 1904 (probably in the end of January), and had walked straight into the exclusively luxurious and highly expensive Grand Hotel. Little did she know that she was only a couple of months away from extraordinary fame and success. During that time she might have considered trying out some more choices to start afresh including dancing, something that she had not tried at the previous attempt. Under any circumstance, she had committed to herself, never to return to Rudolf and his family. She was desperate to leave the MacLeods, and along with them she would have to leave her bourgeois identity forever. That implied an end to her identity as a wife and a mother. She had agreed to accept the consequence rather than to accept the torment any longer. Margarethe had felt free to create a new identity of her own—a new life to live and enjoy, a life free from the control of Rudolf and the MacLeods, free from suspicion and abuse, free from slavery and bondage. Liberty beckoned her, and she was ready to make any sacrifice for that.

---

29 Ibid., 34.
30 It is not clear how she came to know about de Marguerie's travel to Paris at that time, because she had been living in Nijmegen, far away from The Hague. Therefore, it might be supposed that she had called him personally to ask for the favor and the gentleman obliged.

She recalled that after the death of Norman, while they had been living in Banjoe Biroe, she sometimes visited the Balkstra family at Blitar. She liked them very much, enjoyed their company, and became close to the mother and the sisters of Mr. Balkstra. Margarethe was so fond of Mother Balkstra that she had started calling her "mother." As already noted, heart broken by her child's death and shattered by Rudolf's rudeness thereafter, she used to go to them for some solace and to spend time with the two sisters. On their request she had danced informally quite a few times before them in their home and had been incredibly appreciated. Sitting idly in her hotel room in Paris the thought had occurred in her mind like a sudden flash—could she take up dancing as a career then? But Margarethe was not confident because she did not have any formal training in dance apart from her dance classes at the elementary French School in Leeuwarden. She had a penchant for the Javanese dance styles—both the temple and the court dances enthralled her, and while in the Indies she had seen some grand performances by the native people of Java, but had never tried to learn from them. She had also been captivated by the temple sculptures during the time she went strolling alone while staying in Tumpang, near Malang, in East Java. The place had richly been surrounded by many Hindu and Buddhist ruined temples dating back to the ancient times, almost all of which are elaborately carved.[31] The most impressive of those being the thirteenth century ruined temple *Candi-Jago*, which is a blend of both the Hindu and Buddhist architectural styles. Margarethe was irresistibly attracted to the exquisitely carved stone statues and reliefs on the temple walls and observed keenly with awe as she had never experienced anything of the kind in her homeland. She had been following the female figures on the stone panels and the unique postures that they were carved in, which resembled the movements of the Javanese temple dancers. Still she was not convinced that she could make a living simply on the basis of that. She must have thought that she should do something else to start with.

---

31   Julia Keay, *op. cit.*,16.

Mata Hari on horseback in a public park in Paris in 1912
(The Mata Hari Foundation, Fries Museum, Leeuwarden)

As the daughter of an excellent rider Margarethe must have had a knack for riding and had learnt horse riding in the Indies[32] mastering the art. According to the custom of that time she rode side saddle, which made her appear all the more graceful. Probably on the advice of her lover Henry de Marguerie, who remained her sincere friend forever, and as a French diplomat might also have written a letter of introduction for her, she had gone to meet the owner Monsieur Ernst Molier of the famous Molier Circus in Paris. At that time many such shows had been going on in the French capital, like Cirque Rancy of Theodore Rancy, Cirque d'Hiver (established in 1852 as Cirque Napoleon, but renamed in 1870), Cirque Fernando (originally Cirque Medrano), the Royal Romanian Cirque Cesar Sidoli (established by Theodore Sidoli in 1874, and renovated by his son Cesar Sidoli in 1888), and some others, all of which had equestrian shows, but she went to see Monsieur Molier. It is quite plausible that because she had been introduced by her lover de Marguerie, he would only have sent her to someone he knew well, and so he must have known M. Molier personally. However, with her riding skill, a tall and graceful physique, and adequately good looks she had obtained a part-time job as an instructress in his circus. It was an equestrian show with beautiful horses, talented riders, and some other kinds of animals showing off their strange skills and ruling the center stage. Ernst's shows

---

32   Waagenaar, *op. cit.*, 1964, 44.

had been remarkably popular in Paris, the city of entertainment. All the performers, both male and female, came from aristocratic background, and Margarethe felt comfortable in their company. The famous dancer Loie Fuller had participated in a dance show at the circus in 1904. Each of Molier's shows would end with a spectacular pantomime named *The Apotheosis of Ernest*[33] in which the lady members performed a graceful dance together. Margarethe might also have joined the dance show at the circus and might have been noticed by Molier due to her graceful and impressive postures and movements. She had a lovely body, sparkling bright dark eyes, and a dazzling smile—not to be wasted in the circus. Her job at the Molier's had no doubt been respectable, but it did not fetch enough money for her living. Moreover, M. Molier had been facing some difficulty in getting the desirable number of bookings for that season. So he had suggested Margarethe to try out dancing as a viable profession.

Molier was an elderly man who had great sympathy for Margarethe (she might have impressed him with her imaginary narratives), and had taken care to introduce her to the Parisian society women he knew with the hope that they would introduce her to the proper circles. Henry de Marguerie too had taken some initiative for her and as a true diplomat had introduced her to the French salons as a genuine Oriental lady.[34] Margarethe must have narrated her made-up life story to him and to impress her lover had surely invented much about her Oriental lineage. As a Parisian, de Marguerie knew that Orientalism was in vogue in Paris especially from the turn of the century, and it had also been quite appropriate because with her dark complexion, dark eyes, and long black hair Margarethe looked like an ethnic Oriental beauty. The Oriental look however could be due to her Woudker[35] (a gypsy tribe from Asia that had once lived in Friesland) ancestry (from her mother's family), but in no way Indian. As noted earlier, Cléo de Mérode had impressed her audience at the Paris World Fair in 1900 through her Oriental recitals, but because she had very fair complexion, a common European feature, she was criticized for inauthenticity. Margarethe could fill that gap due to

---

33 Pasquin, "Theatrical and Musical Notes," *Otago Witness*, New Zealand; Issue 2633; August 31, 1904, 61; [www.paperpast.natlib.govt.nz]

34 Newman however attributed the entire credit to Camille de Sainte-Croix, editor of *Revue Theatrale*, who, he said, had introduced Mata Hari to people who could guide her in her pursuit; *op. cit.*, 53.

35 Howe, *op. cit.*,16.

her color, and if she could impress the Parisian audience by her beauty and grace as a dancer then fortune would surely bless her. Nevertheless, through the sincere efforts of Molier and de Marguerie, in February 1905, Margarethe had got a chance to make her debut as an Oriental dancer at the salon of Madame Kireevsky, a retired singer in Paris, who used to organize charity shows at her swanky residence, in order to collect money for some social cause, especially for the benefit of the Russian Red Cross which collected money for the war prisoners. As an experienced performer she must have measured the financial prospects of launching an authentic "Oriental" dancer, "fresh from the Indies," at her charity show. She took the trouble to find a musician for Margarethe who would play Indian music on the violin and had introduced her debutant dancer as Lady MacLeod.[36] The evening became exceptional with the mystic aura created by Lady MacLeod through her captivating slow and sensuous movements embracing nudity. As a novice dancer she might have wanted her career to have a good start, and therefore, to be sure, she had resorted to nudity to give a thrusting impact on the audience. She knew it very well that nothing succeeded like nudity, and could certainly create the distinct mood of her Oriental dance with great perfection. The show had been extremely successful making Lady MacLeod a star overnight, and she could, for the first time, attract considerable attention from the press.

Margarethe was not at all prepared for the overwhelming response she had received from the audience on the very first evening. She could not believe anything that was going on around her and had virtually been in a trance. When she had left Rudolf forever in search of her destiny with only 50 centimes in her purse, she could not even dream of that evening. Nothing around her had seemed to be real to her. But she became sure about one thing—she really had something in her to enchant the audience with—it was her splendid nudity and not the authenticity of her Oriental performance. Her nudity had depicted subtlety and divinity, and therefore could not be rejected as crude by the elite Parisians. For the first time Paris had seen nudity devoid of eroticism; had witnessed someone rise above the limitation of merely gratifying voyeuristic masculine

---

36 Waagenaar wrote: "... Margaretha danced in the beginning of February at the 45th celebration of the 'Diner de Faveur' where her name for the first time was given as Lady MacLeod." *op. cit.*, 1964, 46; although Shipman has made a reference to an article regarding Lady MacLeod's debut performance at Mme. Kireevsky's house written by Francis Keyzer (February 4, 1905), correspondent of *The King* from London, who wrote: "Lady MacLeod is Venus." *op. cit.*, 146.

gaze through her performances, and present genuine art. It was not true though that Margarethe had introduced nudity to the Parisian stage, because it had been exhibited on stage by the cancan dancers (Louise Weber, a.k.a. la Goulue of Moulin Rouge, Nini legs-in-the-air, and their likes) for quite some time. Even some of the Salome dancers had resorted to nudity on stage before her. Sarah Brown had introduced striptease at the music hall Moulin Rouge while performing in the role of the Egyptian Queen Cleopatra. She had also appeared nude while modeling as Lady Godiva for a painting by Jules Joseph Lefebvre in 1890, and had continued with her nude art on Parisian stage for quite long, due to which she was impounded and imprisoned by the police in 1893 on charges of public obscenity. Manon la Valle had been her contemporary who bared before the public in Paris, and had been fined 100 francs by the Eleventh Court in 1893 for public nudity. Blanche Cavelli, the Parisian actress and dancer during the last decade of the nineteenth century, was popularly known as the first stripper on professional stage (1894). Cléo de Mérode had appeared nude for a ballet in 1896, at the Casino Municipal in Paris. Clara Ward (a.k.a. Princess of Chimay) had also appeared for public performances at the Moulin Rouge and the Folis Bergère during the end of the nineteenth century barely in a body stocking and also had tableau'd for a while as a nude artist. Much before them, in 1860, the French demimondaine Cora Pearl had appeared inadequately dressed or even in nude on stage quite frequently. Even before that, in 1827, the French ballet dancer Francisque Hutin had appeared in titillating clothes on stage. Although she had never appeared nude for her performances, the audience waited to catch a glimpse of the lower part of her body every time her silk skirt blew in the wind.

But nothing was comparable to what Lady MacLeod had presented at Mme. Kireevsky's house. Her dance appeared to be an expression of eternal serenity through which she could strike a balance between the sacred and the profane. The intellectual stimulation that she could provide through her dances had appealed to the elite society enormously, because the subject matter of her recital was neither god, nor women's submission to the supreme male power, but submission of the finite to the infinite. Her "glorious nudity"[37] simply astounded the French audience, who had been swept off by the audacity she had expressed on stage. It had certainly been evident to the viewers that Lady MacLeod was trying to say something on

---

37 Keay, *op. cit.*, 43.

her own through her dancing, was representing her own interpretation of life, which was far from what the other dancers had been showing on stage. She therefore stood out gloriously from the crowd due to her originality. Several offers had poured in to perform at various other places including the Musée Guimet, and she obliged. She had danced more than 30 times during 1905, at various prestigious places like the Trocadéro music hall, the famous Cercle Royal, the Grand Cercle, and at the homes of rich and famous people including the multi-millionaire banker Baron Henri de Rothschild, the renowned French actress and member of the *Comédie French* Cécile Sorel (May 14), the French chocolate king Gaston de Menier, who had named her "Oriental Dream" (May 19), at the salon of Arthur Meyer, at the house of Jeanne Tourbey, at that of the Countess of Loynes, of the Italian singer Lina Cavalieri, at the house of the most popular soprano of the Belle Époque Emma Calve of the Metropolitan Opera in New York and the Royal Opera in London, and also at various fashionable clubs. Newspapers had started publishing articles about her, her Indian ancestry being the focus. Margarethe had successfully created the magic Paris was longing for. The ground had already been prepared by Loie Fuller, Cléo de Mérode, and others; Margarethe only needed to enkindle the imagination of the Parisians, and so she did with utmost care—creating stories one after the other for the audience and the journalists about her past. At least once she was there on the right time and at the right place. She did shed her past completely and had stepped forward to create her own identity. After long last she could put the right step ahead toward freedom—her most cherished goal since she had been in the Indies with Rudolf.

It is quite comprehensible upto this point. Nothing extraordinary needed to be imagined for her. One could easily foresee that Margarethe would get some more dance contracts for some private performances in Paris, one or two shows at some third grade music halls, a few wealthy lovers, prostitution, and penury at old age—this could well have been the life story of a woman who had fled her marriage to make it big in the entertainment capital of the world where she had truly been an alien. But fate had something radically different in store for her, something very unusual for someone like Margarethe who had started from mere nothing—with no money, no contacts, and no skill whatsoever—Fame. Her courage and tenacity had paid richly. She was confident both of her sexual prowess and of her splendid body, and was destined to become famous in the era of

WHY PARIS?

Art Noveau. Thus, by sheer luck, two people who changed her life forever had been present at the show in Mme. Kireevsky's house—Émile Étienne Guimet, owner of Musée Guimet, a private collection of eastern curios and artifacts housed in a neo-classical building at Place d'Iéna, and his director Monsieur M. Leon de Milloue. Intrigued by Lady MacLeod's Oriental presentation they were struck by the idea to promote their collection through a living expression of the Orient, instead of merely arranging the lifeless exhibits for the visitors, which included many hand-picked collections from India, China, Cambodia, Vietnam, Persia, Greece, and Egypt.

On several previous occasions, Guimet had arranged for showing Buddhist rituals to the visitors to make his collection more interesting for them. So, they had planned to launch Lady MacLeod in a public performance at the museum along with a lecture session on Oriental dance and music. The only thing out of place was her Scottish name; so Guimet had suggested her to adopt a stage name that could be suited to her style. "Mata Hari"—Javanese for the rising sun or the eye of dawn—was her choice.[38] Shipman wrote: "One of her childhood friends in Leeuwarden recalled reading a letter in 1897 or 1898—the first year or two of the MacLeods' residence in the Dutch East Indies—in which she spoke of becoming a dancer and using the name Mata Hari."[39] I presume it could have been in 1898, after her performance in the amateur play *The Crusaders* (September) in Malang at the local Club House, because she had never danced before that. Waagenaar said that it could be sometime before that, because the friend had left Leeuwarden in 1898.[40] However, "*Mata Hari*" must have been a popular phrase in Java because there was at least one lodge by that name, which was owned by the brother of de Balbian Verster of Holland, an old friend of Rudolf who had published the advertisement of marriage for Rudolf in his newspaper. The place might have been visited by the MacLeods while they were living in Sumatra. Mata Hari was nevertheless born on March 13, 1905, at Guimet's domed museum library in full view of the chosen elite Parisians.[41] Margarethe lived no more.

---

38 Ostrovsky said that the natives in Java had referred to her as "Mata Hari" when she lived there; *op. cit.*, 54.

39 Shipman, *op. cit.*, 148.

40 Waagenaar, *op. cit.*, 1964, 46.

41 According to Pat Shipman (*op. cit.*, 150), Julia Keay (*op. cit.*, 43), and Erika Ostrovsky (*op. cit.*, 69), the audience had a strength of 600 aristocrat men and women; according to Tony Bentley (*Sisters of Salome*, 98) there were 300 people in the audience that night, though according to Waagenaar it was a "carefully selected small group of

There had been other versions as well, like the one I found in the *New-York Daily Tribune* ("Sacred Dances of Brahmanism," June 25, 1905, 4). One Parisian correspondent had reported: "... Lady MacLeod Mata Hari, who, under the auspices of several French Academicians, including Henry Houssaye, Victorien Sardou, Edouard Detaille, Henri Lavedan, and of the eminent painters, such as Albert Besnard, and patronized by the Duchesse d'Uzes, Mme. Madeleine Lemaire, Comtesse Mathieu de Noailles and other prominent mondaines, has had the courage to become a sort of terpsichorean personification of Brahmanism." He then went on to say that Molier had actually never appointed her as an equestrian in his circus, instead had asked her to exhibit some of her other talents before him. Lady MacLeod had at once danced *Princess and the Magic Flower*, "... executed with marvelous precision, grace, and energy the war dance indicated in the Rig Veda." Molier had found it to be different from any dancing in Paris and had said: "The only thing that we have had here at all resembling it was the Annamite dances performed some years ago by Mlle. Cléo de Mérode." The correspondent had asserted that because Molier had thought that Mata Hari could earn a handsome living easily and honestly by her dancing, he had personally spoken to the director of the Guimet Museum so that he could utilize her for his courses in Brahminism. The correspondent wrote: "Her dancing, at first witnessed only by students, soon became known to painters and sculptors."

However, Émile Guimet had decorated the stage for Mata Hari from his Oriental collection—the Natarāja (Siva—the cosmic dancer) statue placed at the back on an elevated pedestal was an eleventh century bronze sculpture from the southern part of India (Tamilnadu) created during the Chola period;[42] a big oil lamp in a bowl was placed at the feet of the statue, a sitting stone bull, symbol of Siva's unmatched vigor, had been placed on an alter on the left side of the statue of Natarāja, a stone statue of Lord Buddha in the Abhaya (fearless) posture seated on a lotus depicting his protective mood had been placed on an alter atop a few made-up steps at the right side of the stage, far behind that, at the back of some potted decorative plants, had been placed a stone statue of Lord Subramānya or Skanda, the Hindu god of war, in a standing posture with his peacock mount symbolic of perfection and victory over evils, the huge pillars of the rotunda of the museum library had been decorated with garlands of

guests" (*op. cit.*, 1964, 48).
42 Ostrovsky, *op. cit.*, 69.

flower, the carpeted floor of the library had been strewn with fragrant roses, sandalwood incense had also been lit, and the rotunda was decorated with candle lights to create an ambience of a Hindu temple. On March 13 and 14 at 9 P.M., Mata Hari was to appear on the dance floor as a Hindu temple dancer. She had been surrounded by four girls in black toga, whose presence had merely served a decorative purpose at the beginning, but when Mata Hari shed all her veils and dropped naked (although she wore a body stocking for the occasion[43]) at the feet of Natarāja in a gesture of complete surrender to the Supreme Lord, the girls would immediately cover her with a "gold lamé cloth."[44] She had prepared three dances for the museum show—*The Poem of the Princess and the Magic Flower, The War Dance of Subramānya,* and *The Invocation of Siva*.[45] Her performances did not follow any of the classical Oriental dance forms and had been a blend of "the Javanese ceremonial *Serimpi*, erotic Hindu temple dances, the Egyptian-Arabic *baladi* ... and the Indian street dance *nautch*."[46] Keay wrote: "There were no definable dance steps, no formal structure, it was dancing only because it was obviously not anything else ..."[47] Initially she used to choreograph all her dances in her own distinctive style, which had an aura of audacious boldness and unparallel uniqueness.

On a personal note, I would like to draw attention to Gabriele Brandstetter's opinion about erotic Hindu temple dance. So far as my knowledge goes, I have not known of any Hindu temple dance which is erotic in nature, although it is true that temple dances had originated with the idea to appease and entertain the presiding deities of the temples, but had necessarily been part of the divine offerings. Indian temple dancers or the devadāsis, as they are popularly known, had in fact been married to the principal deities at a very young age (before menstruating age), and through the marriage to the gods they were considered to have become eternally-auspicious women free from widowhood (*nityasumangali*).[48] The devadāsi had thus been dedicated to the deity ('branding') who became her husband and patron, and was assigned with various duties related to the worship of the God including daily rituals during sunrise and sunset through dancing in

---

43   Bentley, *op. cit.*, 102.
44   Howe, *op. cit.*, 41.
45   Gabriele Brandstetter, *Poetics of Dance*, 67; Waagenaar, *op. cit.*, 1964, 52.
46   Ibid., 67.
47   Keay, *op. cit.*, 42.
48   Saskia C. Kersenboom, *Nityasumangali*, ix.

the classical styles and singing auspicious verses and hymns in His praise to boost up her divine husband's mood, singing lullabies during bedtime to ensure good sleep to the God, waving the pot-lamp during morning and evening prayers, weaving flower garlands for the deity, occasionally cooking food for the God, etc. Apart from these, the devadāsis also had to perform special rituals during festivals. They had been considered to be representatives of the goddesses who personify female power and energy including fertility. No devadāsi had ever been scantily dressed for any occasion whatsoever related to the temple, because she used to be in the holy service. Devadāsis had essentially been classical dancers and singers who, at a mature age, would train the newcomers into the classical dance forms. None of Mata Hari's dances had ever resembled any of the Indian classical dance forms. I therefore suppose that Brandstetter might have intended to mean Mata Hari's dancing postures had some resemblance to the erotic sculptures of some of the Hindu temples in India. In that case also his speculation is far from the truth. However, Wheelwright has referred to a dance critic who rightly said: "the secret of Mata Hari's success stemmed from having observed Java's native bayaderes of the Susuhanan of Solos' and Sultan of Jogja's ballet corps."[49]

Carolina La belle Otero in metal breast plates (1901)
(Bibliothèque nationale de France, Paris)

---

49   Julie Wheelwright, *op. cit.*, 17.

Louise Mante in metal breast plates before Mata Hari
(Bibliothèque nationale de France, Paris)

Describing her costume in detail Waagenaar wrote: "Mata Hari ... was dressed in what could pass for an authentic oriental costume, selected by Monsieur Guimet from his rich collection ... she wore a white cotton brassiere covered with Indian-type jewel-studded breastplates. Bracelets of similar design were worn on her wrists and upper arms, while her head supported an Indian diadem that curled up backward above her black hair ... Jeweled bands were clasped around her waist, holding up a sarong which from the hollow of her back descended around her hips towards a point on her belly about half-way down below the naval. The rest was bare."[50] It had been similar to the costume of her first public appearance (image 4 between pp. 134–135, Julia Keay, *op. cit.*) as an Oriental dancer at Mrs. Kireevsky's house in early February that year.[51] It then becomes hard to fathom how the costume for her recitals in March at the museum could come from Guimet's collection. Moreover, neither the Javanese court dancers nor the Indian temple dancers (devadāsis) ever wore bejeweled metal brassieres for their performances. Her head-band barely resembled something of the Javanese style of headgear. It is well known that the classical Indian or Hindu temple dances are chiefly of two styles—the Bharatanātyam and the Odissi. And in none of the styles the dancer's

50   Waagenaar, *op. cit.*, 1964, 48.
51   Shipman, *op. cit.*, 146; Keay, *op. cit.*, 33.

ONE LITTLE ORCHID

costumes include anything even closer to what Mata Hari had used for her performances. It is rather part of the costume of belly dancers from the Middle East and had been adopted by some European dancers even before Mata Hari for participating in the Salome Dance. Louise Mante, Parisian dancer Hagino, and La Belle Otero could be excellent examples in this regard. Maybe due to this reason she had been compared to Salome from the very beginning.[52] Wheelwright mentioned a review in the French daily newspaper *Le Gaulois* after her first performance at Guimet's museum in March 1905, in which the reviewer had commented that she "danced like Salammbo before Tanit, like Salome before Herod." Belly dance had been popularized in the west during the World Expositions of 1889 in Paris, of Chicago in 1893, and of 1900 again in Paris. It had formed the major attraction for the western spectators contributing to commercial success of the Egyptian pavilions at the Expositions. The belly dancers had presented the flavor of Islamic entertainment to the American and European audiences in an eroticized and commercialized manner, and as a matter of fact they had taken the western world by storm. In effect belly dance became closely linked to the Parisian entertainment world casting great influence on the popular cabarets and café concerts during the late nineteenth and early twentieth centuries.

Mata Hari's head gear and metal breast plates
(The Mata Hari Foundation, Fries Museum, Leeuwarden)

---

52   Wheelwright, *op. cit.*, 17.

However, Mata Hari's performance at the museum had lasted for two consecutive evenings (March 13 and 14, 1905), but the reverberation continued for very long. She had drawn attention of the press whenever she had performed—in September 1898, after her performance in *The Crusaders*, a local correspondent of *Weekly for the Indies* wrote: "... it would have been difficult for the public not to be charmed by this elegant amateur;"[53] in February 1905, after her performance at Mme. Kireevsky's house, Francis Keyzer of *The King* wrote: "Lady MacLeod is Venus;" and seeing her at the Musée Guimet the overwhelmed press correspondents simply glorified her in their articles.[54] Most significant was the description of *The Flash*, which wrote: "... an exotic spectacle yet deeply austere." Mata Hari had cleverly blended her nudity with a kind of religious fervor to produce variation in her style—the sacred temple dances of India. During that time the French government and its courts had been censoring nude dancing in public. As a result, some of the renowned dancers had been arrested for creating public obscenity through their nude dancing, but surprisingly Mata Hari was never impounded. And that was precisely what attracted the elite Parisian audience—she had never been vulgar or shameless. She had never presented herself like "meat on the rack,"[55] which other nude dancers of the music halls of her time did. Had she been obscene on stage, the bourgeois Parisians would certainly not accept her so warmly. As she had been inspired by the temple dances of Java, even her nude performances were laden with sanctitude. Wheelwright wrote: "... Mata Hari's greatest gift was her ability to make a clear distinction between the 'nude of art' and the 'nude of commerce'."[56] She had started a lustrous career as a woman of 29, while most of her contemporaries were much younger. She had tried really hard to maintain the madness and excitement surrounding her. One of her tact had been inventing various fanciful stories about her past in order to make her existence all the more mysterious, especially to cover up the imperfections both in her looks and her dancing skill. With her remarkable skill of creating and recreating her fictional past she could intrigue the Parisian audience to believe her stories of having Indian origin. The audience had been obsessed with her and was captivated by seeing what they were made to believe—authentic Indian temple dance,[57]

---

53   Ibid., 47.
54   Shipman, *op. cit.*, 152–154.
55   Gordon, *op. cit.*, 214.
56   Wheelwright, *op. cit.*, 21.
57   Martin Clayton, and Zon Bennett, eds., *op. cit.*, 55; Before Mata Hari it was Marie

and had never doubted that "Her mission in Paris was to initiate the city 'into the classical dances of her adopted country.'"[58] Brandstetter remarked: Mata Hari was "the museum-bred mannequin of erotic dance."[59]

She used to communicate with the enthralled audience not only through her fabulous body, but also by the brilliance of her intellectual ability. Between every performance she used to present a brief speech to describe the style and content of her acts, which she repeated in many languages to impress her audience—French, English, German, Dutch, probably in Italian, and even in Malay (the dialect of Java) to prove her authenticity. She had learnt to speak Malay while she stayed in the Indies, probably to communicate with her local help maids, which paid richly at such occasions. She said, "My dance is a sacred poem in which each movement is a word and whose every word is underlined by music."[60] After the performance was over she joined the audience decked in chic Paris fashion to interact with them, and to provide them a feeling of proximity and an opportunity to compliment her all over again. Such gestures enabled her to establish a sense of intimacy with the spectators, which had contributed positively to her tremendous attraction, because she could make them believe that her aim had not been to show off her splendid nudity, rather "… to educate Europeans into the culture of the Orient and that, when that was done, she would retire to a monastery and spend her life in contemplation."[61] Least did the audience realize that it had been the beginning of her tragic imagination and mythomania,[62] rather her novel ideas had dazzled them to such extent that no other dancer ever could, no matter how famous and popular they had been. Every other day people would learn something new about her from the newspaper reporting and her interviews published in popular magazines, which gave rise to varied speculations about her. Although by doing that she had accomplished her goal for the time being, but had failed miserably in the long run. She had to pay with her life mostly due to such naïve self-mystification.

>Taglioni, the Italian Oriental dancer in Paris, who was known as an Indian Temple Dancer during the 1830s. However, she appeared on stage in daringly revealing dress during that time.

58 Wheelwright, *op. cit.*, 15.
59 Quoted in Eva Horn, *The Secret War*, 180.
60 Shipman, *op. cit.*, 152.
61 Howe, *op. cit.*, 44.
62 The phrase was coined by the French psychologist and psychiatrist Dr. Ernest Dupre in 1905 to mean an excessive tendency for lying and exaggerating.

WHY PARIS?

Mata Hari photographed in fashionable dress
(Bibliothèque nationale de France, Paris)

Mata Hari's meteoric rise to stardom however had left many of her contemporaries envious. Sidone-Gabrielle Colette, the famous writer, columnist, dancer, and actress in Paris during the early twentieth century, who had been greatly praised for her natural nudity on stage (*The Flesh*, 1907), had seen Mata Hari dance at Emma Calve's salon and had commented about her in 1923: "She did not actually dance, but with graceful movements shed her clothes."[63] Howe mentioned a slightly different version of the same account and quoted Colette: "She hardly danced at all, but she knew how to undress herself slowly and move her long, proud, bister body."[64] Misia Sert, the famous Parisian hostess and patron of Diaghilev, had also commented negatively on Mata Hari's dance style—"She was a trite night-club dancer, whose art consisted in showing her body."[65] Mata Hari nevertheless was not convinced about her own dancing skills and

---

63 Shipman, *op. cit.*, 155; Waagenaar, *op. cit.*, 1964, 55.
64 Howe, *op. cit.*, 42.
65 Misia Sert, Moura Budberg, Trans., *Misia and the Muses: The Memoirs of Misia Sert*, 143–144.

had once remarked to her friend and Dutch painter Piet van der Hem: "I never could dance well. People came to see me because I was the first who dared to show myself naked to the public."[66] Dancing not being her forte she knew that it was necessary to apply some trick to succeed on the professional stage, and therefore had planned to punch some element of awe into her performances. What else could be more suitable than nudity, she had rightly guessed. Inspired by her phenomenal success, a cigarette manufacturer had printed her photograph on the tins hoping for more business; so did a biscuit company and also a wine manufacturer from Austria (after her incredible success in Vienna), who had named his product "Mata Hari Absinthe Bohemian." Printing pictures of celebrities on popular domestic consumer products to increase sale was not new, and the Parisian consumers had already liked and bought biscuit tins, soaps, and other products with Mérode's pictures on them. Mata Hari could amazingly reach that level in a remarkably short span of time.

Mata Hari was quickly becoming a stage icon in Paris, and therefore she required someone to organize and manage her shows. With the help of the elderly civil lawyer Edouard Clunet (63 year old at that time), an advocate at the Court of Appeals of Paris who was incorrigibly infatuated with her, she had been introduced to Gabriel Astruc, the well-known producer who had organized numerous shows for many great artists of that era, who had agreed to become the manager-cum-agent for her and had remained her impresario till the end. So it must be admitted that Astruc's contribution to Mata Hari's successful career as an international dancer is undeniable. He had booked her in the autumn of 1905, for a performance of *The Dream* (on August 20) at the prestigious music hall Olympia Theater in Paris. Paul Ruez was the director of the theater who had made plans to introduce Mata Hari to the audience with much grandeur, and therefore had also arranged for some other performances on that evening, viz., mime, Arabian dance, juggling, and violin recital along with some acrobatic acts. It had been her first big show where she was to dance before a sizeable audience. Music for her show was scored by George W. Bing, and it had been a phenomenal success. "Once again," wrote Pat Shipman, "the reviewers struggled to find superlative adjectives with which to describe Mata Hari's dancing." The reviewer for *The Journal* glowingly wrote: "Mata Hari personifies all poetry of India, its

---

66 Shipman, *op. cit.*, 145.

mysticism, its voluptuousness, its languor, its hypnotizing charm ..."[67]

She had started to earn magnificently, which at last could fulfill her dreams to become a grand consumer—of chic and fashionable clothes, cosmetics, jewelry, shoes, furs, hats, and everything money could buy her—everything that she had been deprived of as the wife of Rudolf—everything that she had expected from her marriage with an elderly Scott officer. She had once lamented in a letter to her father and step-mother: "... if I want to buy needles or thread, then I have to beg him for 10 cents."[68] After long last, she was truly happy. She relished every moment of her life as a dancer and did not repent for her broken marriage anymore. Her earning had shot up with every performance she gave, and so did her expenses. Her desire to buy luxury was insatiable, and hence she needed wealthy lovers to fulfill all her dreams and all her desires. People of the rich and elite circle in Paris and in other European cities wherever she performed fantasized of being her lover. At a later date she had told the journalist G. H. Priem: "... I received protection of the richest strangers and I did not lack the skill to profit from that."[69] Did she ever get to read and learn a few erotic measures to lure men from the Indian literary masterpiece *Kāmasūtra* written in the first century AD by the saint-philosopher Vātsāyana? Ostrovsky made a hint to it.[70] Mata Hari had become a craze in Europe among the elite and the ordinary, and equally among the young and the old. Penny postcards of Parisian stage beauties had been very popular during the turn of the century, and her nude picture postcards sold for a high price.

After enthralling Paris by her captivating grace and charm, she had ventured abroad with her shows. The success that she had reaped in Paris was extended to the other European cities by courtesy of Gabriel Astruc, and in January 1906, she had an engagement to dance in Madrid, the capital city of Spain, for 2 weeks. In February[71] she was engaged for Jules Massenet, the most successful and fashionable composer of that time (who had been 64 years of age), in the opera "The King of Lahore" (*Le Roi*

---

67   Ibid., 160–161.
68   Ibid., 110.
69   Ibid., 149.
70   Ostrovsky, *op. cit.*, 52.
71   February 17 according to Waagenaar, *op. cit.*, 1964, 71; also Howe, *op. cit.*, 47; but February 13 according to Elizabeth Nash, *Geraldine Farrar*, 31.

de Lahore) at the beautiful city of Monte Carlo in Monaco. Mata Hari was dazzled with her accomplishment as a dancer and also had been amazed to know that she was being considered as a serious dancer, because in Massenet's opera she had shared the stage with the famous Italian ballerina Carlotta la Zambeli in Act III[72] as an *apsarā* (celestial nymph) in the song and dance sequence, which had depicted the paradise garden of Indra, the King of Gods. A varied version is given by Elizabeth Nash—in the opera Mata Hari had appeared as a solo dancer in the role of Sitā,[73] and the song was rendered by Geraldine Farrar, the most glorious singer and actress of that time from America. Mata Hari however had developed an intimate relationship with Massenet during the show, and had hoped that he would compose a special ballet exclusively for her. The show had been such a triumphant success that none other than Giacomo Puccini, the famed Italian composer who was present at the show, had sent her flowers along with a passionate note to congratulate her for her performance. Shipman aptly wrote: "She left a trail of smitten admirers behind her wherever she went in Europe."[74] Jules Cambon, the leading diplomat and the French ambassador in Madrid, was among the smitten lot, with whom she had initiated an intense relationship. Within only a few days Mata Hari became so special for Cambon that he had arranged for a reception party in her honor, and had introduced her to the guests as "a true ambassadress of France."[75] She had virtually become a *'femme fatale'* in the truest sense, who, in the opinion of the conservatives, could effortlessly sweep men off their rational domain and lure them to danger and destruction through her seductive charms.

---

72   Bentley, *op. cit.*, 105.
73   Nash, *op. cit.*, 31.
74   Shipman, *op. cit.*, 164.
75   Ibid., 163. It is however interesting to note that in a declaration to the Paris correspondent on October 20, barely 5 days after her execution, Cambon said: "Mata Hari was a courtesan. It is proved that she was a spy and the center of a spying system ... She merited no indulgence." "No Comparison Between Women Put To Death," *The Evening Star*, October 20, 1917–Part I; Washington, DC, 8.

WHY PARIS?

Mata Hari posed in the nude for Leopold Reutlinger
(Getty Images Media India Pvt. Ltd.)

It was in 1906 that Rudolf had decided to marry once again, and therefore divorce with his estranged wife Margarethe became essential. He had used one of Mrs. MacLeod's nude photographs (taken by the famous photographer Leopold Reutlinger) in the court to get a divorce on the grounds of desertion, indecency, and adultery. As there had been no reason and no ground for her to contest, the divorce was granted on April 26 that year. Although she had already become a famous dancer and did not have any financial constraints at that time, still she did not claim her daughter's custody, because by then she had certainly realized that having Non around would be impediment for her in many ways. Mata Hari was in no mood to compromise with her long awaited and newfound glory, fame, enormous earning, and lavish lifestyle for any reason whatsoever and therefore must have decided to cherish the sweet memories of her days with her dear Non instead of having her custody. Performance after performance she grew more and more confident about her skills, and a divorce from Rudolf at that juncture had mattered little to her. As her European sojourn had continued unhindered she rather must have felt more liberated after the formal divorce and Rudolf's remarriage. She did not have dearth of wealthy lovers and Rudolf had been reduced to sheer nothing for her.

Mata Hari enjoyed her life as a dancer and a courtesan at the same time moving between the realms of pleasure and leisure. After all, as a lady, she could command respect from the elite and noble upper-class European society, and that had mattered much to her. She had been dictating the world of her lovers and thus had felt like an empress in their company. She had both the license and liberty to choose her patrons, and nothing could compel her anymore. Through her performances she had ultimately found an alternate way of self-expression—the expression of freedom and sanction.

After the divorce Mata Hari's next significant engagement was in Berlin in August 1906. It was her first visit to the historic city of great scientists, philosophers, painters, and architects. That was before Olga Desmond, the German dancer who became well known for her public nudity, had debuted in Berlin. Desmond loved to show off her nude body on stage posing like classical Greek statues. A renowned Russian art critic Nikolai Evreinov had preferred to call Desmond "naked" instead of "nude," because he thought that nudity involved certain amount of modesty and artistry[76] that she had lacked. However, Mata Hari was truly excited, not only because she had been given a chance to enthrall the German audience in the grand city, but also because she had foreseen the prospect to become the mistress of Lieutenant Alfred Kiepert, who was also a rich landowner in Berlin. Mata Hari had met the high-ranking German officer in Madrid a couple of months back (January 1906), and they had also exchanged warmth and passion. He had always been very passionate about Mata Hari and was happy to take her as his mistress in Berlin. He was delighted to put her up in a luxurious apartment in the outskirts of Berlin—away from the watchful eyes of his beautiful and possessive wife, and nonetheless had kept her in opulence. Kiepert had been a very loving companion, with whom Mata Hari could banish the hurtful thoughts of the days spent with Rudolf, and could also console herself of the marital humiliations. As stated earlier, they had often been seen together at chic and expensive restaurants at luncheons and dinners; and also at the Imperial army maneuvers at Jauer-Streigau, Silesia, during the autumn of 1906. They had travelled together not only in Germany, but abroad as well. In 1907, she took a trip to Egypt for a couple of weeks to learn the intricacies of Egyptian dance, and probably Kiepert had accompanied her on that trip. Egyptian dances had formed a significant genre of "Oriental dance" as perceived by the westerners, and had been quite popular among the

---

76 Colleen McQuillen, *The Modernist Masquerade*, 193.

European–American audience since the World Expositions of the late nineteenth century (through the recitals of Little Egypt Fahreda Mazar (Fatima Djemille), La Belle Fathema, and Little India Ashea Wabe). Mata Hari knew it well that her fake Oriental dances could not captivate the audience for long, and therefore, to add novelty to her performances, she must have thought of exploring the Baladi dance (a kind of folkloric style which was being developed in Egypt during the turn of the century). It was before Sent M'ahesa and Ruth Denis had appeared in Berlin (1908) with their self-styled "Egyptian Dance," although their styles had never matched with any of the traditional dances of Egypt.

Nevertheless, during the end of 1906, Mata Hari had received contracts to dance in Vienna at the Secession Hall and the Apollo Theater (15 December-16 January) (a vivid description of her performance at the Secession has been penned by Matthew Isaac Cohen, *Performing Otherness*, 25-26). There also she was accompanied by Kiepert. Through her unquestionable nude performances and fascinating stories about her past she had conquered the Austrian spectators with ease. The *New Vienna Journal* wrote: "Isadora Duncan is dead! Long live Mata Hari."[77] One anonymous correspondent from an Austrian journal had written an article on December 15, 1906, with the title "Brahma Dances in Vienna," in which he had penned the following words in her praise—"She does not dance. She performs a prayer before the idol, as a priest performs a service."[78] However, with each triumph the story of her past had changed for the news correspondents, as she gave newer versions of her Oriental ancestry. Vienna had come to know her as the great granddaughter of a Javanese prince. Enthused greatly by her graceful personality the enchanted audience cherished her splendid presentations. Mata Hari still could not enjoy her victory in Vienna very much. She had to part with Kiepert soon after the Vienna episode, because his wife took a stern legal step against him in order to compel him to abandon his notorious mistress (*femme fatale*). Kipert had become her source of luxury and not having him any further implied compromising with her dreams of opulence. But under penalty of a judiciary council she had been helpless and had to part with him. Kiepert had paid 300,000 francs to her as his parting gift. The relationship was shortly revived in 1914 during her visit to Berlin just before the First World War began.

---

77 Shipman, *op. cit.*, 165.
78 Alexander Kolb, "Mata Hari's Dance in the Context of Femininity and Exotism," *Mandrágora* 15 (15):60.

The Parisian sphere of entertainment had been replete with dazzling beauties and enchanting self-styled modern dancers during the Belle Époque, each one of them distinct in their own rights. Before Mata Hari became an inseparable part of the Parisian world of popular amusement during the early twentieth century, most of them had been performing nude in public and in private salons. The entertainment news columns had never spared a chance to eulogize them because Paris had been in a mood to welcome every novel approach. Mata Hari's dance style had certain similarities with the styles of some of her contemporary dancers, e.g., predominantly solo recitals, bare-foot dancing, natural backdrop, use of reformist clothing[79] without the corset, oriental forms free from rigorous and disciplined movements, etc, but still she did not become part of those who had crowded the Parisian sphere of entertainment at the turn of the century. Her dance style could certainly be marked as "new dance" as opposed to the predominant style of ballet dance that had been very popular in Paris. It could have been due to this reason that Mata Hari had often complained about faking of her Oriental dance style by inexperienced dancers like Mlle Suzy Deguez, one of her contemporaries, who became famous for her Hair Dance.

Mata Hari's professional rival Suzy Deguez
(Bibliothèque nationale de France, Paris)

---

79 The brilliant fashion designer Romain de Tirtoff, alias Erté, had created a theatrical costume for Mata Hari in 1913 for Jacques Richepin's Oriental musical comedy "Le Minaret" in the Renaissance Theater in Paris; *Erté's Theatrical Costumes*; Erté; Preface. Her other designers included Georgette Brama and Lucy Christiana.

However, two strands of the new dance form have been noted by Gayle Kassing—one comprised of "the concepts, techniques, costumes, and stage settings from around the world ...,"[80] while the other had been introduced by the author, performer, and teacher Genevieve Stebbins, who had learned and taught the Delsarte method of expression in dance. Mata Hari did never learn any particular dance method, surely not the Delsarte method, still could use bodily gestures to display emotions through her unique style. Nevertheless, mention of a few names along with their distinct styles would presumably be pertinent to end this chapter—Sarah Brown was a French music hall modern dancer who was known in Paris for her rebellious personality. During the late 1880s, Parisian news correspondents had dubbed her "Queen of Bohemia" and had described her as one of the most notorious women in Paris. Cléo de Mérode, a Parisian ballet dancer who had later ventured into performing Javanese and Balinese dances (Paris World Exposition in 1900), was acclaimed for her Salome dance, and had been mistress of many renowned and high-profile men in Europe, including the Belgian King Leopold II. Maud Allan had hailed from Canada and had been a trained concert pianist in Berlin. She had debuted as a dancer in Vienna in 1903, and had travelled all over the world including Paris with her performances. Allan was mostly popular for her distinct rendition of the Salome dance. Liane de Pougy, Caroline La Belle Otero, and Émilienne d'Alençon, known as the "Grand Trio" of Parisian stage during the turn of the century, had been notorious dancers and famous courtesans of that time. As already noted, Liane de Pougy had suffered a failed marriage and eventually had rushed to Paris for a living, where she became a noted demimondaine and a successful dancer. La Belle Otero had been born in Spain and became a dancer in Paris in 1890. She had performed Flamenco Dance at the Folies Bergère in 1893, which brought her fame, and was photographed in metal breast plates for her postcards in 1901. She was also a Cake-Walk (musical dance performance originally among the plantation workers, which became fashionable and enormously popular as a form of entertainment in Paris during the turn of the century) performer during the Belle Époque. The French born Émilienne d'Alençon was also a Folies Bergère dancer and a renowned courtesan, who had been known for her lesbian liaisons with some eminent society women in Paris. She was also known for her epileptic singing at the music halls in Paris.

---

80   Gayle Kassing, *History of Dance: An Interactive Arts Approach*, 182.

Isadora Duncan was an American dancer who had been inspired by the ancient Greek culture and danced barefoot on stage. She used loose-fitting, translucent Grecian tunics without a corset as her dance costume and imitated the mythological figures painted on the ancient Greek vases. She preferred free style dancing which had made her appearances greatly unconventional. One correspondent wrote: "She was a complete dancer. While the other great dancers dedicated their life to dance, she dedicated her dance to life." Duncan was dubbed as "The greatest tragic dancer of the modern world." Loie Fuller, also an American, was a renowned modern dancer who had been known for her Serpentine dance (1891 in Paris), Fire dance (at the Folies Bergère in 1892), Salome dance, Cake-Walk, and her Oriental dance (*Aladdin's Wonderful Lamp* based on the classic *Thousand and One Nights*). She had been a magician of lights and choreographed her dances on her own. Although she had performed cabaret in her early career, through her later performances she had depicted denial of sexuality and the body culture. There was also the renowned French columnist and dancer Colette, known for writing a sex manual in 1900, who had experimented with her dance on the Parisian stage from 1905, and was acclaimed for her "virginal nudity." She had actively participated in the "culture physique" which had flourished during the Belle Époque. As a gymnast she had a good physique and the Parisians remembered her stunning nude performance in the role of Yulka in *The Flesh* for her "sobriety and dignity."[81] Although she had lived a life of an "erotic militant" she had never made herself sexually available, which marked her distinction from the other licentious women of the stage at that time. Emilie Marie Bouchaud (a.k.a. Polaire) was a celebrity performer in Paris during the early twentieth century. Born in Algeria she was the dark complexioned music hall singer and dancer who had acted in comedy roles at the famous theater halls and also in some early films. Polaire was known as a Cake-Walk performer, a belly dancer, and also for her Scarf dance. Adorée Villany, a French contemporary of Mata Hari in the professional field, had appeared on the Parisian stage in 1905, at the age of 14. She too had been an active patron of the cult of "culture physique," implementing nudity as a piece of art and had performed accordingly in the *Dance of the Seven Veils*. Her naked body was later dubbed as a genuine artwork by the elite people and renowned painters of Germany, who had extended their support to free her after she was arrested in Berlin in 1911 on charges of public obscenity.

---

81   Patricia A.Tilburg, *Colette's Republic*, 135.

There had been so many more names listing of which is virtually not possible here, so I refrain from the exercise. Each had been unique regarding their personality, style, presentation, professional background, and life-philosophy, but one thing was supposedly common between them—all had been significantly frustrated in their private lives. Therefore, when Margarethe came out of her domestic shell and stepped into the spectacular domain of amusement in Paris with the dream to become Mata Hari, it had been a perfectly appropriate arena for her. No other vocation could be suited for her, and no other city could present her with more than what Paris had gifted her—name, fame, admiration, opulence, rich lovers, enumerable admirers, luxury, and freedom. Because none of the other so-called Oriental dancers had been presenting Javanese dance in her chosen way from her special perspective, she could make use of her full potential to thoroughly exploit the Parisian audience in her favor in the name of genuine Oriental art. Paris had satisfied her beyond her expectations and had readily become her second home.

Chapter 4
The Socio-Political Scenario in Europe

It had been during the Belle Époque that Mata Hari had chosen to start her career as an oriental dancer in Paris, which has historically been demarcated as the period starting from the last decade of the nineteenth century till the start of the First World War. Much social change had been noticed during that short period of time mostly regarding the roles of modern women. New Woman was being accepted and popularized in various ways, principally in the consumer world. While women in general had wholeheartedly welcomed their changing identity, it was not so for the orthodox men in France. Misogyny had been a global phenomenon from time immemorial, and the French bourgeoisie had no reason to deviate. I suppose it could have been related to the concept of private property, as women have the biological possibility to bear anyone's child. They had been considered by the bourgeois mindset to have a propensity for immorality, and thus were seen as a danger to the society, being subject to hateful treatment by men. However, modern European misogyny could be linked both to the Napoleonic Code and Victorian morality. According to Bram Dijkstra, it had been a product of European imperialism that upheld a sexist ideology,[1] although according to Michael Solomon, misogyny is always consciously or unconsciously directed toward gaining some contiguous material advantage.[2] Therefore, it can be presumed that popularity of the New Woman had caused men much agony due to the fear of possible loss of the material advantage men were used to enjoy. During that time women were increasingly being seen as potential consumers, not only of domestic products, but also of the upcoming fashion world. They were being initiated in the new trend of advertisements for the consumables meant for them. As noted earlier, women had also started to participate in the social life by aspiring for higher education, by choosing to claim their social-political-legal rights, and also by earning for better living. It had implied more visibility in the public sphere, and

---

1 David D. Bilmore, *Misogyny: The Male Malady*, 178.
2 Ibid., 177.

as a consequence, more wrath of the privileged sex. Significantly, women who had stepped out of their domestic confine in search of freedom had mostly been non-Catholics and Protestants. It provided the scope to club anti-feminist sentiments with anti-Semitism. It has been noted earlier that Mata Hari had been a Protestant by faith, and thus had become target of the anti-Semitic sentiment prevalent in Europe during that time.

Anti-Semitism had overtly been practiced in France for quite long, and the extensive history of conflict between the Catholics and the Protestants cannot be neglected in this regard. It is well known that much anti-Semitic literature was being published in the form of pamphlets, cartoons, newspaper articles, in magazines, periodicals, etc, which had considerable influence on the French psyche. Further, the ESM Saint Cyr (Special Military Academy of Saint Cyr) had a significant, though indirect, role regarding Mata Hari's fate, because, as noted earlier, the defense institute did strongly uphold and spread Catholic and anti-Semitic ideals. Piers Paul Read wrote: "... there was one French institution where the conservative, Catholic Frenchman had reason to believe that he was still in control—the army."[3] Edouard Drumont's *La France Juive* and *La Libre Parole* had repeatedly claimed that the Jews "could not be trusted as officers in the French Army." The academy had been founded by Napoleon Bonaparte in 1802, and quite understandably did uphold the motto "Training for Victory," but during 1870s the motto was changed to "Honor and Homeland." The change was very significant since for the first time in its history a value laden maxim had been introduced as the motto. Study to win (Napoleon Bonaparte) or study to defend the fatherland (Louis XVIII) must surely have had a varied connotation than that of study to defend honor and the fatherland; while the previous ones had a purely objective character, the latter became subjective in nature.

Therefore, the students who had been trained at the institute during that time would certainly have had an attitude of nobility regarding duty toward their fatherland. Victory as the goal had supposedly been replaced by honor of the fatherland. It actually broke the limitations of the goal of triumph in a battle and had extended its scope to include honor in every sphere—no matter if it had been introduced to regain the territories of Alsace and Lorraine, which the French had lost in the Franco-Prussian War of 1870–1871, thereby inspiring the students to restore honor and

---

3   Piers Paul Read, *op. cit.*, 29.

pride of the fatherland. Henri Gouraud, a graduate from Saint Cyr in 1889, wrote in 1890: "These two words, 'Honor and Homeland', encapsulate military duty ... A single sentiment equals them in beauty, in power, (that is) religious faith."[4] The military school obviously had a patriotic fervor, and nationalistic anti-German sentiment was blatantly infused there. It would be surely interesting to note that most of the army personnel present at the trial and court martial of Mata Hari had graduated from Saint Cyr during 1870s and the following decades, i.e., after the miserable defeat in the war with Germany. Therefore, I suppose that, they had been biased against her from the very beginning. Executing her could have been their means of restoring honor of the fatherland that they thought had been tarnished primarily by the changes introduced in the modern industrial society and by the rise of the Jews, secondly by the rise of New Woman during the turn of the century, and finally by the Semitic people who had acted against France during the Great War. Mata Hari's execution, in a sense, had therefore been symbolic.

Not only Saint Cyr, but the role of the other educational institutions in France also seems to be important in her case. State's monopoly in education had been replaced in 1850 (Falloux Law or the Freedom of Instruction Act) by a rapid development of Catholic schools which were run by conservative religious leaders, mostly by the Jesuits and the Assumptionists (founded in 1845 by Emmanuel d'Alzon). It could be possible because the Law had been more inclusive to allow any Frenchman of 25 years or above with adequate qualification to establish a secondary school. Priests were hence not excluded by the Law and had also been eligible to establish their own schools. Therefore, as a matter of fact, the Church had profited significantly by implementation of the Law. Jeffery Haus wrote: "the Falloux Law ... opened the door for the Catholic clergy to reinforce and expand its presence in French education during the Second Empire ... municipal councils often preferred to hire instructors belonging to religious orders ... becoming a significant force in the educational system."[5] Those people had been rivals to the Protestants, the Jews, the liberals, the freethinkers, and the secularists, and believed very strongly that all were together in a conspiracy to destroy the Church. French Enlightenment and the subsequent French Revolution owed much to the freethinkers and therefore had been hated by the orthodox and the Catholics, as they

---

4   Roy M. Dilley, *Nearly Native, Barely Civilized*, 26.
5   Jeffery Haus, *Challenges of Equality*, 46.

could never forget the atrocities perpetrated against their community in the name of the Republic. The Catholics had been patronized both by the aristocrats and the bourgeoisie on the one hand, and by the ordinary classes on the other. So, it becomes apparent that the social ambience of France was being dominated by the conservative Catholic sentiments and ideals in every way during that time.

However, although I have no intention of retelling the Dreyfus story here, still a bit of elaboration on the Affair seems pertinent because it had blatantly exposed the socio-political schism in France during the end of the nineteenth century. Alfred Dreyfus was born in Alsace in 1859 to a Jewish textile manufacturer, and the family had shifted to Paris after Alsace-Lorraine was annexed by Germany (i.e., after the defeat of France in the Franco-Prussian War). Since his childhood he had received French education in Paris and had aspired to join the military service. He had studied in the Military School of Polytechnique (1878) near Paris, where along with military training he had also learnt science. He had attended the artillery school to receive more specialized training, and became a French artillery officer in 1882. In 1891, he was admitted to the War College (École de Guerre), from where he had graduated successfully in 1893, although his grades had been lowered by General Pierre de Bonnefond, one of the panel members who was a diehard anti-Semite, because of his Jewish origin. Bonnefond had awarded him a zero in "Moral Conduct and Personality" as he did not want to see a Jew among the General Staff. Alfred Dreyfus had protested against the injustice by filing a complaint with the Director of the school, but his complaint was rejected. Although General Lebelin de Dionne, Director of the school, wrote: "I have seen many officers at the École de Guerre. I can state that none of them met with any animosity from their superior officers or their comrades. If this was not so for the honorable M. Dreyfus, this was because of his revolting character, his intemperate language and his undignified private life, and in no way because of his religion."[6] By saying "undignified private life" the General must have hinted at Dreyfus's numerous so-called passionate affairs with the Parisian courtesans and demimondaines of his time.

Nevertheless, after his graduation from the War College, Alfred Dreyfus was deputed as a trainee at the General Staff Headquarters in the French Army chiefly due to his remarkable intelligence, inspite of the fact that

---

6   Eric Cahm, *The Dreyfus Affair in French Society and Politics*, 5.

many of his senior colleagues had disliked him.[7] Despite being a Jew, he had become part of the General Staff in France only because of the influential French statesman and four-time Prime Minister Charles Louis de Freycinet, who had been the War Minister from 1888. He was a Protestant and a Republican, and had warned that anti-Semitism would not be tolerated in the army under any circumstance whatsoever, especially after the unfortunate death of the young Jewish officer Captain Joseph Armand Mayer in a duel with the notorious anti-Semite Marquis Amedee de Mores in 1892. Like Dreyfus, de Freycinet had also received his education at the Military School of Polytechnique, and had assisted Léon Gambetta (known as the "Father" of the Third Republic) in his people's war while opposing the Germans in 1870. Gambetta was a Radical and an ardent secularist, and had considered the Church as the enemy of the Republic.[8] Drumont, known as the Pope of anti-Semitism, due to obvious reasons, had referred to him as a "scheming Semite" in his articles published in *La Libre Parole* during that time. He even went to the extent to claim that due to the knowledge of occultism, the Jews could grab high social position and power over French economy depriving the French, and hence it (the occult) should also be the instrument to solve the problem. He therefore had turned to the power of the occult in order to subvert the invisible menace and to give justice to the Catholics and innumerable French people who had suffered because of the Jews (bankruptcy of the Union Generale and sabotage of the Panama Canal). French Jews were devoted to the Enlightenment values and had been supporters of the Republic, although it was clearly hated by the Catholics.

The infamous Dreyfus Affair had started with an incident, quite insignificant, at the German Embassy in Paris, and it is quite interesting to note that Madame Marie Bastian (Auguste), the charwoman working there, had in fact been employed by the French secret service (the Statistical Section) in 1889. She was secretly assigned the task of collecting discarded papers from the waste-paper basket of the Embassy and handing them over to the officers of the Statistical Section, who searched those for any secret information. During the end of September 1894 (20th–25th), in one such exercise, Major Hubert-Joseph Henry, who had joined the French intelligence service in 1879, had chanced upon a torn note (*bordereau*) written on a tissue paper (onion-skin paper) which read: "Without

---

7   Read, *op. cit.*, 84.
8   Ibid., 22.

news indicating that you wish to see me, I am however sending you ... some interesting information ..." It included a list of five documents which the writer of the note had intended to forward to Maximilian von Schwartzkoppen, the military attaché of Germany in Paris. The documents mentioned in the note had been related to functioning of the French military artillery and troop positions.[9] Although the note did not have any signature or date, Henry concluded that there had certainly been a traitor in the French General Staff who was betraying France by providing important secrets to the German counterparts, and had brought the note to the immediate attention of his superior Colonel Jean-Conrad Sandherr, head of the Section de Statistique. Sandherr then drew attention of General Auguste Mercier, the French Minister of War in 1894, to the said note. They had decided to analyze the handwriting. The task had been assigned to Alphonse Bertillon, a French police officer and a biometrics researcher, who was a hardcore anti-Semite. Although he was not a handwriting expert, he had purposefully concluded that the note was written by Dreyfus, and none other. Dreyfus was called in for interrogation. His writing had ostensibly resembled with that of the note. It was then concluded unanimously that the perpetrator of such heinous treason could have certainly been none other than Alfred Dreyfus. Dreyfus was arrested on October 15, 1894, on charges of treason against France.

Political analysts of that time had speculated that a scandal of the magnitude of the Dreyfus Affair had become necessary for France to distract public attention from the strong social and political turmoil which had resulted from mass unemployment, falling prices, widespread hunger, and the ruined wine industry. Therefore, it becomes evident that Dreyfus had been a victim of France's internal conflict. France had been under extreme pressure from the anarchists for a considerable span of time (from 1885). The Third Republic had failed to provide what it had pledged to the people, and the conservatives had been looking for an opportunity to bring down the Republic. Long hours of work in unhealthy conditions and low wage gave rise to militant trade unionism (syndicalism). Financial collapse of the Union Generale bank (1882) had resulted in recurring economic crises, followed by frequent outbreak of strikes and riots. Influx of refugees from Russia had jeopardized the employment sectors in France. Political activists like Mikhail Bakunin, Peter Kropotkin, Leo Tolstoy, Elisée Reclus, and others had cast much influence on the

---

9   Tom Conner, *The Dreyfus Affair and the Rise of the French Public Intellectual*, 57.

French society through their powerful writings. Many French writers had joined them as they found their ideology quite convincing, e.g., Octave Mirbeau, who had later been an ardent Dreyfusard and had supported Dreyfus in his fight against his wrongful indictment and exile. Only a couple of months before Dreyfus was arrested the fifth French President Marie François Sadi Carnot was assassinated in Lyon (June 24) by a young Italian anarchist Sante Geronimo Ceserio. The unexpected gruesome incident had resulted in an outbreak of widespread violence in the country. Hence, France had desperately needed a scapegoat to sail over the social and political conflagration, and Dreyfus had been the target. He was the only Jew in the French General Staff, came from a wealthy background,[10] and moreover, had not been a yes-man of his superiors in the army. Right from his days at the School of Polytechnique he was disliked by many people of rank, and it had continued even after he had been appointed in the General Staff. He had never been popular among his colleagues. Tom Conner wrote: "Dreyfus's superior officers never did like him, not only because he was Jewish, but also because he always had a dour and forbidding demeanor and was so very punctilious about everything he did."[11] He had been a captain in the artillery, and unfortunately for him, the information that was being secretly divulged to the German attaché through the note had been related to the artillery. Moreover, some of the investigating officers had observed that since Dreyfus's brothers chose to stay back in Alsace after its annexation by Germany (1871) and became German citizens, Dreyfus would surely be a sympathizer of Germany due to his family background. He was therefore fitted to become the victim.

Nevertheless, the French Prime Minister Charles Alexandre Dupuy, the military Governor of Paris General Félix Gustave Saussier, and the Foreign Minister Albert Auguste Gabriel Hanotaux had not been the least convinced of Dreyfus's guilt of treason. So, Major Hubert-Joseph Henry had no other way but to forge and fabricate important documents (seven letters written by Dreyfus to the German Kaiser and also one reply from the latter) in order to build a case against Dreyfus and get him convicted, although Henry could never prove Dreyfus's motive to spy for Germany. It had precisely been the weakest aspect of the prosecution's

---

10 Wealthy Jews had been an eyesore especially to the Catholics since the collapse of the Union Generale and the Panama scandal, as the Jews were held responsible for both the disasters, although with virtually no evidence.
11 Conner, *op. cit.*, 61.

case. Dreyfus was a loyal French, a patriot having the intent to serve his country, as a successful and hard working cadet he had a bright future in the French army, he was happily married with two children, had been wealthy enough not to have the need to earn money through espionage, he was a morally upright person, and had not been a womanizer (although, as noted earlier, people in the French army believed that he had passionate relationship with some Parisian courtesans). Therefore, it becomes all the more difficult to fathom why he would become a traitor and would want to betray France. Further, the handwriting experts had also expressed disagreement regarding the writing of the note, which raised doubts about his guilt. Still he had been convicted for treason and was imprisoned in the Devil's Island in April 1895. The French intelligence service had left no scope for Dreyfus, had manufactured documents to use against him, had spread preposterous rumors, and had used various propaganda techniques to pin him down. The French Catholic newspaper *La Croix* took a leading role in the anti-Dreyfusard campaign due to its anti-Semitic disposition, encouraging even reactionary outcomes. One of the rumors had been regarding the imperial *bordereau*, in which there was reportedly a note written by the Kaiser Willhelm II, which had identified Dreyfus as a German spy.

In early March 1896, the French intelligence service got hold of a note (or an unsent telegram) called *le petit bleu* or 'The Little Blue' (in an identical manner that the *bordereau* had procured and then was handed over by the same charwoman) written by von Schwartzkoppen to Ferdinand Walsin Esterhazy, who, although was an officer in the French army (he had served in the French counterintelligence service for some time), had been on the payroll of Germany for spying on France. Lieutenant Colonel Marie Georges Picquart, who was chief of the Statistical Section at that time after Commandant Nicolas Jean Conrad Sandherr became paralyzed, had been Dreyfus's teacher at the War Academy. He was given the responsibility to investigate Dreyfus's case. Curiously Sandherr had been a native of Mulhouse in Alsace, the same place that Dreyfus came from, and had his military training from Saint Cyr, due to which he must have hated Dreyfus because of his Jewish origin. He had played a significant role in arresting and convicting Dreyfus. However, Esterhazy had sent two letters to Picquart with the request to transfer him to the War Office. Picquart recognized the handwriting immediately and discovered that the note for which Dreyfus had been incriminated was actually written by Esterhazy. Esterhazy was known to have had a penchant for women[12] and gambling, and therefore had always been in debt. Moreover, it was revealed that he had a curiosity for secrets about the gunnery. Significantly, Major Henry was a long-time friend of Esterhazy as both had worked in the same military office from 1877 to 1880, and might have known from the very beginning that the note that he had busted was not written by Dreyfus at all, but it was the creation of his friend. Major General Charles-Arthur Gonse, who was directly involved in the investigation of the Dreyfus case, and some officers of the higher ranks in the French army did not want to pursue the case further, and President Félix Faure had been the main obstacle for Dreyfus's retrial. Still it had primarily been due to Picquart's initiatives that the case was reopened in June 1899, after much furor, and eventually Dreyfus was proved not guilty by the court. He was vindicated in July 1906, and had been reinstated in the French army as a squadron leader. He had subsequently been awarded with the Legion of Honor for his service to France. I wonder whether his service for his country had included being a scapegoat at the time France needed one.

Although the American historian Albert S. Lindemann wrote: "... anti-Semitic prejudice does not seem to have played a primary or decisive role among those officers who concluded he was the culprit. Much more significant seem to have been ... the spy mania, the desperate concern to root out the traitor in the inner councils of army, Dreyfus's status as one of a very few possible suspects, the similarity of his handwriting to that on the *bordereau*, and the 'D' documents ...,"[13] all the Dreyfusards were of the opinion that Dreyfus had been falsely implicated because of his Jewish origin. Kevin Passmore came up with an entirely novel explanation related to the new recruitment policy of the French army. He wrote: "... the condemnation for espionage of the Jewish staff officer Alfred Dreyfus ... owed much to discontent among monarchist and aristocratic officers at new methods of recruitment to the General Staff. Older, largely Catholic officers from the Saint Cyr military academy resented a new promotion system that favoured younger, more secular graduates of the

---

12   Leslie Derfler, *The Dreyfus Affair*, 97; One of his mistresses (Madame de Boulancy) to whom he owed a huge amount of money had revealed his letters in *Le Figaro* on 28 November 1897, which were filled with hatred against France and loyalty toward Germany.

13   Albert S. Lindemann, *The Jew Accused*, 101.

École Polytechnique ..."[14] Passmore hinted at a fracas between the left and the monarchists on the Affair and wrote: "The left saw the forgery as evidence of a military monarchist, and Catholic conspiracy against the Republic, while the right defended the honour of the Army ..."

Relevance of the Dreyfus Affair in Mata Hari's case could however be presumed to have taken a binary form—its indirect influence on her case, and the similarities between both the cases. In 1917, France had evidently been suffering due to the devastating war, and added to it was the scar of the Dreyfus Affair that had tainted honor of the country at the turn of the century—especially because of the bitter battles between the republicans and the conservatives regarding the Affair. Morale of the French people had already been at a low when the war broke out. So, it is not improbable that Mata Hari's arrest and her subsequent execution might have served some significant socio-political purpose of the French government at the time of their national crisis. Moreover, as the French Criminal Code considered treason (breach of trust perpetrated by any citizen of France) to be a political crime not punishable by death penalty, Dreyfus had been deported to the Devil's Island. The judgment was largely criticized in France as people demanded for the severest punishment for such heinous crimes against their country, and as a consequence death penalty had been introduced for crimes of espionage (breach of trust against France perpetrated by people of other origins) during wartime. Mata Hari's fate was sealed by the implementation of that law. Further, there are much similarities between both the cases, which are too striking to be ignored, and could be enumerated in the following way—first, Dreyfus and Mata Hari both had been incriminated for spying against France; second, like Dreyfus, Mata Hari had also been a victim of the prevailing anti-Semitic sentiments of the French society, although their religion had never featured during the trials; third, quite significantly almost all the judges and officers of the military court had been Saint Cyrians in both the cases; fourth, like Dreyfus, Mata Hari had also been made a scapegoat to suppress the socio-political turmoil that had disturbed the tranquility in France; fifth, in both the cases army officers of the intelligence section had used forged and fabricated documents to convict their victims; sixth, some of the officers involved in both cases had also been working for personal gain; seventh, like Dreyfus (Scoundrel D. letter—*"ce canaille de*

---

14 Kevin Passmore, *The Right in France, from the Third Republic to Vichy*, 101.

$D.$"[15]), Mata Hari too was never informed about the fabricated documents (telegrams in her case) created against her for her conviction in the name of national security; eighth, like Dreyfus's case, her trial was also held *in camera* to prevent public awareness and thus to provide an upper hand to the prosecution from the very beginning; ninth, like Dreyfus, Mata Hari had also hoped in vain that the French army would realize their mistake very soon and would set her free; tenth, deliberate spreading of rumor and propaganda through the print media had played significant roles in both cases; eleventh, like Dreyfus she had also suffered miscarriage of justice in the hands of the French army; and last but not the least, both Dreyfus and Mata Hari had been convicted by the press even before their official trials had ended.

I would now like to focus on the Great War, and since Mata Hari had been executed by the French army, perspective of the Allied forces would plausibly be appropriate to start with. It is well known that the war had been triggered by the assassination of the Archduke Franz Ferdinand of Austria, which could be counted as the proximate cause of the great conflict, but its roots certainly went a bit further in the past—the ultimate cause comprised of several political and economic factors arising out of conflicts among the great European powers which had played the nemesis, including the Franco-Prussian War of 1870–1871, when France had lost Alsace-Lorraine to Germany. The French had since pledged to get the lost territories back by any means and avenge their defeat. Therefore, inspite of the best efforts of Joseph Jean Jaurès, the anti-militarist who had been committed to the left-wing socialist stand of a civilian army and defensive wars, for reconciliation between France and Germany in order to avoid war, the conflict became inevitable. The French commoners would not stop before taking revenge on the Germans for their defeat in the Franco-Prussian War, and getting back Alsace-Lorraine which they believed that the enemies had annexed wrongfully. Jaurès's anti-war campaign and his call for a general strike against war had been retaliated by hatred from the rightist nationalists, who considered him to be pro-German, and therefore had been instrumental to his assassination on July 31, 1914. It had clearly indicated an internal conflict in France even before the war was declared. France had already been divided on the question of the Dreyfus Affair—the Dreyfusards and the anti-Dreyfusards, and on that of feminism and anti-feminism. Added to it were the nationalists (the

---

15   Conner, *op. cit.*, 68.

rightist anti-Semites and anti-Dreyfusards) who had been up in arms to eradicate their socialist opponents even by taking resort to violent means.

Before the war happened, not only France, but nearly all the major European powers had suffered from a feeling of threat and decline,[16] and as the only remedy to overcome the weakness they had entered into a decisive armed conflict. Assassination of Franz Ferdinand had only been a ploy for the great European powers to embark on the époque-changing conflict. Germany wanted to expand its borders and therefore had responded positively to the Austro-Hungarian request for support (the Kaiser commented "Now or Never" on July 4, 1914, a note that he had scribbled on the letter sent to him by Heinrich von Tschirschky in this regard) in order to avenge the Archduke's murder. France wanted Alsace-Lorraine back. Russia had alliance with Serbia, and wanted to stand by its friend at the time of crisis. According to the Franco-Russian Military Convention, the secret military understanding of 1892 (signed by Nicholas II in 1894) between Russia and France, both countries had committed to help each other "immediately and simultaneously" if anyone was attacked by Germany or its allies. "Wilhelm II signed the order for general mobilization at 5 PM on August 1 ..."[17] and on the same day Chancellor Theobald von Bethmann Hollweg had wired to Count Heinrich L. von Tschirschky, the German Ambassador to Vienna, "If the dice roll, may God help us all."

The war broke out during the very first days of August, involving most of the European countries followed by—the Battle of the Frontiers (August 14–25)—fought along the eastern frontiers of France and Belgium. The Battle of the Frontiers, comprising of four major conflicts—the Battle of Lorraine (August 14–25, 1914), Battle of the Ardennes (August 21–28, 1914), Battle of Charleroi (August 21–23, 1914), and Battle of Mons (August 23, 1914)—did not turn out to be favorable for the Allied forces. Germany had reasons to celebrate as the Imperial Army could establish its superiority at the frontiers. The first offence on Liège (Belgium) had resulted in its siege on August 7, 1914, by the Germans. At the Battle of Mulhouse (August 8–25, 1914), the French army had attempted to recapture Alsace from Germany. Even after occupying it twice they had to lose it on both the occasions. The British Expeditionary Force (BEF) had

---

16   R. F. Hamilton, and H.H. Herwig, eds., *The Origins of World War I*, 443.
17   Holger H. Herwig, *The Marne, 1914*, 14.

to retreat at Mons on August 23. In an attempt to get back Lorraine the French army had initiated an offensive at Ardennes, but due to strategic error was miserably defeated by the German Imperial Army on August 23 and had to retreat providing an opportunity to the Germans to enter France unhindered. Namur in southern Belgium had been occupied by Germany on August 25, on August 29 French army had to retreat at the Battle of Guise, and on September 6 Maubeuge had surrendered to Germany following heavy bombardments on the fortress which was in possession of the BEF. According to the war historians, the Battle of the Frontiers had been catastrophic for the Allied forces due to various reasons—lack of coordination between the battalions, inaccurate planning, inadequate intelligence, and moreover, underestimating German strength. But it had only been the starting blow for them, and they could ultimately overcome the defeat.

At the start of the World War I, with the intention of attacking and destroying Liège near northern France and combating an expected attack by the French that had threatened safety of the German Empire, on August 4, 1914, the German troops had invaded Belgium through Gemmenich (as part of the 1905 Schlieffen Plan) which had already proclaimed neutrality. It was absolutely necessary for Germany to abolish the powerful network of fortresses in Belgium at once in order to capture its land and infrastructure for passage through the country, which the Belgian government had persistently denied them (the last ultimatum had been served by the German government to Belgium on August 2, 1914).[18] Possession of Liège had been considered by the Chief of German General Staff Helmut von Moltke to be the *sine-qua-non* for crushing France at the beginning of the war. During the following couple of weeks the Germans had epitomized unparalleled savagery and barbarism through their acts of atrocities on the civilians (Rape of Belgium), which had started with the attack on Liège on August 4. Gerald J. Meyer wrote: "... the Germans ... would have to attack and destroy the powerful network of fortresses that the Belgians had constructed at Liège just inside their border with Germany. For this reason German mobilization required an immediate invasion of Belgium: Moltke's entire strategy would collapse if the Belgians were given time to ready their Liège defenses."[19] In

---

18 Jameson Patrick Ryley, "The Historian Who Sold Out: James Bryce and the Bryce Report," *Iowa Historical Review*, 1(2); 2008, 67.
19 G. J. Meyer, *A World Undone*, 97.

the beginning of the war, General von Moltke certainly knew that unless Liège was conquered the Schlieffen Plan would not work, and therefore possession of Liège was the "*sine qua non*" of Germany's war effort. He was somewhat convinced that the French guerrilla fighters, along with the Belgian civilians, had been attacking them from the very instant they had entered Belgium, and so, it was necessary to defend German interest. The German troops had been terrified with the guerrilla techniques used by France since their experiences in the Franco-Prussian War and had considered the guerrilla fighters as criminals who must be grinded by all means. They believed that by use of terror against the guerrilla fighters they could succeed in repressing the violent situation created by the civilian shooters. William Le Queux wrote: "The atrocious acts committed by the troops of the Kaiser have staggered the civilized world."[20] Violating the Hague Convention resolutions they had bombed ill-fated and unwarned civilians from zeppelins at Antwerp in the dead of night, killing most of the women and children who had been asleep. They had burnt the ancient city of Louvain on August 26 along with the well-known university library which had a rich collection of manuscripts, leaving many dead and homeless. In the same vein they had vandalized and burnt Visé while captivating its inhabitants.

The fate of Dinant was no different with the killing of nearly 675 civilians and burning of more than 1,200 houses on August 21 and 23, 1914. The action had been ordered by Commander Major von Schlick of the 1st Battalion of Grenadier Regiment 101, who had later justified the killings and arson as a measure taken only as an act of self-defense. In a report on the street-fighting in Les Rivages (Dinant) on August 23, 1914, he wrote: "... men of every age women and girls—fired madly on us ... and that the remedy taken only constituted an act of self-defense."[21] The companies of von Schlick had massacred towns and villages, slaughtered innocent noncombatants, tortured defenseless civilians, violated women, mutilated children, ransacked and looted houses, and had committed indescribable sins against humanity. Hospitals and churches had also not been spared. Richard Harding Davis, the renowned writer and one of the war correspondents from America who had arrived in Belgium to report the war, wrote in the *New York Tribune* on August 23, 1914: "The

---

20 William Le Queux, *German Atrocities*, 12.
21 E. N. Bennett, *The German Army in Belgium*, 154.

entrance of the German army into Brussels has lost the human quality."[22] The Bryce Commission Report of 1915 has recorded all of it in minute detail, although is not considered to be above question.[23] Le Queux indeed wrote: "The blood of those martyred innocents cried aloud to God for vengeance, and such vengeance must surely come upon the Kaiser ..."[24] Sven Anders Hedin, the Swedish explorer and travel writer, however wrote: "The destruction wrought by the Germans in their advance has partly been involuntary, and has partly had its cause in the conduct of the civilian population. But the Germans have never destroyed simply for the love of destruction."[25] The *Manifesto of Ninety-Three* (4 October, 1914), which was subscribed by eminent German scientists, artists and scholars, defended the invasion of Belgium in the same vein. It is however plausible that defying the Hague Convention resolutions (1907), the Germans had unleashed a reign of terror in Belgium due to two reasons—first, since they had believed that Belgian neutrality had been violated by the French Army;[26] and second, to remain in control of its territory throughout the war in the interest of their own war effort. Records of the war show that inspite of receiving support from the BEF 5,000 civilians had been massacred in Belgium by the Germans during the first couple of weeks of the war. Having been a neutral country it had been beyond their anticipation. The Allied forces had used such enemy barbarism to build up widespread propaganda campaign against Germany during the war. Even a "German Crimes Calendar"[27] had been published as a propaganda machination in order to memorialize German atrocities on each day of the year.

---

22 N. Lande, *Dispatches from the Front*, 173; reprinted as "Saw German Army Roll on Like Dog," in *The Farmer and Mechanic*, NC: September 8, 1914; 10.

23 Ryley, *op. cit.*, 69 & 74.

24 Le Queux, *op. cit.*, 19.

25 Sven A. Hedin, *With the German Armies in the West*, 208.

26 Coleman Phillipson, *International Law and the Great War*, 17. In early August, 1914, while crossing its borders toward the south at Gemmenich, the German General Otto von Emmich had distributed a declaration in Belgium which proclaimed that the German troops were crossing the Belgian borders due to the fact that: "... Belgium's neutrality having been violated by the French officers, who, in disguise, crossed Belgian territory ... in order to make their way to Germany."

27 Jane Potter, *Boys in Khaki, Girls in Print*, 70.

AU PEUPLE BELGE

C'est à mon plus grand regret que les troupes allemandes se voient forcées de franchir la frontière de Belgique. Elles agissent sous la contrainte d'une nécessité inévitable. La neutralité de la Belgique ayant été violée par des officiers français qui, sous un déguisement, ont traversé le territoire belge en automobile pour pénétrer en Allemagne.

BELGES !

The declaration of Otto von Emmich
(Internet archive, no known copyright)

Since the war had been continuing beyond the expected limit, more and more people started contributing to the endeavor in their own manner—patriotism being the chief sentiment of the lay citizens. A brief mention of the case of Miss Edith Louisa Cavell would be pertinent here as her name had been used widely by the Allied forces to promote the war efforts—be it for recruiting soldiers in the army or as a propaganda tool against German atrocities. Miss Cavell was an English nurse and her connection with Belgium had started in the 1890s while working as a governess with the François family of Paul François in Brussels. She had been inspired to become a nurse when she was in Bavaria as a governess and had visited the Free Hospital there. Back in London she had worked as a junior nurse at the Fountain Fever Hospital (Lower Tooting) for a few months from December 12, 1895; and in September 1896, determined to take up nursing as her career she had enrolled for her nursing training at the Royal London Hospital. After completion of her studies in 1900, Miss Cavell had worked as a probationary nurse at the same hospital. She had then worked as a night superintendent and also as an assistant matron at the Saint Pancras Infirmary in London from 1901. She had also worked in Manchester for some time before she was recruited as the matron in-charge at the Berkendael Medical Institute in Brussels in 1907. Belgium was invaded and had been under German rule during the First World War, and the institute was granted a permit to continue work as a Red Cross hospital in 1914, in order to take care of both the German and the Allied soldiers who had been wounded in the war. Miss Cavell truly dedicated herself in the service of the sick and the wounded soldiers at Dr. Antoine Depage's clinic at The Graduate School for Belgian Nurses.

She did not marry, and thus the hospital became her life where she used to spend most of her time among the war sufferers. With her selfless service to humanity she had become quite popular in Belgium. She had been exceptionally brave, intelligent, hardworking, very compassionate, and had voluntarily shouldered various responsibilities, especially those that concerned nursing and caring for people.

In the month of September, Herman Capiau, by profession an engineer who had guided the BEF and had assisted them during the end of August 1914, to set up a field hospital after the defeat at Mons, had informed Miss Cavell that some of the Allied soldiers were trapped behind the German lines and in nearby forests after the retreat at Mons, and that the Germans had been shooting them indiscriminately. The German army had in fact put up notices at the border areas suggesting that the Allied soldiers who did not surrender would be shot. Lieutenant Colonel Dudley Coryndon Bodger and Sergeant Major Fred Meachin[28] had been among the many soldiers wounded in the war and were in dire need for treatment. They were running from shelter to shelter for quite some time, and at the end had been helped by Capiau to reach Cavell's hospital both for treatment and for refuge. Bodger and Meachin had stayed there in Cavell's care for a couple of weeks before they were ready to leave for England. Both of them had then approached Miss Cavell to arrange for their safe return and were the first ones to be assisted by Miss Cavell to escape safely through the borders of Holland.[29] Although Bodger was arrested en route by the German officers, Meachin had reached England safely. The success of that small effort had encouraged Cavell intensely, and therefore from then onward she had been using her hospital premise secretly to shelter Allied soldiers and to send them back to their homeland through The Netherlands. She had singly been responsible for helping 200 Allied soldiers (prisoners/fugitives) escape to safety within less than a year. What had started as a sheer necessity eventually became a network of refuge for the fugitives, an elaborate escape mechanism, and also a recruitment centre for the willing Allied soldiers. Miss Cavell took active role in recruiting and sending French, Belgian, and English soldiers to the war front, for which she was assisted by more than 35 people in Brussels, including Prince Reginald de Croy and his sister Princess Marie de Croy, Countess Jeanne de Belleville, architect Phillipe Baucq, chemist Louis

---

28 Katie Pickles, *Transnational Outrage*, 23.
29 Diana Souhami, *Edith Cavell*, 63.

Severin, engineer Hermann Capiau, advocate Libiez, chemist Derveau, Mrs. Bodart, Louise Thuliez, a French school mistress who had acted as an escape guide,[30] and others who helped the Allied soldiers with providing forged documents and false passports either to escape to their own countries or to reach their army headquarters. Miss Cavell persistently and diligently had been doing it not only as her duty toward her homeland, but also due to her compassion for the sufferers.

During that time much had been going on also at the seafront. In May 1915, RMS *Lusitania*, sailing from New York to Liverpool, had sunk off the south coast of Ireland, which was torpedoed by the German navy as they had suspected it to be carrying ammunitions. The dreadful incident had sent a shockwave among the Allied countries as hundreds of innocent lives had been massacred deliberately (nearly 1,200 people had died), and as a result anti-German sentiment exploded across the globe. Newspaper articles severely condemned the barbaric act. Some wrote about the horror and terror that the Germans wanted to spread through the wreck; some wrote that the act was in the truest sense "devilish." The German intelligence service became even more active following the incident and its widespread repercussions. However, in early July 1915, the German secret service had been alerted about Philippe François Victor Baucq (probably by the Frenchman Georges Gaston Quien, who had been a German secret agent and was allegedly known to have betrayed Miss Cavell and others of her group.[31] Later he was arrested and imprisoned by the French army, although he had persistently claimed innocence), an architect from Brussels, who had been carrying on recruitment of the English and the French soldiers for the war front. He was suspected of espionage and was subsequently arrested along with Louise Thuliez on August 1 (actually on the night of July 31) from his residence. His belongings included a letter from Edith Cavell, which had been the direct proof of her involvement in anti-German activities, and thus her medical institute came under suspicion. On August 5 Miss Cavell was arrested by the German counterintelligence service and had been charged with enemy espionage. On August 8 she had confessed about her guilt: "I acknowledge that between November 1914 and July 1915, I have received into my house, cared for, and provided funds to help them reach

---

30   Katie, *op. cit.*, 23.
31   Souhami, *op. cit.*, 225.

the front and join the Allied Army."³² She was bold, truthful, and would never speak lies under any circumstance.

During her trial she told the juries that she had been under the strong impression that if she did not help the Allied soldiers to escape then the German army would shoot them. She ardently believed that she had been serving humanity by doing what she did, and so, nothing could have refrained her from helping the Allied refugees. For her it did not amount to spying.³³ Although Miss Cavell had contemplated that it was better to help the fugitive soldiers instead of them suffering silently and becoming martyrs, but for the German counterintelligence service she had certainly been indulging in enemy espionage. Both Baucq and Cavell had been put up in the St. Gilles military prison in Brussels. Cavell had been kept in cell number 23 for 8 weeks followed by solitary confinement for the last 2 weeks of her life before her execution on October 12, 1915. Her trial was kept a top secret by the German authorities, and at the dead of the night she had been executed barely within 9 hours of announcement of her death sentence, not giving her the rightful opportunity to seek for clemency. The modus operandi proved that Germany had been in a hurry to execute Miss Cavell. She had been accused of violating Paragraph 58 of the *German Military Code*, which however could only vaguely apply to her case. James M. Beck mentioned of an unknown source in his book, who affirmed: "... the true meaning of the law was perverted in order to inflict the death sentence upon her."³⁴ It had been a deliberate move not only to punish an enemy ally, but also to facilitate reinforcement of German occupation in Belgium. Therefore, it would not be wrong to assert that Miss Cavell had suffered miscarriage of justice in the hands of Germany. Countess Maria von Kallenbach, a doctor turned spy for Germany, had later claimed that it had been she who betrayed Miss Cavell, and not Gaston Quien, who, during his stay in her hospital, had reportedly befriended Miss Cavell in order to betray her.³⁵ Edith Cavell had nevertheless been venerated by England as a martyr and was considered to have been a selfless angel who had bravely

---

32 Ron Christenson, ed., *Political Trials in History*, 66.
33 Although in 2015, Stella Rimington, a former Director-General of MI5 in the 1990s, claimed that she had found some evidence in the Belgian military archive which could conclusively prove Edith Cavell's role in supporting her organization in spying for the Allied forces, BBC Radio 4, News broadcast on 16 September, 2015.
34 James M. Beck, *The Case of Edith Cavell*, 43.
35 Ione Quinby Griggs, "Woman Who Betrayed Edith Cavell Boasted of Part to Milwaukeean," *The Milwaukee Journal (Green Sheet)*, 2 May 1934: 19.

sacrificed her life for her country, but she was not only a patriot (as she had said: "patriotism is not enough"), her sacrifice had transcended nationalism as she had sacrificed her life not only for England, but for humanity. Gordon Brown wrote: "Her compassion new no nationality."[36]

Similarly, the case of Louise de Bettignies, a Frenchwoman from Lille who had founded the notorious Alice Network (Alice Ring) in order to collect secret information against Germany during the war, also calls for a mention here. She had been working under the pseudonym of "Alice Dubios," and probably was the most efficient spies for England and the Allied forces during the First World War. She had been a polyglot having fluency in English, German, Italian, and also in some other European languages. Sometime in January 1915, Major Cecil Aylmer-Cameron, joint head of the (General Head Quarter) GHQ's intelligence wing and a spymaster for England, had met her by sheer chance at Folkestone, his workplace (Folkestone Bureau) on the English Channel, and had immediately weighed her potentiality as a spy. He had been assigned with the responsibility of developing espionage networks in Belgium and northern France, and therefore did not waste the opportunity to recruit her for the Allied forces, especially for England. Louise had undergone extensive training for espionage in Britain, and then had returned to her hometown Lille to engage in her assignments as a secret agent for England. Her network of sub-agents exceeded a hundred with both male and female members enrolling enthusiastically. Marie-Leonie Vanhoutte (alias Charlotte Lameron) had become her co-conspirator against Germany. It is needless to mention that they had been exceptionally brave and daring. Louise had actually been active in the field for merely close to 9 months, and within such a short period was instrumental in saving the lives of more than a thousand British soldiers by helping them escape to The Netherlands.

Impressed by her espionage skills her superiors had nicknamed her "The Queen of Spies." After the armistice a British soldier had remarked about her: "The services Louise de Bettignies rendered are inestimable. Through her we learned ... all the movements of the enemy, the exact position of their batteries, and a thousand details that were of great help to our headquarters."[37] Significantly, the Alice Network had been working with the French Second Bureau (Deuxième Bureau) from May 1915, and had

---

36   Gordon Brown, *Courage*, 35.
37   Quoted in Kathryn J. Atwood, *Women Heroes of World War I*, 78.

provided definitive information about German preparations for an attack on Verdun planned for February 1916 (The Battle of Verdun). It could well have been possible that Georges Ladoux was using the network to collect information against Mata Hari while she had returned to Paris in December 1915. However, Louise and her accomplice Marie-Leonie was captured by the German counterintelligence in October 1915, tried, and had been sentenced to death in March 1916. Both of them were kept in the St. Gilles prison. Although, due to some unknown reason (probably due to the outcry over the execution of Edith Cavell) the death sentences had later been commuted to rigorous life imprisonment, following very harsh treatment in prison Louise had died in September 1918 of physical ailment (unsuccessful operation for a pleural abscess). Marie-Leonie was released after the armistice and had lived till old age, but Louise's arrest and consequent death had shattered the Alice Network, due to which the British had to suffer a serious setback regarding collection of wartime intelligence.

There were nevertheless many other Allied martyrs who had sacrificed their lives for their countries. Mention of Gabrielle Alina E. M. Petit, a 22 year old Belgian lady who had been recruited in July 1915, and trained by the British intelligence at the GHQ to spy on Germany from Brussels, would also be pertinent to the present context. She was nicknamed Miss Legrand by the British intelligence and had been designated to report to one Mrs. Collet-Sauvage. As her fiancé Maurice Gobert was sent to the war as a soldier of Belgium, she had also felt the need to perform duty toward her country and had volunteered to work as a first-aid maid for the Belgian Red Cross in Brussels. This provided her with the opportunity to collect precious information from the wounded German soldiers whom she nursed. She then conveniently passed on those secrets to her British employers through Mrs. Collet-Sauvage by using invisible ink. Petit had been responsible for collecting information on the movements of enemy troops, their size, location, train movements, and also for collecting technical information.[38] She had also been making arrangements for the fugitive soldiers to escape to Belgium through the borders of Holland. She had been quite clever and had used multiple identities (door-to-door sales woman, newspaper vendor, fisherwoman, nanny, barmaid, bakery delivery woman, and even a beggar)[39] to accomplish her

---

38 Tammy M. Proctor, *Female Intelligence*, 116.
39 Atwood, *op. cit.*, 58.

goal during wartime. She had been extremely courageous and confident of herself to have done all those difficult things at such a young age. Petit was suspected for enemy espionage due to a betrayer who had posed as a Dutchman, and eventually was arrested in February 1916, by the German counterintelligence service. During her interrogation she had refused to divulge any of the names of her accomplices, instead she had adamantly declared before the court: "... Kill me. I will only be replaced ..." Like Miss Cavell, she was also kept in the St. Gilles prison in Brussels and had been executed on April 1, 1916, at the Tir National shooting range in Brussels. The Germans even had tried to defame her after her execution by spreading rumors that she had been spying for money and not for love for her country. However, their trick did not work, and after the war was over she had been hailed as a national pride.

As on the land, sea warfare had also been an important aspect of the war, and there was no dearth of martyrs who had laid their lives after being captured by the German counterintelligence. Captain Charles Algernon Fryatt had been one among them. He was not an army man and therefore had not been a combatant during the war. He was captain of the unarmed merchant ship S. S. *Brussels* and had been ordered by the British Admiralty to stop and destroy German U-boats during his voyages. On 28 March, 1915, on his way from Harwich to The Netherlands, Fryatt did accordingly, but his attempt had failed as he could not destroy the U-33 (submarine), which had a close shave at the last moment. Fryatt however had succeeded to navigate safely to Rotterdam. His bravery was published widely in some European newspapers, and subsequently he had also been rewarded for his gallantry. The German government was enraged by the outcome of the incident, and although Fryatt had been a civilian, he was captured on 25 June, 1916 after more than a year of the incident. He had been tried by the Field Court Marshall of the German Naval Corps and was found guilty on three counts—(i) for being a free-shooter, (ii) for his deliberate attempt to sink a German U-boat, and (iii) for engaging in civilian hostility against Germany. He was therefore condemned to death. On July 27, 1916, he had been executed in haste (within only 2 hours from pronouncing the death sentence) by the firing squad. Altogether 16 bullets had been pumped into his 43 year old body giving him instant death. Fryatt's execution was depicted in England as the judicial murder of an innocent civilian by Germany, and his sacrifice had been celebrated as heroic. Britain had lost one of her brave and courageous patriots to German exasperation. His wrongful and brutal execution had stirred up a huge international condemnation because of the fact that Fryatt had only rightfully tried to defend his vessel and the passengers from enemy attack, and hence his act could hardly be classified as war crime. Civilians had virulently shouted slogans and had marched on the streets of England against Kaiser Wilhelm II, whom they wanted dead. As the Allied forces did not leave any opportunity to stir up civilian sentiment against Germany, posters and pamphlets had been published in France and Britain as part of propaganda against the wrongdoings of Germany during the war.

It might however seem somewhat perplexing to contemplate how the case of Mata Hari, a dancer and courtesan (an adventuress as per the common perception), could have any likeness to those of the patriot spy martyrs of the Allied forces. Herein the hypothesis of French revenge against Mata Hari could presumably find its way. She might have been entrapped by the Allied forces to avenge the wrongs perpetrated on their patriots by the enemy, including captures and executions of the brave sons and the "selfless angels" who had worked passionately during wartime, and by captivating them the German counterintelligence had destroyed the espionage network that the Allied forces had established and had relied on. Further, her execution might also have had a cathartic effect on the French people to vent out their hatred against Germany for losing Alsace-Lorraine. Mata Hari had been an eminent public personality, and so had attracted media coverage on every possible occasion. Therefore, her capture, trial, and execution could apparently create the necessary sensation to serve the purpose of exposing some German conspiracy to the French people for revitalizing their morale during wartime, thereby taking revenge on and diminishing confidence of the enemy. Rampant propaganda in the British and French press had been incited against German aggression and atrocities in Belgium and in other neutral places.

Keay wrote about a Conspiracy of Optimism,[40] which had encouraged the citizens to keep aside all their sorrow and despair in pretence of cheerfulness in order to encourage the soldiers who had been toiling at the Front. "Defeat was a forbidden word" she wrote. The British authority had used various propaganda techniques to encourage the war effort (propaganda through war photographs, cartoons, and literature, including the Bryce

---

40 Julia Keay, *op. cit.*, 92.

Commission Report of 1915, which was published barely 5 days after the sinking of *Lusitania*). Varied images of womanhood and motherhood had been used to that end; even Miss Edith Cavell's death had been used to propagate mass agitation against Germany in order to enhance the number of soldier recruitments for the war front. Alan Wilkinson wrote: "Forgetting her last statement, "Patriotism is not enough," British propaganda used Edith Cavell's death for the cause of the war effort. A postcard was printed showing a spike-helmeted German looking with satisfaction at the dead body of a sylph-like girl radiant in heavenly light. The caption reads: Miss Edith Cavell Murdered, Remember!"[41] Instead of bringing the culprits to book and punishing the killers, British government was more inclined to exploit the plights of the martyrs in their own interest. As mentioned earlier, Charles Fryatt's execution had also been used for the purpose of propaganda in favor of the war effort by the British, marking his memory as an inspiration for the soldiers. Most of the anti-German posters had been aimed at the objective of recruiting soldiers.

Keeping my concern limited to the issue of Mata Hari's trial and execution I would bypass detailing on the war, and instead would embark on the military crisis in France which, according to some of her biographers, had very much been pertinent to her case. At a very crucial time of the war the crisis had taken form of a mutiny among almost half of the French army as 54 divisions had got involved in the rebellion during the months of May and June in 1917. (It is significant to note that Mata Hari had been arrested in February 1917, and was under judicial trial during the months of May–June in that year). In December 1916, Robert Georges Nivelle was handed over the charges from the French Commander in-Chief Joseph Jacques Césaire Joffre due to the latter's removal after his debacle in Verdun and Somme (in February 1916, and July 1916, respectively). Under Joffre's leadership the French had to give up Fort Douaumont to the Germans without any resistance, which was situated at the most prime position regarding the war. The German army had then used the well-protected fort as their army shelter and operational base. Weakening French power, more than 100,000 lives had been massacred after the capture of the fort, and as a consequence the social and political atmosphere in France had suffered a deep setback. After removal of Joffre, Nivelle could prove his worth by recapturing the fort. It had immediately boosted the morale of the soldiers along with that of the civilians which

---

41 Alan Wilkinson, *The Church of England and the First World War*, 96.

quickly made him a national hero, and thus he had gained confidence at the highest levels—of the War Minister Louis Hubert Gonzalve Lyautey, and also of the Prime Minister Aristide Briand. So, in April 1917, when Nivelle came up with his plans for a huge aggressive assault with 5,300 guns and 129 Schneider tanks against Germany he had received the necessary faith and support from Briand, although Hubert Lyautey had not been quite happy with Nivelle's tall claims and high aspirations.

Nivelle had planned to attack his enemies off the guard and had anticipated defense of a nominal number of German soldiers against his offensive in the Second Battle of Aisne on the Chemin des Dames. He was therefore confident to conquer a sweeping victory for France within only 48 hours; but he had missed to take into account the major espionage network Germany already had in Europe. Nivell did not care to keep his plans secret as he had sought for all-out support from the French people and had wished to cheer them up for the imminent victory. The German General of Infantry Hans von Boehn was well aware of the French assault plans as his men had succeeded to capture all the relevant documents in a trench raid at least a week before the attack. Nivell obviously knew nothing about the mishap and had proceeded with his plans nonchalantly. His offensive however had to be delayed due to bad weather, and on April 16, at an early morning attempt, his brainchild was launched. The German troops had been ready with all measures to mow down the French assault. They had already built anti-tank trenches at advantageous positions for their soldiers in order to demolish the French offensive, and their artillery had been ready to fire on the French tanks to destroy the mighty efforts of the enemy.[42] The front line had been interspersed with thousands of concealed German machine-guns to open fire indiscriminately on the French infantry in order to kill instantly and disperse them with immediate effect. The French troops had been caught off the guard in the open field resulting in massive loss of lives (40,000 casualties) on the very first day. By April 25 the number of death had reached 95,000, whereas the total number of French casualties exceeded 187,000 and approximately 29,000 had been taken as war prisoners in the Second Battle of Aisne (from April 16 to May 10). None of Nivelle's tall claims regarding the offensive could be materialized, and it had diminished the high expectations of the soldiers who had put their lives at stake to regain French glory and honor. The Nivelle Offensive had failed devastatingly, which

---
42 Spencer C. Tucker, ed., *World War One: The Definitive Encyclopedia*, 54–55.

had catastrophic results including demoralizing the soldiers to the point of revolt.

The disastrous failure of the Nivelle Offensive had resulted in the French Army Mutiny of May 1917. A total number of 119 incidents of revolt had been recorded, of which nearly 90 were marked as serious offenses against the country. The typical mutinous acts comprised of outrageous exhibition of dejection regarding war, breaking windows by stone-pelting, arson, refusal to follow orders of the high commands to return to the Front, display of red flags, singing of revolutionary songs that had inspired more men to join the mutiny, heavy drinking, disconnecting train engines from the bogies carrying troops and ammunition, manhandling railway employees and military police, etc. To suppress the rebellion the French army had imprisoned many mutineers and had tried them under the Army Rules. A total of 23 rebels had been executed for mutinying collectively against France, while many had escaped with lesser punishments. The French government had held the defeatist campaigns responsible for the mutiny, "but the actual causes were much more deeply embedded in the trying experiences of the nation."[43] No lesson was apparently learnt by France from the Somme Offensive (started on July 1, 1916), which had been the fiercest battle of that century with more than 100,000 soldiers wounded and dead. The wounded soldiers of the French troops had suffered at that time from medical inadequacy and unplanned, amateurish attitude of the government toward them.

However, on May 20, 1917, at the meeting of the 128th Regiment of the 3rd Division, the soldiers had voiced their grievances against the Nivelle Offensive, based on which the reasons for the mutiny might be summarized as the following—inaccurate planning of Nivelle for the offensive; inadequate intelligence on the part of the Allied forces, especially of France, due to which Nivelle did not have any idea about the German trench raid before the attack; lack of coordination between the French troops; underestimation of the strength of German militia; extreme fatigue of the French soldiers from the long and tiring war that had claimed countless lives at the front; the enormous casualty figures unnerving the troops; suffering dreadful conditions at the war front including inadequate medical facilities, along with substandard and unhealthy food;

---

43   Ebba Dahlin, *French and German Public Opinion on Declared War Aims: 1914-1918*, 122.

awareness of and worry about the political corruption at the highest levels of leadership which had been pushing the soldiers to the brink of refusal; lack of repose thwarting physical and mental revitalization of the army; dissatisfaction regarding grant of leave; upsurge of pacifist and anti-war literature affecting morale of the soldiers; newly appointed military commanders effectuating loss of confidence giving scope to the troops to question their competence; wretched conditions of the "rest camps;" effects of the Russian Revolution of February 1917; delay in the arrival of American troops; etc. It became absolutely clear that the soldiers who had hoped to get back their lost lands of Alsace and Lorraine even at the cost of their lives, and thus to take revenge on the enemy for the wrongs perpetrated against France, had become extremely frustrated with the French government.

To revert the condition in the army Nivelle had promptly been replaced by Philippe Pétain, who took care to improve the conditions in the French army in order to restore normalcy among the troops. But the mutiny had spread so wide that it could not be stopped in a short time, and even in July 1917, incidents of revolt had continued to occur. The unrest spilled over into the civilian life as well with rampant labor strikes due to inferior working conditions, high cost of living, and also due to the influence of anti-war propaganda. As the situation snowballed, the French government had started invoking the blame game. The Interior Minister Louis Jean Malvy had been a well-known sympathizer of the syndicalists and the defeatists (in 1914, at the outbreak of the war, he had spoken against arresting those anti-militarists who had been named in the Carnet B), and hence was blamed by Georges Clemenceau, Léon Daudet, and other conservatives for the disaster. [As a result on August 30, 1917, Malvy was forced to resign because he had been accused of handing over French deployment plans to the enemy.] Not only Malvy, this had been true for some other French officers as well. But people at the highest ranks of the French government had soon realized that blaming each other would not yield the required results and therefore had cleverly tried to put the blame on hundreds and thousands of imaginary spies who had supposedly been working on the French soil on behalf of Germany to jeopardize the Allied war efforts. They had then played the last trick—by blaming Mata Hari for the entire debacle they had virtually tried to prove to all Frenchmen that the plan for the attack on Germany could succeed but for spies like her. Mata Hari was already imprisoned on charges of enemy espionage, and on July 25 she had been sentenced to death. It should be noted that the Allied forces all along knew that there had been no material proof to confirm that Mata Hari was a spy, of any country whatsoever. It had therefore been a conspiracy hatched on their part to implicate her falsely in order to gain political mileage during the war. Mata Hari had been an easy prey for them, and had she not been there, it would have been someone else who would certainly become the scapegoat in her stead. In fact, the French army had desperately required a scapegoat to put the blame on, and unfortunately Mata Hari was there. Due to her characteristic naivety she had made herself readily available to them. Therefore, as already noted, her death sentence had been symbolic in a sense and was used by the French as a propaganda tool against Germany at the time of mass war hysteria.

The news of Mata Hari's death sentence had spread like wild fire as the newspapers and magazines encased French sentiment. At the time of a national crisis it was convenient for France to use her diabolically as a scapegoat projecting her as a symbol of evil incarnate—as if the French people could ultimately take revenge on Germany for the devastation perpetrated against them in the battles by taking away her life. The French citizens had considered her capture as a phenomenal victory of the French counterintelligence, which had a cathartic effect on them. In order to divert people's resentment that is exactly what the French government had wanted at that time. The French propaganda machinery had started spreading rumors that Mata Hari was responsible for the failure of the Nivelle Plan as she had dispatched sensitive information to Germany about use of tanks[44] by the French army in the war right from the beginning of the Battle of Somme, and also for the menacing army mutiny.[45] As in common perception of the French people courtesans, demimondaines, prostitutes, and mistresses were linked easily to espionage (incidents of Napoleon III and Georges Clemenceau had still haunted them[46]), it compelled them to believe that at the least 50,000 French soldiers had lost

---

44 Michael Foley, *Rise of the Tank*, 71. I would also like to quote from a newspaper report of 1917 on this issue: "... Mata Hari learned vaguely of tanks early in 1916 ... It is rumored that a deputy inadvertently gave her the first information about tanks. And the rumor is strengthened by the fact that Mata Hari had plenty of coal for her apartment during the fuel famine last winter." "Mata Hari—Spy," *Manawatu Daily Times*, Vol. XL (13760); 13 December, 1917, 2.

45 Keay, *op. cit.*, 208.

46 Julie Wheelwright, *op. cit.*, 50.

THE SOCIO-POLITICAL SCENARIO IN EUROPE

their lives in the wars because of Mata Hari's highly efficient espionage strategies during the Battle of Verdun (February 21–December 20) and Somme (July 1–November 18) in 1916 (notably, Mata Hari had returned to Paris for the second time on June 16, 1916). Although there are controversies regarding the number of dead, wounded, and lost soldiers, there is no doubt about the devastation suffered by the French army in those battles. As the war had effectively removed all the barriers between facts and rumor, all these issues had been raised during her trial. Hence, one becomes compelled to presume that she was sentenced to death for the military expediency of France, no matter whether she had actually done any harm to the country and its people or not.

Nevertheless, after the defeat in the war of 1870–1871, France had realized the urgency to establish an official intelligence service, which had been possible due to the earnest efforts of the then War Minister Georges Boulanger. He had introduced the counterintelligence law of France in April 1886, which had distinctly defined the nature, kind, and scope of information that could be deemed as illegal. In order to ensure safety to the people and property of France, he had also implemented an elaborate system to identify and capture spies working against France. It had included preparation of two lists (1887) of foreigners who had been of military age and were residing in France (Carnet A), and also of French and foreign nationals who could potentially spy against France (Carnet B—The Red Book). Both the lists were prepared by the Deuxième Bureau (French counterintelligence service), and the French police had started working on the Books immediately filling them up with names of French and foreign nationals who had either been suspected to be a threat to France or were potential national enemies. The Ministry of War had also permitted for surveillance of those named in the lists. By 1911, Carnet B comprised of three categories of individuals[47] who were considered to have been potential enemies of France—(1) foreigners who had been suspected or marked as enemy spies, (2) Frenchmen who had been suspected to be enemy spies, and (3) French nationals akin to leftist radicals, syndicalists, trade unionists, pacifists, and anti-militarists or defeatists, who were opposed to war (in their opinion "All war is criminal") and could disrupt army mobilization for war. According to the French records, by June 1914, before the war had started, Carnet B listed almost 2,500 names as potential threat to France. It could be quite possible that Mata Hari's

---

47   Paul B. Miller, *From Revolutionaries to Citizens*, 89.

name as a foreigner had also been listed under the first category of Carnet B, especially soon after the start of the war, or at least after the British had warned France on her antecedents in early 1916, and therefore she had been under surveillance for quite some time. According to a circular of September 1911, of the War Ministry, police could immediately arrest anyone during war whose name had featured in the lists, their target being mostly the anti-militarists because they had been considered by the conservatives as serious internal threats (although the third category of the list was relaxed during the war as most of the enlisted persons had joined the war on behalf of France). But others had not been spared. Almost 560 foreigners who resided in France had been named as potential enemy spies, and some were even interned at the outbreak of the war. Mata Hari had also been implicated by the French government due to several reasons, overlapping curiously, that benefited France in wartime.

CHAPTER 5
THE SCAPEGOAT

The scene had opened in Berlin on the eve of the First World War, while Mata Hari was present in the city. The Germans were being made to believe that it was going to be a war to defend their homeland, and therefore there had been a lot of enthusiasm regarding the war among the common citizens (Spirit of 1914), besides the fact that most Germans were daily wagers working in various factories, agricultural fields, or mines for their livelihood. They lived a moderate life as they did not own lands or did not mint money from other sources to sustain their families; and in case a war broke out they would have suffered the most. During the turn of the century the whole of Europe had been divided on the issue of each country's ulterior motives, and tension never ceased to prevail between them. Britain had pledged to counter any effort that would have opposed British hegemony, while Germany wanted to do the same—to acquire unlimited power in order to establish German domination in Europe and ultimately throughout the world. General Helmut von Moltke, Chief of the German General Staff, had believed very strongly that only Germany was capable of delivering spiritual progress to mankind, and it was the only nation that could lead mankind toward a higher destiny. That obviously resulted in frequent conflicts between the two countries and their allies. Lay citizens of all the countries had always been the worst sufferers as they were hit directly by such mindless unrest. Still, due to deliberate and well-organized war propaganda by the government, common German citizens had believed that at the end they would surely be victorious.

Although anti-war demonstrations had pulled huge crowds in July 1914, August 1 had seen the largest patriotic gathering in Berlin with nearly 50,000 war enthusiasts cheering jubilantly for the ensuing war. Amid the mood of ecstatic joyousness in early August people from other countries who had been holidaying or working in Germany had rushed to the borders to return to their homeland, Mata Hari being one of them. She had gone to Berlin from Italy (Milan) either to research for and compose a new dance recital (with the assistance of the renowned Egyptologist Professor Johann Peter Adolf Erman, Director of Egyptology department at the Royal Museum in Berlin, who had been known to Émile Guimet) which she had wished to base on ancient Egyptian culture, or to get new contracts for a few dance shows in the German capital, or could have been both. On May 23 she had signed a contract with the famous director Richard Schultz to dance (*Thief of Millions*[1]) at the Metropol Theater for 6 months, which had been scheduled to start on September 1 that year. The dance contract had become very significant in her story of espionage and therefore deserves special mention. In Berlin Mata Hari however had enough time to prepare for her shows, to make new friends, and even to renew her relationship with some old ones. Her romantic adventures had also been pursued through the July Crisis, while the most powerful nations in Europe including Russia, Austria–Hungary, The Netherlands, France, Britain, Germany, Serbia, and some others were preparing for a war against the other besides the fact that there had been considerable efforts to avert any devastating confrontation. Mata Hari could not possibly be unaware of the happenings around because on one night during the end of July, while dining with her friend Herr Griebel, the Superintendent of Police in Berlin, she had been witness to scaringly noisy demonstrations of a massive crowd that had congregated in front of the Emperor's Palace shouting "*Deutschland über Alles*" (Germany above all). Quite evidently the socio-political situation in Europe, especially in Germany, had been tense during the end of July, and in the first week of August war was declared. Anti-foreign frenzy had quickly taken a wild form, and citizens of the Allied countries (Triple Entente) were being harassed ruthlessly everywhere by self-styled German patriots. Due to Mata Hari's complexion the German police had mistaken her to be a Russian and had treated her very badly stopping and checking her on the streets of Berlin several times. Suddenly Berlin became an alien city to her, and soon she had realized that it would no longer be safe for her to stay on in Germany. Disgusted with the sudden changed situation she wanted to return to Paris for Neuilly, where she had a house (Villa Rémy) that had been gifted to her only a couple of years back by her ex-lover Felix Xavier Rousseau.

Due to the declaration of war all the theaters in Berlin had immediately closed, and it became necessary for her to break the contract with the

---
[1]   Sam Waagenaar, *op. cit.*, 1965, 109.

Metropol. Mata Hari had made a mistake by leaving her valuable furs and jewelry in the custody of her costumer, a feeble looking tough man, who had refused to give up his dues under any circumstance. But as the show had been cancelled Mata Hari did not want to make any payment to him—after all it was not her fault in any way. A scuffle had become inevitable and the costumer had then confiscated all her expensive furs and jewelry in order to get his dues. He had refused to return the valuables unless full payment was made to him. Stuck in an awkward situation she could think of no other way, and therefore had contacted her German agent for money. She had been informed that as she was a resident of France the German bank had frozen her account at the start of the war. Mata Hari became extremely annoyed and frustrated at the turn of the events and had desperately wanted to get out of Germany as early as could have been possible for her. All of a sudden a strange sense of loss had gripped her from nowhere. On August 6 she had tried for the first time to cross over to Switzerland on her way to Paris via Zurich by boarding a train, but due to lack of necessary identity papers in support of her neutral Dutch nationality to cross the German borders she was nabbed at the Swiss border.

At the border she had naively informed the guards that she was going to return to France, without even realizing the gravity of the wartime changed situation. The German guards had informed her that she could not proceed any further without proper documents, although her luggage would be sent ahead. They did not allow her to take her bountiful luggage off the train and had forced her to return to Berlin even without a single dress for a change of clothes. Mata Hari had been a frequent traveler in Europe for many years, but had never faced such an irksome situation. After 9 days, on August 15, she could somehow manage to obtain the required Dutch passport from the Dutch Consul General of The Netherlands, Mr. H. N. F. van Panhuys, in Frankfurt am Main, who had identified her as "Mrs. Margaretha Geertruida Zelle, divorced wife of MacLeod, born in Leeuwarden and living in Berlin."[2] She could then cross over to Holland (due to the Battle of the Frontiers all routes through the Swiss borders had been sealed) with the help of an elderly Dutch gentleman known only as Mr. K., who, knowing about her plight, had generously bought the train ticket for her to reach Amsterdam as she had no money with her (absolutely intriguing, but strangely true).

2   Waagenaar, *op. cit.*, 1964, 120.

ONE LITTLE ORCHID

It had been the only time in the life of Mata Hari that she could get help from a man without applying her romantic tricks. On August 16 she was however back in her homeland after 10 long years. Did her heart pound at the imagined probability to see her daughter who had almost been 16 by then? She had quickly planned to flaunt her enormous success before the MacLeods and to rescue Non from them. Least did she realize that nothing any longer was going to happen the way she wanted to, because like many others she had also been under observation of the British secret service from the day she had first tried to cross the German borders.

During that time, the Battle of the Frontiers had already cast deep shadow on the Dutch society. Schools had been closed for the students and were converted into refugee camps. All necessary consumables including food became scarce. Toward the middle of August, after the siege of Liège by Germany, the Dutch citizens became extremely scared, and inspite of their neutrality no more did they feel secure. As Mata Hari had severed all ties with Margarethe, her step-mother and her brothers were no more related to her. So she had to put up in a hotel, which was essentially a splendid one. She had settled at the adequately luxurious Victoria Hotel in Amsterdam. Mata Hari could virtually do nothing in such unfavorable situation and had to wait idly for the trouble to subside. Adam had died in 1910, but his "little orchid" did not even come to attend his funeral, nor did she contact the bereaved family to express her sympathy and solidarity at the moment of grief. She had been too engrossed with her life as a professional dancer and with her lovers. So, after 10 years, when she had returned to her homeland, she did not want to meet any one of them. Mata Hari had left Margarethe far behind and did not want to look back again. However, once in Holland, using her feminine charms, she had started looking for someone who would keep her in opulence, because Paris had been out of her reach she did not know for how long. The Dutch banker Mr. van der Schalk had soon been in her net, who had mistaken her to be a Russian and was overwhelmed with his foreign coy mistress. The naïve banker had gladly helped her to restore her wardrobe from his own pocket and had kept her in luxury for 2 months, before her fraud had been exposed to him. It was then by chance that Mata Hari had found her aristocratic old beau Baron Edouard Willem van der Capellen, a Colonel commandant in the Dutch Cavalry (Second Hussar Regiment, Eindhoven), who, at the age of 52, had gladly accepted her as his mistress and had guaranteed her of all her material needs.

Assured and rejoiced she had decided to pursue her dancing profession once again. By approaching several producers in Holland she could bag a contract with the French Opera, and on December 14 had performed at The Royal Theater in The Hague. She had been 38 years of age at that time, and being aware of Non's presence in the city she did not dare to wear revealing costume for the ballet she had performed in. Mata Hari however could win the hearts of her audience with her characteristic ease even in a period costume that she had worn for the evening. But soon she had realized that she would not be able to depend on the theater agents in The Hague for more dancing contracts, and therefore she had to abandon her aspiration to flourish as a dancer in Holland. With the support of her lover she had then moved out of Amsterdam to settle in The Hague, where van der Capellen had rented a beautiful old house for her along the canal at Nieuwe Uitleg. With full enthusiasm she had started to renovate it in the way that she had imagined would reflect aristocracy.

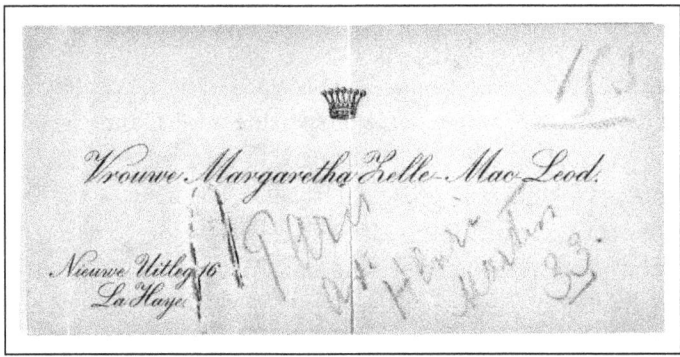

Mata Hari's visiting card
(The Mata Hari Foundation, Fries Museum, Leeuwarden)

Soon Mata Hari had been in short of funds and as a result the renovation work was delayed which bothered her greatly. Waagenaar wrote: "Mata Hari was terribly short of money during those first eight months in The Hague."[3] It had been from the beginning of 1915 until the month of August that year, while she was staying at the Hotel Paulez in The Hague. The carpenter Mr. Soet, whom she had hired for the renovation work of her new house, was worried about her limited resources and had started distrusting her regarding his payment. Consequently, the issue had taken

---
3   Ibid., 125.

a bitter turn and Mr. Soet had even insulted her in front of one Monsieur Wurfbain at the latter's office. Wurfbain, a banker and friend of her Dutch lover van der Schalk, who had been a known German sympathizer, was working to provide food supplies among the German occupiers in Belgium. As mentioned earlier, it could have been sometime during that financial crisis that Kroemer had turned up to her with his offer to spy for Germany;[4] and it is quite understandable why she had readily accepted his offer. Moreover, Mata Hari had always wanted to be in Paris, the city of celebrations, and at her Villa Rémy in Neuilly-sur-Seine. Nearly a year back, when the war broke out and she had been trying to cross the borders of Germany to reach a safe place, she could only think of Paris and had desperately wanted to return to her "own city." It had been quite long (from February 1914, when she went to Italy and Berlin unto August 1915) that she could not go to her city of love due to the war situations, and she was not ready to lose any chance to return to the French capital. Accepting Kroemer's offer could provide her with an opportunity to visit Paris again and that was enough for her at that moment.

Therefore, it can well be presumed that Mata Hari had accepted Kroemer's offer exclusively due to her personal considerations, and her intentions in no way comprised of helping Germany at the time of war. And when he had offered a hefty sum of 20,000 francs in advance for the shady task Mata Hari was overwhelmed, because she had considered it as reimbursement for her confiscated valuable furs and jewelry by the German costumer. She had plausibly sighed of relief that after all Germany had paid her back for her lost possessions. In order to carry on with the assigned secret service for Germany Kroemer had also given her three bottles of invisible ink, which she later said that she had thrown away into the canals from the ship en route to Paris. All the while Mata Hari knew that she would not spy for the country that had insulted and harassed her unnecessarily during the outbreak of the war without any fault of hers. She was not, as already noted, the "forgive and forget" type. Nevertheless, her only condition for accepting Kroemer's proposal was that she would not use her name for any correspondence with him, and Kroemer had then provided her with the fatal code H21 for the purpose—"H" indicating that she was supposed to report to Captain Hoffman of German secret service.[5]

---

4   Waagenaar wrote that Mata Hari was introduced to Kroemer by Wurfbain in January 1915; ibid., 237.

5   Pat Shipman, *op. cit.*, 187.

With Kroemer's money she had merrily headed for France in December 1915, on the pretext of selling off her personal belongings at Neuilly and signing professional contracts for some engagements in South America, never contemplating whether her story would at all be believed in wartime. Keay wrote: "The excuse she gave for going to Paris was surely too vacuous to convince even the preoccupied baron ..."[6]

With a visa granted to her on November 27 to travel from Holland Mata Hari had started from The Hague on November 30 via Tilbury on her way to Paris and had travelled through the British port at Folkestone on December 3, where, as a routine exercise, she was questioned along with other passengers onboard. The officials at the port had not been convinced with her explanation for traveling to Paris during wartime. Her case was further referred to MO5, and when questioned by the counterintelligence officer Captain S. S. Dillon about her wartime sojourn to Paris she communicated a story quite different from the one she had told before—selling her home in Neuilly in order to settle in The Hague where she already had a house. Such contradictory replies had not been received without suspicion by the port authorities. Although nothing incriminating was found on her, the officer had remarked "not above suspicion" in his report on her questioning, which was signed by the PC Sergeant Frank Bickers and the Superintendent P. Quinn. Mata Hari was not apprehended by the British Police, but the note on her had been sent to all the British ports, a copy of which had certainly reached France. Blissfully unaware of the fatal tags put beside her name she had completed her journey toward her paradise on the British ocean-liner S. S. *Arundel*. Shipman has hinted at another reason for the officers to find Mata Hari to be "most unsatisfactory." She wrote: "The real problem was probably not what Mata Hari said but who she was, she was a woman, traveling alone, obviously wealthy and obviously an excellent linguist—too educated and too foreign to make a British officer comfortable. Worse yet, she was ... one who admitted to having a lover. Women like that were immoral and not to be trusted."[7] Shipman might have been partially right, but, I suppose and have already mentioned earlier that the British counterintelligence service had definite knowledge of her connection with Karl Kroemer, the honorary German consul in Holland, even before she had left Holland for Paris, and therefore it was not, as speculated by Shipman,

---

6   Julia Keay, *op. cit.*, 93.
7   Shipman, *op. cit.*, 190–191.

a simple case of misogyny on part of the British officers.

Paris had been declared to be an entrenched war camp, and knowing nothing about it Mata Hari had landed in the city with her own agenda of amusement. Once in Paris she was baffled with the drastic change that the city had gone through merely in a year. Keay wrote: "The extraordinary fashions that had prevailed in the pre-war years ... had no place in a world where practicality ruled supreme."[8] Describing the war ridden city she further wrote: "Enticing window displays had been replaced by patriotic tableaux draped with the national flag and by posters announcing fund-raising events for the benefit of wounded soldiers. No more motor buses trundled along the streets, no luxurious private cars ... speeding cars flying the tricolor ... great grey lorries, loaded with foodstuffs, uniforms, wire netting, barbed wire, ammunition and every possible kind of war material rushing through Paris on the way to the Front."[9] Keay further commented: "The stark contrast between the idle, glittering past, and the grim, functional present was too shocking to be ignored."[10] Mata Hari had never witnessed anything of that scale in a war and had somewhat felt out of place in her favorite city, but still on December 24 she wrote to her old friend and agent Gabriel Astruc expressing her wish to perform in Diaghilev's Ballet Russes. He had however declined possibly due to wartime difficulties. It could be speculated that while in Holland she might have known from some sources that Diaghilev was still in Paris, and as there did not seem to be any scope to pursue her profession on the stage in her own country (because the French Opera, with which she was engaged in The Hague, did not arrange for regular shows), she had quickly planned to approach him for an opportunity to perform in his group—if not for money, at least to mend her diminishing fame and prestige. So, it could also have been part of her plan to visit Paris in 1915.

However, Paris, during that time, had been a place where soldiers of all friendly countries were being seen, and to spend her days in good humor, Mata Hari had renewed her romantic liaison with her first lover Henri de Marguerie. She had also befriended a 42 year old Belgian officer named Fernand, in the mean time, who had been the Marquis de Beaufort, a Major in the 4th Belgian Lancers of the 1st Division of cavalry, had been

---

8 Keay, *op. cit.*, 93.
9 Ibid., 98.
10 Ibid., 106.

serving in the Army of the Yser,[11] and most significantly was ready to pay for her exorbitant bills and other requirements. While the Parisian women, with grief-stricken haunted eyes, were being seen struggling and toiling to meet their ends, Mata Hari was busy with her old and new lovers. Nothing could ever persuade her to shift focus from her self-love. However, only within 3 months she was fed up with the somber wartime mood of Paris, and in the middle of February 1916, had decided to return to The Hague. She had preferred to be with van der Capellen in Nieuwe Uitleg, where the war was not menacing, and had hoped that the newly renovated home would be more exciting than Paris. Newman wrote: "She had given up the lease of her villa at Neuilly in March 1914 ...,"[12] but its contents were kept safely with the Maple warehouse. In February 1916, with 10 big cases full of table silver, furniture, shoes, hats, jewelry, and clothes brought from the firm, she had started for Holland via Spain and Portugal.

Much had been going on in the mean time regarding her at the British end that Mata Hari was completely unaware of. As noted earlier, there was a crucial report (February 3, 1916) sent by Richard Tinsley to the MO5 in London with regard to her accepting money from the German Embassy in The Netherlands, which had expressed his suspicion: "One suspects her of having gone to France on an important mission that will profit Germans."[13] So, the British counterespionage service had evidently been keeping watch on her, and within 2 weeks, after Mata Hari had reached The Hague in February, another British report said that she might travel to France once again to collect money that the Germans had deposited in a bank for her services rendered to them. So, it might cogently be speculated that it had been due to Tinsley's adverse report against her to the MO5 during the war that the prejudice of her being an enemy spy had taken wind, which never freed her again. On February 22, 1916, the British secret service MO5 had informed their French counterpart by issuing a circular (61207/MO5-E),[14] which said that "If she (Mata Hari) comes to this country she should be arrested and sent to Scotland Yard."

---

11   Russell Warren Howe, *op. cit.*, 80.
12   Bernard Newman, *op. cit.*, 61; though I wonder why would she do that, because she was supposed to return to Paris after her visit to Berlin, and even at her first attempt to get out of Germany at the outbreak of war she had wanted to return to Paris. But in that case why did she keep her belongings with the firm does not appear to be clear.
13   Shipman, *op. cit.*, 193.
14   Keay, *op. cit.*, 118.

Mata Hari had not been a French national, but still instead of informing Holland the British had informed the Deuxième Bureau about their plan to arrest her. It might therefore be speculated that through the said circular the British secret service had practically wanted to caution the French about her suspected activities during wartime, and as France was an ally of Britain in the war, it must have been binding on them to treat her similarly. None other than Major-General Sir Vernon G. W. Kell, the distinguished middle-aged British army officer having an illustrious military career serving around the world with knowledge of many European and Asian languages, had co-founded (along with Captain Sir George Mansfield Smith-Cumming of the Navy) and was heading the Home Section of the British Security Service Bureau (which had been a part of the MO5) during the First World War.

Once back in The Hague Mata Hari had soon started missing Paris so much that even van der Capellen's money and luxury could not hold her back for long. She had later said that her life in The Hague "was very sad"[15] because van der Capellen was busy at the frontier, and being known as his mistress she could not take another lover at her home in a small city like The Hague. During that time she had received a message from her latest lover in Paris, the Marquis de Beaufort, who had felt incredibly lonely without her and had begged her to return to Paris. So, she did not once hesitate to make up her mind to go to Paris for a second time. Mata Hari had immediately applied for an entrance visa to travel to France, which had been granted on May 12, 1916 (she got it from the French Consul in Holland on May 15) with a note that stated—"Not valid for the war zone" (Paris was indeed in the war zone), although it is not quite clear why the French government did not refuse her an entry visa despite getting two secret negative notes about her from the British counterespionage service long back on December 9, 1915, and also on February 22, 1916. It could have been indicative of a diabolical scheme of the French which had been planned well ahead to frame the dancer (it is important to note that the 9 month long Verdun offensive had started in February 1916, and it was soon called "Hell" due to the miserable condition of the soldiers and the huge casualties suffered by them. So, France might have foreseen the need for a scapegoat quite long before she had actually been framed). Mata Hari, however, had also wanted an English visa that time, because she had planned for a stopover in Britain on her way to Paris, but

---

15   Waagenaar, *op.cit.*, 1965, 190.

was refused. It is curious to note that France had plans to use tanks in the war, and Britain had been manufacturing those in 1916.[16] Therefore, her interest to visit England during that trip had probably sent an alarm to the British counterespionage officials.

She however had taken the refusal as an insult and became desperate to procure the permit by any means. She could never stand the idea that someone else would control her life. So, during wartime, Mata Hari was being frequently seen visiting the Foreign Office in The Hague with the request for assistance to get an English visa. On April 27 a telegram had been sent by the Dutch Foreign Minister to the Dutch Legation in London, with a request to pursue Mata Hari's visa application which said that the Dutch national in question wanted to visit Paris for "personal reasons" and wanted to stop over in London en route, but because under no circumstance she could be allowed to enter the "prohibited areas" in England, a refusal message from the British office was forwarded to Holland on May 4, which read—"Authorities have reasons why admission of lady mentioned your 74 (i.e., the number of the Dutch wire) in England is undesirable."[17] The reply should have been extremely alarming for Mata Hari, but she was not informed anything by the Foreign Office in The Hague about the reason for her visa refusal. One could presume from her bold and desperate personality type that she would have undertaken the journey anyway even if she was informed about the genuine cause of her entry refusal to Britain, and so she practically did. I would like to borrow Erika Ostrovsky's words for her—"Nothing appeared to warn her. She seemed blind to all danger ..."[18] Mata Hari had always demonstrated her love for living on the edge, and hence, failing to get a travel visa she had reluctantly dropped her plan for a stopover in England, although had continued with her plan to travel to Paris. She had completely overlooked the note on her French visa, which did not allow her to travel to the war zone. The war by then had well been into the second year, and she was going to enter the entrenched war camp for the second time without any valid excuse apart from "for personal reasons," so it was undoubtedly going to become her fatal journey, which she should have avoided by all means. Her limitless naivety was to take an unfortunate turn because war had its own rules, and that surely did not match up to Mata Hari's naïve expectations.

16 "Wickedest, Most Dangerous," *The Pittsburgh Press*; PA: 25 December, 1921, 67.
17 Waagenaar, *op. cit.*, 1965, 136.
18 Erika Ostrovsky, *op. cit.*, 134.

Was it only because she missed Paris that she had taken the risk to travel during war for a second time? Was it her wanderlust that compelled her to undertake the trip? The phrase "for personal reasons"[19] in the telegram addressed to the Chief of Dutch Legation in London is extremely vague and could well mean anything—including espionage. I presume the case must have been slightly different, and would like to speculate that after returning to The Hague from Paris in February 1916, she must have been in contact with Kroemer, who might have sought for a feedback regarding her task in Paris. That might have given her the reason to visit Paris for a second time on the pretext of personal reasons, because she had done absolutely nothing to please Kroemer on her first trip (no matter what the British agents had reported), and therefore owed a justification to him for the 20,000 francs. Mata Hari later said that Kroemer had handed her three bottles of secret ink in May 1916, which she had thrown into the waters of the canals. But plausibly she had confused her dates as she had been doing always. However, on May 24, 1916, Mata Hari had started sailing from Amsterdam aboard the Dutch steamship S. S. *Zeelandia*. The fateful voyage was scheduled to take her via the Iberian route to Vigo in Spain through the English Channel stopping at the Port of Falmouth for regular check; from Vigo she was supposed to proceed to Madrid in order to take a train to Paris. Everything seemed quite easy to Mata Hari as she had travelled on the same route before. She was confident and proud of herself as always, and also of the situation she had thought she was in, never apprehending anything wrong. So, onboard *Zeelandia* she had been as usual in her charming self and in a joyful mood as she was too excited to visit Paris once again—it was only a matter of a few more days and she would again be in her cherished city, among her old friends, and hopeful for some new ones as well. Quite normally for her she did not want to recall how she had felt in the war ridden city only a few months back, and had wished to find Paris the way she had always found it before.

---

19   Shipman, *op. cit.*, 194.

THE SCAPEGOAT

Onboard S. S. *Zeelandia* in May 1916
(The Mata Hari Foundation; Fries Museum; Leeuwarden)

Henry Hoedemaker, a Dutchman from Amsterdam, had been co-passenger of Mata Hari on the *Zeelandia*. A salesman by profession (a diamond smuggler in the South American States in peace time[20]) and a self-styled spy hunter that he had been (although his name did not occur in the list of British secret agents working in Holland), Hoedemaker had been quite curious about her from the very beginning of the journey and had searched her cabin in her absence. He told the other passengers that as he had been working for the British counterintelligence service and was responsible for patrolling the Channel to keep watch on potential spies travelling to and from Holland, it was absolutely right for him to enter Mata Hari's cabin in her absence. But if he was merely an over-enthusiast patriot, and not on the British payroll, then how did he know that she had long been a British suspect? So, it might be supposed that even if he had not been on the spy-catcher list,[21] he might have been close to some British officials of the counterintelligence service and might have

---

20 "Has Marga Mac Leod-Zelle (Mata Hari) Been Executed?" www.nationalarchives.gov.uk, KV-2/1.

21 Shipman, *op. cit.*, 195.

learnt about Mata Hari from them. He in fact was often seen with the British officer at Falmouth who checked all passports. However, Mata Hari, in her own typical way, had later analyzed that he had created lot of trouble for her because she had refused to sleep with him in her cabin. Nevertheless, another Dutchman on the ship, Mr. Cleyndert, a rice merchant from Zaandam in Holland, had sympathized with her for the harassment and then took the trouble of informing her about the "dirty" Dutchman Hoedemaker. She had been dumbfounded at first by knowing that someone had the audacity to sneak into her cabin in her absence. She became so infuriated that she had confronted the man personally seeking for an apology. Following his denial her temper and the situation both went out of control too quickly, and as a consequence she had slapped him while on the deck, in full view of many passengers; the blow had been so hard that it caused oozing out of blood from his nose. Mata Hari had felt triumphant after the incident, but Hoedemaker felt vengeful. How could he take such a public humiliation from a debauch woman?

The ocean liner had already crossed Falmouth, and she was not detained by the British officials there. One of her American fellow passengers (a varied version says that he was an Uruguayan consul) knew Hoedemaker personally and had alerted her to beware of him because he was sufficiently dangerous to cause difficulty for her at the immigration office either at the Port of Vigo or in Handaye, the French frontier post where she would be crossing the Spanish border for France. Sure enough, Hoedemaker had chosen the latter office to create trouble for her in order to take his revenge, and consequently French officials at the immigration service in Handaye had told her that she could not enter France. They had further advised her to consult the Dutch consul in San Sebastian to get help in order to cross the border for France. Mata Hari was desperate to reach Paris at any cost and had skillfully used her tricks. She wrote a letter in haste to her old beau Jules Cambon, who had been the Secretary General of the Ministry of Foreign Affairs in France. Then instead of sending it to Cambon she had brandished it before the French officials in Handaye, and quite surprisingly it had worked for her. She was allowed to cross the French border to proceed toward Paris. Mata Hari had been too happy with her triumph, and on June 16 she had proudly checked into the Grand Hotel in Paris. Least did she apprehend that she was truly in deep trouble, and that she had virtually stepped into her death trap. Paris was no more safe for her.

The next segment of her tragic tale had started at this point. Mata Hari had landed in Paris at a time when barely at a distance of 200 miles the Battle of Verdun was in its third phase. It could not have been possible that she knew nothing about the massacre at the battlefields, as all the local newspapers were brimming only with battle stories, although censored to a great extent. But she had been nonchalantly turning away from the grave reality. Even the enormous death toll that had shattered French morale, both at the home and at the war front, did not impact her in any way. She was rather delighted to see an abundance of soldiers in uniform in the streets of Paris like never before. Sitting idly at the window she must have been watching the sight, because for her it certainly implied more choice of men she could have liked to be with. While a delighted Mata Hari had continued with her pleasure projects from her luxurious apartment at the Grand Hotel in Paris, Captain Georges Ladoux, head of the Deuxième Bureau, on the advice of his British counterpart, had appointed two inspectors on June 18, Tarlet and Monier, only 2 days after her arrival in the war ridden city, to keep constant watch on her, obviously without her knowledge. Those two inspectors had been shadowing her to every possible place from morning to late in the night, and it is amazing to know that it took three full days for Mata Hari to realize that she was indeed being tailed. On June 21 she had complained to the hotel staff that she was being followed by two men everywhere, but she had failed to notice that the duo had actually been getting most of the information about her from the hotel itself. They had been painstakingly listing names of each and every visitor she entertained in her room at the Grand, and also in great detail had been noting down the places where she went, who she met for luncheon and dinner, who she talked to on the telephone, etc.

One of the visitors at the Grand Hotel was Second Lieutenant Jean Hallaure of the French cavalry, whom she had known since her first visit to Paris in 1903. The 13 year old horse trainer at the Molier Circus had been transformed into a tall and handsome cavalry lieutenant with remarkable wealth, and therefore Mata Hari was glad to spend some intimate moments with him. At 26, Hallaure had been infatuated with her to the extreme, and had been openly going around with her quite frequently. Nothing seemed unusual to Mata Hari, but her fate had betrayed her on every other situation during the war, and her friendship with Hallaure would only prove it once again. Hallaure was posted at the Deuxième Bureau of the Ministry of War at that time and had been warned by one of his friends (Captain Christian de Mouchy) about the suspected woman he was frequently being seen with.[22] Hallaure had played a significant role in her life (and death thereof) some time later, which might have been due to his jealousy or to his patriotic sentiments. Nevertheless, although there was no dearth of passionate visitors at her hotel room, still she had been waiting for the Marquis de Beaufort to return to Paris on leave from the war front, because it was solely due to his request that she had come to Paris at that time. On July 14 in the evening, he had arrived at the Grand Hotel and had left for the Front on the morning of July 19. Mata Hari had enjoyed his wealth and his company to the fullest in those 5 days; but as soon as he had left Paris she was seen in the company of other men, although not all were men in uniform, one of them being the Parisian liquor baron Antoine Bernard.

However, sometime in July, before the Marquis de Beaufort had arrived on leave in Paris, the 40 year old past-her-prime dignified dancer had by chance met with a young Russian soldier, who was a Captain in the 1st Russian Special Imperial Regiment, posted at Mailly near Reims in the province of Champagne (although according to Ostrovsky, he was an aviator positioned at the newly developed airbase in Contrexéville near Vittel[23]), and was almost 19 years younger to her—born in the same year as of her late son Norman,[24] and hence must have been even younger to him—Vladimir de Massloff (Vadime). He was 21 years of age, but with a slender stature looked even younger. They had first met at the salon of the Grand,[25] the same hotel where he had put up with Nicolas Gasfield, one of his colleagues from the army, during his leave, and soon Mata Hari had realized that she was in love with the blue-eyed young Russian Captain. It was real and intense love from her side, might have been "love at first sight" (she had first seen Vadime in uniform, did she remember that she had first met Rudolf also in uniform?), something that she had never experienced before for any man in her life. Mata Hari, the famous demimondaine and the immensely popular dancer of the European entertainment world, had become Vadime's "Marina" overnight, inspite of the fact that Vadime did not have enough money even to keep her with him, no

---

22 Ibid., 200.
23 Ostrovsky, *op. cit.*, 135.
24 Eva Horn, *op. cit.*, 187.
25 Howe, *op. cit.*, 84. Shipman however has a varied version of this first meeting—at Mme Dangeville's salon probably on July 29, *op. cit.*, 202.

matter whether in luxury or otherwise. Keay wrote: "All her reservations were swept away, all her resolve forgotten ... Suddenly emotion was the most natural thing in the world—all the love she might have given to Rudolf, all the care and devotion she might have lavished on Norman and Jeanne-Louise, all the tenderness and concern that had been denied an outlet for so many years were now Vadime's for the asking."[26] But why did she get romantically involved with a much younger soldier at a supposedly mature age? Was it due to her feeling of insecurity and mid-life crisis as Russell Howe has hinted at?[27] Or was it due to the crisis of a deprived mother? She had been deprived of caring for her children (Rudolf did not trust her with the children), and had been burdened with a feeling of guilt all through her life for not being able to take proper care of them that had resulted in death of her son at a very young age.

But why was Vadime attracted toward her? Although not much is known about the personal life of the young soldier, one might guess that like all others he too had been smitten with the charm of the famous dancer, and the lure of her proximity naturally became irresistible to him. The feeble young man might also have felt comfortable with a robust mother-figure like her. Fate however had played the nemesis once again, and everything was going to change for her very soon. With all the sincerity of passionate love for her Vadime she had wished to be with him forever, and did not want to part even for a while. She wanted to marry him and to get settled with him at some secluded place where none of her admirers could ever be able to trace them. Their first meeting however had been short because Vadime had to report back to his Regiment, but he had returned to Paris probably toward the end of July. Smitten by her charm he had also wanted to be with her. Reuniting with him had been so joyous for Marina that she had quickly made plans to be closer to her lover even while he would have been at the Front. Therefore, on the pretext of taking the spring water for a hydrotherapy cure at the spas in Vittel, on July 31, Mata Hari had applied to the Police Commissariat for permission to visit Vittel on August 7. At the same time she had also applied for a safe-passage for Calais, which might have been as an alternative arrangement in case due to the war situation she needed to return to Holland. She had been refused both the permits, especially the permit for Vittel, as the area was dangerously closer to the war front and came in the war zone.

---

26 Keay, *op. cit.*, 124.
27 Howe, *op. cit.*, 85.

Contrexéville airbase was also very near to Vittel.

Hydrotherapy and thermal cure had been known in France for quite long and was especially sought by the colonials for tropical ailments. There had been quite a number of such spas in France, most popular among them being Vichy, La Bourboule, and Vittel. Vittel is situated in the east of Paris, nearer to Nancy. Although there were many water sources at Vittel, but two main sources had generally been utilized for public use— the Grand Source and the Source Salée. The waters of Vittel had usually been cold and rich in minerals and were beneficial for a variety of diseases[28] like arthritis, kidney ailments, urinary disorders, gallstone, liver ailments, gouts, diabetes, neurasthenia, bronchial catarrh, enlargement of the prostate gland, juvenile epilepsy, etc. What made the waters of Vittel most popular had been the proportion of minerals present in it, which were sufficient for cure, but not excessive. The spa had been a pleasurable destination for the visitors because of the numerous good hotels, restaurants, a nice casino, and also a modern theater that had been built in a beautiful surrounding. With the large number of colonials thronging for cure to Vittel, the place typically became exuberant and quite attractive. It was therefore absolutely normal for Mata Hari to have chosen Vittel for a cure. She could have instead gone to La Bourboule in the south of Paris which did not fall in the war zone. That had also been a quiet and beautiful place for cure as it was situated on the mountains overlooking the Alps of Switzerland. It is not clear though whether she had actually been ill at that time or not, and also whether she had desperately needed the cure or not. I suppose that the following factors might plausibly have caused her decision to go only to Vittel, and not to any other hydro-cure spas—first and foremost, the proximity of Vadime from Vittel; second, the easy accessibility of Vittel (for her it had been a satisfactorily pleasant and luxurious destination for a change) from Paris; third, she had visited Vittel in 1911, and had used the waters for cure, therefore its curative effects and the place both were known to her; last but not the least, she must have been pleased with the treatment of Dr. Pierre Bouloumie (Shipman wrote Dr. Boulommier[29]), who was the superintending physician, medicine consultant, and one of the directors of the Vittel spa. Her intentions to visit Vittel in August 1916 surely did not comprise of spying against France. So, in accordance to her habitual spirit, Mata Hari could

---

28   Edward Lassere, *The Mineral Waters of Vittel*, 5.
29   Shipman, *op. cit.*, 223.

not accept refusal for the permit and had blunderously sought advice from Hallaure in order to get the permission at the earliest. She could not wait because Vadime was supposed to leave shortly for the war front, and she was not ready to bear separation from him even for a moment. Keay wrote: "... for Margarethe it was not just an affair. It was a cataclysm."[30] She was completely lost in love, otherwise she might have read the vengeful eyes of her 26 year old French lover Jean Hallaure.

Hallaure had possibly been waiting for such an opportunity. He certainly did not like Vadime's intimacy with his lady love. Mata Hari treated him dispassionately, which he might have thought had been due to her intimacy with Vadime. While he had repeatedly sought her intimate company waiting for long hours at the hotel, she had curtly turned him down on every occasion. For her he had merely been one among her many admirers, but it was not so for Hallaure. He had felt bitterly cheated by her adventures with his rival Vadime and had apprehended that the cause for her urge to go to Vittel was only Vadime, and nothing else. Jealousy and humiliation had taken him over quite quickly and what else than revenge could have been in his mind? Like a true patriotic Frenchman he had then entrapped her during the war, although not for her German links, but for her intimacy with Vadime and her indifference to him. He had been a young officer, and I would like to speculate that he might have wanted to rise in his army career by helping the Deuxième Bureau nab her as a German spy. Vittel had been situated barely at a distance of 25 miles from the battlefield of Verdun and 5 miles from the Contrexéville French air force base, which was being newly developed during the First World War to launch bombing raids on German arms and ammunition factories, and therefore her desperation to go there in the ploy for cure could definitely raise suspicion against her. Oblivion of all wartime troubles, Mata Hari had continued to be her usual narcissist self. Hallaure had cleverly advised her to visit the Military Bureau for Foreigners to pursue for her permission to go to Vittel. That apparent piece of good and friendly advice did not raise any doubt in Mata Hari's mind inspite of knowing that she was being followed everywhere by two odious men. She moreover had no knowledge about the fact that the Foreign Office was located in the same building in which the Deuxième Bureau was also located—282 Boulevard Saint-Germain—the address that was going to ruin her life. Hallaure must have purposefully informed Captain Ladoux

---

30   Keay, *op. cit.*, 123.

well in advance about the possibility of her visit to the Foreign Office for a travel permit for Vittel.

It was due to her sheer ill fate that Mata Hari had knocked at the wrong door at the right address. When the door opened she had found herself in front of "a fat man with very black beard and very black hair, and spectacles ... He was tall and fat ..."[31] It was Georges Ladoux,[32] head of the Deuxième Bureau of the Army Headquarters. He was a self-styled spy-hunter, who had thought that enemy espionage was the greatest threat to France in the time of the devastating war, and had been determined to nail any such danger to his homeland. He was the man who had received the warning from the British counterespionage service regarding Mata Hari, and being a graduate of the Military Academy of Saint Cyr he had naturally equated debauchery with espionage. Shipman wrote: "Ladoux needed an attention-grabbing case; he wanted to capture a spy as a major victory."[33] So, like he had assigned two inspectors to keep watch on Mata Hari, he also had started intercepting all her mails. Mata Hari did not have the faintest idea that Ladoux had already targeted her, and therefore when she had confronted him by chance on August 1, 1916, she had suspected nothing. Ladoux was quite impressed by her fashionable appearance and had presented himself with all gentility. Mata Hari found that he knew about her application for a permit to visit Vittel and that he was the person who could provide one. Out of sheer stupidity she had requested him to do something to withdraw the surveillance of the two policemen who shadowed her day and night. Ladoux had no intention to appease her. Later in his memoir he wrote that on seeing her he at once knew that she was indeed a German spy.

According to Mata Hari's description of their first meeting, Ladoux had offered her to render him "a great service" by spying for France and had promised to give her the permit on condition that she would not seduce any French officer at Vittel. This beats all reason. How could the head of the French counterintelligence service even think of appointing someone to spy for France when he had already known that she was an enemy spy?

---

31 Shipman, *op. cit.*, 208.
32 Ostrovsky stated: "Ladoux had been one of the visitors to the Villa Rémy before the war and had attended her dance recitals in the garden, along with other dignitaries." *op. cit.*, 138.
33 Shipman, *op. cit.*, 207.

THE SCAPEGOAT

Why did his experienced eyes not see through her novice and immature mind in order to measure whether she would at all be able to do the job he had been assigning her? Moreover, why would he knowingly permit an enemy spy to enter the war zone at Vittel when France was already facing devastation in the Battle of Verdun? Therefore, it is not difficult to assume that Ladoux had been working with a definite motive and according to a definite design. His motive had been his own advantage along with that of his country at the time of national crisis; and he therefore needed a perfect scapegoat to fulfill his binary purpose; and only someone like Mata Hari could have been the appropriate prey. Trapping her could have served a dual purpose for him—first, rise in his military career, and second, as Shipman hinted at: "… Ladoux may have had an even more sinister motive. He may well have been working as a double agent for Germany … so, he needed a scapegoat to divert attention and suspicion from his own activities even more than he needed someone to blame for the French suffering."[34] It is interesting to note that Ladoux in fact had later been arrested by the French counterintelligence service on charges of enemy espionage, although was released due to lack of conclusive proof.

In the mean time, Mata Hari had learnt that her dear Vadime had been wounded in the Battle of Somme from an exploding shrapnel of the German army which had hit his left eye blinding him partially and that poisonous phosgene gas had left his throat and lungs choked. She had also known that he was being treated at the military hospital in Vittel. Vadime could well have been taken to any of the numerous hospitals in Paris which was not very far, as was usually done regarding most of the wounded soldiers at the Front, but fate had again been playing a cruel trick with Mata Hari. The unfortunate news had come as a blow to her, and forgetting everything else she had just wished to be by the side of her beloved Vadime at the time of his great trauma and to take care of him. Vittel could therefore be her only destination, and any delay to reach Vadime due to any reason whatsoever could not be tolerated by her. She was in frenzy to get the permit for Vittel, and had applied both to the Police Commissariat and to the Prefecture of Police with the hope to get it at the earliest from any one source. She had also visited the Foreign Office many times with the same objective. Unfortunately, her paroxysm had set an alarm for the Deuxième Bureau as it was already known to the

---
34   Ibid., 207.

French army that Germany had been trying to find out every detail about the upcoming aerodrome near Vittel. Mata Hari was being suspected for quite long of having allegiance to Germany, and therefore Ladoux had concluded that she must have been using a ploy to reach Vittel with the intention to help the enemy. He had immediately decided to keep an eye on her in case she was permitted to visit Vittel. However, the whole month of August was spent toward that effect by the lovesick naïve woman, but she did not stop seeing other men in the mean time because it had been her source both of joy and of sustenance. She had also met Ladoux many times at his office during that time, and on August 21 had assured him that she would accept his proposal for the task he had offered her, but only after returning from Vittel. She had actually taken 3 weeks to decide on his proposal and had also consulted her longtime friend Henry de Marguerie regarding the matter, who did not discourage her. Could he have been in the know of the French design to entrap her? However, she got the permit on August 29 from the Police Commissariat, a black booklet with the stamp "VALID FOR THE WAR ZONE," and had started for Vittel on the morning of September 1, 1916. Mata Hari was inevitably and secretly being shadowed in Vittel by the same duo Tarlet and Monier. She had chosen to stay at the Grand Hotel there (room 363 had been allotted to her), and on September 3 met Vadime, who came to see her with his left eye covered with a bandage (according to Keay they had met at the military hospital[35]).

Mata Hari's heart had pounded at the sight of the wounded young man, who looked utterly frightened and defeated. Was the mother in her evoked at that instant? Did her dear little Norman's helpless eyes flash in her mind for a moment? She had felt that Vadime needed her care and love even more at that horrible time and had then and there decided that she would never deceive him for any reason. Was it sort of a commitment to compensate Norman's loss? In an intimate romantic moment of their togetherness on that night Vadime had proposed her for marriage and she had agreed immediately. She might have found a justified reason to work for Ladoux because she knew that she would need more money to marry Vadime and to be with him forever as his "Marina." With her dear Vadime she had dreamt of being the "happiest woman on earth." After living a notoriously public life of an extravagant nude dancer and constantly struggling to keep up to her graceful public image, well past her

---

35   Keay, *op. cit.*, 133.

years of youth at the age of 40, Mata Hari might have realized the need to settle down with someone she loved and to lead a peaceful life. None of her lovers could give her so much mental comfort and solace as Vadime did. In Vittel being all the time together for 4 days that Vadime had been on leave they had enjoyed each other's company to the fullest. "It was a wonderful lovers' holiday"[36] wrote Shipman. I would also like to borrow a few words from Keay who wrote: "... joy was more sublime, love more precious and the thought of loneliness made infinitely more unbearable by the threat of imminent separation."[37] Mata Hari was prepared to leave her cherished identity of a "Red Dancer" to become Vadime's "Marina" for the rest of her life, and only wanted enough money so that his parents did not discard their mismatched relationship. But fate had other things in store for her.

Vadime had been under treatment for only 10 days because his wound was not much severe, and after he returned to the Front on September 7 Mata Hari had spent some more days in Vittel in the company of a few rich men, which the police duo had noted down diligently. Then on September 17 (September 13 according to Julia Keay and Russell Howe[38]) she had returned to Paris and had walked straight into her death trap 2 days later—Ladoux's office—the Deuxième Bureau—with the intent of getting the job of serving France finalized in return of good amount of money. Although van der Capellen did unfailingly sent her enough money every month from The Hague, but in the changed situation with the plans to marry Vadime she had considered it insufficient. Further, she must have thought that after the wedding she would retire and would not keep any connection with any of her previous lovers. She wanted to be loyal only to Vadime and none other. She had strongly felt that Mata Hari must die to be reborn as Marina, like Margarethe had done for Mata Hari. She had already accepted some money from Kroemer in Holland, and in order to marry Vadime needed even more. Did she realize the implications of accepting money from Ladoux yet again? Did she think that she could really fool both the French and the Germans through her charm, like she had skillfully done as a dancer for many years, by pretending to do service for their country? Nothing did she know of the British reports and the counterespionage network of the Allied forces in Europe,

---

36 Shipman, *op. cit.*, 218.
37 Keay, *op. cit.*, 133.
38 Ibid., 134; Howe, *op. cit.*, 96.

especially in Holland, with regard to her case, and the subsequent warning about her to the Deuxième Bureau which had been received by none other than Georges Ladoux himself. Therefore, she had also been unaware of the fact that Ladoux already knew that she had accepted money from one German agent to do secret service for his country. Mata Hari, on the basis of her naïve and vacuous reasoning, did not consider it to be wise to reveal that she had taken money from Kroemer presumably due to two reasons—first, she might have thought that if she revealed the fact then Ladoux would pay her less; and second, she had not considered the 20,000 franks given to her by Kroemer as an advance fee for her secret services to Germany, rather for her the amount had been reimbursement for the confiscated valuables in Germany. That was the gravest blunder that she could have made during her wartime ventures in Paris as it had been the first weapon she herself did provide to Ladoux, which he later had utilized against her with utmost skill.

Mata Hari had offered to do the task for Ladoux in return of 1 million francs, not because she thought that amount to be worth for her service to France, but because she might have considered that amount to be sufficient to impress Vadime's father, and to settle down with her beloved after marriage, even after repaying her outstanding debts. She had told Ladoux that if necessary for France she could even become the mistress of the Crown Prince of Germany Friedrich Wilhelm Victor August Ernst (a.k.a. Prince Wilhelm), who had been staying 30 miles north of Verdun at Stenay in occupied France during the war, and under whose commands the 5th Army had started the Verdun offensive. She had believed that she could seduce anyone at any point of time with her characteristic mastery. Her eyes must have sparkled with the prospect of enslaving the carnal desires of the Crown Prince for 1 million francs in the name of service to France. Ladoux was quite surprised to know of her confidence, and to assure him Mata Hari, with great idiocy, had then come up with the name of Kroemer as her acquaintance who she believed could help her in the matter. Ladoux was "giving her sufficient rope to hang herself," and Mata Hari "placed her head right in his noose."[39] Ladoux knew Kroemer very well and his suspicion therefore had instantly turned into certainty—for him she had indeed been a German agent recruited by Kroemer. All of the British warnings appeared to be true to him. It was later revealed that she had been agent H21 of Germany, and learning

---

39 Ibid., 134.

from the British secret service Ladoux had also believed her to be AF44, although without any proof, an agent who had been trained and recruited by Doktor Schragmüller of Antwerp. The French had never cared to collect sufficient proof against her in order to convict her, and it had only been the start of her unending torment. She had been so engrossed with her self-styled plans of a settled future with Vadime and of the enormous amount of money she had believed she could get with much ease that she must naively have thought that because she did not have any deceitful motive against France there should be no question of suspecting her. She had rather been explicit and frank with Ladoux with her plans to serve France, which she had wrongly assumed would please him. Even after all that she had faced since the past couple of months—from visa refusal for England, the incident with Hoedemaker, difficulty to get into France at the border in Handaye, being shadowed in Paris and also in Vittel by two policemen, delay in getting permit to visit Vittel, etc, she had failed to get the alarm and had continued to believe that she could subjugate the whole world by her seductive prowess. For her nothing in the male-dominated world had ever existed outside the purview of her erotic skills.

Ladoux had assigned her to work from Belgium. She had been reluctant to return through Germany (because she did not do anything in return of the 20,000 francs that she had taken from Kroemer, and had reasonably feared trouble), and therefore had requested him to arrange for her hassle-free return via the Channel. She had quite normally been apprehensive after her bitter experience on her last journey through the Channel. Ladoux did finally get an opportunity to tail her in Spain where he had his agents and finally a possibility to entrap her at the British port, and so had readily agreed to her plans. He told her to return to Holland and to await further instructions from him. Significantly, he did not pay even a single centime to her in advance for the work, not even for her travel expenses. Mata Hari should have apprehended danger from Ladoux at least at that point, which she did not. Instead she was all prepared to proceed to Belgium with her silly plans to seduce the Crown Prince, and as usual had required some extravagant clothes to impress him. In an open mail to Ladoux addressed to his office she had requested him for money, not to travel to Holland, but to buy some new fashionable clothes. She did not even care to know how she was supposed to communicate with Ladoux in order to send information to him. She was so eager to get the promised money from him that she had started exploring more scope to impress the French spymaster.

Mata Hari had remembered Monsieur Wurfbain, the Belgian businessman who she knew was close to General Moritz Ferdinand von Bissing, the 72 year old highly acclaimed German officer, who was then in command of occupied Belgium. As she knew Wurfbain for quite long she had thought that he could be her contact in Belgium to get introduced to von Bissing. Mata Hari certainly did not know that von Bissing was the person who had signed the warrant for Miss Edith Cavell's execution only a year before, and foolishly believed that she could use her coquettish means to extract secrets from the General. She had contemplated that to win the Crown Prince would not be difficult at all for her as she had planned to seek help from Kroemer in this regard. The first thing that came in her mind was that to fulfill the important task she would certainly require a wardrobe filled with latest exquisite fashion, and therefore had written again to Ladoux for money. She had naively assumed that everything would happen the way she wanted to, because she believed that she had the skills to impress anyone and get things done accordingly, which would ultimately ensure her 1 million francs from Ladoux. She had then expressed her wish to make a grand coup in one go and had told Ladoux that she would quit after that. Her sole interest being marriage with Vadime, she knew that she could not continue collecting small bits of information for long. When Ladoux had asked her why she wanted to serve France, her reply had been: "I have no other interest except that of becoming able to marry my lover and be independent."[40] Ladoux had promised to pay her handsomely only after she came up with some results and not before that. Mata Hari had agreed because she could not detect his design, had been too confident of herself, and had no reason to distrust her prowess. For Ladoux she had only been a freelance secret agent without a specific mission, without any codename, without even any money, who had not yet proven her loyalty to France.

Desperate to get some money to buy new clothes Mata Hari had rushed to the Deuxième Bureau on September 20, and had confronted Ladoux, who bluntly refused her in the name of his superior Colonel Goubet. She had been worried for money because she did not have much in her account as van der Capellen had not sent her monthly allowance yet. She had also apprehended that if he knew about her latest adventure he might even stop sending money to her or might even disown her. Ladoux then wanted to test her nerves and looking straight into her eyes had told her

---

40   Shipman, *op. cit.*, 230.

that one French person with the codename AF44 would contact her in The Hague and would give her further intimation. Mata Hari had been nonchalant. She did not know of any AF44 before, but Ladoux did not stop pressing her. He had asked her whether she recognized the number, which was given to her at Antwerp by Fräulein Doktor, the chief trainer of the German spy training school. She had retaliated at the dirty trick and had flatly threatened Ladoux that if he continued with such deplorable suggestions with her then she would not do anything either for him or for his country. She must have started believing that she was indispensible for France during the war and that she had been doing great favor by providing her expert service to the country. After all it was Ladoux who had approached her, not she. Did Mata Hari realize what the prerequisites for being a secret agent could have been? She had been too stupid, too public, too egoist to have become one. It was only due to the lure of 1 million francs that she had agreed to collect secret information for Ladoux, which, according to her understanding, had been equated merely with seducing some influential people of the enemy camp in order to extract secrets through pillow talks. Ladoux must also have known her very well, then why did he try to appoint her as a secret agent for France? His intentions must certainly be questioned. In order to impress her spymaster Mata Hari however had offered to renew her relationship with the Duke of Cumberland and to mold his allegiance toward the Allied forces. The Duke was an old man with whom Mata Hari surely did not have any relation. He had become the "Traitor Duke of England" by becoming a Major in the German army and by taking up arms against the British Empire. Therefore, she must have meant his son Prince Ernest Augustus of Cumberland (Duke of Brunswick) who had married Princess Victoria Louise, the only daughter of the German Kaiser Wilhelm II, and became a Major-General in the German army during the First World War. It is immaterial whether she could actually mold the Duke in favor of the British Empire or not, the most significant thing to be noted here is boasting of her own flirtatious talent with utter stupidity.

Ladoux had evaded her repeated request to grant her money in advance for the job. Being sure that he would not give her anything before she proved her worth to him, Mata Hari had to fall back on van der Capellen, her only source of sustenance at that point in time. She also had to settle some financial debts in Paris before she was to leave for Holland, and therefore, in mid-October, had impatiently written to her maid Anna

Lintjens in The Hague to request the Baron on her behalf to send her 6,000 francs without delay. Although the money had already been sent to her by her lover, might have been due to wartime difficulties it had reached the Comptoir National d'Escompte de Paris not earlier than November 4, 1916. Relieved of the financial anguish she however wanted to inform the Dutch Legation in Paris about her return to Holland. Although Ladoux did not have any objection to her proposal, he had strangely concluded that she was indeed an enemy spy. Waagenaar wrote: "Ladoux ... 'was now convinced' of her being a spy, although one wonders why. Did the fact that Mata Hari wanted to inform the Legation of her own country about her return to Holland prove that she was a spy? For some mysterious reason Ladoux thought so. It would seem that to the Chief of the French Intelligence Service any move by Mata Hari proved that she was a German spy."[41] This could have been possible only if it had been predesigned. Ladoux however in the meantime had sent Mata Hari to Henri Maunoury, the French War Police at the Prefecture of Police, who had been responsible for law enforcement in the city of Paris, from where she could procure a visa for Holland via Spain. He moreover had given her the names of six secret agents who had been working in Belgium at that time for France and the Allied forces. Ladoux in fact had instructed her to carry some messages for them. Waagenaar wrote: "Five of them were double agents, spying for both France and Germany, and therefore known to the enemy. The sixth was spying for France only ..."[42]

In the evening of November 5 Mata Hari had left for Madrid as usual with full enthusiasm for embarking on something novel, not knowing that it was going to be the fateful last journey of her life. She had reached Vigo on November 9 from where she had boarded the Dutch ocean-liner S. S. *Hollandia* to reach Holland through the Port of Falmouth. The ship had reached the English port on November 13 where the British counterintelligence service and the Scotland Yard had jointly been scheduled to check every passing ship of any country as a wartime rule. Bernard Newman wrote: "In those days the British Navy was the mistress of the seas, and no one might travel in wartime save by its permission."[43] So, all the passengers of *Hollandia* had been examined in a routine manner by the Scotland Yard officials, but for Mata Hari the trouble had just begun.

---

41 Waagenaar, *op. cit.*, 1965, 150.
42 Ibid., 148.
43 Newman, *op. cit.*, 62.

She was searched thoroughly, and then had been questioned in detail by George Reid Grant and his wife Janet Grant, who were special officers of MI5/E branch. They had mistaken her with one Clara Benedix, a German spy from Hamburg, who had been a trainee at Antwerp under Fräulein Doktor, for whom the British authorities (MI5 and the Department of Interior Defense) had circulated a notice in May 1916, tagged with her photograph, to arrest her if she arrived in Britain and to be brought to the Scotland Yard. Nevertheless, in all probabilities it might not have been a mistake on the part of the British secret service, because Mr. Albert Frederick Calvert, a distinguished British author, traveler, mining engineer, and scientist, had spotted Mata Hari in Madrid at the Ritz Hotel, and subsequently had informed officers at the British port about the plans of her journey to Holland via England. He had suspected her of espionage and therefore wanted to warn the British authorities about her prior to her journey.[44] So, when the passengers of *Hollandia* were being searched at Port Falmouth by the British officials, Mata Hari had been targeted.

Mr. Grant however had shown the photograph of Clara Benedix to Mata Hari claiming their identity,[45] which she had refused for obvious reasons. She wondered how she could suddenly become Clara Benedix. Miss Benedix had been living in Spain during that time as a flamenco dancer, and MI5 had definite information that she was travelling on the same ship with a fake passport. In the photograph Benedix was seen in a Spanish dress with a white mantilla covering her head and a fan in her right hand. The mantilla, which covered women's head decoratively, had been part of the Spanish women's traditional costume, and as Mata Hari had been in Spain quite many times, some of her photographs show her

---

44 Albert F. Calvert, Letter to the editor, "Women Spies," *Daily Mail*; July 30, 1917. The National Archive; Reference KV-2/1; www.nationalarchive.gov.uk

45 This might apparently seem to be quite surprising, but actually it is not, because I have noticed similar cases of misidentification by the people involved in her examination at Falmouth. The book *Queer People*, for example, written by Basil Thomson contains an image between pages 184 and 185, which shows a woman in an Indian dancing costume holding a snake in her hands that is coiled around her waist. Basil Thomson has identified the photograph as that of Mata Hari's, which is a glaring misrepresentation. The lady in the said picture does not even look like Mata Hari from any angle. *The Evening News* had published that image on 31.07.1917, (UK government National Archive, Reference KV-2/1) with the caption "MARGUERITE ZELLE," from which the mistake might have originated. This could explain the inaccuracy of identification regarding Mata Hari at the Falmouth port. Shipman also wrote about some inaccuracies in Thomson's reports about Mata Hari, *op. cit.*, 237.

in a black mantilla, but she did not resemble the lady in the photograph in any way. Some of the Dutch passengers onboard who knew Mata Hari personally had tried to clarify the confusion with Mr. Grant, but of no avail. Even the Captain of the ship had tried to aver for her, but nothing helped. It has been indicated by Wheelwright: "Grant's confusion probably stemmed from MI5's list of suspects."[46] The detail in the list had consisted at least of two mistakes—her height was noted wrongly as 5ft 5 in, while she had actually been gifted with five inches more; and her spoken languages wrongly included English and Italian besides French, Dutch, and German,[47] but she actually did not speak either English or Italian (although there are varied opinions regarding the languages she actually spoke). Miss Benedix fitted perfectly into the wrongly documented description of Mata Hari in the MI5 list, and therefore Mr. Grant would not be dissuaded by any means. She had then been frisked, strip searched by Janet, and although nothing incriminating was found on her, she was apprehended by them, disembarked at Port Falmouth and escorted to London along with her large number of luggage with which she always travelled.[48] Brief description of her belongings, while she had been detained at Cannon Row, is being given here[49]—(1) one small wooden box containing a gilt clock; (2) hat box containing hats, hat-pins, etc; (3) trunk containing boots, shoes, furs, chemises, gloves, umbrella, blouses, dirty linen, hair ornament, etc; (4) boot box containing various kinds of shoes, etc; (5) trunk containing corsets, veil, bodices, petticoats, jackets, towels, blouses, dresses, etc; (6) trunk containing a mirror, combs, coats, ornaments, shoes, visiting card in the name of Vadime de Massloff, dresses, gloves, etc; (7) wooden box containing China tea service; (8) gladstone bag containing jewelry, boxes of cigarettes, night dresses, bodices, gloves, handkerchiefs, cash box, currency notes of various European countries, keys, etc; (9) one travelling rug; and (10) one fitted lady's dressing bag. In addition to the list mentioned above her belongings included two letters, a French identity book, French passport, and annex to the French passport book, one Dutch passport, and one French agreement. However, what

---

46   Wheelwright, *op. cit.*, 55.
47   British Intelligence File; Ref. W.O. 1,101; Secret 140, 193/M.I.5.E; December 15, 1916; The National Archive; Refrence KV-2/1; www.nationalarchives.gov.uk
48   Shipman gave the list of her belongings as enlisted by MI5 after her arrest at Falmouth, *op. cit.*, 244–245.
49   The complete list is to be found in The National Archive; Reference KV-2/1; www.nationalarchives.gov.uk.

transpires from contains of the luggage is her taste for elegance and class.

Mr. Grant however had sent a note to London saying "... It is believed that she is the woman 'Clara Benedix', a German agent ..."[50] While sending an official note about his "belief" Grant did not once reflect on what could be the effect of his "belief" on Mata Hari if she had truly been innocent. If it had merely been his "belief," then he could have checked the authenticity of her passport with the Dutch Foreign Office in London before arresting her, which he did not do. He could also have gone through the British documents of December 1915, when she had been searched and interrogated at Folkestone while travelling to Paris. Even her French identity book and the passports that she had on her person while travelling could prove that she was not Clara Benedix, but Grant preferred to follow his belief. Why? The *Daily Mail* had reported on 31.07.1917 ("Condemned Woman Spy"), that she had actually been arrested under DORA (Defense of the Realm Act)[51] which had been passed in August 1914, right after the war had started, and had specifically targeted single women travelling alone.[52] The 1914 Alien Restriction Act (ARA) had the provision to target and arrest undesirable people who were not British by birth. The OSA (Official Secrets Act) of 1911 also dealt sternly with espionage in Section I, which clearly stated "purpose prejudicial to the safety or interests of the State." Proctor wrote: "The 1911 Act made it easier to prosecute those accused of espionage by assuming a subject was guilty unless proven innocent."[53] So, it might well be presumed that the British secret service merely needed a ploy to arrest Mata Hari. One might wonder whether Grant had also been working as a part of the whole plan. Mata Hari had obviously panicked at the turn of the events. The Grants had escorted her first to the Scotland Yard in London, and then had handed her over to the Chief Inspector Edward Parker. Basil Thomson at that time had been the head of the Special Branch of the Scotland Yard. A barrister by profession he had also been a distinguished officer with an illustrious career in various departments of the British government and at that moment was in-charge of interrogating captured spies. Mata Hari had been taken to the Criminal Investigation Department in London (November 14) for interrogation, so she was supposed to face Thomson.

---

50   Shipman, *op. cit.*, 237.
51   The National Archive; KV-2/1; www.nationalarchives.gov.uk
52   Tammy M. Proctor, *op. cit.*, 34.
53   Ibid., 32.

ONE LITTLE ORCHID

Photograph of the dancer Basil Thomson (and correspondent of *The Evening News* of July 31, 1917) had mistakenly identified as Mata Hari's in his book.
(Alamy Images India)

The 55 year old experienced colonial ex-civil servant had evidently been impressed by Mata Hari's appearance. During her interrogation she admitted that she had met Clara Benedix while travelling from Madrid to Lisbon early that year and had also dined together at a restaurant, but nothing more did she know of her. She had repeatedly denied that she was Clara Benedix. Later Thomson wrote about his experience with her: "... a severely practical person who was prepared to answer any question with a kind of reserved courtesy, who felt so sure of herself and of her innocence that all that remained in her was a desire to help her interrogators."[54] Although Thomson had found no evidence against her at any point, still he was convinced that she was a German secret agent. This certainly quells all reason. Why? Why had all the people been hell bent against her to stamp her as an enemy spy even without a single proof?

---

54   Basil Thomson, *Queer People*, 182.

The well-known historian Phillip Knightley aptly said: "... not because she was a dangerous spy, but because ... what she was."[55] I suppose and have already noted before that Tinsley's report of February 1916, against her regarding her accepting money from a German official had been the telling reason. However, during her interrogation Mata Hari had confessed to Thomson that she was indeed a spy, not of Germany, but of France. He quoted her in his book as saying: "I am a spy, but not, as you think, for the Germans, but for one of your allies—the French."[56] She had then revealed all that had happened between Ladoux and herself during the past months. Thomson had been quite astonished to know it from her, because he knew that the British secret service had already warned France about the lady. He failed to understand how, inspite of the warning, the head of the French counterintelligence could employ her to spy for them.

Thomson had interrogated her for 2 days. Captain William Reginald Hall, the director of Naval Intelligence, and his assistant Lord Baron ("Dick") Herschell, head of the diplomatic section of Room 40 who ran an agent network in Spain, had also been present through the sessions. Thomson had asked her every possible question related to her life spanning from her childhood until very recent happenings, and Mata Hari surprisingly had told mostly the truth. She had been interrogated for the most part by the assistant chief constable in the presence of the three stalwarts, and his questions had been focused mainly on two issues—first, her identity, and second, the 20,000 francs that she had received in The Hague through the Londres Bank. He had made a hint that because the Londres Bank was the bank of the German embassy, she had actually received money from them. Mata Hari had never accepted the allegations. To defend herself she had then given the names and addresses of 12 people who she had believed could help her in some way to get out of the mess and could depose in her favor. The list had comprised of the following people—(i) her Dutch lover Baron van der Capellen, (ii) Mr. D. van Houten of The Hague, (iii) Messrs Hymans Brothers (Barristers) in The Hague, (iv) Dr. Evart van Dieren, the social-critique and amateur philosopher in Amsterdam, (v) Mr. Albert Keyzer, the Belgian correspondent for the *Daily Mail* and

---

55 Phillip Knightley, *The Second Oldest Profession*, 49.
56 Thomson, *op. cit.*, 183. Her confession about being a French spy had however been distorted by Bouchardon to report (22.05.1917) that she had admitted to being a German spy, although in November 1917, after her execution, Lieutenant Colonel Hercules Pakenham had accessed her MI5 files and had found that she never made a true confession about her involvement in German espionage; Andrew, *op. cit.*, 80.

the "*Era*" in London, (vi) Henri Edmond Rudeaux, the renowned French artist and painter, (vii) the Marquis de Beaufort, her Belgian lover, (viii) Émile Guimet, Director of the Guimet Museum in Paris, (ix) Monsieur Maunoury, the Police Chief in Paris, (x) Georges Ladoux of the French counterintelligence service, (xi) Count van Limburg-Stirum, Dutch Legation in Paris, and (xii) Mr. Otto David Eduard Bunge, Consul de Holland in Paris.[57] To prove her identity she had even made a reference, although indignantly, to her biography written by her father.

However, the interrogators had eventually realized that they had indeed mistaken her to be the German spy in question. In his memoirs Thomson wrote: "... she had no intention of landing on British soil or of committing any act of espionage in British jurisdiction, and with nothing to support our view we could not very well detain her in England ..."[58] Mata Hari was then allowed to return to Spain, but was not allowed to proceed to Holland, where she had originally been headed to. Thomson did not forget to give her a fatherly advice before releasing her—"give up what you are doing." Mata Hari must have decided not to heed his warning, because enticement of the 1 million francs had been much stronger for her. Ladoux had nevertheless played a diabolical trick with her. When he was communicated by Thomson to verify Mata Hari's version, he became enraged by her stupidity. He had taken it as a humiliation, because he might have thought that she had deliberately put him in an awkward position in front of the British allies by telling them that he in fact had assigned her with the task of spying against Germany. He denied all that she had told Thomson, and although it was by his order that Mata Hari had started for Holland, he actually had advised Thomson to send her back to Madrid by writing—"Understand nothing. Send Mata Hari back to Spain." Ladoux could have had at least two reasons to advise Thomson to send her back to Spain. Howe wrote: "... at this point he didn't want her in Holland, where she might well complain to her government and to the press, thus embarrassing his much-higher-ranking British counterpart Thomson ...;"[59] and second, he had already laid the trap in Madrid for the naïve dancer. Her name was Marthe (Betenfeld) Richer (a.k.a. 'The Lark'), a double agent working both for France and Germany (German secret service code number S32), who had been appointed by Ladoux himself and

---

57 The National Archive; Reference KV-2/1; www.nationalarchives.gov.uk
58 Thomson, *op. cit.*, 183.
59 Howe, *op. cit.*, 113.

THE SCAPEGOAT

was on the French payroll. Marthe was sufficiently intelligent and had been gifted with all that was needed to succeed as a spy. She had been the first French female aviator, who had lost her husband Henri Richer in the war early that year, and had pledged to destroy the enemy. Therefore, like her husband, she had also joined the French secret service to serve her country and had proved herself as a supremely efficient French spy during the First World War.

Mata Hari had naively thought that the mix-up was certainly an accident. She could never see through the design of her trap, and that is exactly what had given advantage to Ladoux. After her release from the Scotland Yard on November 28 she had stayed for a couple of more days in London (at the Savoy Hotel, in room no. 261), and in the mean time, with the object to return to Holland, had applied for a Dutch visa. She had tried in vain as she was denied by Basil Thomson, and had been allowed to proceed only to Spain. Although she could not accept the situation, she did not raise any objection either. She might have by then started to realize that she could not have her way always. On December 1 Mata Hari had left London to board S. S. *Arguaya* on her return journey to Vigo to reach Madrid. Her fate had always played the nemesis, and it had not been an exception at that time either. Even before she could reach Madrid a letter from the Dutch Minister of Foreign Affairs in The Hague had reached the Dutch envoy there warning him about her arrival in the capital. Wherever she went she had invariably carried the burden of stigma that was being attached to her name by those who had worked out the design. Mata Hari had put up at the Hotel Continental in Vigo on December 6 and soon had started to renew old acquaintances in the city. She could never sit idle, out from public attention, and had always wanted to be in the limelight. So, not knowing anything about the warning against her, she had gone to see the Frenchman Mr. Martial Cazeaux, who had been secretary to the Dutch consul in Vigo, and after exchanging general greetings she had told him every bit that she had to go through in the past couple of days, including meeting a Belgian couple by the name of Allard onboard *Hollandia,* whom she had found to be quite intriguing, because while she knew that the husband worked as a secret agent for England, the wife spied for Germany. She had also said that the Captain of the ship had told her about them.[60] Mata Hari did not even care to realize that

---

[60] Waagenaar wrote that this incident had actually occurred after Mata Hari had returned to Vigo from London, *op. cit.*, 1965, 148; Shipman also subscribed to his

ONE LITTLE ORCHID

Cazeaux was a Frenchman, and could use the information against her at any point of time in his own interest. She seemed to have had blind trust for all those she considered to be her friend.

Curiously Cazeaux, on that day, had offered her to spy for Russia during the war. Had he truly been serious about the proposal? Or was he merely testing her integrity and loyalty toward his own homeland France? It is quite normal to ponder what had been so special about her that within a span of only 5 months she had been asked to spy for Germany (Kroemer), for France (Ladoux), and also for Russia (Cazeaux), while in fact she was not even suited for the job. However, by revealing the name of Allard to Cazeaux, the last nail had been drilled into her coffin, which she was obviously ignorant of. Mata Hari had chosen to be noncommittal to Cazeaux and had left for Madrid on December 11. In Madrid she had put up at the Ritz Hotel. She was absolutely perplexed at that point. Everything had become topsy-turvy because it had been completely contrary to the planning that she was supposed to execute as per the orders of Ladoux. She certainly knew nothing about his reply to Thomson and his original plan to entrap her either at Falmouth or in Madrid. She had simply been looking forward to the 1 million francs that she believed Ladoux would give her if she could prove her worth as a spy; only which she had thought could ensure a dream life with her beloved Vadime. She was not ready to lose either Vadime or the money, and not being able to reach Holland as planned therefore had worried her extremely, because only Holland, and then Belgium, could have been the perfect starting point for her new adventure. She had desperately tried to contact Ladoux from Madrid, but could not. He did not reply to any of her messages, which perfectly suited his program against her. He had just been waiting for her to commit some mistake in distraught. Shipman wrote: "Ladoux was no longer her protector or employer, but instead her worst enemy and the last person she should have asked for advice."[61] If only Mata Hari could realize that!

Her life no doubt had been full of mistakes, but from this point onward she had been committing only blunders. Mata Hari had never been

---

view, *op. cit.*, 248; while Keay wrote it had happened en route to Holland, before she was arrested at Falmouth, *op. cit.*, 141; Julie Wheelwright endorsed her view, *op. cit.*, 59; Howe however wrote that Mata Hari had met the couple on *Arguaya* on her way back to Vigo, *op. cit.*, 114.

61 Shipman, *op. cit.*, 250.

politically aware; her first priority being both pleasure and opulence, she had never even thought about political intricacies and repercussions. She did surely read newspapers whenever she could, but her focus had always been advertisements of the latest fashion houses, of the latest cosmetic products, and of course stage. So, it is quite understandable that she would fail miserably in the new game that she had plunged into for money. In Madrid she had waited in vain for Ladoux's instructions, and then had thought of doing something on her own to prove her worth, thereby to please Ladoux. The time frame is particularly noteworthy to get a glimpse of her mindset—she had stayed in Vigo from December 6, reached Madrid on December 11, and wrote to Kalle the following day. She might have foolishly expected to get a prompt reply from Ladoux, failing which she had become so impatient that she ridiculously took the ball straight into her own court. At the Ritz Hotel she looked into the pages of the German diplomatic list to find names of some high-ranking German personnel to start her adventure with, and had stumbled on the name of Captain Arnold Kalle, the German military attaché in Madrid, who had chiefly been responsible for gathering intelligence for his country in neutral Spain. His position in the army had attracted her, and therefore she had decided to start with him although she did not know that Kalle had been promoted to the rank of Major by that time. On December 12 she had written to him asking for an appointment on the pretext of seeking an explanation about her arrest at Falmouth as Clara Benedix, which was promptly settled for the following afternoon at his residence.[62] Kalle was sure that Mata Hari could not have been from the enemy circle, because she had addressed the letter to him not as "Major" but as "Captain," which he had not been adding as a prefix to his name for the past 10 months. An enemy spy should have certainly known his proper designation, he had rightly thought. Mata Hari had been quite happy with his reply, but what was she going to do with him at the meeting? She was to simply impress him, something she had been exceptionally good at, and then she might have thought that she would try to get some German secrets from him by using her seductive prowess. All seemed to be very easy for her, but she was not at all clear about how much intelligence would get her the 1 million promised francs from Ladoux.

---

62 Shipman wrote that the first meeting between them took place on December 23, 1916; *op. cit.*, 252. I find this hard to believe, as that date would fail to explain the reason for Kalle's first message to Berlin about her on December 13, the very day they had met for the first time.

However, even at the age of 40 she could triumph over the German military attaché on the very first meeting and succeeded to extract some information about dropping of German and Turkish officers in the coastal French zone of Morocco. During a casual discussion Kalle had revealed to her that Germany had the key to the French cipher and could read all radio traffic sent by them. (It is really intriguing as to why a senior German officer did disclose some of the war secrets to a lady he had met for the first time). Regarding the issue of her arrest at Falmouth Kalle had assured her that he would get the facts clarified from the chief of German counterespionage Baron (Misrachi) von Rolland, who was based in Barcelona. She too had shared her views with Kalle about—(i) French resentment of British direction of the war; (ii) mounting opposition to the Aristide Briand government due to the circumstances of the Verdun offensive; (iii) how the Greek princess Marie Bonaparte had been using that sentiment and her proximity to Briand for her selfish purposes to make her husband Prince George the king of Greece, although he was not the bona fide successor to the throne; and (iv) the Allies' plan to launch a spring offensive against Germany (had she been talking about the Nivelle Offensive?). How stupid could Mata Hari indeed have been to leak French intelligence to Kalle in return of a bit of unconfirmed German secret? To top it, after returning from her adventures with Kalle, she had written on that night to Ladoux through a public mail about the whole story of her triumph over the German military official and the secret information she had collected from him, and did not forget to mention that Germany had deciphered the French radio code, and had also mentioned the name of von Rolland as the German counterespionage chief in Barcelona during the war. What she did not reveal in that letter was her fees of 3,500 francs that she had received to entertain Kalle.

Sadly as always, she did not know that Kalle, in the mean time, had already checked her antecedents with the German intelligence in Holland, and after meeting her for the first time on December 13 in his study he was convinced that she had been sent to him by the French. He also came to know that she had taken 20,000 francs from Kroemer more than a year ago, but did nothing for Germany in the mean time, and therefore her pretence became evident to him. Kalle was certain that Mata Hari had betrayed Germany. Keay wrote: "... she had double-crossed the German intelligence service, and he was not prepared to let her get away with it."[63]

---

63 Keay, *op. cit.*, 156.

He might moreover have wanted to avenge killings of the 11 German spies at the Tower of London from 1914 to 1916.⁶⁴ Kalle however did not want the French to take any political mileage from her detention by the German army, and therefore had set up the trap for her in such a way that the French would certainly arrest her. The Madrid–Berlin traffic sent by him stands proof to that. There could have been other reasons also for Germany to entrap Mata Hari. Interestingly, in one contemporary newspaper I have found two more grounds for Germany to act against her— "(1) that the German espionage chief at Amsterdam, who had an affair with her, was enraged at her treachery to him and wished to betray her; or (2) that the German government, alarmed at the seductions she was exercising over their own officers, decided to betray her to the French."⁶⁵

This image was published in the Dutch monthly magazine *De Kroniek* in June, 1916; taken from the published documents of the UK government (KV-2/1)

Ladoux had however been immediately informed about Mata Hari's adventures with Kalle by his agents in Madrid, plausibly by Marthe Richer,⁶⁶

---

64   *British Military and Criminal History: 1900 to 1999*; http://www.stephen-stratford.co.uk; "Spying, The Tower of London."

65   "Wickedest, Most Dangerous – War Spy of All," *The Pittsburgh Press*; 25 December, 1921, 67.

66   Waagenaar however wrote that Marthe did not know about the liaison between Mata Hari and Kalle even until April 1917, and had only learnt about it from the

who had been staying at the same Ritz Hotel in which Mata Hari had put up, and was the mistress of the German naval attaché Hans von Krohn. Significantly, von Krohn had shared a considerable amount of German secrets with his lady love whom he had never suspected to be a French spy. It might be a matter of speculation that whether it had been due to von Krohn's blind love for Marthe or due to her superb espionage skills. However, Ladoux did not delay for a moment to order interception of all the traffics passing through the Eiffel Tower between Madrid and Berlin, because he knew that Kalle would surely communicate with the German counterespionage chief Major Walter Nicolai of Section III B in Berlin regarding Mata Hari. Moreover, he must have quickly thought that it was the appropriate time for him to finalize the design in order to implicate her directly and conclusively as a German spy. As radio transmission came into use shortly prior to the First World War, all the countries involved in the war used coded messages to communicate state secrets. Combatants had continually devised secretive ciphers to communicate in an undetected way, while the opponents untiringly made efforts to crack them down.

Ever since the war had broken out occurrence of certain incidents at the sea had become exceedingly significant for the signals intelligence of the combatant camps. On August 5, 1914, the day war broke out, the British cable-ship C. S. *Telconia*[67] had dragged up Germany's transatlantic telegraph cables that had been spread through the English Channel and had destroyed all of them (five in total) by cutting them apart. It had rendered the Germans vulnerable to interception as they were then compelled to use their adversary's signaling system for their own war effort. Recovery of three German codebooks toward the start of the war had enabled the Allied forces to gain advantage over the enemy. In the beginning of September, the Russians had fished out the body of a German signals under-officer who had drowned on August 26 along with 14 other crew members in the wreckage of the German light cruiser S. M. S. *Magdeburg* of the Imperial Navy. It had been deployed to the Baltic as a warship to bombard on the Russian war fleets.[68] The German soldier had been carrying three secret codebooks which he could not

---

newspapers in Paris; *op. cit.*, 1965, 170–171.
67   Barbara W. Tuchman, *The Zimmerman Telegram*, 10; although modern scholars differ with her in this respect.
68   Robert M. Grant, *U-Boat Hunters*, 34.

destroy before the ship had wrecked in the firing by the Russian boats. All the three books had been recovered by the Russians on his body and in other parts of the wreckage. Toward the end of October those books were handed over to their British counterpart in London. It had been the most crucial recovery of the basic German Naval Codebook known as the *Signakbuch der Kaiserlichen Marine* or the SKM Codebook. The second recovery had been made on August 11 by Captain John T. Richardson of the Royal Australian Navy, with the capture of the German Line Ship *Hobart* at Port Philip Heads in Australia. It was the most vital HVB (*Handelschiffsverkehrsbuch*) Codebook. Recovery of the third VB (*Verkehrsbuch*) Codebook was made on October 17 from the wreckage of the German torpedo boat SMS *S119*, at the Battle off the Dutch Island of Texel. Armed with the three codebooks the Allied forces could successfully find the key to all German ciphers used at least in the preliminary stage of the First World War. The British Intelligence Division 25 (ID25, a.k.a. Room 40) and the French Cipher Bureau both had been extremely efficient in the task of deciphering coded German messages, and therefore the Germans had evidently been at the back foot from the very start.

Ladoux had been fully prepared to pounce on his unsuspecting prey by all means. Mata Hari had become too precious for him and he could not let her away. He had recalled how doctored evidence had been manipulated to implicate Alfred Dreyfus barely a couple of decades before. So, if necessary, he must have thought, he could follow the precedence. By anyhow arresting her Ladoux wanted to achieve the well-calculated results, and therefore did not care for the means. Spy hunting had been a familiar phenomenon both in the Triple Entente and in the Triple Alliance; and therefore, one more hunt would not have made any significant difference except for the mileage Ladoux wanted to reap out of that. In the mean time, probably on the evening of December 17, Mata Hari had met Colonel Joseph Denvignes in the lounge of Ritz Hotel through a common friend Mr. G. de Wirth (or de Witt). Although at that time Denvignes had been an aging French military attaché and in-charge of French intelligence in Madrid, but still her magic worked on him, and in an instant he became infatuated with the iconic diva. She had then revealed unto him her experience at Falmouth, her meeting with Kalle, and whatever information she could extract from him. He had advised her to get back to the German attaché as soon as possible in order to get more precise information about German plans of the Morocco landings, because presumably he might have wanted to let his superiors know that he had been instrumental in achieving such important information for France. Kalle had 19 years of experience in German military service and had been the intelligence expert in Madrid for quite some time. Therefore, although he had been intimate with Mata Hari at the first meeting, he was in no way overwhelmed by her repeated presence in his house. He had rather been somewhat sure about her intentions for her frequent visits to him and obviously had started sending messages to Berlin about her. The first message from Madrid to Berlin sent by Kalle about Mata Hari had been dated December 13, while the last was sent bearing the date December 28, 1916. Those 15 days and a couple of radio traffics between Madrid and Berlin had been extremely crucial to seal her fate.

Nevertheless, Denvignes was to return to Paris in a short time along with the visiting French War Minister General Louis Hubert G. Lyautey and must have wanted to spend some more time with his lady love in Madrid; so he had frequented the Ritz in order to join her everyday at lunch and at dinner. He had been emphatically expressing his love for the dancer and had requested her to stay with him after he returned from Paris. Before leaving he had even taken a violet from her dress along with her handkerchief as souvenirs. Mata Hari had handled such over enthusiast lovers for quite long and therefore did not distract herself. Her sole focus being the 1 million francs she had requested him to explain her achievements to Ladoux while they met in Paris, and also told him about her plan to be in Paris early in January 1917. Denvignes had been delighted by the possibility of being with her in Paris and had passionately told her to look for him at the Grand Hotel d'Orsay after she reached the city of joy. Therefore, it is evident that he had planned to stay in Paris toward the start of the year. In a cold December night during the Christmas they had parted after warm and intimate exchanges. Bearing some information from the Germans and without any reply from Ladoux, Mata Hari must have thought that she needed to rush to him in Paris in order to prove her worth as a spy, to claim an explanation from him for his silence, and to get some amount of the promised money which she had been in dire need of at that moment. She had not received any money from van der Capellen for quite long and even Ladoux did not send her a single centime for her "invaluable" services to France. She had been compelled to survive barely on the money that Kalle had given her. Insufficiency of money was sufficient to infuriate her, and so she had been. Toward the end of December Mata Hari had received a letter from Senator Emilio Junoy, who had been her lover once and had still been her well-wisher. He had specifically warned her saying that one French secret agent had visited him in recent time and had told him that she was considered "to be hostile to the Allies." But, instead of warning Mata Hari his letter had simply outraged her. She had gone all out for an explanation from Junoy. He had been astounded by her reaction and hopelessly anticipated more trouble for her. However, on January 2, 1917, she had arrived in Paris, sadly for the last time. It had been too cold in Paris in early January that year. All of France was covered in a vast sheet of ice, and life in Paris had almost come to a standstill. Moreover, there had been severe dearth of coal and other home fuels due to the war. So she had cleverly decided not to stay in the house that she had rented for Vadime and herself, and hoping to get money both from her Dutch lover and Ladoux she had happily settled at the newly built magnificent Hotel Plaza Athénée on Avenue Montaigne.

Mata Hari must have thought that "The information she had gleaned in Madrid would surely guarantee her the warmest of welcomes and the heartiest of congratulations from Ladoux; why, the whole of France would owe her a great debt of gratitude for her achievement"[69] wrote Keay. But her "mission Ladoux" did not work as he had refused to meet her right at that time, but he did two things immediately—one, he had appointed the duo Tarlet and Monier[70] to keep constant watch on her right from the day of her arrival in Paris, and two, had informed about her arrival to Captain Pierre Bouchardon, the 46 year old chief investigating officer of the military tribunal (Third Council of War) to whom he reported. Ladoux was ready by all means to wind up his net around her as there was pressure "from the President's palace to catch more spies."[71] At the hotel she was handed a note from Ladoux asking her to stay in Paris, and committing to contact her within 7 days. With her characteristic naivety she had thought that he might have been preoccupied with the war effort and still had hoped to get her dues in near future, not having the faintest idea about what had been happening behind her in Madrid and also in Paris. It was related to the radio traffic between Madrid and Berlin with

---

69   Keay, *op. cit.*, 162.
70   According to Howe the two inspectors appointed by Ladoux were not Tarlet and Monier, *op. cit.*, 129.
71   Ibid., 144.

regard to her that had been intercepted toward the end of 1916 and early 1917 (from December 13, 1916, to January 5, 1917, to be specific), by the French counterintelligence at the Eiffel Tower. A total of nine radio messages had been sent by Kalle to Berlin, two of which are missing in the French counterintelligence files[72] (no. 238 of December 14 and no. 239 of December 18), and he had received three replies from Berlin. So, even before Mata Hari had returned to Paris in search of Ladoux and the promised 1 million francs, he knew everything about her by virtue of the intercepted messages, and it might have specifically been the reason for him not to meet her.

However, on her arrival in Paris she had immediately started to look for her latest lover Denvignes, and not finding him at the Grand she went to the Deuxième Bureau with the hope to locate him. It is quite amazing that rushing in a taxi through the snow covered streets of Paris in early January Mata Hari had frantically been looking for Denvignes only to know whether he had informed Ladoux about her successful Madrid ventures. The news was extremely important to her because she had truly believed that it would fetch her handsome amount of money from Ladoux that she needed to marry Vadime. Nothing had been more important to her any longer. She was utterly shocked to know that Denvignes had already left for Madrid. She wondered how he could go away without even informing her anything. She had then chased him to the railway station and could finally capture a glimpse but nothing transpired. She had felt terribly bad and betrayed due to such behavior from someone she had relied heavily on, but still did not suspect anything wrong. Ladoux must have told Denvignes about the radio traffic, and therefore the smitten lover had taken a sheer u-turn to get out of Paris as soon as he could, although it is important to note that Ladoux did not inform anything about the radio messages to Bouchardon, who was going to be the key person of her pre-trial interrogations. Mata Hari had no other option but to wait for 5 days to hear from Ladoux, and eventually had met him on January 7 at 282 Boulevard Saint-Germain. She had learnt from him that Denvignes had not informed him even a bit of her achievements in Madrid. She had then informed Ladoux all that she could collect from Kalle—(i) the Germans had already broken the French code and could read all radio traffic sent by them; (ii) they had specific knowledge about the French pilot who dropped Allied agents behind the German lines; (iii) German

---

[72] Ibid., 171.

secret agents carried invisible ink crystals under their fingernails; and (iv) the Germans had planned to drop German and Turkish officers in the coastal French zone of Morocco. Ladoux had doubted Mata Hari because he could not believe that the German cryptanalysts had truly deciphered the French code, which was prepared by highly efficient cryptologists who had been guided by the supremely talented Colonel François Cartier, head of the French cryptologic service. Ladoux had only needed a ploy not to pay her, and his disbelief provided him the reason for nonpayment of the promised sum or a part thereof to Mata Hari. She became impatient for the money and had gone three more times to the Deuxième Bureau looking for him, but every time she was refused under some plea. Mata Hari had understood absolutely nothing.

As she had no money at that moment she could not send any to Vadime and had helplessly kept worrying about him. She kept busy with writing loving cards and letters to him every day requesting him for his company in Paris, but all her letters reached Ladoux instead. The addressee received only those that Ladoux had approved, and the same had been true also for her. She received letters which had either been steam opened secretly or had been delivered to her with a note "Opened by the censorship." It is needless to say that Mata Hari had all along been in the dark about Ladoux's mischiefs. Nothing much had been happening for her and she could do nothing about that. Life seemed to have stagnated for her. She had then started renewing her relations with some of her old friends in order to find solace in their company. One of them had been Jules Cambon, the secretary-general of the Foreign Office. Cambon had been overwhelmed to see his old flame in Paris once again, and had welcomed her heartily even by neglecting his official duties in order to be with her all the time. She was quite upset with Ladoux and his promised 1 million francs had appeared to her to be a mirage. In order to get over with the frustration she had decided to relax and to enjoy Paris along with the variety of men in uniform the city offered during wartime, accompanying them to luncheons and dinners, to theater and music halls, and obviously to bed, although her dear Vadime's wellbeing had never ceased to occupy her mentally. Her sole objective at that point of time had been substantial amount of money in order to be able to marry Vadime. Therefore, without heeding to the fact that her letters were being intercepted, on January 11 Mata Hari had written a note in desperation to Cazeaux in Vigo enquiring about whether the Russians still needed someone to work secretly in Vienna. She did not have the slightest idea that in no time Ladoux would know about her letter, and would surely interpret her intention as that to double cross France. Ignorant of everything else in war ridden Paris, she had kept herself busy by doing her favorite things like shopping, visiting her hairdresser, her jeweler, and her dressmaker. Due to financial constraints[73] she had been changing frequently to cheaper hotels during that time. She had received only 5,000 francs from van der Capellen on January 16 (five bills of 1,000 francs each) through Mr. Otto David Eduard Bunge, the Dutch Consul in Paris, and had sent 3,000 francs to Vadime from her account.[74] The Dutch colonel had written to his deluding mistress that he could no more continue to pay for the rented house if she did not return to Holland soon. The very first reaction of Mata Hari to that letter had been of fear, because she was terribly afraid of losing her only source of sustenance at that moment. She had been aging fast and with her fading youth she knew it for sure that finding another smitten lover as her patron would not at all be easy for her, and therefore she had immediately wanted to return to The Hague, at least to console her indignant lover for the moment and to ensure his continual financial support.

The ever unsuspecting dancer did not know anything about Kalle's planted traffic or about what had been going on in Ladoux's mind regarding her. Keay wrote: "... Margarethe had become the package in a merciless international game of pass-the-parcel."[75] By January 12 she had finally smelt something wrong as she had noticed the police duo shadowing her once again. She wrote to Ladoux asking for money and for clarification about the two policemen who had been following her everywhere. She had also visited the Dutch consulate in frenzy to ask for protection and had desperately wanted to leave Paris for Holland. She wanted to see Vadime once again before leaving for Holland and had requested her old friend Adam Wieniawski, a member of the Russian Red Cross, to share with her any information that he could collect about Vadime at the Front. Informed about her arrival in Paris Vadime had managed to get leave on January 13 only for a day, and although his superior had warned him

---

73 According to Howe it had been due to "the unfriendly attitude of the staff at the Plaza Athenee"; *op. cit.*, 136.

74 This amount differs from 3,000 to 5,000 as varied versions have been represented by her biographers.

75 Keay, *op. cit.*, 156.

against the "dangerous lady," he had rushed to Paris to be with his dear Marina for that night—the last night that they had stayed together. While they met at the hotel lounge, out of sheer eagerness to share with her, he had showed the colonel's warning letter to her. Enraged due to the fear of separation with her lover Mata Hari at first had thought that Ladoux must have been trying to ruin her romance, but then had accused Denvignes for being jealous with Vadime and for instigating the Russian colonel to issue a warning letter against her. She however had concealed her feelings from Vadime as she did not want to disturb him with her own agonies on that precious night. She did not even tell him anything about her dealings with Ladoux or with Kalle, or even about the difficulties she had faced at Falmouth. She did not indulge in passionate love with him on that night, but had only expressed tender feelings for her dear Vadime who had slept on her lap like a little boy. The next morning Vadime had left for the war front not realizing that he would never see his Marina again.

Mata Hari had rushed to the Dutch consulate as soon as Vadime departed and had applied for a visa to go to Holland through Switzerland. She then went to Maunoury at the Prefecture of Police with the request for a travel permit to go to Holland, but had been told by him that because Ladoux was away from office for 3 weeks she could get the permit only after his return. In desperation she then went to the Ministry of Foreign Affairs asking for a permit for Holland. It appears to be the fact that everyone in France had been conspiring against her, and all except Mata hari knew pretty well about her fate. Never did she suspect that she would not be able to get the permit to leave France because someone of the French army had been trying to trap her. She did not even realize that her desperate attempts to get a permit to leave the country would put her into immense trouble beyond her capacity to handle. The French government did not want to spoil more time on the matter, and on February 10, 1917, the warrant for her arrest had been written and signed by the Minister of War Hubert Lyautey, who had significantly been a graduate from Saint Cyr. It was then sent to the General of the Division, Military Governor of Paris Auguste Dubail, Office of the Military Justice, with the word "Secret" stamped on it. Howe wrote: "On February 10, just before her arrest, an unsigned report was made ... from the ministry of war to the military governor of Paris ... The document—number 1 ... summarizes briefly the reasons why someone (Ladoux? Goubet?) was asking for her arrest. It says "Zelle is strongly suspected of being an agent in the service of Germany." This statement of mere suspicion is bizarrely followed by a statement of fact: that she "belongs to the Cologne intelligence center, where she is listed under the designation of H21."[76] Colonel Goubet was chief of the Fifth Bureau, by whom Ladoux had been appointed and to whom he reported, although Mata Hari had never met him and might never have known of him either. However, the glaring discrepancy in the report did not deter the French government to proceed on its preplanned line of action. On February 12 she had returned to the Foreign Office to inquire about her travel permit only to know that the papers were not ready yet. The arrest warrant was issued for her on that day itself, which had accused her of enemy espionage. Next morning, while she was having breakfast at 9 o'clock, Mata Hari was arrested from room 131 of the Elysée Palace Hotel by the Police Commissioner Albert Priolet, who had led a team of five inspectors (Mercadier, Curnier, Des Logeres, Quentin, and Pinson[77]) to her hotel suite to seize all documents, bank details, messages, and letters available with her. Mata Hari still did not suspect that she was being led to prepare for her final performance, which was not to be related to the stage and would not be composed by her anymore.

---

76 Howe, *op. cit.*, 152.

77 Wheelwright, *op. cit.*, 67.

CHAPTER 6

MISCARRIAGE OF JUSTICE

It will certainly be an understatement to say that Mata Hari had been shocked by the sudden turn of events, she in fact panicked—she was simply horrified. The woman who had always been happy in the company of men in uniform was for the first time afraid of them. On the previous night when she went to bed after having a sumptuous dinner, she did not have the least idea about what the morning next would have to offer her. Even when she had woken up in the morning of February 13 everything went according to her daily routine and nothing had really seemed to be unusual. She had ordered for her breakfast, taken a good shower like the other days, had applied light make-up on her middle-aged face that made her more attractive with a loosely tied hair-knot, dressed well, and then had settled on the table with the daily newspaper awaiting food. The chambermaid had served her breakfast on time and she had been enjoying it, when the door knocked. To her utter dismay she had found the policemen inside her room with the arrest warrant for her, which read: "The woman Zelle, Marguerite, known as Mata Hari, living at the Palace Hotel, of Protestant religion, foreigner, born in Holland on 7 August, 1876, five feet ten inches tall, being able to read and write, is accused of espionage, tentative complicity, and intelligence with the enemy, in an effort to assist them in their operations."[1] Even before she could realize anything the five inspectors had ransacked her room in order to collect every bit of paper and all other items that they considered could be invaluable for her case, and enlisted them[2] which included—a French visa issued at The Hague in 1915 (before her first wartime visit to Paris), a travel permit for Vittel (1916), a residence permit to stay in Paris (1915), an extract in her name from the registry of enrollment for aliens, a document issued in London pertaining to her French visa to go to Hendaye in December 1915, her Dutch passport, some correspondences, bills, papers pertaining to her bank transactions, some addresses and visiting cards, a few photographs,

---

1 Sam Waagenaar, *op. cit.*, 1964, 171.
2 Pat Shipman, *op. cit.*, 277–278.

a pendulum clock, some gifts, toiletries, and a few bank notes and currencies. The graceful dancer of yesteryears stood there absolutely dumbfounded witnessing the manhandling of her personal possessions. Due to obvious reasons she had not been given a chance to defend herself and was taken straight to Bouchardon's office (the Third Council of War) at the Palace of Justice on the quai de l'Horloge. Everything that had happened was so unexpected to Mata Hari that she had no time to fathom the eventuality of the raid. It was 11 in the morning and she had found herself seated opposite to the chief interrogator; and after his questioning was over she had been taken to the prison of Saint Lazare.

It was the ultimate test of her forbearance. She had simply broken down. Saint Lazare prison had been notorious for "housing prostitutes, delinquent girls, and other women prisoners and convicts,"[3] including thieves, spies, debauched women, and female criminals of every sort. Mata Hari could not even think of finding herself among such rogues. As almost all of the prisoners had belonged to the shady world of Paris they had been suspected to be carriers of venereal diseases, and therefore, as a mandatory rule, the prison doctors examined them thoroughly on arrival. Mata Hari hated the idea. She had immediately wanted to run away from the dirty clutches of the prison officials, and from all the meaningless exercise that was being conducted against her will. She knew that she was innocent. She had even expressed that to the investigating magistrate Captain Bouchardon at his office during her first interrogation. Bouchardon had been a tough and unremitting investigator, and hence was nicknamed "The Grand Inquisitor" by Georges ("The Tiger") Clemenceau. His colleagues knew him to be somewhat obsessive regarding the cases that he was responsible for investigation, and because his mission had been to eradicate the "enemy within," he had strived to know every detail about the detainees. A bit of information about Bouchardon, which appears to be pertinent to Mata Hari's case, might briefly be furnished here: "Bouchardon was especially merciless with Mata Hari because of her immorality. Bouchardon had recently discovered that his own wife had taken a lover. His personal notes indicate that he had decided upon Mata Hari's guilt from their very first meeting, if not beforehand."[4] Julia Keay wrote: "... his objectivity was tinged with prejudice. Bouchardon was

---

3 Rev. Edward R. Udovic, "Saint Lazare as a Women's Prison, 1794–1932," 1; Virtual Exhibition of DePaul University; 2011. Internet archive.

4 Shipman, *op. cit.*, 281.

no more immune than the next Frenchman to the current epidemic of xenophobia, and ... was convinced from the start that Margarethe was guilty."[5] Instead of probing her case from all possible angles with an open mind Bouchardon had deemed her to be guilty from the very first day he had met her in his office. Keay quoted Bouchardon: "She was a born spy. She had all the qualifications. Feline, supple and deceitful, accustomed to amusing herself at the expense of anyone and everyone, without scruples, attracting men with her body, devouring their fortunes, and then breaking their hearts."[6]

His scorn for Mata Hari evidently demonstrates that she had been regarded as an enemy spy due to her moral laxity, and not for what she had actually committed. Rosie White wrote: "... Mata Hari represented a disturbingly mobile femininity. Her trial was an attempt to fix that mobility ... it was thus not important what Mata Hari had actually done, but rather what she represented."[7] Keay moreover wrote about two of the Captain's initial disappointments that could have had some effects on the handling of his detainees, including Mata Hari—he had dreamt of becoming a doctor, but because he was very weak in mathematics, he had to give up his dream to become one; and second, although he was appointed as the Commander of the Territorial Infantry by virtue of his seniority in the battalion, he had to give up because he did not have the essential skill of horse riding.[8] Due to his lack of equestrian skill he moreover had to endure scornful looks from his colleagues. Although he had been posted to Paris as the chief investigating magistrate of the Third Council of War, he could really never get over with the despairing experience. It is needless to mention that Mata Hari knew nothing about Bouchardon's personal life and had been expecting him to be a sensible French officer who would handle her case logically and sympathetically; and because she was confident of her innocence she had told him that she did not need a lawyer to defend her case. She actually did not care too much because she had somewhat been sure that as she was at the service of France someone in the French counterespionage must have been playing a vile game with her, and the entire drama had taken place due to some

---

5   Julia Keay, *op. cit.*, 178.
6   Ibid., 178.
7   Rosie White, "Mata Hari and the Myth of the Femme Fatale," Helen Hanson, and Catherine O'Rawe, eds., *The Femme Fatale*, 74.
8   Keay, *op. cit.*, 174.

misunderstanding on his part. Therefore, as soon as the questioning was over Mata Hari had risen to her feet to move out of Bouchardon's office, because she might have thought that she had effectively clarified the misunderstanding. The small statured and tense-looking man, instead, had sent her to Saint Lazare.

In prison, Mata Hari was identified by number 721 44625. On February 13, 1917, her sparkling persona had been reduced to a mere number. Within a couple of hours her identity had taken a drastic turn which was beyond her wildest imaginations. As per the prison rules, on the first night she had been kept on the eastern part of the prison enclave in a padded cell in order to prevent any attempt to commit suicide. Mata Hari loved herself too much and would never commit self-destruction under any circumstance. She was moreover convinced that the French army had made a grave mistake by captivating her unnecessarily and would surely release her in a short time. She could never apprehend that they had conspired to entrap her in order to fulfill their own wartime purposes, and therefore was not serious about the charges brought against her. She did not even think of employing an expert lawyer to deal with her case, instead had foolishly requested her long time admirer Edouard Clunet, who, being an expert in international corporate law, was absolutely inept regarding war rules or espionage suits. The most admired and attended demimondaine, who had been enjoying privacy of the enormously luxurious hotels and chateaus in Europe, was shoved into a room which was "dark, damp, filthy, rat-infested, unheated, and furnished primitively."[9] She had been provided with a dirty straw mattress to sleep on the floor. The prison cells had peepholes on the doors to enable the guards to keep watch on the inmates, depriving the internees of privacy. She did not get an opportunity to take a bath all the more due to scarcity of water for use of the inmates. Shipman wrote: "The fastidious woman who had insisted on a private bathroom in every hotel was restricted to a small bowl of cold water in the morning for her ablutions."[10] They had not even been provided clean clothes every day, having the privilege barely once in a week. The prison cell that she had been put in did not have any window, and after dark she had to manage with a weak streak of gas light from the street that peeped through the barred opening high up on the brick wall of the prison. Meals provided in Saint Lazare

---

9   Shipman, *op. cit.*, 283.
10 Ibid., 283.

were no better either.[11]

Mata Hari did not feel like eating anything there. The dinner that was served on the first evening had comprised of a thin soup, bread with boiled vegetables, and some wine. Meat in paltry amount was served only once in a week making the meals all the more dull. Breakfast and lunch made no difference for her. Worst, she was even compelled to pay for her food as per the prison rules. She did never have such nauseous food even when Adam had left them due to his bankruptcy. After her transformation as an eminent dancer she only had the privilege of dining in the most famous and the finest restaurants with men who madly loved her. The whole environment of Saint Lazare had simply been repulsive to her but she was helpless. She stood at the receiving end at that moment, and however brutal it might have been she could only passively take what was being provided to her by the prison authority. Still she wanted the privilege to have a telephone in her prison cell while the inmates had even been denied the basic amenities like daily bath and clean clothes, but was obviously refused. Mata Hari had realized at last that she had been duped by Ladoux, but could do nothing about it at that time. She had naively thought that she would better rely on Bouchardon for justice and had waited patiently for her hearing on the next day thinking all the time that her ordeal was going to end the moment she would clarify the misunderstanding to him. Bouchardon had called her on February 15, the day after, for the second pre-trial questioning. Mata Hari obviously did not know that the person she wanted to trust over Ladoux had already convicted her as an evil woman, an unashamed whore, and nothing better, and would not spare her by any means. Tammy Proctor wrote: "Historically, female spies have been categorized either as self-sacrificing patriots bent on saving their own countries, or as whores with an inherent character weakness driving them to treason and betrayal for the sake of money or fame."[12] Society was made to identify the two types distinctly as either the celebrated or the hated. As per the common perception Mata Hari could only be identified with the latter. Newspaper articles too had been using the following words about her—"The woman with the body of a goddess and the charms of a demon." ("Cruelest Lie – or Truest Mercy?" *The Washington Times*, August 29, 1920, 3.)

---

11 Waagenaar however wrote that the food was "not too bad," *op. cit.*, 1965, 174.
12 Tammy M.Proctor, *op. cit.*, 7.

On the second day of her interrogation she had again refused to take legal help because she was not only convinced about her innocence, she actually did not doubt that some sort of diabolical scheming could have been taking place against her. She moreover had confidence on her French admirers and must have naively thought that the French people who loved and admired her very much could never do any injustice to her. As per the French law, Edouard Clunet had been allowed to stay at the questioning on that day from her side. On most of the other days (save only the last) only three people had participated in the questioning sessions— the accused Mata Hari, the interrogating magistrate Bouchardon, and the court recorder Manuel Baudouin. Bouchardon had asked her to talk about her life in detail, and Mata Hari had spoken elaborately with great tenacity mixing up the dates as usual and representing fictitious stories about her past, mostly about her life with Rudolf, "to create a more favorable impression"[13] as Wheelwright has put it. Her life in the East Indies, her children, Norman's death, Rudolf's devilish treatment towards her, her loneliness—she had revealed every bit of her torment before Bouchardon. She had then narrated about her very first visit to Paris in 1903, about how she had started her career in the great city, how she had met Émile Guimet, about her success as a dancer, and also about her European sojourn. She had also boasted about her lovers in great detail and had described how they had rightfully treated her like a queen. She did not however forget to make a mention of her lover Colonel van der Capellen in The Hague, who she said had been sending money regularly for her maintenance at that time. She had also mentioned her former lover Alfred Kiepert, who, right before the outbreak of war in Berlin, had promised to meet her in Paris very soon. She had also spoken about her relationship with Herr Griebel, the Police Superintendent in Berlin in 1914, and had stressed that at that point of time she had no way to know that war was imminent. She had also spoken about the trouble she had faced while leaving Berlin early in August after the war broke out, about her first wartime visit to Paris in December 1915, about Marquis de Beaufort, and about everything that had happened to her during that time. Bouchardon had patiently given her adequate time to spill her beans, but could not catch her on the wrong foot. After the questioning was over for that day she had requested Bouchardon for her dressing gown, which, she said, was indispensible for her, and with great hope had also told him: "I am in Saint Lazare under conditions that I cannot withstand and ask that you

---

13   Julie Wheelwright, *op. cit.*, 72.

have me examined from the point of view of health. I am suffering greatly and need special care."[14] She had also informed him that she had vomited blood earlier on that day. Bouchardon had immediately ordered for her examination by the prison doctor, who had found her to be "in good physical health," although quite nervous, and had recommended for changing her cell if possible.

On February 19 she was shifted to a slightly better cell,[15] meant especially for prostitutes and spies, known as the Ménagerie (the Animal House), where rats, fleas, and lice accompanied her along with errant women of the prison. The cell was better because it was furnished with "two wooden beds with straw mattresses and coarse brown blankets, a brick floor, whitewashed walls and a skirting board of tar."[16] The new cell had somewhat been a bit brighter with a dim light in the evenings and a window on the wall for daylight, but Mata Hari's fate was not to shine anymore. She had been isolated from the world outside for the past one week as no visitor apart from her lawyer-lover Clunet was allowed to her cell, but he was more a helpless lover than an efficient lawyer. Her arrest had been kept secret by the French government (was it because Miss Edith Cavell's arrest had also been kept secret by Germany?), and therefore she was not allowed to write letters to her friends, and any newspaper reporting on her was also strictly forbidden by the French army. She was not permitted to write to the Dutch Legation in Paris as Bouchardon had considered her crime too heinous to allow the normal course. Even the Dutch Legation had not been informed about her arrest prior to April 23. Her repeated requests to write to her beloved Vadime had also been turned down. She was extremely worried about Vadime as she knew he would not know what his loving Marina had been going through. She had never even imagined being in such isolation and quite normally had been finding it hard to cope with the situation in prison. In utter anguish and acrimony she had been writing letters frequently to the interrogating officer Bouchardon complaining about the filthy and nightmarish conditions she had to face in captivity, about her vermin-infested bed, about the dull meals and tasteless wine served by the prison cook Sister Auréa, about the ever diminishing size of bread and meat, about scarcity of water for a refreshing bath, about lack of soap for her use, about insufficient

---

14   Shipman, *op. cit.*, 286.
15   According to Keay it was on February 17, *op. cit.*, 182.
16   Wheelwright, *op. cit.*, 72.

clean bedspreads and clothes to change, about her toiletries that she had left in the hotel, her laundry, her comfortable bedroom slippers, etc, assuming that he would realize how special she was, would do her justice as she had truly been innocent, and would surely set her free very soon. She had also wanted her debts to be paid off before her apprehended release from the jail, and had written in detail to Bouchardon what amount she wanted to pay and to whom. But slowly and evidently she had been losing her cool because she still dreamt of a life with her fiancé Vadime and had desperately wanted to be free.

In the new cell Mata Hari was allowed to take some rest for 2 days, and on February 21 she was called in for the third interrogation (second, excluding that on the day of her arrest) at Bouchardon's tiny 8 foot office. He had the habit of biting his fingernails while questioning his subject, pacing up and down in nervous steps, tapping the pencil on the table, etc, which was quite unbecoming of an officer like him. Mata Hari often became irritated with his ways of dramatizing the interrogations, more so because she had found the whole affair to be superfluous, although for the French it was extremely necessary, because they had set hands on a perfect scapegoat. France had found, according to Howe, "... this pretentious, over-aged, overweight, over-priced harlot ... She was foolish, reckless, impulsive, and impetuous ...,"[17] and that was exactly what France needed at that moment. Wheelwright wrote: "She had become the victim of her success."[18] Bouchardon however had refused Clunet's repeated requests to be present at the questioning sessions as he knew that there were more secrets to hide in her case than to reveal in the presence of a desperate lover. At the beginning of his questioning on that day he had asked Mata Hari about her first wartime visit to Paris in 1915, and she had replied confidently that her purpose to come to Paris in December 1915 had been, first, to collect some expensive toiletries that she had left in her Neuville house which she did not find available in The Netherlands, and second, as she had decided to settle down in her new house in The Hague, she had also planned to collect some of her belongings from Paris and sell off the rest that were lying at the Maple warehouse. In reply to Bouchardon's question about the reason for her second visit to Paris in June 1916, she had said that her lover Marquis de Beaufort had invited her to come to Paris and she had obliged him. During her questioning

---

17   Russell Warren Howe, *op. cit.*, 236.
18   Wheelwright, *op. cit.*, 84.

on that day, for the first time, she had taken Vadime's name, and had told Bouchardon how much she loved her Russian fiancé whom she had met in July 1916. Mata Hari wanted to convey that she had nothing to do with German intelligence and had sincerely wanted to settle down with Vadime. She told him that if she could marry Vadime "I would be the happiest woman on earth." But she did not know that Bouchardon had been doing his homework by digging her past with great diligence. He did not even believe the story about her visit to Vittel to see Vadime who had been wounded in the war—Vittel was too close to the war front. She had then revealed Ladoux's name who she said had asked her to spy for France in return of money and told Bouchardon that because she wanted to marry Vadime she needed a lot of money which she had thought could be earned by accepting his proposal. Mata Hari tried to assure her investigator that there was nothing more to her espionage venture, but he had been relentless. "He had commissioned a team of police investigators, led by Inspector Carnier,[19] to investigate her past activities ..."[20] wrote Keay. Carnier had fulfilled his assignment by collecting all the detail about her, from her birth, marriage, divorce, her life in Paris, her professional engagements in Europe, list of her lovers, etc, but nothing had been reported by him about her being a German spy.

Bouchardon's forehead wrinkled as he was surprised by the findings, because he had strongly believed that the woman had indeed ditched France and had finally expected to get some concrete proof against Mata Hari from Carnier. Utterly dissatisfied with the report he had decided to call in all her lovers from Carnier's list and also to call those who could be traced from the visiting cards found in her hotel room. Summoned by the Second Bureau during wartime they had been compelled to make a beeline to Bouchardon's office, but none had testified against Mata Hari— she had never discussed war or any diplomatic matter with any of them. The committed interrogating officer was not satisfied with the outcome of his effort, and then had decided to follow her money trail. He had been sure about and hence was determined to prove her guilt. Every bank in Paris therefore had received a note from the French counterintelligence service to find out if Margarethe Zelle had any secret account with them, where she could have deposited her ill-gotten gains, but nothing of Bouchardon's interest had transpired. He had then chosen to call in

---

19 Shipman spelt "Curnier," *op. cit.*, 290.
20 Keay, *op. cit.*, 184.

her dressmakers, hotel maids, the jewelers, and shop assistants—all those who had known Mata Hari personally at some or other point of time. His interrogations at last had yielded some result, because quite a few made-up stories against her had been conveyed by them either to please the high-ranking officer or under the influence of the propaganda against her that had started to make the rounds in the Parisian newspapers by that time. Most significant among them included the story of her involvement in the tank disaster at the Battle of Somme. Bouchardon however knew that such baseless stories could not prove anything against her in the court of law. It had become absolutely necessary for the French army to spread fabricated and exaggerated stories about her in order to make her a national foe in the public mind, so that her punishment could have the required cathartic value in wartime crises. The French propaganda machination had worked diligently toward that goal, and needless to mention, had also succeeded to a great extent. She was even reported to have demanded for a daily milk bath in jail, while the children in France could not be nourished properly. Who else than a despicable traitor could ever do that? Therefore, the conspiracy hatched against her by the French government was being implemented at both the levels—official (political) and social—because a dual attack on her could only serve their wartime purpose.

Mata Hari had no means to know the French conspiracy against her, and after a long and tiring questioning session, in the evening of February 21 wrote to Bouchardon earnestly pleading one more time for permission to see her beloved Vadime. She knew that Vadime would also worry for her and would become impatient by not hearing from his dear Marina for so long, but she did not know that all her love letters from Vadime were being intercepted and confiscated by Ladoux midway. She wrote begging to Bouchardon: "I have never—never—done anything bad toward you. Give me my freedom."[21] The lady who always had enjoyed freedom on her own terms had been compelled to seek authority from others, most importantly from men—who she knew had ever been ready to do anything for her and whom she had taken delight in captivating through her charm. Her heart-rending appeal however had echoed in vain within the dingy walls of her prison cell with no effect on Bouchardon. She had next been called in for interrogation on February 23. For the first time Bouchardon had raised Kalle's name on that day to know exactly what

---

21   Shipman, *op. cit.*, 289.

relationship they shared in Madrid, designing his questions in a way to indicate that the French government knew that she had been working for German secret service. Mata Hari denied his charges and had said that she had found Kalle only from the Diplomatic Book of Hotel Ritz where she had been staying in Madrid and had contacted him because she wanted to prove her worth as a spy to Captain Ladoux in order to impress him to get the promised money. She had also told Bouchardon proudly that in the course of time she had realized that Kalle had fallen madly in love with her to the extent that she could extract any information from him that could have benefited France in the war. Her boastful claims had irked Bouchardon even more because he knew how vacuous she could have been.

Mata Hari did not care to know how wrong she had been. The interrogating magistrate then had raised question about the 5,000 francs that she had received in Paris in January 1917, which she had claimed came from her lover van der Capellen's account, and not from the German Embassy in Amsterdam. Bouchardon could have verified her claim at least in three ways—(i) he could have checked the Baron's brief note sent to her along with the money, which had mentioned that if Mata Hari did not return to The Hague soon he would give up the house in Uitleg. That curt note could prove her claim conclusively; (ii) there was also a letter from her maid Anna Lintjens which mentioned that van der Capellen had already sent the money to Paris; and (iii) he could also have examined the account from which the money had been sent to Mata Hari. But Bouchardon purposefully did not take the trouble to find out the truth, instead, he had found none of her explanations to be acceptable, as he had already considered her to be undeniably unscrupulous and hence guilty. For him a woman of questionable disposition like her could never speak truth, although on that day itself he had received a report that not a single drop of secret ink, nor anything incriminating had been found among her seized belongings which were checked thoroughly by the police. Invisible ink could be made from a varied range of chemicals commonly found in items of daily use like soap, face cream, perfume, anti-pregnancy or spermicidal solutions, etc (items found among her possessions), from saliva, urine, lemon juice, onion juice, wine, vinegar, honey, even from milk, and amazingly fresh semen could also make excellent secret ink that could be developed through heating the paper. The First World War had seen rampant use of such means by all the quarters, both the Triple

Entente and the Triple Alliance, as it had commonly been a useful tool in espionage. So, it was quite normal that the items confiscated from Mata Hari's hotel room on the day of her arrest would be examined for invisible ink. Nothing had been found in her possession which could prove her guilt, but Bouchardon was determined to prove her crime and would not stop before that.

On the next day, February 24, Mata Hari was again called in for interrogation at the magistrate's office, and then again on February 28 and March 1. The sole purpose had been to break her nerves and push her to her wit's end so that she might confess her crime. Bouchardon had questioned her about her acquaintance with Ladoux and how she got to spy for him. He had also questioned her about what information she did collect from Kalle and what did she do with that. Mata Hari told Bouchardon that inspite of her repeated efforts in Madrid to contact Ladoux for his instructions she did not get any reply from him regarding her course of action. She had then contacted the French military attaché in Madrid for advice. She had revealed the name of Colonel Denvignes to whom she had handed over all the secrets that she could collect from Kalle, and also told Bouchardon about how Denvignes had requested her to return to the German military attaché in order to collect more concrete information about their plans against France. She had also revealed how Denvignes had been madly infatuated with her and how he had ditched her in early January that year. Mata Hari could not forget the humiliation by Denvignes. However, by that time her lawyer Clunet had made a petition for her provisional freedom (application for parole), which was refused[22] on February 26. The bold letters across the envelop read "REJECT" which had hit Clunet directly on his face, because under the circumstances he had been deeply worried about Mata Hari's sanity. His repeated appeals had all been denied, and Mata Hari could not get freedom. She was failing to cope with the filthy condition of the prison and had fallen very ill toward early March. She herself had written many letters to the prison authority as well as to Bouchardon complaining about the inhumane arrangement in which she was compelled to live in the jail, but no one heeded to her desperate appeals.

She had always thought that as she was innocent she certainly deserved better treatment from the French government, but she did not know that

---
22   Ibid., 292.

they had already convicted her—even before the trial. For them she was the most heinous criminal who had connived with the enemy in order to harm France and the people in the time of war. French propaganda thoroughly influenced the spy-scared commoners who had been made to understand that it was due to her that they might not ultimately get back Alsace and Lorraine from Germany. Although the surveillance report against her failed to come up with a single proof about her involvement in enemy espionage, still she was reported to have been arrested "red handed" for the crime. As the French Law of Armed Conflict Manual did not consider a spy to be a combatant in war, it did not grant the prisoner-of-war status to a person found guilty of enemy espionage. It says: "A spy has no right to prisoner-of-war status and is subject to the national legislation of the territory where he is captured."[23] Therefore, Mata Hari could not claim the status of a war prisoner. Had she been treated as one she could get some protection under the regulations of The Hague Convention of 1907. But she was helpless, so was her lawyer Clunet. She had to look forward to Bouchardon's decision at every step. Even if she was ill she had to get permission from him for the prison doctor's visit to her cell, who would meticulously write a report, on most occasions, to please Bouchardon—be it for Mata Hari or for any other prisoner in Saint Lazare.

Due to her severe illness in early March, Mata Hari had requested Bouchardon to postpone her interrogations for a few days. She had been suspected by the prison doctor Bizard of having syphilis, and because at times she coughed up blood she was also suspected to have tuberculosis. Bouchardon therefore had called her on Monday, March 12, as had already been requested by her, instead of 9th as had been previously scheduled; and in her presence had examined the contents of the sealed packets seized from her hotel room. Nothing significant to her case was found and the interrogation had ended in a short time. It is although important to note that on March 6, even after her arrest in Paris, one more radio message had been intercepted on the Eiffel Tower, which had been written in the broken code and was sent from Berlin to Kalle in Madrid enquiring about the work of H21. Clunet however had been requesting Bouchardon repeatedly for her hospitalization, but in vain. An appeal for a second opinion upon her health condition had been granted, but

---

23 Quoted in Jean-Marie Henckaerts and Louise Doswald-Beck, eds., *Customary International Humanitarian Law*, II (I), 2569.

on March 26 her condition was reported to be satisfactory by the prison doctor. Staying continuously in an unhygienic and soiled cell had been affecting her health badly. Mata Hari repeatedly requested Bouchardon and also the military governor of Paris for provisional liberty pleading that she had never spied against France, but had been refused every time. France could not let its catch go free. Bouchardon continued questioning people whose visiting cards[24] had been found in her hotel room (the dancer had been an avid collector of calling cards of men she had met, even if she met them only for once), but nothing had transpired as all of them deposed before the magistrate that she had never discussed war with them. Even Ladoux was called in for questioning and in a stern voice he told only that which suited his purpose. He insisted on her loose morale and on her numerous affairs with men in uniform of any rank, any age, and any nationality. And because she had been of dubious character, Ladoux asserted, she had to be an enemy spy. Bouchardon subscribed to his view because he too had been of the same opinion. "It was a short leap, in his eyes, from sleeping with a man for money to milking him for information which could be profitably sold to the enemy"[25] wrote Wheelwright.

Ladoux had also revealed that his arrangement for tailing Mata Hari in Spain did not bring forth any significant result, but he still did not disclose anything about the radio messages to Bouchardon and had kept waiting for the opportune moment. If those messages had been so important to her case and were conclusive evidence to implicate her then why did he hide them from the interrogating magistrate? Did he have some ulterior motive toward his own end or for the good of France, or was he acting according to someone else's instructions? It might also have been that Ladoux could not complete the process of effectively doctoring the messages by that time, and therefore had withheld those from Bouchardon. However, in severe illness Mata Hari had been praying to Bouchardon again and again for her release or at least to shift her to the prison hospital, but all her cries had fallen into deaf ears. She wrote to him "I am completely mad. I beg of you, put an end to this. I am a woman. I cannot support [myself] above my strength."[26] Bouchardon had remained silent to her trauma, because he wanted to punish her for her sins against his homeland, and thereby to break her. For a whole month she had nothing

---

24 Waagenaar, *op.cit.*, 1964, 205.
25 Wheelwright, *op. cit.*, 74.
26 Ibid., 74.

to do apart from taking brief strolls in the prison courtyard, resting, and thinking of Vadime who she had no means to reach. Bouchardon had intimated her about her Russian lover in the mean time—that Vadime had been severely wounded and was under treatment at the Hospital Epernay. Mata Hari became even more desperate to get out of the jail in order to see Vadime and to be by his side at the moment of his despair. But the gap had become so painfully unbridgeable, that she could do nothing about it. Mata Hari had never found herself in such a helpless situation before.

On April 12 Bouchardon had summoned the psychologically shattered former demimondaine exactly after a month for another session of questioning, and had started his interrogation by asking her direct questions about Alfred Kiepert and her spying for Germany.[27] She had previously told him that she considered herself to be an "international woman" and therefore had many friends across Europe. Shipman wrote: "An international woman was a worldly woman, a cosmopolitan woman, and by extension, a woman of loose morals. In Bouchardon's eyes, Mata Hari's labeling herself an international woman only reinforced his low opinion of her."[28] He had twisted her statement in his own typical manner to indicate that she had indeed been a German spy. Mata Hari although had denied the charge: "The fact that I have had relations with certain people in no way implies that I have done espionage work. I have never done any espionage for Germany, nor for any other country, with the exception of France."[29] She was then asked about the liquid contents of two bottles found in her handbag—one was a solution of oxycyanide of mercury while the other was a potion from a bottle labeled 'TOXIC' which contained *bylodure de mercure dans lyodure de potassium*,[30] both had commonly been used as contraceptives by the prostitutes and courtesans of France. Mata Hari had bought those from a chemist shop in Paris under the prescription of a Spanish doctor who she had consulted in December 1916, while she was in Madrid, and had been using for the same purpose.

A chemical analysis report of the contents of her handbag had reached Bouchardon on April 10, which said that although the liquids of the two bottles found in her possession had therapeutic use, those could also be

---

27 Waagenaar, *op. cit.*, 1964, 208.
28 Shipman, *op. cit.*, 302.
29 Waagenaar, *op. cit.*, 1964, 208.
30 Keay, *op. cit.*, 190.

used as excellent invisible ink if diluted with plain water in a certain proportion. Armed with the report he had felt delighted as it was a concrete proof against her that he had been searching for so long. But Mata Hari had disappointed him by replying that she was using them for therapeutic purpose only and not as invisible ink. She in fact did not even know that the liquids she had been using for quite long could have espionage value. Bouchardon had then informed her about questioning people whom she knew and had asked her to present names of those whom she wished to be interrogated in her favor. Mata Hari was comfortable with anyone's interrogation in her case and had provided names of some of the officers she knew could help her, but had pleaded not to call Vadime. She did not want her fiancé to be dragged into the mess that she had been in. She only wanted good things to happen to their relationship, which she had feared could be ruined by calling him for questioning in relation to a suspected spy. With great earnest she had requested Bouchardon not to interrogate Vadime: "... the mere idea of seeing him again in these circumstances has already made me cry ... Since he is the man I love the most in all the world, he is also the only one that I don't have the strength to see ..."[31] Due to some unknown reasons Bouchardon heeded to her request, and instead of calling Vadime to his office, the Russian soldier's previous note regarding his relationship with the former dancer had been taken into consideration as evidence. As none of the nine questioning sessions did unearth any evidence whatsoever against her, on April 16 she was permitted, for the first time since in prison, to write to the Dutch Legation. It had been more than 2 months after her arrest that she could finally inform van der Capellen in The Hague about her plight through the Dutch consulate in Paris.

Mata Hari had still hoped to get bail in a short time, and also had worried about her house in Uitleg. She had written to the Dutch consulate in Paris asking to advice her maid Anna on her behalf to make necessary domestic arrangements there, because she had thought that she would return to her lover van der Capellen in The Hague soon after she got provisional liberty. However, because nothing of any material relevance to the case in question could be grasped by that time, on April 20, deeply frustrated, Bouchardon had made up his mind to give up. He had told Ladoux that "my investigations have ground to a standstill."[32] To be sure

---

31 Wheelwright, *op. cit.*, 75.
32 Keay, *op. cit.*, 190.

about Mata Hari's innocence he could have called in van der Capellen and Anna Lintjens to testify that the 5,000 francs which had been sent to her on November 4, 1916, was actually sent by him and not by Kroemer; but Bouchardon simply refused to do that because the case had been kept confidential and therefore no civilian witness could be called in to depose in her favor. Ladoux had been startled by Bouchardon's plans to quit. It was far from what he had schemed against Mata Hari, and therefore had been desperate to stop Bouchardon by all means from terminating the interrogation. As mentioned earlier, the Nivelle Offensive had already started on April 9 with the promise to win over Germany within a few days, and by the 16th the French army had proceeded towards the Chemin des Dames ridge which had been occupied by the German soldiers. It had been a crucial moment of the war, and the French citizens had anticipated triumph over Germany as a result of the offensive. Ladoux had been aware of the French soldiers' dissatisfaction over the huge number of deaths in the war from early 1917 and was sure that Mata Hari, as a suspect of enemy espionage, could not be freed by any means at that point of time. She was too precious due to her propaganda value and hence could be made to do more for France. For Ladoux it had been the most opportune moment to play his trump card, and therefore, on the next day, Saturday, April 21, he did send a secret note regarding the Madrid–Berlin radio messages[33] to Lieutenant-General Dubail, the military governor of Paris who had been rejecting all of Mata Hari's bail appeals for so long. Like Bouchardon, Dubail too had not been informed about the radio telegraphs previously, and they obviously did not know that those were written in the broken code. Ladoux, quite tactfully, had kept it secret in order to use them later in his own interest. The immediate next step taken by the Ministry of War had been sending copies of the intercepted radio messages between Kalle (Madrid) and Berlin to Bouchardon for consideration regarding the case.

All of a sudden everything became crystal clear to Bouchardon as he could evidently see the motive behind each and every heinous act of the vicious woman. Curiously neither Dubail nor Bouchardon did think of verifying the contents of the messages, of examining their originality, or of questioning about why those were written in the broken code, because

---

[33] Howe mentioned that there had been three sets of the same messages—12 intercepted by the Eiffel Tower (Eiffel Tower set), 9 given by Ladoux to Bouchardon (Bouchardon set), and 14 given by Ladoux to Dubail (Dubail set); some of which are missing in the files; *op. cit.*, 178.

Bouchardon was sure that the Ministry of War must have verified each one of them before passing them on to him. As the interrogating magistrate he only needed some concrete proof, and at last had been in possession of the clinching evidences against the accused. Bouchardon could not be happier. From that point of time the focus of his interrogation was bound to take a sharp turn. The woman who had merely been a suspect of espionage was going to be considered a criminal. He was all the more happy because his anticipation about the debauch lady had been proven to be true. After all he was sure that he could not go wrong. Bouchardon might have felt triumphant all the more because by punishing Mata Hari he could at last console his injured ego after his wife had deserted him. He was absolutely certain that whatever she had done against France would result in nothing short of her death sentence. In his memoirs he later wrote: "Margareth-Gertrude Zelle had furnished von Kalle with a whole series of information ... it was considered by our services, and especially by Supreme Headquarters, as containing a part of important truth. It confirmed ... that the spy had been in touch with a number of officers and that she had cleverly been able to ask them certain perfidious questions. At the same time her association with other circles had enabled her to get information on our political situation."[34] Pathetically, Mata Hari was not aware of any of these developments, and still had aspired for freedom. She did not stop writing letters requesting Bouchardon for her provisional liberty and had also insisted Clunet to write on her behalf. On April 23, Clunet, not knowing about surfacing of the radio messages, wrote to the interrogating magistrate: "No proof has been furnished against her that supports this indictment. It is not possible any longer to maintain such state of things against this unhappy woman, or at least it is necessary to give her provisional liberty ... It would be unjust and cruel to prolong this situation."[35] Bouchardon knew exactly what to do.

Mata Hari was next interrogated on May 1. It had been a closed door affair to maintain utmost secrecy, and even the press had been bluffed carefully by spreading the news that Bouchardon would be going to some other prison for hearing another case. Mata Hari was made to sit face to face with him for the questioning, and between them on the table had laid the heap of "clinching evidence" of the Third War Council. He had accused her directly of the following—(i) of being the German agent

---

34   Quoted in Waagenaar, *op. cit.*, 1964, 210.
35   Shipman, *op. cit.*, 306.

H21[36] belonging to the Central Information Bureau in Cologne, and sent to Paris on their instruction twice during the war (in 1915 and 1916) to spy against France by collecting important state secrets; (ii) for accepting 5,000 francs in November 1916, for her services to Germany; and (iii) for providing Kalle with information about France of political, diplomatic, and military importance.[37] Mata Hari did not know how to react. Keay wrote: "The more she struggled to extricate herself from her nightmare the deeper she seemed to sink into its vicious grasp ... Where had these radio messages come from? Who had sent them? Who had *invented* them? Was it von Kalle? Kramer? Ladoux? Why? Over and over and over again, why? There seemed to be no logic, no understanding, no answer ... Her composure was in shreds, her pride in tatters. Her behavior became irrational and unpredictable."[38] Mata Hari had denied the charges straightaway and had told Bouchardon that he was making the same mistake as Ladoux who believed that she was AF44 from Antwerp, and also the officer of the Scotland Yard, who had thought that she was undoubtedly Clara Benedix. Both had later been proved wrong. Bouchardon had then shown her the complete text of the first telegram sent by Kalle to Berlin on December 13, 1916, which read: AGENT H21, BELONGING TO THE CENTRAL INFORMATION BUREAU IN COLOGNE, WHO WAS SENT TO FRANCE FOR THE SECOND TIME IN MARCH, HAS ARRIVED HERE. SHE HAS FEIGNED TO ACCEPT THE SERVICES OF THE FRENCH ESPIONAGE BUREAU AND TO CARRY OUT A TRIAL-MISSION TO BELGIUM ON THEIR ACCOUNT. SHE WANTED TO GO FROM SPAIN TO HOLLAND ABOARD THE HOLLANDIA BUT WAS ARRESTED IN FALMOUTH ON THE 11TH OF NOVEMBER BECAUSE SHE WAS MISTAKEN FOR SOMEONE ELSE WHO IS KNOWN TO ME AND WHO IS IN MADRID. ONCE THE MISTAKE WAS RECOGNIZED, SHE WAS SENT BACK TO SPAIN BECAUSE THE BRITISH CONTINUED TO CONSIDER HER SUSPECT. SHE NOW INTENDS TO GO TO HOLLAND VIA PARIS AND SWITZERLAND. SHE HAS FURNISHED VERY

---

36   Although it appears that Ladoux had known about her code name H21 from the radio messages, H. R. Berndorff however was of the opinion that "Le Doux" had come to know about it from the Comte de Chilly, who had been romantically associated to a nurse named Hanna Wittig, and was working secretly for France in 1916, during the war. Hanna had overheard a confidential conversation of some German army men at a restaurant about H21 and how the agent had informed about movement of French troops; and realizing the importance had subsequently informed the Comte; *Espionage*, 192.

37   Waagenaar, *op. cit.*, 1964, 212.

38   Keay, *op. cit.*, 193.

COMPLETE REPORTS ON THE ENCLOSED SUBJECTS, BY LETTERS AND BY TELEGRAMS. SHE RECEIVED 5,000 FRANCS IN PARIS IN NOVEMBER AND IS NOW ASKING FOR 10,000. PLEASE GIVE ME INSTRUCTIONS RAPIDLY. Bouchardon gazed sternly at her indicating that the person in question could certainly be none other. Mata Hari had told the story of her torment at Falmouth to the interrogating magistrate during one of her questioning sessions, and therefore Bouchardon unmistakably knew that the telegram was talking about her.

Howe has indicated that the radio traffic had been Ladoux's fabrication. His justifications are[39]—(i) the original Eiffel Tower interception had been that of the message dated December 13, 1916, which had been "about the Franco-Greek princess, Briand, and British "control" of France; but in Ladoux's set the date had been mentioned as December 31, 1916; (ii) Mata Hari's second visit to Paris during wartime had been in June 1916, and not in March. Ladoux might have made the mistake while he had altered the transcripts; (iii) he had also inadvertently made a mistake in the amount of money that Mata Hari received from her lover in The Hague—she had received 5,000 francs, but Ladoux had made it 10,000 francs in the message; (iv) Kalle had identified the agent by a code number in the message to maintain anonymity, and hence it appears to be superfluous to mention all the detail of the activities undertaken by the agent (that too in the broken code) that must have been already known to Berlin; (v) the message mentioned about "Cologne center" from where the agent was being controlled, which seems to be unacceptable to reason. If H21 was heading for Belgium then it would have been quite normal for Germany to control the agent from Antwerp, which was a city in Belgium occupied by them, and not from Cologne; (vi) the suggestion in the message that a radiogram can enclose letters and telegrams is quite strange.

Shipman seems to have subscribed to this view by saying "... these telegrams did not exist—or did not exist with the alleged contents ..."[40] Her justifications could be summarized in the following manner—(i) if the radio messages did really exist while Mata Hari had been arrested then why did Ladoux take almost 3 months to inform the chief interrogating magistrate about them? More so, because Bouchardon had been literally toiling to unearth some conclusive evidence against her in order to

---

39 Howe, *op. cit.*, 166–169.
40 Shipman, *op. cit.*, 312.

implicate her on charges of espionage; (ii) if Ladoux already had such incriminating proofs against the accused then why did he arrange for shadowing her day and night from early January 1917, right after she had arrived in Paris from Madrid? What new evidence did he expect to unearth while all his previous attempts to tail her had failed to obtain anything suspicious against her? (iii) the messages had contained nothing of military importance except merely that the German counterintelligence already knew that the French had deciphered their code. Then why did Ladoux withhold those from Bouchardon as well as from Dubail for so long in the pretext of secrecy? Moreover, why did he not inform Bouchardon that the messages had been sent in the broken code? (iv) only Ladoux had authenticated the telegrams which had been challenged by none, and therefore it might be presumed that he had deliberately doctored them to distract French attention from the genuine double agents who were certainly known to him as those who had also been working for Germany; (v) while in Madrid Mata Hari used to give her letters to the hotel bearer for sending them to the post office instead of going in person for the purpose. Ladoux's men must have collected all her letters and telegrams from the menial staff of the hotel, steam opened them to note down all information she wrote in her letters, and hence Ladoux could easily manipulate the radio messages regarding her.

Léon Schirmann however is convinced about the authenticity of the telegrams, but it is notable that none of the traffic contained any gap and garbled passages typical for intercepts. There should ideally have been some remark indicating defective text in the radiograms, which is evidently not there. Nevertheless, in the book review of Schirmann's *Mata Hari: Autopsy of a Machination*,[41] Hilmar-Detlef Brückner opined, it could be speculated that the cryptology section of the French Ministry of War might have been instructed to reconstruct the defective passages of the telegrams, which had provided an opportunity for editing the texts in a discreet manner. In Mata Hari's case "information may have been inserted facilitating considerably the identification of the former dancer as 'H21'." Brückner has quoted Elsbeth Schragmüller in this regard—"In our telegrams only H21 was mentioned, and the person of Mata Hari was never referred to." Therefore, it is apparent that Ladoux, at some point, must have been instrumental to insert text into the telegrams in order to

---

41   Hilmar-Detlef Brückner (Review), "Mata Hari," Léon Schirmann, *Journal of Intelligence History*, 4 (1), 2004: 117.

implicate Mata Hari for enemy espionage. I regret not knowing French, and therefore Schirmann's point of view remains unexplored in this book. Although authenticity of the radio traffic had not been established at any point during her trial, Mata Hari was still implicated by the interrogating magistrate and subsequently by the French military court.

One however wonders what might have prompted Ladoux to present two sets of the same messages—one to Bouchardon (9) and the other to Dubail (14)—during the interrogation. One more justification might be added to those mentioned above in support of the view that Ladoux had in fact manipulated the telegrams—why was the defense lawyer Clunet not allowed to see the messages which were to determine the fate of his client and why was he not allowed to be present at the hearings regarding the messages? Using secrecy as a ploy he was refused permission every time he had sought for. The 1916 law regarding functioning of the French military tribunals permitted the counsel of an accused to be present at all the questionings, and this right had been guaranteed by the law of 1899 as well, but was ignored deliberately. In a letter written to Bouchardon, Clunet had pointed out that he was entitled by the French law to peruse the entire dossier of his client, and his right could not be denied in the name of secrecy. But still he was not allowed to defend Mata Hari in the proper way. Bouchardon had sought advice from Major Jullien, the chief military prosecutor, mentioning the Madrid–Berlin radio messages to have been of "ultra-confidential" nature; and did not forget to mention that because Clunet had once been her lover there was no reason to trust him either as an efficient lawyer in her case or as one who would maintain the required secrecy in the case. Jullien nevertheless had supported Bouchardon and had rejected Clunet's appeal.

However, Mata Hari had repeatedly denied being the German agent H21, and also all the other accusations that Bouchardon had tried to raise against her. She told him that she had met a couple on *Hollandia* who had also been arrested at Falmouth on the same day that she had been, and she speculated that one of them might have been H21.[42] Bouchardon

---

42 Shipman, *op. cit.*, 314; although there are varied versions in this regard—according to Waagenaar it was Mata Hari who had taken the name of Mrs. Blume during the questioning, and had also mentioned that Mademoiselle Blume was travelling from Holland, and therefore was not on the same ship with her; *op. cit.*, 1964, 213; Howe however wrote that Mata Hari had said that Beaufort had informed her about the German spy who was arrested at Falmouth on December 15, 1916; *op. cit.*, 182.

later had initiated an inquiry into the matter and toward the end of May he was reported by Colonel Goubet that Elise Blume (a.k.a. Lisa/Ilsa), a German national, had indeed been incarcerated in England for espionage during that time. So, Bouchardon knew that Mata Hari was not lying, although he was certain about the identity of H21 because Kalle had mentioned in his radio message that H21's maid lived in Holland whose name was Anna Lintjens. He had then referred to another message of December 23, sent from Madrid to Berlin, which said that she had asked for more money from Kalle for her services, in reply to which Kalle had been ordered by the German secret service to pay H21 the amount of 3,000 francs. It was the exact amount that Mata Hari had received from van der Capellen at that time, and hence Bouchardon had simply assumed that it was German money. Kalle had paid her 3,500 pesetas in Madrid and had informed Berlin about it on December 26 through a radio message. The message also said: *H21 WILL REQUEST BY TELEGRAM VIA THE DUTCH CONSUL IN PARIS THAT A FURTHER AMOUNT BE PAID TO HER MAID IN ROERMOND AND WANTS YOU TO ADVISE CONSUL KROEMER IN AMSTERDAM ABOUT THE SAME.* Another radio message dated December 28 had mentioned: *H21 WILL ARRIVE IN PARIS TOMORROW. SHE REQUESTS FOR AN AMOUNT OF 5,000 FRANCS TO BE SENT TO HER IMMEDIATELY AT THE COMPTOIR D'ESCOMPTE IN PARIS THROUGH THE INTERMEDIARY OF CONSUL KROEMER IN AMSTERDAM AND HER MAID ANNA LINTJENS IN ROERMOND, WHICH SHOULD BE PAID IN PARIS TO DUTCH CONSUL BUNGE.* Therefore, it was quite clear to Bouchardon that within a couple of months Mata Hari had received more than 12,000 francs from German funds for her services rendered to them. Mata Hari had tried her best to make him understand the state of affairs, but in order to implicate her, the interrogating magistrate did not need any further proof.

Bouchardon persistently went on questioning Mata Hari about the telegrams, focusing on the message sent on December 14 (one of the missing radiograms) by Kalle to Berlin, which had mentioned about the British secret agent Mr. Allard, a Belgian national. She had emphatically denied having told about Allard to Kalle, but recollected that she had taken his name in Vigo; and as mentioned earlier, the person who she had confided in Vigo was Martial Cazeaux, a French sympathizer. Bouchardon however had refused to believe that there might have been paid people of Ladoux at Hotel Ritz who could have truly intercepted her letters and could have then communicated the contents to Ladoux. Bouchardon thereafter had embarked on the issue of invisible ink referring to the same message of December 14 in which Kalle had reported to Berlin that agent H21 had told him that the French knew how to develop secret ink that was being used by the German. Mata Hari denied any knowledge whatsoever about German invisible ink and had replied that she doubted Denvignes of doing the mischief. By taking his name she might have tried to take revenge on the French military attaché because of two reasons—first, she had doubted him to be the author of the letter against her that had reached the head of Vadime's Regiment, who then had alerted her fiancé against her; and second, she was somewhat sure that Denvignes had reported her findings in Madrid to Ladoux without taking her name, thus stealing all credit of the information collected by her. She still believed that Ladoux might not have paid her because of Denvignes's malfeasance. As Denvignes was not significant in any way to the French intelligence service, Bouchardon did not heed to her allegation against him. He instead had shown her a message of March 6 written to Kalle from Berlin, which said: *PLEASE LET US KNOW WHETHER AGENT H21 HAS BEEN TOLD THAT FOR ALL COMMUNICATIONS SHE SHOULD USE THE SECRET INK WHICH WAS GIVEN TO HER, AND WHETHER SHE HAS BEEN SHOWN THAT THIS INK CANNOT BE DEVELOPED BY THE ENEMY.* She repeatedly told Bouchardon that she knew nothing about German invisible ink and had reiterated that it was Ladoux who had offered her money to do secret service for France, not *vice versa*. Bouchardon could have given her the benefit of doubt, but he did not. No argument, no evidence in her favor, was any more relevant to him.

Mata Hari was not called by Bouchardon for the next 3 weeks, and on May 15 she had written to him praying once more for her provisional freedom. She wrote: "You cannot degrade a woman, day after day ... I am here because of a misunderstanding. I beseech you: stop making me suffer. I cannot take any more, truly, truly."[43] She had received no reply as usual from him because he had deliberately been making her suffer for her sins against France. On that day she had also written a letter to Clunet in a plaintive tone—"... Where will it end? Does he wish to kill me? Must he kill me? Or give me my liberty?" She had evidently been losing her head, and "was shattered in spirit, mind, and body;"[44] but Clunet

---

43 Shipman, *op. cit.*, 318.
44 Ibid., 320.

was helpless because he stood alone by her side against the whole of the French authority, who wanted to use her life as well as her death in the interest of France in the war. It had been as if she was supposed to pay off every bit that France had given her once. Mata Hari had been called in for the next interrogation on May 21. During that time, in May 1917, the army mutiny resulting from the failure of the Nivelle Offensive had been continuing in a bizarre way, effectively weakening both the French war effort and the morale of the French soldiers. It has already been mentioned that the French government was going through a trying time in order to resolve the problem, which had also affected the home front significantly. Something really big was required to make an effect on the society, and also on the mutinying army, to bring back their confidence on their homeland. No one could be a more appropriate sacrifice than Mata Hari at that point in time, and hence, Bouchardon had been particularly instructed by the Ministry of War to implicate her on charges of espionage. The French government had strongly anticipated that the people of France would surely regain courage to fight back the enemy when they knew that their government had effectively obliterated the enemy within.

Mata Hari had desperately wanted to get a way out of the mess, and on that day, without any provocation from Bouchardon, for the first time she had explained the entire episode that had happened with her in Amsterdam when Kroemer had called at her door. The story was quite lengthy and she did not try to make it short, explaining every nuance that she could recall. She had confessed that she did not disclose the incident to Ladoux because she did not consider it to be necessary as she had not done anything for Kroemer in return of the money she had received from him. She had also told Bouchardon that inspite of recruiting her with the promise of huge amount of money, Ladoux had abandoned her. His plan to send her to Belgium did not work due to the incident at Falmouth. She had told Bouchardon that she was extremely worried with her mounting bills and no money to fend for herself in Madrid, and therefore had to search for ways to earn some money to sustain. She had also told him that she went to Kalle sheerly due to that fact, and did not intend to divulge any French secret to him (she obviously had no knowledge of any French secret either), but only had seduced him to bed for money. In return of her intimate favors Kalle had offered her a ring, but she had refused to take it as she did not like the ornament. He had then substituted with money. Therefore, the 3,500 pesetas that he had given her was her lover's gift and not payment for any espionage work. Bouchardon however did not believe her and had asked her to pinpoint whom did she serve betraying whom—Germany or France? Mata Hari boldly replied: "If my attitude towards the Germans and the French was different, then it was because I wanted to hurt the first ... and help the second."[45] Her words had fallen into deaf ears. Bouchardon then told her that he had questioned Jean Hallaure regarding her visit to 282 Boulevard Saint-Germain in 1916, but Hallaure did not subscribe to her version. He had also pointed out that her surveillance in Paris and Vittel had revealed that she had been going around with many army officers of various countries, which, according to him, was not quite normal. Mata Hari had then replied: "I love officers. I have loved them all my life. I prefer to be mistress of a poor officer than of a rich banker. It is my greatest pleasure to sleep with them without having to think of money. And moreover I like to make comparisons between the various nationalities."[46] Bouchardon had skillfully distorted every word she uttered in a manner to suit his purpose and had wrongfully claimed that she made a confession for her involvement in enemy espionage on that day [On May 22, Bouchardon reported to Colonel Goubet about the alleged confession, and detailed on the three bottles of invisible ink that was given to Mata Hari by Kroemer, although she had never admitted to have used them. He also made up stories against her in his reporting which did not have any factual bearing. www.nationalarchives.gov.uk (KV-2/2)]. It was however absolutely normal for him to trust the French army officers instead of believing a debauch woman, who had reportedly done great harm to France during the war (by divulging secrets of the tanks to the enemy).[47]

Bouchardon had again grilled her on the next day, May 22, regarding her meeting with Kroemer and Kalle, and regarding the 20,000 francs that was given to her by the former. His simple logic was that the Germans were no fool and would therefore never give her such a hefty sum for doing nothing for them. So, he had concluded that she must have been paid for some of her previous services to Germany. He had then mentioned about her two wartime trips to France, her sending letters to her maid Anna in The Hague through the Dutch consulate instead of using

---

45   Waagenaar, *op. cit.*, 1964, 221–222.
46   Ibid., 223.
47   Ernest Dunlop Swinton however had varied opinion on this issue; *Eyewitness*, 204-205.

normal post, implying that those had been meant not for the maid but for Kroemer, and also about her confession to Kalle that she was H21 whom Germany did not consider to be a traitor (apparent from the radio messages). As Clunet was not allowed to attend the hearings Mata Hari had to face Bouchardon's charges merely with her own style of reasoning, which, although had been nearer to truth, could never please the interrogating magistrate. Against all the charges that had been raised by him she had replied each time with denial. She had never bored from expressing and explaining the real circumstances to Bouchardon in minute detail thinking desperately each time that her reply would ultimately satisfy him and would fetch her liberty, but nothing really worked because the magistrate already had the final decision in his pocket.

However, on that day Ladoux was finally called in to depose in front of Mata Hari, and a bitter verbal duel had immediately ensued between them as she had initiated a hateful altercation with him. She had been waiting for that moment and would not leave Ladoux easily, although her misconception about the promised 1 million francs was eventually put to rest. Ladoux said: "When Zelle-MacLeod told me that she could actually penetrate as far as German Headquarters, I asked her whether she really believed that she could get us information on the operational plans of the German army. When she answered in the affirmative, I said: "For that kind of information we would pay a million."[48] He did not fail to mention that she had suppressed facts about her being an agent of Germany while he had talked to her about rendering services to France and denied that he had recruited her as a spy, because he claimed before Bouchardon that he did not provide her with a code number, did not give her a mission, nor any money, or any means of communication that were essential for a secret recruit. Ladoux had said that he suspected her. Then why did he allow her to re-enter France in 1916? His reply perplexed Bouchardon as he said that it was not his duty to allow or oppose her visa for re-entry into France, and by exposing her he had only done his duty toward his homeland. What he did not mention was that he had been intimated by the British counterintelligence about her possible involvement in German espionage as early as in February 1915, but still he had advanced with his adventures with the former demimondaine. Strangely, Bouchardon could not see the ambiguities in his replies, and instead focused only on Mata Hari, because that is what he had been assigned to do. Bouchardon

---

48 Waagenaar, *op. cit.*, 1964, 227.

insisted her to explain why she had not revealed to Ladoux about the Kroemer incident, to which she had replied: "I did not tell you my plans because you did not want to pay me ..." Bouchardon then told her that according to the French law "maintaining such contacts with the enemy is equivalent to the actual transmitting of information." Mata Hari became furious. She had said: "Then your law is frightful."

Although Bouchardon had already decided on her guilt and had also been reporting concocted stories against her to his superior in order to establish his views, she was again called the next day, on May 23, for questioning. For him, after nearly 13 days of interrogation, Mata Hari had never spoken the truth, while it was both him and Captain Ladoux to whom the case had been crystal clear. So, the questioning had followed an almost repetitive pattern—mention of her first meeting with Kroemer in Amsterdam, his reaction after she had returned to Holland from France in February 1916, the 20,000 francs that he had given to her for her services to Germany, her sending message to Anna Lintjens through the Dutch diplomatic channel, her being known to Antwerp which was evident from the radio messages, and the like; and Mata Hari's replies had been the same as before. It could have been Bouchardon's trick to test her confidence. On that day he had also read out Denvignes's official statement about her, which she had endorsed to have been closer to truth but for the relationship that he had shared with her while she had been in Madrid. Denvignes, due to obvious reasons, must have suppressed his feelings about her in his official statement to Bouchardon, but it was absolutely certain from his statement that he did not consider her to be a German spy. To establish her version of the relationship Mata Hari had disclosed some detail regarding Denvignes's conduct in Madrid, but Bouchardon was not convinced. Nothing from her could ever convince him in any way.

During the last week of May he had still continued interrogating more witnesses for the case, and the list included Vadime de Masloff, although, as requested by Mata Hari, he was not called in to depose at Bouchardon's office in Paris, instead he was allowed to send his statement to him. Vadime had categorically stated that his relationship with the former dancer was not at all important to him, and therefore in March 1917, he had gone to Paris to ensure a breakup with her, but had found that she had already been incarcerated for her involvement in enemy espionage. Russia had been going through a very bad political phase during that time due to the army revolt (February Revolution of 1917), and Tsar Nicholas II was eventually forced to resign in March. Vadime could take no chances with his career in the army, and therefore renouncing the relationship could have been the best alternative for him at that point. All of a sudden Mata Hari's whole universe had fallen apart and she only had a stony reaction after knowing about Vadime's statement. She could not utter a word. How could her dear Vadime be so rude to her? They had planned to marry and to live together for the rest of their life, they had shared so many passionate moments, she had showered so much love and care on him—how could all that joy suddenly become unimportant to him? Mata Hari, as always, could not understand what had gone wrong. She could never even envisage that for Vadime, at that point in time, the most important thing could only have been his army career, which, by no means, would he put at stake for the elderly former dancer. He had been wise enough to end a dissimilar relationship which surely headed to nowhere. Vadime's spell was over, and therefore his beloved Marina remained no more.

On May 30 Mata Hari was called in for another questioning session when Denvignes had been the focus of interrogation. Mention of the Crown Prince Friedrich W. V. August Ernst and his only brother-in-law (husband of Princess Victoria Louise of Germany) Ernest Augustus C. G. III, the Duke of Cumberland, was also made to seek clarification from her on the matter. She admitted that she had mentioned them to the French colonel, but not with regard to anything of military significance, because she had known the Crown Prince only through some intimate interactions while she had been the mistress of Mr. Kiepert in Berlin. Bouchardon nevertheless did not believe her. For him she was definitely guilty and her money trail had proved it beyond any doubt. Therefore, the continuation of her interrogation had been repetitive and meaningless to some extent; still she was called in for two more sessions on June 1 and 12, plausibly in order to be sure over and over again. Once again she was questioned about Kroemer's money and her relationship with him. In her own peculiar manner she had replied with repentance that she could not progress with the relationship with him because her house in The Hague had not been completely furnished by then, and she did not have good linen or proper silver crockery even to serve tea to a gentleman. What else could have been Bouchardon's understanding of the situation from her reply apart from that she was eager to develop a passionate relationship with

Kroemer if she had a well-established home? On the question about the 20,000 francs she reiterated that she had accepted the money as reimbursement of her confiscated furs and jewelry, and not as payment for any secret service. Then why did she take the name of Kroemer and tell Kalle that she was in the service of the Germans? She said that she had to pretend like one because she wanted to become reliable to Kalle so that he would confide to her about important German plans during wartime. She had further told to the ever cynical Bouchardon that all that she had done in Madrid was purely in the interest of France and not of Germany.

He had picked up the issue of Vittel once again, to which she replied that the trip was meant for recovering her health, and she had been in a hurry because the season was about to end. Her absence from Paris in 1910–1911 had been known to the French intelligence service as her period of training at the Fräulein Doktor's spy training school in Antwerp, which she had readily denied. She had actually been staying as Mrs. Rousseau at Esvres in the Chateau de la Dorée during that time, but Bouchardon did not believe her. He could have called in Mr. Felix Rousseau or even his servants to depose in the matter, but he did not want to do that as that would have jeopardized his interest. Mata Hari, as if, deserved no justice. In the interest of France Bouchardon would not do anything that could prove her innocence. She was then asked about the director of a bank in Berlin through whom she had received some money from Holland. Mata Hari said that he was Constant Baret who had been her lover while she was in Berlin in 1914, but she had denied knowing Kroemer at that time. On June 12, at the next questioning session, Mata Hari had complained that the French was guilty of arresting her without giving her an opportunity to defend herself—in order to clarify the accusations of espionage she wanted to talk to Ladoux first, but had not been given an opportunity to do so. She had then requested the magistrate to call her long-time friend Henri de Marguerie as her witness, who had been closely connected with her during her stay in Paris in 1915, and knew about all her activities during that time, but was not permitted. Marguerie knew that she had no other intention than to rejuvenate her mood with her old friends and to mix with new people who aspired to be entertained during the tiring war. It had been a considerably short session that day with unfolding of no new evidence.

Mata Hari was called in for the final interrogation on June 21 and on that day, for the last time, she had tried in vain to convince Bouchardon, because she knew that it was going to be her last chance to do so. Once again she had narrated her first encounter with Ladoux in detail and her reason to accept his offer to work for France. She asserted that Ladoux had appointed her officially, especially because he had talked to her regarding the matter in the office of the War Department, and not in any Paris restaurant or in any private apartment, from where he had sent her to the government office of Maunoury in order to get her exit visa for Vittel. She also revealed her plans that she had chalked out while in Madrid in order to prove her capability to Ladoux, to render service to and also to facilitate France in the war. She admitted that she had willingly taken the responsibility from Ladoux, although with the aim to earn some money in order to marry and settle down with her fiancé Vadime. Waagenaar quoted her: "I had been the mistress of the brother of the Duke of Cumberland, who ... had married the daughter of the Kaiser ... I knew that the Duke's brother-in-law, the Crown Prince, had made him solemnly swear that he would never reclaim the throne of the Kingdom of Hanover. He did swear this, but only for himself—not for his descendents. He and the Crown Prince hate each other violently. It was this hate which I intended to exploit in the interests of France ... I would have resumed my relations with the Duke of Cumberland and would have done all I could to detach him from Germany and get him over on the Allied side."[49] She went on with giving explanations to Bouchardon about her basic nature and about all that she had been doing in France during the war. It was the day that marked beginning of the summer solstice. Although the earth receives the most daylight on that day, it had been the day of utmost darkness for Mata Hari—the eye of dawn. All through the questioning sessions she had tried to put her point across by arguing from the best of her knowledge and capability, but had failed to convince Bouchardon, and therefore was destined to face trial in the military tribunal. As it was the last day of interrogation Bouchardon was under legal compulsion to allow Clunet to be present for his client at the session, and he had been allowed to do so, although he was no more in a position to change her fate. Mata Hari had been chosen as the sacrificial victim by France.

Although the pre-trial had ended on June 21, not much was changed for Mata Hari. Many of the Dutch newspapers had published articles

---
49 Ibid., 239.

about her during that time, and ultimately on June 30 Mr. Hannema, the Secretary-General of the Dutch Foreign Ministry, had shown some concern over her plight asking Clunet to keep him informed, though with no significant outcome. On July 20 she was however released from Saint Lazare and had been moved to the Concièrgerie because her trial was scheduled to start on July 24 at the Palace of Justice, and as per the common practice she was supposed to be kept closer to the venue. Mata Hari had been kept in the same enclave that had housed Queen Marie Antoinette in 1793, and also Maximilien Robespierre during the Reign of Terror in France. It had however not been difficult for Bouchardon to decide on the fate of his subject. On the basis of a few doctored evidences, conclusive according to him in the case, but still without any "strong case" against Mata Hari, he had written a report from his own perspective of beliefs and had referred the case to the Third Council of War for further action. Shipman wrote: "The telegrams said that she was a German spy but did not even hint at any information she passed, and they contained peculiar inconsistencies."[50] Yet on June 21, the highly prejudiced Bouchardon had formally concluded on the sin of the former dancer, who, according to him, was a predatory woman and a dangerous creature.

It was absolutely shocking for Mata Hari because she failed to understand why a simple misunderstanding had eventually become so grave for her, and why the interrogating officer had all along refused to see the truth. Due to her characteristic naivety she could never see the pattern that had been concocted by the French government to implicate her falsely in the interest of France—the country she had believed to be her own. She still hoped to get justice and had earnestly believed that the worst possible thing that would happen to her could be either getting expelled from France forever or being sentenced to hard labor.[51] As she was confident of her innocence she could not think of any harsher punishment. But Mata Hari had been mistaken. From the very beginning the trial court had known that on the basis of certain clinching proofs the interrogating magistrate had found her to be guilty, and therefore the line of judgment had somewhat been predetermined. Waagenaar wrote: "Mata Hari's actual trial was of little importance, except insofar as it dealt with the verdict and sentence ... But the real case was Bouchardon's."[52] Shipman

---

50   Shipman, *op. cit.*, 323.
51   Udovic, *op. cit.*, 2.
52   Waagenaar, *op. cit.*, 1965, 178.

wrote: "There were only three types of evidence against her. One was the contents of the intercepted telegrams about agent H21; a second was her receipt of monies through the Dutch consulate ... the third was her admission that she had taken money from Kroemer ..."[53] Although there had been no evidence of Mata Hari's interest in military matters or her using invisible ink for her liaisons, still her fate was sealed. No more was she a suspect, she was a convict. Mata Hari was convicted without any conclusive proof against her for something she had never done, and she had been a victim of the then European culture and politics.

In his report Bouchardon had cleverly twisted and distorted all of Mata Hari's statements that she had placed before him justifying her acts and had brought a total of the following eight charges against her,[54] focusing mainly on her suspected intentions on various occasions—

1. She had entered the entrenched camp of Paris in December 1915, with the intention to obtain secret information and documents to help Germany during wartime.

2. In Holland she had procured documents and information for the German consul Kroemer during the first half of 1916, in order to bring damage to the military endeavor of the Allied forces during the war.

3. In May 1916, she had maintained contact with Germany through Kroemer in order to help their war enterprises.

4. She had entered the war zone of Paris in June 1916, with the intention to procure documents and information in the interest of Germany.

5. Since May 1916, she had maintained contact with Germany from Paris in order to facilitate and assist them in the war.

6. In December 1916, she had established and maintained contact with the German military attaché in Madrid with the aim of assisting Germany during war.

7. In Madrid during the same time she had provided secret

---
53 Shipman, *op. cit.*, 337.
54 Ibid., 339–340.

information pertaining to the Allied forces to the German military attaché in order to damage and endanger the military services of the former. The information divulged by her to Kalle had been related to—(i) the interior politics of France, (ii) the upcoming spring offensive, (iii) discovery of the German secret invisible ink by the French along with the methods to develop, and (iv) disclosure of the name of a secret agent in the service of France.

8. In January 1917, she had maintained contact with Germany with the intention of harming the war efforts of the Allied forces, thereby helping the enemy.

It is quite surprising as to how Mata Hari's supposed intentions became so evident to Bouchardon, inspite of the fact that on every occasion she had emphatically denied his charges. Moreover, Mata Hari had not been in Paris in May 1916, and Bouchardon did not even care to rectify his mistake while preparing his report against her. He had never thought of contemplating her version because from the very beginning she had been a "dangerous creature" for him who spoke several languages with equal ease, had lovers all over Europe, and confessed to be an "international woman." Mata Hari was therefore guilty. The Third Council of War would certainly not do any justice to this unscrupulous and condemned woman. After more than a month later, on July 24, her trial had begun at the Palace of Justice, which was held only for two consecutive days. Everyone present at the courtroom was amazed to see the woman, once renowned for her grace and glamour, in a visibly transformed state—with her carelessly dressed graying hair and lack of make-up she looked absolutely ruined—although she still strived to maintain her posture of dignity. She was calmly seated in front of seven distinguished military personnel,[55] all members of the Third Permanent Council of War of the Military Government of Paris, and so had been appointed by the Military Governor General Auguste Dubail (a Saint Cyrian of the 1870 batch)—Lieutenant-Colonel Albert Ernest Semprou (President of the Tribunal), while the other six men had all been judges in her case—Major Fernand Joubert, Captain Lionel de Cayla, Gendarmerie Captain Jean Chatin, Lieutenant Henry Deguesseau, Second Lieutenant Joseph de Mercier de Malval, and Sergeant Major Berthomme. Lieutenant Andre Mornet had been present as the Trial Counsel and Sergeant Major Rivière as the

---

55 Waagenaar, *op. cit.*, 1964, 253.

clerk. The only person present from her side was the elderly lawyer and friend Edouard Clunet. Although in his memoirs Major Emile Massard (Mata Hari's biographer) had claimed to be present as the representative of Governor Dubail, no documentary evidence had been found to substantiate his claim. Bouchardon also had claimed to be present at the trial, but there is no record to prove his claim either.[56]

Three law books, supposed to be followed in the case, had also been kept on the table—the *Military Code of Justice*, the *Criminal Instruction Code*, and the *Ordinary Penal Code*—with which Clunet was not well conversant. Significantly almost all the people present at the trial were Saint Cyrians, and therefore, as per the general trend, had been both anti-Semitic and misogynic. Mata Hari was an independent woman who had walked out of her marriage on her own will abandoning her husband and daughter, and therefore had to bear the wrath of the judges' personal preferences. Moreover, due to some strange reasons, she had been considered to be a Jew,[57] which made her guilt all the more unpardonable. The Articles of the law books, on which the proceedings were supposedly going to be based, had little bearing. The proceedings had started at 1:00 PM in the crowded Court of Assizes room[58] where the spectators had curiously gathered to see the former glamorous sex symbol of Europe. She had appeared for the trial elegantly dressed in a large dark blue coat over a low-cut blouse, and to cover up her graying hair had sported a large tricorn hat. But as her trial was supposed to be a secret affair it was necessary to be held *in camera*, and hence the courtroom had been cleared of the over enthusiast spectators. The press was also debarred from being present at the trial. The courtroom guards had been ordered to keep them at a distance of at least 30 feet from the closed door in order to maintain absolute secrecy in the case. Regarding the sources about the trial Shipman wrote: "The only available accounts of the trial are the official judgment ... which does not detail the lines of questioning; a letter about the trial written after the fact by Captain Jean Chatin, one of the judges; and eyewitness accounts written years later by Bouchardon and Massard, who may not have been present at the trial."[59]

---

56   Shipman, *op. cit.*, 347.
57   It was common understanding among the French that Mata Hari had been appointed as a German spy by Walter Nicolai, and since most of his spies were Jews, so Mata Hari was necessarily a Jew.
58   Wheelwright, *op. cit.*, 85.
59   Shipman, *op. cit.*, 347.

Artist's impression of the trial of Mata Hari
(The Mata Hari Foundation, Fries Museum, Leeuwarden)

The jurors had Bouchardon's report in front of them and were to decide on all the eight accusations made by him against Mata Hari. However, President Semprou was the first to open the trial by questioning her about her relationship with Griebel in Berlin and why she had been in his car on the day war broke out. The President had however confused Griebel, merely an officer in the German Police Force, with Berlin's Metropolitan Police Commissioner Traugott von Jagow, who dealt with espionage matters during that time and had accused her of accepting secret service against France on the request of her Commissioner lover. Mata Hari was astounded to hear some such thing from the august court, because she had never been in the company of von Jagow while in Berlin and therefore had strongly denied the charge. Trial Counsel Lieutenant Mornet had thereafter started with the question of her allegiance with men in uniform and she repeated what she had told Bouchardon earlier on the matter—that she simply was fascinated with men in uniform. She said: "To me, the officer forms a race apart ... I never noticed whether they are German, Italian or French."[60] She had further added that she did not have any malicious intention for that. The second question by Mornet had been regarding her visit to Vittel during the war, and her reply was the same as she had said during her pre-trial hearings—to take the water for cure and to meet her fiancé Vadime. Mornet scowled at Mata Hari,

---

60   Quoted in Wheelwright, *op. cit.*, 87.

because if she was not well and had urgently needed the cure, then at the same time how did she write to her lover van der Capellen in Holland that she had been doing perfectly well. How could Mornet know what might have been going on in the thoughts of a package of entertainment like her? She had replied that as she did not want to upset the Baron who paid her handsomely for her living, she did not inform him about each of her personal matter.

As the jurors had necessarily based their interrogation on the submitted pre-trial report of the interrogating magistrate, the questions followed a similar pattern, and her replies had also been almost the same; and it is needless to mention that like Bouchardon the jury was also not convinced with her replies, because even before the case was started the jury had already known exactly what to do and what to establish. Money trail could have been an appropriate way for Mornet to pin down the accused, and therefore taking out a cheque for 5,000 francs from the file before him in a dramatic gesture he had raised the issues of the 20,000 francs that was paid to Mata Hari by Kroemer, and the payments that she had received through the Dutch consulate in Paris. Mata Hari only had to say what she had already told Bouchardon about Kroemer's payment and had added that the other amounts had come from her various lovers in return of her sexual favors to them. She had also clarified that the cheque for 5,000 francs (one of the two that she had received) was sent to her from Holland by van der Capellen as her regular allowance. A teetotaler and a vegetarian Mornet had immediately assessed that the amounts had certainly been more than what could have been required for her sexual favors and had concluded that it therefore must have been for some other important service that she had rendered to the Germans, which, for him, had clearly indicated at some kind of secret service of military significance that she had engaged in to facilitate them during the war. He did not also believe that the two drafts of 5,000 francs had actually come from van der Capellen and taking Bouchardon's line had thought that those were in fact sent to her by Kroemer. For him every bit of her money stank of German conspiracy against France. Mornet had pointed especially to the 3,500 pesetas that came from Kalle, which had been paid from the government funds allocated to pay the secret agents who worked for Germany. But how could Mata Hari be responsible if he had misappropriated government funds to pay his mistresses? Mornet however had no doubt that the money had been paid to her for her intelligence services to Germany, because it somehow was apparent to him that Germans did not pay such high prices to their mistresses merely for their sexual favors. Waagenaar although referred to Marthe Richer's book where she had stated: "I bring you evidence that he (the German Naval Attaché in Madrid von Krohn) kept me with the money he had at his disposal to pay his spies with."[61] This might have been a common practice among the German government officials of that time, which Mornet might not have been aware of.

The next question from Mornet had been related to her association with Ladoux and to the reasons for why did she hide that she had already been paid in advance by Kroemer for her secret services to Germany. Mata Hari could not understand what was so wrong in that—women have always used various covert means to achieve their goals, which had certainly been beyond men's capability even to fathom. Moreover, there was no reason for her to reveal all her secrets to Ladoux because he had not even given any money to refurbish her wardrobe that was absolutely essential to seduce the highest ranking German people in Belgium; and all the more because she had never done anything for Kroemer after taking money from him. She had also said that she wanted Ladoux to trust her outrightly, because only then would he pay her the promised amount of 1 million francs, which could support her to marry Vadime and settle down happily with him. According to Howe, Mata Hari told the jury that she had planned to "announce her recruitment into German intelligence after getting back to Holland, making it her first coup for France—just as she had used her recruitment by Ladoux to try to impress Kalle."[62] He further speculated that she refrained from confiding in Ladoux about Kroemer because she knew that Ladoux "had her shadowed for 6 months in France, from May to November 1916, and had openly expressed suspicions about her."[63] She moreover had apprehended that Ladoux might not allow her to go to Vittel if he knew about her connection with Kroemer and might probably confine her in Paris.

However, in reply to Mornet's question about her relationship with Kalle in Madrid she had said that it was only because Colonel Denvignes had advised her to return to Kalle in order to collect more specific information

---

61   Waagenaar, *op. cit.*, 1964, 257.
62   Howe, *op. cit.*, 239.
63   Ibid., 239.

on the German war plans that she had gone to his house again. It is significant to note that she did not visit Kalle while she had proceeded toward Holland in November through Madrid, and only went to see him when she had been sent back to the Spanish capital by the British counterintelligence; but the jury had deliberately overlooked this. If she had already known Kalle then it would have been quite normal for her to see him while she was travelling through the city en route to Holland. Mata Hari had then told Mornet that she had wanted to use her liaison with Kalle for personal reasons also—to get a permit in order to return to Holland through Germany as she would never again try to travel through England, especially after her experience at Falmouth. Mata Hari had naively thought that because she was being absolutely honest and perfectly logical in her replies the jury would certainly realize that she was innocent and would set her free in a short time. With all sincerity she had argued that if she had been truly guilty of enemy espionage she would not dare to return to Paris during wartime, at least after her unexpected arrest at Falmouth. Nevertheless, her sincere logic had failed to impress the jury.

Mornet had then picked up the issue of her code name H21, which she had admitted of knowing, but had denied having ever used for any purpose. The prosecution had the set of radio messages (Bourchardon's set of 9 messages) along with Bouchardon's report, which clearly mentioned her as a "born spy," and therefore Mornet had simply brushed aside her reply regarding H21. The French government was convinced that it had been due to her relationship with Kalle that the German Naval Force could torpedo several ships carrying Allied troops to Morocco. Without any concrete proof she had been accused of "collective assassination" because she was believed to be responsible for the death of fifty thousand French soldiers in the Battle of Somme in 1916. The allegation hinted at her supposed involvement in the tank drama at the battle, when the German army had used a sophisticated version of the anti-tank guns (especially the Krupp guns) to jeopardize and destroy the French efforts. The logic was very simple—somebody who could desert her husband and children for her own pleasure, one who could cause death to her own child, was certainly so vile that she could undoubtedly massacre any number of French soldiers in return of money, especially because she was a *femme fatale* who had been working for the enemy. It had moreover been rumored that the former dancer had plenty of coal for her personal use during the pinching fuel famine in France in the winter months of 1917, indicating at her positive involvement and ill nexus with some top officials in the tank disaster.

Mata Hari tried to defend herself saying that she had actually informed Ladoux that the Germans were sending soldiers to the Moroccan coast by submarines and did not tell Kalle anything about the Allied soldiers. She had also tried to justify herself saying that she could not even think of killing a single person, so the question of her causing death to 50,000 soldiers was absolutely absurd. Her reply however had no impact on Mornet. He had next called in five witnesses for the prosecution in order to justify his accusations—(i) Inspector Monier, one of the duo who had kept watch on Mata Hari for quite long, (ii) Police Commissioner Albert Priolet, (iii) Captain Ladoux, (iv) his superior Colonel Goubet, and (v) a furrier named Albert Ramillay. Although none could furnish any evidence of her involvement in enemy espionage, all had somehow been convinced about her crime. Monier had testified about her luxurious way of living and her friendship with high-ranking men, Albert Priolet had testified about the circumstances of her arrest from a hotel on February 13, Goubet had made the following statement: "one of the most dangerous that counterespionage ever captured."[64] Mornet therefore wanted to call in more people, especially Vadime de Massloff and Lieutenant Jean Hallaure, but none had appeared before the War Tribunal, instead had sent written statements. Later Mornet had called in some other people as witness—the manicurist to whom Mata Hari frequented while she was in Paris, and a fortuneteller to whom she had paid a visit in January 1917, after returning to Paris from Madrid. She might have wanted to know when she would get the 1 million francs from Ladoux and when she would be able to marry Vadime. None of them however had spoken about anything that could strengthen Mornet's stand. The trial had been closed at 7 o'clock in the evening that day, with President of the Tribunal's order to continue on the next morning at 8:30. Mata Hari was taken back to her prison cell in the Concièrgerie accompanied by Sister Léonide and the prison guards.

In the morning of July 25 the court room looked exactly the same as the previous day. The public and the press had not been allowed as usual. Mata Hari was brought into the room, along came Edouard Clunet, as

---

64 Shipman, *op. cit.*, 349.

it was supposed to be the last day of hearing, and her lawyer was legally entitled to attend. Lieutenant-Colonel Semprou had started the session with written statements of the two witnesses Vadime de Massloff and Jean Hallaure, which had been read out loudly by the clerk Rivière before the jury. None of their accounts had revealed anything adverse about the accused. Edouard Clunet had invited some people to depose in favor of his client who included her long-time friend Henri de Marguerie and the secretary-general of the Ministry of Foreign Affairs Jules Cambon. Marguerie, an expert cryptanalyst for the Ministry of Foreign Affairs,[65] told the jury that when he had met Mata Hari during the war in 1915 they had only discussed Indian art and nothing that bore any military or political significance. He had openly expressed his opinion about Mata Hari—that she could not be a spy. His version was echoed by some other witnesses who had testified that she spoke only of art, theater, books, and music, but never of war. Cambon had also taken a similar stand saying that she had never probed him for anything related to war (it has although been stated earlier that on October 20, only after 5 days of her execution, he admitted to a Paris correspondent of *The Evening Star* that Mata Hari had indeed been an enemy spy). Adolphe-Pierre Messimy, the French Minister of War during the outbreak of the war in 1914, had also been summoned to the court, but did not appear in person. His wife had sent a letter to President Semprou stating that her husband had never been linked to Mata Hari. Messimy's name had not been mentioned in the court, and he was identified only as M—y, due to which Louis Malvy, the Minister of Interior, was widely presumed to have been her lover, which was however not true. Nevertheless, in April 1926, Messimy had admitted his romantic liaison with the dancer,[66] and it became apparent that the German spymasters might have taken keen interest to employ her as a secret agent because of her proximity to the then French Minister of War. (It does not however make any sense, because during the end of 1914 or at the beginning of 1915, at the time when Kroemer had met Mata Hari, Messimy was no longer the War Minister, his tenure had ended in August 1914). Although, as the defense counsel, Clunet had tried to make his point absolutely clear about the inconsistencies and weaknesses in the prosecution's case, it had no impact on the members of the Tribunal because they were convinced by the prosecution's accusations. Curiously,

---

65   Wheelwright, *op. cit.*, 89.
66   Ebba D. Dahlin, *French and German Public Opinion on Declared War Aims: 1914–1918*, 121.

even at the final trial, neither van der Capellen nor Anna Lintjens had been called to testify for her. Eva Horn wrote: "Bouchardon is following a logic of war that does away with all ambiguities. War renders the alluring mysteries that populated the glamorous salons of the belle époque deeply suspicious ... Mata Hari falls victim to this iron logic."[67] She had been demystified too harshly as all the mysteries that she had carefully woven around her had been torn off by "all too serious men" during her trial.

Mata Hari's fate had already been decided, and by then she must also have understood that she was not going to be freed easily. Anticipating further confinement she must have been in a trauma, still she had confidently pleaded her innocence saying "My defense is to speak the truth. I am not French. I have the right to have friends in other countries, even those at war with France. I remain neutral. I count on good hearts of French officers."[68] Her confident defense did not move Mornet, and he commented: "... defendant Zelle be declared guilty of all acts brought against her[69]... This is perhaps the greatest woman spy of the century."[70] Shipman wrote: "Where was the evidence that she had harmed France? Where were the secrets she was supposed to have passed?"[71] Nothing seemed to be necessary in her case anymore as President Semprou had declared the hearing closed. Clunet had pleaded for her forgiveness, but was obviously rejected. Mornet had accused her of the following[72]—(i) she gave information to Kalle about (a) the intentions of Prince George of Greece, (b) the politics in Paris, (c) opposition of the French people to Briand's government, and (d) the fear and resultant anxiety of the Frenchmen of English domination in the war; (ii) she had discussed with Kalle about (a) the possibility of a spring offensive, (b) the dropping of French spies behind the enemy lines by the French aviator Jules Védrines, (c) travel limitations imposed upon French officers during wartime, and (d) the French knowledge of German secret inks; (iii) she had links with a spy chief in German intelligence service named Griebel as her lover and controller; (iv) she had penetrated the war zone in Paris twice (in December 1915 and June 1916) with the mission to collect documents and information in

---

67   Eva Horn, *op. cit.*, 186.
68   Shipman, *op. cit.*, 352; Wheelwright, *op. cit.*, 90.
69   Waagenaar, *op. cit.*, 1964, 261.
70   Wheelwright, *op. cit.*, 90.
71   Shipman, *op. cit.*, 352.
72   Wheelwright, *op. cit.*, 90.

order to facilitate the German war endeavor; and (v) she had maintained intelligence with Germany through Kroemer in Amsterdam and Kalle in Madrid. Mornet had concluded that her accepting money from Kroemer and Kalle, and even the two drafts of 5,000 francs each that came from Holland (Mornet did not hesitate to mention Baron van der Capellen as "straw man" for Kroemer[73]) proved beyond doubt that she was an enemy spy.

The jury had to decide on all the eight points raised by Bouchardon in his report, and although there was no evidence, took merely a couple of minutes to vote. Wheelwright gave a detailed account on the issue.[74] She said, on the first accusation that on her first wartime visit to Paris in 1915, she had collected important military information and communicated it to the German intelligence, there was no evidence. On the second accusation that she had given secret military documents and information to Kroemer in Amsterdam, there was no evidence. Mata Hari had denied handing over anything whatsoever to the German consul and had only admitted accepting 20,000 francs from him as compensation for her furs and jewelry confiscated in Germany in August 1914. The third accusation was related to her intention to supply information to Kroemer in return of the money accepted from him, which could be proved in no way. The fourth accusation had also been related to her intention to enter Paris in 1916, in order to collect documents and information in the interest of Germany, which could not be proved either. The fifth accusation that she had actually maintained contact with German intelligence in 1916 with the aim of assisting them in the war could not be proved because of lack of evidence, as the two policemen appointed by Ladoux to shadow her during that period could not produce any proof of her contact with German spymasters or the secret agents. The sixth and seventh accusations had been related to her relationship with Kalle in Madrid and her imparting information of military importance to him. During her interrogation Mata Hari had claimed that she had shared with Kalle only such news that she had either overheard at the restaurants or had read in the newspapers. It is highly improbable that such information could be considered as constituting of any intelligence value.

The prosecution however had relied solely on the Madrid–Berlin traffic

---

73 Howe, *op. cit.*, 241.
74 Wheelwright, *op. cit.*, 91–92.

in this matter, which (i) did not mention anything about what intelligence the former dancer had revealed to them, and (ii) lacked authenticity because those had been written in the broken code, and therefore in all probability might have been work of manipulation. Someone at some level had certainly engineered the radio traffics. Moreover, according to Howe, Kalle had referred to two missions in France in the messages, which in fact could not have been known by him, as he only knew about Kroemer's attempt to recruit Mata Hari as a secret agent for Germany in 1916, "and therefore he would not have made that mistake himself. That was Ladoux's *surenchère*—upping the bidding—to help clinch the case."[75] Howe further said that if the doctored messages were used merely to get a confession from the accused it would have made sense, but those had been included by the prosecution as evidence against Mata Hari, which amounted to deception by the French government.[76] More so, during the trial no one had been allowed to question the authenticity of or even to ask for proof regarding the existence of the messages. However, Wheelwright remarked that the final accusation that Mata Hari had maintained contact with Germany in January 1917, while in Paris, could not be proved as Ladoux's agents had constantly followed her during that time and still had failed to come up with single evidence to this effect. Therefore, it is quite evident that, the prosecution did not have any genuine case against her and she was being made a scapegoat by the Deuxième Bureau. At the end of the trial on July 25, 1917, Mata Hari had been found guilty of all the eight charges brought against her and was condemned to death by the prosecution. Although "No one accused of spying can be punished by a court of law without the production of conclusive orthodox evidence"[77] wrote Coulson, no one had the courage to challenge the prosecution. The then moral giants of the Third Republic had defeated the enemy within. According to Schirmann it had been a court-ordered assassination, while her sympathizers said that it was a judicial murder. Jacques Reboul, who had directed the French counterintelligence in Switzerland during the First World War, later said: "The case against Mata Hari was invented out of nothing at all."[78]

Waagenaar mentioned something quite curious regarding the jury

---

75 Howe, *op. cit.*, 238–239.
76 Ibid., 242.
77 Major Thomas Coulson, *op. cit.*, 107.
78 Jacques Reboul, "Spy Scare Grips The World," *Auckland Star*, June 30, 1934, 4.

votes[79]—all the seven members were not fully in agreement on all the eight points—while six members had agreed on all the questions, the seventh member categorically said 'No' every time he had been asked whether he thought that Mata Hari had disposed off information she had collected against France, because he was convinced that there was no proof. That man had voted negatively three times—on the second, fifth, and the seventh questions. Waagenaar further opined that it was all the more strange that even after the jury unanimously confirmed about Mata Hari's contacts with enemy intelligence while she had been in Paris in 1917, "none of these German agents had been caught, brought in as witnesses, or been brought to trial. Nor was Mata Hari ... ever seen talking to them. The jury simply confirmed what Captain Bouchardon had suggested."[80] Odder still, according to Waagenaar, had been the abrupt change of mind of the seventh member of the jury, who did not think that she was an enemy spy, yet for some unknown reasons, agreed to her death sentence. However, the court clerk Adjutant Rivière had been asked by President Lieutenant-Colonel Semprou to read out the verdict aloud and he had obliged. The words poured into Mata Hari's ears like molten metal. Although she had anticipated some harsh sentence, she had no idea what she was awaiting. She could not believe her ears, and only mumbled "It's impossible! It's impossible!" After signing an appeal for re-examination of her case she was taken to cell number 12 at Saint Lazare, which was demarcated for condemned women of repute. It was a spacious cell that had previously housed notable prisoners like anarchist Rirette Maîtrejean, stage actress Valentine Merelli, a rich Parisian Madame Peockes, who had supposedly murdered her husband, the social revolutionary Louise Michel, the money launderer Therese Humbert, Madame Henriette Caillaux, wife of former French Prime Minister Joseph Caillaux, and the courtesan Marguerite Steinheil, mistress of President Félix Faure. Marguerite Francillard, the teenage dressmaker who had acted as a courier for the German secret service and was sent to the firing squad on January 10, 1917, had also been captivated in that cell. Like them Mata Hari too had been given special treatment there as the quality of her food had improved, she had been allowed to read and smoke, and two female prisoners had been appointed on voluntary guard duty for her along with two nuns to take her care—Sister Léonide and Sister Marie. Sister Léonide, the Sister Superior of the prison nuns, was a middle-aged

---

79 Waagenaar, *op. cit.*, 1964, 262.
80 Ibid., 263.

bold lady who had been given the nickname "Bostock"[81] by the prisoners after the famous lion tamer Frank Charles Bostock of that time, possibly because of her tough temperament. Mata Hari however became her favorite within a short while, to the extent that the middle-aged tough nun could not hold her tears back at the time of her execution.

Although Mata Hari had been permitted to read inside her prison cell she had no knowledge that the French press had continued with their propaganda scheme against her frequently reporting fabricated stories about her (like her demand for a daily milk bath in the prison or about her involvement in the tank disaster at Somme). It had possibly been a strategy to instill trust for the government in the French soldiers as well as the civilians by publicizing about its capability to destroy the enemy within. The Netherlands government however had started to follow her case closely, and on July 28 the Foreign Ministry in The Hague had requested its personnel in Paris to try for a reduced prison sentence for her. The case of Leopold Vieyra might have inspired such action. Vieyra had been a Dutch subject based in London, who was tried by the British for his direct involvement in enemy espionage, and was condemned to death in November 1916, although later his sentence had been commuted to life imprisonment. There had been other cases as well when the death sentence was subsequently commuted to life imprisonment; so there was sincere effort from the Dutch government to save Mata Hari from the firing squad. The Council for Revision was composed of five people—Judge Couinaud and four other judges, mostly from military service, who had heard her case on August 17 and had taken almost no time to declare that the Third Council of War had made no violation of the Law regarding her case, and hence her plea for revision had been rejected immediately. Clunet did not have the courage to inform his client that her request for revision had been rejected. Still no one else knew it better than Mata Hari that the judgment of the Third Council of War had been unjustified. Waagenaar wrote: "All those who were supposed to be her friends had deserted her—out of fear, out of jealousy, out of revenge perhaps."[82]

On September 2, not knowing that the Council for Revision had already denied her request, she had written an emotive letter to The Netherlands Legation seeking every possible help and saying that she felt deserted.

---

81   John N. Raphael, *The Caillaux Drama*, 48.
82   Waagenaar, *op. cit.*, 1964, 267.

Only two possible ways had been left to save the former *grande dame* from the firing squad—the Court of Appeals and a request for pardon to the French President. On September 26 Clunet had appealed to the Appellate Court challenging the Third Council of War's right to judge Mata Hari's case. On September 27 the case was heard at the Court of Appeals where Mr. Reynal had represented her (as Clunet was not inscribed at that court he was not allowed to speak on her behalf). He did not take any interest in the case of a condemned woman and had left the decision to the Court. The Court of Appeals merely discussed on the competence of the Third Council of War to hear espionage cases during war, and as the question had been answered unanimously in the affirmative, the case was dismissed barely within 15 minutes. On the next day, The Netherlands Legation had called Clunet to get some feedback on her case, in reply to which he did send the latest edition of the Journal of Tribunal containing the decision. The Legation had informed The Hague, where the Dutch Foreign Office took immediate steps by sending a wire to Paris with the request for pardon to Mata Hari on humanitarian ground, which had the signature of the Dutch Foreign Minister John Loudon. She did not sit idle either, and on September 22 had written a letter to Ridder van Stuers, the Dutch legatee in Paris, desperately seeking his interference for presidential pardon. Clunet earnestly believed that President Poincaré would not allow the graceful lady to perish in that manner. Every moment was too precious to her as would usually be for a convict on the death row. Mata Hari wanted to live—if not for Vadime anymore, at least for her teenage daughter. Margarethe, the mother, had lost to Mata Hari, the dancer, in 1905, but at the moment in time Mata Hari, from the deepest core of her heart, had wanted to lose the game to Margarethe and her Non. Being closer to death she must have realized that all her aspirations, all her wealth and enjoyments had simply been worthless. She had only wanted to hold her dear Non closer to her heart and hoped that at least she would certainly understand her mother.

President Raymond Poincaré, a conservative by allegiance, with his well-known strongly anti-German sentiments and unemotional disposition, had not been moved by the appeal for pardon of a traitor, and as he firmly believed that traitors did not deserve mercy, he had rejected all such appeals on principle. Poincaré would not consider Mata Hari's clemency appeal mercifully all the more because the political situation of France would not permit such a move at that point of time, and also because the entire effort of the French government to find and destroy the enemy within would fail. Major Thomas Coulson wrote: "Would any President have dared to inflame public spirit when it was clamouring to have its social structure purged of all Defeatist elements and all cosmopolitan parasites destroying the security of France, by exercising his prerogative of clemency in favor of a woman who had sent thousands of French soldiers to their deaths and who still remained proudly unrepentant if not actually proud of her infamy?"[83] Could Queen Wilhelmina of The Netherlands intervene to save Mata Hari at that juncture? Probably yes, but even if she could, she would not, because that would mean her direct interference in the war matters of France, which, being in a neutral position,[84] she was not supposed to do. Moreover, Wilhelmina could not take the risk of jeopardizing the bilateral relationship of The Netherlands with Britain merely to save a former demimondaine from the firing squad.

However, the President's rejection letter had reached Clunet on Saturday, October 13, 1917 (must have been a calculated move). On that day at least six Dutch newspapers in Holland had reported that Mata Hari had already been executed. The news came as a shock to the Dutch people in The Hague as they had certainly expected her presidential clemency. None of her near relatives had been informed about her fate, nor had they been allowed to contact her in the prison. In Rotterdam her brother Johannes Hendriks Zelle had earnestly tried to procure a copy of the judgment along with a copy of the accusations against her from the Dutch Foreign Affairs Minister John Loudon, but strangely no such copy was available with the ministry at that time. There was no way left to save Mata Hari from the firing squad, still Clunet had vowed to cling on to the faintest hope for his lady love and to try for the last time. Since the next day was a Sunday he had to wait till Monday, October 15, to place his appeal. Least did he know what had been going on at the prison end. On Sunday, October 14, the order for her execution had been signed in the morning, and the resident physician of Saint Lazare Dr. Leon Bizard was informed that the execution had been scheduled for the next morning. Sister Léonide had also been informed accordingly, because they were the two people who had to prepare Mata Hari for the final moment. The convict was obviously not informed about the plan, and worse, she did

---

83 Coulson, *op. cit.*, 291.
84 Holland's policy of neutrality during the war might have been inspired by the first international conference in The Hague in 1913.

not even know that her mercy petition had been denied by the President. In the night of October 14 she had gone to sleep with the hope that the following morning would surely offer her some favorable news from the President's office.

In the wee hours of next morning Edouard Clunet had been officially informed to be a witness to the execution at the Vincennes ground, so were Captain Thibaut, the chief military recorder for the Third Council of War, Lieutenant-Colonel Semprou, and Lieutenant Choulot, a Tribunal judge who had not been present at her trial. The event had been scheduled to be carried out by the Fourth Regiment of the Zouaves sharply at 06:15 hours. Many people had gathered at Saint Lazare before dawn—Captain Bouchardon being the first to arrive. He must have been too excited with his triumph over the predator woman. The prison doctor had followed Bouchardon along with his assistant Dr. Bralez. Within a short while had arrived Major Massard, Captain Thibaut, Counsel Mornet, Lieutenant-Colonel Semprou, Edouard Clunet, Major Jullien, the medical officer Dr. Soquet, director of the prison Monsieur Jean Estachy, and the Solicitor General Wattine. Pastor Jules Arboux had been present to accompany them to the execution ground. Some reporters had also gathered at the prison compound to get first-hand news of the episode—"Former demimondaine and the most dangerous enemy spy executed by France"—could surely become the hottest headline in the morning newspapers. In the cold morning of October 15 Mata Hari had been woken up, for the last time, by Sister Léonide at 5 o'clock. Taking a few bold steps Monsieur Estachy had entered cell 12 and had informed Mata Hari that her mercy request had been rejected by the President. He had then instructed her to get ready for the final moment. In the dim light of the prison cell she could see many people standing behind Estachy.

Suddenly she could realize that there was no time left for her and the moment for the final performance had been imminent. Like a spectacular performer she had wished to make her exit perfect and memorable. As noted earlier, she reached out for the black "neat Amazonian tailored suit, specially made for the occasion,"[85] requested for permission to put on

---

85 Brenda Wineapple, *Genêt: A Biography of Janet Flanner*, 129. Shipman's version however differs from Janet, because she said that on the day of her execution Mata Hari had worn the same outfit that she had worn for her trial; Shipman, *op. cit.*, 364; a different version is available in an article published in *The Pittsburgh Press* of December

her corset, pinned up her graying hair in a back knot, picked up a straw tricorn hat, and carefully chose the best pair of ankle boots she had at her disposal. She did not forget to pick up a pair of long buttoned new white gloves that she needed to complete her get-up. Even without any jewelry she looked truly elegant. Clunet however looked shattered. It had been extremely difficult for him to accept such an end for the famous dancer and his one-time sweetheart, and therefore, as the last resort, he had appealed through a letter addressed to Massard to invoke Article 27 of the French Penal Code, which prohibited a pregnant convict to be executed until she gave birth to her child. Everyone present in her cell had been startled by the news. How could she be pregnant when no stranger had been allowed to enter her prison cell for the entire 8 months that she had been captivated? Clunet had no other way but to claim that Mata Hari had been impregnated by him. He was ready to put even his hard earned reputation at stake to save her from the bullets. But as mentioned earlier, Mata Hari was not ready to barter with the glaring lie. She had denied Clunet's claim with a graceful smile. The perennial liar that she had been all through her life had strangely refused to resort to one at the end. She had probably lost all hope—for love, for care, for dignity. Probably life did not mean anything anymore to her. Probably in death she had found a novel way to be in the limelight forever. In her diary she had written: "... it is much more desirable to live a short, tense life to its fullest value than to drag oneself tiresomely through a long life into old age without beauty ..."[86] She did what she had believed to be the most desirable.

On October 15, 1917, when the whole of Paris had been covered in a veil of winter mist, 11 bullets had pierced Mata Hari's body[87] sharp at 06:15. With the first light of the rising sun peeping at the horizon the "Eye of

---

25, 1921, in which the correspondent wrote: "... she wore a diaphanous costume of Indian silk trimmed with gold lace ...," "Unmarked Grave Holds Danseuse Executed as Spy," 67; Henry G. Wales had covered Mata Hari's execution for the William Randolph Heart's International News Service, where he had reported in detail that she wore a black velvet cloak trimmed with fur, black stockings, and high-heeled slippers with silk ribbons tied over the insteps; Roger Kahn, *A Flame of Pure Fire*, 10.

86 Annonymous; *The Diary of Mata Hari*, 2005, 150. It is not certain whether this biographical work had actually been written by the dancer herself.

87 Wheelwright, *op. cit.*, 99, although there are much disagreement regarding the actual number of bullets that pierced her body.

Dawn" had left her mortal body. At daybreak the sky appeared to have become redder to the 66 year old Sister Léonide, who stood at a distance with moist eyes. She had indeed dearly loved the "little orchid."

Conclusion
Mata Hari Syndrome Revisited

Margarethe Zelle MacLeod's life had ended abruptly. She had died "with decorum, courage, and modesty"[1] leaving a trail of rumors and myths that made Mata Hari somewhat immortal. Toni Bentley wrote: "In death the real woman was quickly forgotten, and Mata Hari became the object of mythical projections."[2] The French felt triumphant and certainly had heaved a sigh of relief as the danger had been destroyed. She did not even get the lawful benefit of doubt at her trial. Some of her biographers have accused France for using her death in their own interest, and some, without having a shadow of doubt about her sins against France, have opined otherwise showering praise for effectively destroying the female evil. The official press release reported that Mata Hari had paid for her heinous crimes against France. No one wanted to question the official position, and hence the British, American, French, and other European press followed it. No one who had once been connected to her wanted to admit it publicly after her execution. Wheelwright wrote: "Criticism of her execution was deemed unpatriotic or even pro-German."[3] Her much loved and admired willowy body had also not been claimed by anyone for a decent funeral. Coulson wrote: "Oh, ingratitude! The lovely amber-tinted body that had danced for the delight of so many was despised and rejected by all her numerous lovers when death had stilled its allurements."[4] Therefore, it had been sent to the Paris Medical College in order to facilitate the medical students.[5]

There she laid bare, for the first time in public view, on the dissection

---

1   Roger Kahn, *op. cit.*, 11.
2   Toni Bentley, *op. cit.*, 127.
3   Julie Wheelwright, *op. cit.*, 134.
4   Major Thomas Coulson, *op. cit.*, 309.
5   There are varied opinions in this regard. On October 16, 1917, *The Pittsburgh Press* had reported: "Following her execution as a spy yesterday, the body was secretly buried," "Unmarked Grave Holds Danseuse Executed as Spy," Paris, 1.

table for serving the people whom she would never even want to glance at. Those who could never have had the opportunity even to see her from a distance, had been permitted to touch her most cherished body, and even to explore it at their free will. France had taken revenge on Germany both for killing the saintly mother figure Nurse Edith Cavell[6] and for taking away Alsace-Lorraine from them. Much private and government funds had been utilized in France first to create and then to defame the profane female enemy, the socio-cultural and political icon of betrayal in the highly puritan and xenophobic society, a prototype that might have been necessary to encourage the French population against pacifism toward the war. Wheelwright wrote: "The story of Mata Hari's execution during the First World War had meaning as a triumph over female evil."[7] Truth could not have been important for that purpose. Her charm and fame was enough for France to condemn her. Strangely, not even the freedom-loving French liberals, intellectuals, or republicans had taken any interest to stand by Mata Hari, and although she might have been only one among the 87 people executed by the French army in 1917, but through her execution the nationalists and conservatives could assuage their ego that had been battered after Dreyfus' vindication.

The *femme fatale* prototype of Mata Hari, that made her the iconic female spy of the First World War, had also been instrumental to design the *Mata Hari Syndrome*. It supposedly indicates at the use of predatory style of seduction to gain control over men in order to corrupt them. Mata Hari had been identified as the most depraved woman of the early twentieth century Europe, who had abandoned her husband merely to fulfill her selfish megalomaniac dreams through her sexual talents, and she was labeled as the greatest female spy of that era who had used her sexual charm to gain access to French secrets. In life she had gained the disrepute of being a nymphomaniac,[8] who lived off the material wealth of her lovers, exploited them, and eventually destroyed them completely by driving them to bankruptcy. The prototype of Mata Hari "... bleeds men of their money and their morals."[9] It is interesting to note that women in

---

6   Although there are speculations that the British government deliberately did not try to save her from the German firing squad by providing expert solicitors for her during her trial as her execution had enormous propaganda value during the war.
7   Wheelwright, *op. cit.*, 145.
8   Charles Wighton, *The World's Greatest Spies*, 67.
9   Wheelwright, *op. cit.*, 135.

the early twentieth century European society had generally been seen as agents of destruction, especially those who did not "... conform to any of the 'good woman' images" and were "automatically seen as prostitutes ..."[10] Any woman who wished to comply to sexual freedom was ostracized by the society, and inclusion of the excluded was never possible either socially or morally. So, the myth of *Mata Hari Syndrome*, propagated chiefly by the then bourgeoisie intellectuals, had been extended to include the meaning of sexual perversion as well. It reflected male fantasies about female sexuality and fears of their betrayal, and therefore does not pertain to any reality in the realm of espionage. I call it a myth because it had been based upon false perception of the characteristic traits of the famous dancer-courtesan (mysterious, erotic, and dangerous) which might have been impacted by the spy novels of the Edwardian era. It could also have been associated with the portrayal of the New Woman as sexually overactive and morally corrupt. Common perception had depicted Mata Hari as an over-sexed woman who had indulged in having sex with new men each night—every night different experience—which is far from truth. It is far from the truth that Mata Hari alone had chosen the means of intense seduction or the technique of sexual entrapment, if at all, to execute her secret mission. Most of the spy novels, propaganda literature, and news reporting of that time indicate at pillow talks as the most effective way of collecting secret information, because men in general have always been most vulnerable in the company of a seductress.

She was dangerous because she had been irresistible. "... *sexual* intercourse with women opened men up to *verbal* intercourse with their seductress, creating an opportunity in both the official and the popular mind for women to gain the secrets of nations."[11] Magnus Hirschfeld wrote: "All were equally careless in their intercourse with women and at the height of their passion would whisper, into the ear of their companion-in-lust, secrets that were never meant to be thus used."[12] Proctor has also mentioned Elizabeth McIntosh where she had used the term "Mata Haridans" to describe the adventuress women spies who did not go through any spy training program before or after recruitment as secret agents, instead had used their skill of seduction and sexual talents whenever necessary. Exploiting the erotic instincts of men, the women

---

10 Klaus Theweleit, *Male Fantasies* (Vol. I), 171.
11 Tammy M. Proctor, *op. cit.*, 123.
12 Quoted in Ibid., 123.

spies performed their duty as secret agents by intruding effortlessly into their private space where women belonged naturally and socially. All the Forces involved in the war had made great use of the gender theatrics. The seductress–mistress–courtesan prototype of female spy had since been epitomized, at least until the Second World War. "The romantic link between espionage and sexuality was confirmed by her example" wrote Bentley.[13] Wheelwright wrote: "... she became the worst kind of war profiteer ... Mata Hari sold sex and stole secrets that would endanger thousands of lives, to maintain her decadent desires."[14] This is precisely what *Mata Hari Syndrome* is all about. Spy novels, theaters, movies, and musicals had identified and popularized Mata Hari's perceived traits as those necessary to succeed as a grand secret agent of the enemy force. Her foreignness might also have contributed significantly toward that myth. Henry de Halsalle wrote: "Her 'Eastern Empress' looks, her hypnotic eyes and capricious, fickle, vain and vengeful temper, made her a perfect agent."[15] Wheelwright wrote: "... the spy-courtesan was a convenient receptacle for men's desire to blame women for the horrors of war." She added: "Mata Hari had become a potent metaphor for the war's death and destruction ..."[16]

Sarah Lewison wrote: "In medicine, a syndrome refers to a number of symptoms occurring together and characterizing specific disease ... Mata Hari ... who devises a survival mechanism out of the running together of the fevers of colonial imperialism, demimonde culture, embryonic feminisms, and material avarice. The combination is infectious, and creates a cult following."[17] Lewison continued: "She takes advantage of opportunities the way a parasite infests a host ...," and stressed on the model of parasite–host relationship to explain her version of the syndrome. Although when I had communicated with her regarding her explanation of the syndrome, she replied that it was not related to the dancer's biography per se, but was an expansion of performative forms of spectacle in the late nineteenth century. Nevertheless, the simile of parasite with Mata Hari had also been used before. Howe wrote about her: "... an elegant

---

13 Bentley, *op. cit.*, 127.
14 Wheelwright, *op. cit.*, 136.
15 Quoted in Ibid., 137.
16 Ibid., 134.
17 Sarah A. Lewison, *Mata Hari Syndrome: Every Night Different*, 8.

parasite in a corrupt society ..."[18] Wheelwright in the same vein wrote: "She was an 'international woman' who fed like a parasite on the moral rot of France ..."[19] Even if I do not contradict Howe and Wheelwright who had spoken about the dancer's characteristic trait, I do not however subscribe to the version of Lewison regarding the syndrome, neither do I endorse the common belief regarding the issue, and rather strongly contend that *Mata Hari Syndrome* should consist not of anything even remotely related to espionage or to war. I suppose instead of naming the political account of the syndrome after Mata Hari it would have been more appropriate to extend the *Delilah Syndrome* (promiscuous women who seduce the partners to render them weak and helpless) to the political sphere of espionage as well.

Shipman however wrote: "She sent uncoded letters to Ladoux through ordinary mail; she telegraphed him openly; she called at his office repeatedly. She even sent intelligence to Ladoux by confiding it to a French diplomat she met by chance. What chance had such a woman of being a successful spy, much less a double agent?"[20] Transcending the limitations of any particular country or any period in time secret service always had specific rules to adhere to, and the agents required to follow them with utmost sincerity. Elsbeth Schragmüller (a.k.a. Fräulein Doktor), the greatest and the most trusted German secret agent and spymaster during the First World War, had enlisted the psychological aptitudes essential for secret service—(i) the ability to empathize; (ii) knowledge of human nature and leadership skills; and (iii) the ability to imagine and feel the possible situations that may arise during an operation.[21] Mata Hari possessed none of these capabilities, but still she had been proclaimed by the French army and the western press as the greatest female spy of the twentieth century. Marthe Richer wrote: "... this service requires complete subjugation to the demands and assignments of an intelligence agency ..."[22] She had also indicated that there is no scope for any sort of ambiguity in secret service. According to Robert Baden-Powell, founder of the Boy Scout movement, "To be a really effective spy, a man has to be endowed with a strong spirit of self-sacrifice, courage, and self-control ... quick at observation and

---

18 Russell Warren Howe, *op. cit.*, 235.
19 Wheelright, *op. cit.*, 88.
20 Pat Shipman, *op. cit.*, 374.
21 Eva Horn, *op. cit.*, 194.
22 Ibid., 185.

deduction ..."[23] To add the view of Sun Tzu, the greatest Chinese expert on war and espionage, would presumably not be impertinent here. He had mentioned intuition, acumen, ingenuity, and subtlety as the qualities that each spy must possess. According to the ancient Indian texts a spy should essentially be truthful, greedless, unsluggish, and must have the power of argument.[24] Mata Hari had been far away from all these attributes; she was not even aware of the requirements, neither did she care to adhere to any of the norms of secret service and, as has been mentioned before, took decisions in her own style that suited her temperament perfectly. Newman wrote: "Secret service is secret. Spy-masters never mingle with their spies—above all, are never seen with them: very often spies do not even know their spy-masters. But Mata Hari never attempted to conceal her friendship with German intelligence officers, appearing blatantly in public with them. Did this indicate recklessness or innocence?"[25]

Classification of spies might have followed a common pattern[26]—(i) military officers who volunteer for secret work; (ii) professional and specially trained secret agents; (iii) hired spies who serve temporarily for some pay; and (iv) traitor spies, who by bribery, threat, or blackmail, could be forced to betray their own country. Mata Hari, if at all, could be put only under the third category. Spies were variously classified and, as Keay has pointed out,[27] had been working on three levels—at the basic level there were the small-time unskilled paid informers who were used for collecting information on public sentiment, troop movements, rail networks, transport facilities, etc; on the second level there were spies with specialized knowledge who were assigned the work to report on communications, armaments, fortification levels in strategic areas, and technological advances of the enemy forces; and at the highest level there were the infiltrators who could effectively take responsibility to extract information of enemy plans from the horse's mouth. On which level had Mata Hari supposedly worked? As she was not assigned to watch and report about the French troop movements or the rail networks, nor had she been one having specialized knowledge of communications, armaments, fortifica-

---

23 Robert Baden-Powell, *My Adventures as a Spy*, 22.
24 Kedareswar Chakraborty, *Art of Spying in Ancient India*, 146.
25 Bernard Newman, *op. cit.*, 183.
26 George Fielding Eliot, "Espionage," in *Collier's Encyclopedia* (Vol. 9), ed. Bernard Johnston, 312.
27 Julia Keay, *op. cit.*, 110.

tions, etc, she was accused to have belonged to the highest level—she was suspected to be a German infiltrator who was supposed to extract information from the high-ranking French officers. But that was utterly misleading, because none of the officers had testified against her during the trials. She had never discussed war with any of them.

Therefore, even if *Mata Hari Syndrome* had been a political concept, which was limited to the genre of espionage, it had been a gross misrepresentation. Her so-called intense passion for sex was part of the propaganda against her, a subjective construct, kind of social perception that had been inspired not only by the prevailing spyscare, but also by the changing social role of women of that time, and had also accompanied her fame, and therefore had no objective merit. It had been a clear misrepresentation, because Mata Hari had never wanted to be in the espionage game. It was only due to her desire to marry her beloved and the subsequent lure of a million francs that she had agreed to do some secret work for Ladoux. Therefore, I propose to uproot the concept from the political genre where it had always belonged, and to transport it to the psychological plane where it should have been fitted perfectly. In the present technologically improved world there is no place for spy-courtesans, and hence *Mata Hari Syndrome* remains no more relevant as a political tool. In the fast growing and consumerist world *Mata Hari Syndrome* must be psychologically more relevant today than politically. It is however highly ironical that the person who had never been interested in anything political actually had a supposed political malfunction named after her.

Symptoms like Margarethe Zelle's childish naivety coupled with Mata Hari's extreme narcissism, unmatched vanity, lack of prudence, and great aspiration for a good life complete with the desire for grand opulence should form the basis of the syndrome that had been named after her, and not sexual hedonism, nymphomania, or cruelty, because even if it is true that she had been a sexual hedonist, I suppose she was not at all a nymphomaniac in the truest sense, and irrespective of all anti-propaganda nor had she ever been cruel to anyone. Her fabulous dramatics did not start with the desire for sex or fame, but surely with the craving for freedom and luxury. She took great delight in affluence and always had passionately ridden her fancy's wings. Using sex and self-mystification to earn money had merely been a means for her in the goal of enjoying a luxurious lifestyle. Although she enjoyed male company immensely still that does not indicate that she had been doing it under the compulsion of nymphomania. In her diary Mata Hari wrote: "What do I care about men? They are a means to a goal."[28] Therefore, her desire for taking highly placed and powerful men as her lovers and patrons had been an instrumental desire for her and not a terminal or intrinsic desire. Since her childhood she had been admired by her friends and family, due to which she had surely developed inflated self-esteem. It had been badly battered during the years she had spent with Rudolf and his family. So, admiration in any form naturally made her extremely happy and she would never miss a chance to win. Mata Hari had resorted to every possible tricks of seduction unmistakably to win over male libido, not because she was a pervert nymphomaniac, or like a parasite she had wanted to feed at the expense of and eventually to destroy her lovers, but simply because they had been the means to her opulent living. Her insatiable craving for consumer goods had been pathological because it blurred her rational senses, affected her thought processes, and certainly altered her destiny.

The paradigm of *Mata Hari Syndrome* therefore should be shifted from the political sphere of espionage to the psychological realm. It should ideally comprise of the symptoms of pathological desire for consumption, or of Compulsive Buying Disorder (CBD) which naturally contains intense self-love, intense desire for money, and for vanity, coupled with utter naivety, added with the talent to seduce, mythomania, knack for self-mystification, and craving for unhindered attention and enjoyment. CBD is defined as "a consumer's tendency to be preoccupied with buying that is revealed through repetitive buying and a lack of impulse control over buying." People affected with CBD are generally believed to be insecure and materialistic and are desperately in constant need to appear to be attractive. This, I presume, fits ideally with Mata Hari's personality, because she had strangely felt secure in the company of uniformed people whom she found naturally strong, her "expectation to be desired forever,"[29] and her desire to appear attractive are unquestionable. As noted before, I find her disorder to have been effectuated by her father Adam Zelle and her husband Rudolf's behavior toward her. She must have felt truly helpless when Adam had abandoned her or when Rudolf had treated her like a rogue. Therefore, it had been quite natural for her to use her

---

28 Anonymous, *op. cit.*, 2005, 142.
29 Lewison, *op. cit.*, 8.

only weapon, her talent to seduce, in order to win the men of power and strength. It had no relation whatsoever with nymphomania. However, although Léon Schirmann had reportedly found evidence in the German archives about her recruitment as a secret agent in the middle of 1915 by Walter Nicolai, Chief of the German intelligence service during the First World War, but Mata Hari had never truly been into any secret service; and therefore, it becomes absolutely superfluous to name a politically motivated attitude after her. This merely reflects the then French psyche of comprehending woman spy as the villain—enemy of the Fatherland. Ladoux and Bouchardon "… believed in the witch who had put a hex upon France. To save France, it was their desperate duty to exorcise the demon by exposing Mata Hari and executing her."[30]

Darrow wrote: "… Mata Hari did not have, had never had, an impartial jury. All the parties in her drama … found her instantly suspicious; she so resembled what they thought a spy should be."[31] But now, after a century of her unlawful execution or judicial murder, I suppose we should agree that Mata Hari's true disposition and her innocence of espionage must be respected. I earnestly believe that at least now, after a century has past, she should be vindicated of the wrongful charges of being the godmother of female spies.

---

30 Margaret H. Darrow, *op. cit.*, 290.
31 Ibid., 289.

Appendix A
Detailed Timeline of Margarethe/Mata Hari's Life

Birth (Leeuwarden, Friesland)	1876, August 7
Gift of goat carriage by Adam	1882, August 7
Lived at 28 Groote Kerkstraat	1883, January 1
Miss Buy's school	1883
Adam's bankruptcy	1889, February 18
Cammingha State School	1889
Parents' divorce	1890, September 4
Mother's death	1891, May 10
Shifted from Leeuwarden to Sneek	1891, November 12
Haanstra's School in Lieden	1892
Ousted from the school	1893
Responded to Rudolf's marriage ad of 11 Feb, 1895	1895, middle of March
First meeting with Rudolf MacLeod	1895, March 24
Engaged to Rudolf	1895, March 30
Marriage	1895, July 11
Honeymoon to Wiesbaden (Germany)	1895, July
Left Louise Frida's house to a rented apartment	1896, April
Norman John's birth	1897, January 30
Started for Dutch East Indies	1897, May 1
Reached harbor near Batavia	1897, June 7
Jeanne Louise (Non)'s birth	1898, May 2

Stage debut (Java)	1898, September
Arrived in Medan	1899, May 26
Both the children fell ill	1899, June 25
Norman's death	1899, June 28
Rudolf's retirement from work	1900, October 2
Back to Holland	1902, March 19
Separation with Rudolf	1902, August 30
Rudolf pleaded poverty to the court	1902, September 10
Returned to Rudolf after separation	1902, November 4
Left Non with Rudolf forever	1902, December
First travel to Paris in search of a profession	1903, January
Second travel to Paris in search of a profession	1904, Spring
Worked in the Molier Circus	1904, Spring
Danced at private salons as Mrs. Lady MacLeod	1905, February
Debuted at Musée Guimet as Mata Hari	1905, March 13
Named "Oriental Dream" by Gaston de Menier	1905, May 19
Met impresario Gabriel Astruc	1905, Autumn
Danced in Madrid	1906, January
Danced in Monte Carlo	1906, February
Divorce with Rudolf	1906, April 26
Danced in Berlin	1906, August
Danced in Vienna	1906, Dec. to 1907 Jan.
Went to Egypt	1907
Declared "Star of Dance"	1908
Lived as Mrs. Rousseau	1910–1911
Performed with accompaniment of Inayat Khan	1913, December 14
Prewar visit to Germany	1914, May

APPENDIX A

First World War started	1914, August 4
DORA implemented in England	1914, August 8
Return to Amsterdam	1914, August 16
Met German Consul Karl Kroemer in Amsterdam	1915, January
Accepted money and code name H21 from Kroemer	1915, Autumn
Registered as a resident of The Hague	1915, August 11
First wartime visit to Paris	1915, December
Questioned by MO5 at Port Folkstone	1915, December 4
Her file at the MO5 Register of Aliens marked 'Secret'	1915, December 9
British warned France against her (1st circular)	1915, December
Return to Holland	1916, January
Richard Tinsley reported against her to MO5	1916, February 3
Deuxième Bureau warned by MI5 (2nd circular)	1916, February 22
Second wartime visit to Paris	1916, June 16
Battle of Somme started	1916, July 1
Met Vadime de Masloff first	1916, July 29
Met George Ladoux	1916, August 1
Accepted Ladoux's proposal to spy for France	1916, August 21
Went to Vittel to be with Vadime	1916, September 1
Took espionage assignment from Ladoux	1916, September 17
Started from Paris to reach Belgium via Spain	1916, November 5
Arrested as Clara Benedix at Falmouth by MI5	1916, November 14
Released by the Scotland Yard	1916, November 28
Sent back to Spain by MI5	1916, December 1
Met Arnold Kalle in Madrid	1916, December 13
Final return to Paris	1917, January 2

Met Vadime for the last time	1917, January 13
Arrested by French police	1917, February 13
Pre-trial	1917, February 13–June 21
Trial	1917, July 24–July 25
Death sentence pronounced	1917, July 25
Revision Court rejected her appeal	1917, August 17
Court of Appeals rejected her appeal	1917, September 27
Clemency petition rejected by President Poincaré	1917, October 13
Executed by the French army	1917, October 15

Appendix B
List of Mata Hari's Mistakes throughout Her Life

A series of mistakes and wrong decisions taken by her after Adam had shifted his loving "little orchid" out of Leeuwarden had surely changed the flow of Mata Hari's life, some of which are enlisted here. Although, in the present global society and in the changed social milieu, most of these might not be considered as mistakes anymore, but had certainly been over a century ago. Toni Bentley wrote: "At every turn she might have saved herself ..." (*Sisters of Salome*; 127) but she had chosen to act differently in desperation leading her to an undesirable end.

1. Trying persistently to get things done in her own way; e.g., the incident with Herr Haanstra at the Kindergarten training school in Leiden.

2. Never looking at anything beyond her own perspective and setting enjoyment as the only parameter of her life.

3. Marrying Rudolf MacLeod who was more than double her age.

4. Not consulting any senior member of her family before engagement and trying to take the relationship with Rudolf in her own stride.

5. Never understanding the responsibilities of marriage and refusing to perform household duties of a wife, including duties towards the children.

6. Hating Louise Frida and her two daughters and never trying to become friendly with them.

7. Defying the bourgeoisie rules of the society while still expecting social security.

8. Developing high self-esteem, conceit, and over confidence and never realizing that.

9. Nurturing exorbitant aspirations, due to which she chose the profession of a dancer.

10. Having unrelenting craze for luxury, affluence, attention, and self-mystification.

11. Being a shopaholic and always spending beyond her means.

12. Having obsession for uniformed men and people of high social strata.

13. Nurturing wanderlust while the society expected women to be confined to the private domain.

14. Engaging in sexual freedom in a highly misogynic society.

15. Going around with Kiepert openly while in Berlin (1906) and traveling frequently with him inspite of knowing about his over-possessive wife and also renewing relationship with him before the war in 1914.

16. Leaving her valuable furs and jewelry with the costumer in Germany before her performance at the Metropol Theater in 1914.

17. Not returning to Paris at the end of July even after witnessing pro-war demonstrations in Berlin and waiting till the war had started.

18. On August 6, 1914, while attempting to cross the German borders, informing the German border guards that she wanted to return to Paris.

19. Taking up dancing contracts in Holland unnecessarily during the early days of the war.

20. Accepting Karl Kroemer's offer to spy for Germany in return of money, without having any serious intention for doing anything.

21. Going to Paris in 1915, which was an entrenched area during the war.

APPENDIX B

22. Telling different stories about the reason for her visit to Paris in 1915 when questioned by MO5 officials at the Folkestone Port.

23. Planning for a second wartime visit to Paris in 1916 with a stopover in England.

24. Applying for a British visa in 1916.

25. Not consulting a lawyer even after receiving a refusal letter for her British visa.

26. Not realizing gravity of the wartime situations—both social and political.

27. Not abandoning her plans to travel through the Channel even after her British visa was refused.

28. Going doggedly ahead with her plans to go to Paris in 1916 even after receiving the French visa with a note which said—NOT VALID FOR THE WARZONE.

29. Slapping Henry Hoedemaker in full public view on board S. S. *Zeelandia* in 1916 en route her second wartime visit to Paris.

30. Carrying large number of baggage even during her wartime trips through the Channel.

31. Trying to earn through prostitution and continuing with her lover-hunting soirees in war ridden Paris (1916).

32. Falling madly in love with Vadime at the matured age of 40 and losing all insight.

33. Trying fervently to visit Vittel in 1916, also a warzone, during the disastrous Battle of Somme, even after being refused a permit.

34. Not returning to Holland in 1916 inspite of applying for a permit to reach through Calais.

35. Seeking advice from Hallaure in order to get permit to go to Vittel.

36. Earnestly believing that Vadime would marry her and would settle down together.

37. Blindly relying on all those whom she had considered to be her friends—Hallaure, Cazeaux, Henri de Marguerie, Denvignes, and others.

38. Believing Ladoux who had offered an extraordinary amount of money for her service to France during wartime.

39. Accepting Ladoux's offer without even knowing the basics of espionage—without receiving any money in advance from him, without being given any code name by him for the purpose, and also without any contact information that was absolutely necessary for her.

40. Not revealing to Ladoux that she had already accepted money from Kroemer.

41. Revealing Kroemer's name to Ladoux and thus exposing her connection with the Germans.

42. Revealing the German banker Wurfbain's name (who she thought would introduce her to the high ranking German officials), a close associate of General von Bising, to Ladoux.

43. Telling Ladoux that she could reach von Bissing in Belgium, the man who had signed Nurse Edith Cavell's death warrant only a year back.

44. Telling Ladoux in order to convince him of her capability that she could surely mould the Duke of Cumberland's allegiance towards the Allied side.

45. Requesting Ladoux to arrange for her hassle-free travel through the Channel in order to reach Holland as per the assignment.

46. Informing the Dutch Legation in Paris (November 4, 1916) about her return to Holland.

47. Naming Ladoux as one of her deponents to the Scotland Yard officials after her arrest (as Clara Benedix) at Port Falmouth.

48. Revealing the name of a British secret agent, Allard, to the Dutch consul secretary in Vigo.

49. Trying desperately from Madrid to contact Ladoux for his advice in the changed situation.

50. Contacting Kalle in Madrid on her own without being instructed by or informing Ladoux.

51. Trying to deceive Kalle by pretending to be friendly to Germany.

52. Revealing some French secrets, however frivolous, to Kalle.

53. Not paying any heed to the warning of her well-wisher Emilio Junoy while in Madrid in 1916.

54. Going back to Paris from Madrid in January 1917 with the hope of getting the promised sum of 1,000,000 francs from Ladoux.

55. Sending personal letters to her maid Anna Lintjens from Paris through the Dutch diplomatic channel both in 1916 and 1917.

56. Continuing prostitution in Paris during the war insisting on having soldiers and officers of the Allied army as her clients.

57. Writing to Cazeaux in Vigo from France in January 1917, inquiring about whether the Russians still required someone to work for them secretly.

58. Relying on the interrogating magistrate Bouchardon for justice during her pre-trial.

59. Repeatedly refusing to hire a competent lawyer after her arrest in 1917, and also during her pre-trial; and depending solely upon a lawyer who did not have any experience in the international espionage law.

60. Naively assessing her case to have been merely a mistake on the part of the French army.

Appendix C
Sketchy list of Mata Hari's lovers

Mata Hari had innumerable lovers and patrons during 10 years (1905–1915) of her career as a dancer-courtesan, and even after she had stopped giving performance. It is quite difficult to collect all the names and details after more than a century. The following list is compiled here for ready reference.

1. Adolph Pierre Messimy (1914)—French minister of war
2. Alfred Kiepert (1906)—Lieutenant in the German Army
3. Antoine Bernard (1916)—distiller and stockist of fine liquors
4. Baron Edouard Willem van der Capellen (1914)—colonel in the Dutch Hussar Regiment
5. Baron Henry de Rothschild (1905)—French banker
6. Captain Lieutenant Paul Kuntze (- ? -)—chief of the German seaplane station at Putzig airbase
7. Constant Bazet/Baret (1914)—director of a bank in Berlin
8. Edouard Clunet (1904)—lawyer
9. Emilio Junoy (- ? -)—Spanish senator
10. Enrique Gomez-Carrillo (- ? -)—Spanish-American writer (relationship not confirmed)
11. Felix Xavier Rousseau (1910)—French banker and stockbroker
12. Gabriel Astruc (1905)—playwright, impresario and theatrical agent
13. Gaston de Menier (1905)—French politician and owner of the chocolate empire near Paris

14. George Wilhelm (- ? -)—brother of the Duke of Cumberland (Ernst August Wilhelm)

15. Giacomo Antonio Puccini (1906)—famous Italian composer

16. Henri "Robert" de Marguerie (1905)—Second Secretary to the French legation in The Hague

17. Henri Kapferer (- ? -)—zeppelin pilot

18. Herr Griebel (1914)—police superintendent in Berlin

19. Jean-Helie Hallaure (1916)—Second Lieutenant at Deuxième Bureau of the Ministry of War

20. Joseph-Cyrille Denvignes (1916)—colonel of the French embassy in Madrid

21. Jules Emile Frederic Massenet (1906)—famous French composer

22. Jules-Martin Cambon (1906)—French ambassador in Madrid

23. Koanda (1915)—wealthy Rumanian of dubious character

24. Major Arnold Kalle (1916)—German military attaché to the embassy in Madrid

25. Major von Specht (- ? -)—chief of German secret service in Amsterdam

26. Marquis de Beaufort Fernand (1915)—Belgian major in Paris of the Army of the Yser

27. Marquis Pierre de Montessac (- ? -)—pilot in the French flying corps

28. Monsieur Mege (- ? -)—Nothing known

29. Nicholas Jovilchevich (- ? -)—Montenegrin major in Paris

30. Paul Oliver (1913)—music critic in Paris

31. Van der Schalk (1914)—Dutch banker

32. Vadime de Massloff (1916)—Captain in the Special Imperial Russian Regiment

Select Bibliography

BOOKS

Allen, Ann Tylor. 2005. *Feminism and Motherhood in Western Europe, 1890-1970.* NY: Palgrave Macmillan.

Andrew, Christopher. 2010. *Defend the Realm.* London: Penguin Books Ltd. (Vintage Books Edition; NY).

Anonymous. 1832. *A Guide through Wiesbaden and its Environs.* Wiesbaden: H. W. Ritter.

Anonymous. 2005. *The Diary of Mata Hari.* Paris: The Olympia Press.

Atwood, Kathryn J. 2014. *Women Heroes of World War I.* Chicago, IL: Chicago Review Press.

Baden-Powell, Robert. 2011. *My Adventures as a Spy.* NY: Dover Publications, Inc.

Beck, James M. 1916. *The Case of Edith Cavell.* NY: G. P. Putnam's Sons.

Bel, Jacqueline, and ThomasVaessens, eds. 2010. *Women's Writing from the Low Countries 1880-2010: An Anthology.* Amsterdam: Amsterdam University Press.

Belzen, Jacob A., ed. 2001. *Psychohistory in Psychology of Religion.* Amsterdam: Rodopi.

Belzen, Jacob A. 2010. *Towards Cultural Psychology of Religion.* NY: Springer.

Bennett, E. N., Trans. 1921. *The German Army in Belgium.* NY: B. W. Huebsch, Inc.

Bentley, Toni. 2005. *Sisters of Salome.* London: University of Nebraska Press.

Berndorff, H. R. 2014. *Espionage*. Washington, DC: Westphalia Press.

Bilmore, David D. 2001. *Misogyny: The Male Malady*. Philadelphia, PA: The University of Pennsylvania Press.

Bloembergen, Marieke, and Beverley Jackson, Trans. 2006. *Colonial Spectacles*. Singapore: Singapore University Press.

Boghardt, Thomas. 2004. *Spies of the Kaiser*. London: Palgrave Macmillan UK.

Branca, Patricia. 2013. *Silent Sisterhood*. London: Routledge.

Brandstetter, Gabriele. 2015. *Poetics of Dance*. NY: Oxford University Press.

Braybon, Gail, ed. 2004. *Evidence, History and the Great War*. NY: Berghahn Books.

Brown, Gordon. 2008. *Courage*. NY: Weinstein Books.

Brustein, William I. 2003. *Roots of Hate: Anti-Semitism in Europe before the Holocaust*. Cambridge: Cambridge University Press.

Buckton, Oliver S. 2015. *Espionage in British Fiction and Film since 1900*, MD: Lexington Books.

Burnap, George Washington. 1848. *The Sphere and Duties of Woman*. Philadelphia, PA: John Murphy.

Burton, June K. 2007. *Napoleon and the Woman Question*. Lubbock, TX: Texas Tech University Press.

Cahm, Eric. 2013. *The Dreyfus Affair in French Society and Politics*. London: Routledge.

Caird, Mona A. 2010. *The Morality of Marriage and other Essays on the Status and Destiny of Women*. Cambridge: Cambridge University Press.

Chakraborty, Dr. Kedareswar. 2002. *Art of Spying in Ancient India*. Kolkata: Sanskrit Book Depot.

Christenson, Ron, ed. 1991. *Political Trials in History*. Piscataway Township, NJ: Transaction Publishers.

Clark, Christopher. 2012. *The Sleepwalkers: How Europe Went to War in 1914*. London: Penguin UK.

Clayton, Martin, and Bennett Zon, eds. 2007. *Music and Orientalism in the British Empire, 1780s–1940s*. Hampshire: Ashgate Publishing Ltd.

Cohen, Matthew Isaac. 2010. *Performing Otherness*. NY: Palgrave Macmillan.

Conner, Tom. 2014. *The Dreyfus Affair and the Rise of the French Public Intellectual*. Jefferson, NC: McFarland & Company, Inc., Publishers.

Corsini, Raymond J., ed. 1994. *Encyclopedia of Psychology* (Vol. 2). London: Willey and Sons.

Coulson, Major Thomas. 1956. *Mata Hari: Courtesan and Spy*. London: Robert Hale Limited.

Dahlin, Ebba D. 1933. *French and German Public Opinion on Declared War Aims: 1914–1918*. Redwood City, CA: Stanford University Press.

Darrow, Margaret H. 2000. *French Women and the First World War*. Oxford: Berg.

Davis, Richard Harding. 2015. *About Paris*. NY: Scholar's Choice Publisher.

DeBerg, Betty A. 2000. *Ungodly Women*. Macon, GA: Mercer University Press.

Derfler, Leslie. 2002. *The Dreyfus Affair*. London: Greenwood Press.

Dijkstra, Bram. 1986. *Idols of Perversity*. NY: Oxford University Press.

Dilley, Roy M. 2014. *Nearly Native, Barely Civilized*. Boston, MA: Brill.

Drysdale, Charles R. 1880. *The Nature and Treatment of Syphilis*, Fourth Edition. London: Baillière, Tindall, and Cox.

Erté. 1979. *Erté's Theatrical Costumes*. NY: Dover Publications, Inc.

Everdell, W. R. 1997. *The First Moderns*. Chicago, IL: The University of Chicago Press.

Ex-Intelligence Officer. 1915. *The German Spy System from Within*. London: Hodder and Stoughton.

Feldman, Martha, and Bonnie Gordon, eds. 2006. *The Courtesan's Arts: Cross Cultural Perspectives*. NY: Oxford University Press.

Foley, Michael. 2014. *Rise of the Tank*. South Yorkshire (England): Pen and Sword Military.

Fournier, Alfred, and P. Albert Morrow, Trans. 1882. *Syphilis and Marriage*. NY: D. Appleton and Company.

Freud, Sigmund. 2003a. *On Metapsychology*. New Delhi: Shrijee's Book International.

Freud, Sigmund. 2003b. *On Sexuality*. New Delhi: Shrijee's Book International.

Garval, M. D. 2012. *Cleo de Merode and the Rise of Modern Celebrity Culture*. Burlington, VT: Ashgate.

Gordon, R.D. 2009. *Dances with Darwin*. Burlington, VT: Ashgate Publishing Company.

Gouda, Frances. 2008. *Dutch Culture Overseas*. Singapore: Equinox Publishing (Asia) Pte Ltd.

Grant, Robert M. 2003.*U-Boat Hunters*. Cornwall: Periscope Publishing Ltd.

Hamilton, R.F., and H.H. Herwig, eds. 2003. *The Origins of World War I*. Cambridge: CambridgeUniversity Press.

Hanson, Helen, and Catherine O'Rawe, eds. 2010. *The Femme Fatale*. NY: Palgrave Macmillan.

Haus, Jeffery. 2009. *Challenges of Equality*. Detroit, MI: Wayne State University Press.

Hedin, Sven Anders. 1915. *With the German Armies in the West*. NY: John Lane Company.

Heller, Sharon. 2005. *Freud A to Z*. NJ: John Wiley & Sons, Inc.

Henckaerts, Jean-Marie, and Louise Doswald-Beck, eds. 2005. *Customary International Humanitarian Law*, II (I), Cambridge: Cambridge University Press.

Herold, J. C. 2002. *The Age of Napoleon*. NY: Mariner Book.

Herwig, Holger H. 2009. *The Marne, 1914*. NY: Random House.

Holt, Tonie, and Valmai Holt. 2014. *Till the Boys Come Home*. South Yorkshire (England): Pen & Sword Military.

Horn, Eva. 2013. *The Secret War*. Evanston, IL: Northwestern University Press.

Howe, Russell Warren. 1986. *Mata Hari, the True Story*. NY: Dodd, Mead & Company.

Jeffery, Keith. 2010. *MI6: The History of the Secret Intelligence Service, 1909–1949*. London: Bloomsbury.

Johnston, Bernard, ed. 1987. *Collier's Encyclopedia* (Vol. 9). NY: Macmillan Educational Company.

Kahn, Roger. 1999. *A Flame of Pure Fire*. NY: Harvest.

Kassing, Gayle. 2007. *History of Dance: An Interactive Arts Approach*. Champaign, IL: Human Kinetics.

Keay, Julia. 1987. *The Spy Who Never Was*. London: Michael Joseph.

Kernberg, Otto F. 1985. *Borderline Conditions and Pathological Narcissism*. NY: Rowman & Littlefield Publishers, Inc.

Kersenboom, Saskia C. 2011. *Nityasumangali*. Delhi: MotilalBenarasidass Publishers.

Knightley, Phillip. 1987. *The Second Oldest Profession*. NY: W. W. Norton & Company, Inc.

Lachkar, Joan. 1992. *The Narcissistic/Borderline Couple: A Psychoanalytic Perspective on Marital Treatment*. Philadelphia, PA: Brunner/Mazel.

Lande, N. 1996. *Dispatches from the Front*. Oxford: Oxford University Press.

Lassere, Edward. 1912. *The Mineral Waters of Vittel*. NY: U. S. Agency.

Le Queux, William. 1914. *German Atrocities*. London: George Newnes, Limited.

Lee, Khoon Choy. 1999. *A Fragile Nation*. Singapore: World Scientific Publishing Co. Pte. Ltd.

Lewison, Sarah A. 2001. *Mata Hari Syndrome: Every Night Different*. San Diego: University of California Press.

Lindemann, Albert S. 1991. *The Jew Accused*. Cambridge: Cambridge University Press.

Linton, Eliza L. 1883. *The Girl of the Period* (Vol. I). London: Richard Bentley & Son.

Lowen, Alexander. 1985. *Narcissism: Denial of the True Self*. NY: Touchstone.

Maddox, Lucy, ed. 1999. *Locating American Studies*. Baltimore, MD: Johns Hopkins University Press.

Marshall, Bill, ed. 2005. *France and the Americas*. Santa Barbara, CA: ABC-CLIO, Inc.

McQuillen, Colleen. 2013. *The Modernist Masquerade*. Madison, WI: The University of Wisconsin Press.

Meem, Deborah T., ed. 2002. *The Rebel of the Family* (Linton, Eliza L.). Canada: Broadview Press.

Meyer, G. J. 2006. *A World Undone*. NY: Random House.

Michael, Robert. 2008. *A History of Catholic Antisemitism: The Dark Side of the Church*. NY: Palgrave Macmillan.

Mill, J. S. 1869. *The Subjection of Women*. London: Longmans, Green, Reader, and Dyer.

Miller, Paul B. 2002. *From Revolutionaries to Citizens*. London: Duke University Press.

Nash, Elizabeth. 2012. *Geraldine Farrar*. NC: McFarland & Company, Inc., Publishers.

Newman, Bernard. 1956. *Inquest on Mata Hari*. London: Robert Hale Limited.

Ostrovsky, Erika. 1978. *Eye of Dawn*. NY: Macmillan Publishing Co., Inc.

Panayi, Panikos. 1991. *Enemy in our Midst*. Oxford: Berg.

Passmore, Kevin. 2013. *The Right in France, from the Third Republic to Vichy*. Oxford: Oxford University Press.

Patmore, Coventry K. D. 1854. *The Angel in the House*. London: John W. Parker and Son West Strand.

Phillipson, Coleman. 2005. *International Law and the Great War*. NJ: The Lawbook Exchange, Ltd.

Pickles, Katie. 2007. *Transnational Outrage*. NY: Palgrave Macmillan.

Poliakov, Léon, and George Klin, Trans. 1977. *The History of Anti-Semitism: Suicidal Europe, 1870–1933*; (Vol. 4). Philadelphia, PA: University of Pennsylvania Press.

Potter, Jane. 2005. *Boys in Khaki, Girls in Print*. Oxford: Oxford University Press.

Proctor, Tammy M. 2003. *Female Intelligence*. NY: New York University Press.

Raphael, John N. 1914. *The Caillaux Drama*. London: Max Goschen Ltd.

Read, Piers Paul. 2012. *The Dreyfus Affair*. London: Bloomsbury Publishing.

Richelson, Jeffery T. 1995. *A Century of Spies*. Oxford: Oxford University Press.

Schenkar, Joan. 2001. *Truly Wilde*. Cambridge: Da Capo Press.

Scott, Jill. 2005. *Electra after Freud: Myth and Culture*. NY: Cornell University Press.

Sert, Misia, and Moura Budberg, Trans. 1953. *Misia and the Muses: The Memoirs of Misia Sert*. NY: The John Day Company.

Shamir, Haim, ed. 1990. *France and Germany in an Age of Crisis, 1900–1960*. NY: E. J. Brill.

Shipman, Pat. 2007. *Femme Fatale*. London: Weidenfeld & Nicolson.

Silverman, Debora L. 1992. *Art Nouveau in Fin-de-Siècle France*. Berkeley, CA: University of California Press.

Souhami, Diana. 2010. *Edith Cavell*. London: Quercus.

Steele, Valerie. 1988. *Paris Fashion: A Cultural History*. NY: Oxford University Press.

Swinton, Ernest D. 1933. *Eyewitness*. NY: Doubleday, Doran & Company, Inc.

Theweleit, Klaus. 2003. *Male Fantasies* (Vol. I). Minneapolis, MN: University of Minnesota Press.

Thomson, Basil. 1922. *Queer People*. London: Hodder and Stoughton Limited.

Tierney, Helen, ed. 1999. *Women's Studies Encyclopedia* (Vol.1). CT: Greenwood Press.

Tilburg, Patricia A. 2010. *Colette's Republic*. NY: Berghahn Books.

Tuchman, Barbara W. 2014. *The Zimmerman Telegram*. NY: Random House.

Tucker, Spencer C., ed. 2014. *World War One: The Definitive Encyclopedia*. Oxford: ABC-CLIO.

Waagenaar, Sam. 1964. *The Murder of Mata Hari*. London: Arthur Barker Ltd.

Waagenaar, Sam. 1965. *Mata Hari: A Biography*. NY: Appelton-Century.

Wark, Wesley K. 1991. *Spy Fiction, Spy Films and Real Intelligence.* NY: Routledge.

Wessels, J. W. 2005. *History of the Roman-Dutch Law.* NJ: The Lawbook Exchange, Ltd.

Wheelwright, Julie. 1992. *The Fatal Lover.* London: Collins & Brown Limited.

White, Rosie. 2007. *Violent Femmes: Women as Spies in Popular Culture.* NY: Routledge.

Wighton, Charles. 1965. *The World's Greatest Spies.* NY: Taplinger Publishing Company.

Wilkinson, Alan. 2014. *The Church of England and the First World War.* Cambridge: The Lutterworth Press.

Willcox, R. N. 1900. *Paris Exposition.* Ohio: Willcox Print.

Wineapple, Brenda. 1989. *Genêt: A Biography of Janet Flanner.* Lincoln, NE: University of Nebraska Press.

Woods, B. F. 2008. *Neutral Ground.* NY: Algora Publishing.

Zeldin, Theodore. 2000. *A History of French Passions, 1848–1945.* Oxford: Clarendon Press.

PERIODICALS

Brückner, Hilmar-Detlef (Review). "Mata Hari." Léon Schirmann. *Journal of Intelligence History.* (Vol.4, No. 1). London: Summer 2004. Print.

Brummelman, Eddie; Bushman, Brad J. eds. "Origins of Narcissism in Children." *Proceedings of the National Academy of Sciences*; Vol. 112. No. 12. Washington, DC: 24 March 2015. Internet archive.

Fisher, Edward D. "Syphilis in its Relation to Diabetes." *The Journal of Nervous and Mental Disease*; Vol. 17 (7). Chicago: July 1892. Internet archive.

Grand, Sarah. "The New Aspect of the Woman Question." *North American Review*, Vol. 158, No. 448, NYC: March 1894. Internet archive.

Griggs, Ione Quinby. "Woman Who Betrayed Edith Cavell Boasted of Part to Milwaukeean." *The Milwaukee Journal (Green Sheet)*. The Journal Company. Wisconsin: 2 May 1934. Print.

Kolb, Alexander. "Mata Hari's Dance in the Context of Femininity and Exotism." *Mandrágora*; (Vol. 15, No. 15). Sao Paulo: 2009. Print.

Ryley, Jameson Patrick. "The Historian Who Sold Out: James Bryce and the Bryce Report." *Iowa Historical Review*; Vol. 1, Issue 2. University of Iowa. 2008. Print.

Udovic, Rev. Edward R. "Saint Lazare as a Women's Prison, 1794–1932." Virtual Exhibition of DePaul University; 2011. Internet archive.

NEWSPAPERS

"Condemned Woman Spy." *Daily Mail*. 31 July 1917. Print.

"Cruelest Lie—or Truest Mercy?" *The Washington Times*. 29 August 1920. Print.

"Mata Hari—Spy." *Manawatu Daily Times*; Vo. XL; Issue 13760. (Palmerston North, N.Z.) 13 December 1917. Print.

"No Comparison Between Women Put to Death." *The Evening Star*. 20 October 1917—Part I; Washington, DC. Print.

"Sacred Dances of Brahmanism." *New-York Daily Tribune*. 25 June 1905. Print.

"Theatrical and Musical Notes." Pasquin. *Otago Witness*. Issue 2633. (New Zealand) 31 August 1904. Print.

"Unmarked Grave Holds Danseuse Executed as Spy." *The Pittsburgh Press*. 25 December 1921. Print.

"Wickedest, Most Dangerous—War Spy Of All." *The Pittsburgh Press*. 25 December 1921. Print.

Calvert, Albert F. "Women Spies." *Daily Mail*. 30 July 1917. Print.

Cox, John H. "Alsace Blighted by War Horrors." *New York Tribune*. 23 August 1914. Print.

Davis, Richard Harding. "Saw German Army Roll on Like Dog." *The Farmer and Mechanic*. NC: 8 September 1914. Print.

Nguyen, Huy. "Movie depicts don ca tai tu artists in early 20th century." *The Saigon Times*. 2 August 2015. Internet archive.

Reboul, Jacques. "Spy Scare Grips The World." *Auckland Star*. (Vol. LXV, Issue 153). 30 June 1934. Print.

WEBSITES

Netherland's Patriciaat. (From the official website of Centraal Bureau voor Genealogie).

www.paperpast.natlib.govt.nz

www.nationalarchives.gov.uk

www.stephen-stratford.co.uk

www.chroniclingamerica.loc.gov

www.bbc.co.uk/ Rimington, Stella. "Secrets and Spies: The Untold Story of Edith Cavell." BBC Radio 4, 16 September 2015.

Image Acknowledgements

Fries Museum, Leeuwarden
  (i) Goat carriage gifted to Margarethe by Adam
  (ii) Teenager Margarethe
  (iii) Rudolf and Margarethe after the wedding
  (iv) Artist's impression of Mata Hari
  (v) Mata Hari in a uniform
  (vi) Mata Hari on horseback
  (vii) Mata Hari's headgear and breast plates
  (viii) Mata Hari's visiting card
  (ix) Mata Hari on board Steamship *Zeelandia*
  (x) Artist's impression of the trial of Mata Hari

Bibliothèque nationale de France
  (i) Carolina la belle Otero
  (ii) Louise Mante
  (iii) Mata Hari
  (iv) Suzy Deguez

Getty Images Media India Pvt. Ltd.
  (i) Mata Hari nude

Alamy Images India
  (i) Dancer with snakes

Author's collection
  (i) Image of tropical insects

Internet Archive
  (i) Marriage advertisement of Rudolf MacLeod
  (ii) Marriage announcement of Rudolf MacLeod and Margarethe Zelle MacLeod
  (iii) Image of the pamphlet of Otto von Emmich
  (iv) Images of mannequin with gold headgear

Others
  (i) Image of Mata Hari published in *De Kroniek*, 1916, taken from the published documents KV-2/1 of the UK government

Word Index

1million francs, 164, 166, 167, 174, 176, 182, 215, 228
20,000 francs, 146, 152, 165, 173, 178, 214, 216, 218, 225, 231
282 Boulevard Saint-Germain, 159, 184, 214

A

Aceh War, xxviii, xxix, 63
Adultery, xxxvii
Aerodrome, 162
AF44, 165, 167, 207
Alcoholic, 19, 55, 56
Alice Network, 130, 131
Allan, Maud de, 16, 107
Allard, British secret agent, 175, 176, 211, 258
Allied forces, 121, 122, 123, 125, 126, 129, 130, 133, 136, 138, 163, 167, 168, 180, 181, 221, 222
Allied network, 24
Alsace-Lorraine, 26, 121, 122, 242
Amsterdam Court, xxxvii
Amsterdam Tribunal, xxxii
Angel of the House, xxx, xliii, 39
Angkor Wat, 78
Annamite, 92
Anti-feminism, xlii, 11, 13, 112
Anti-militarist, 121
Anti-propaganda, ix, xliii, 234

Anti-Semitism, xlii, 13, 14, 112, 115
Anti-tank gun, 227
Antoinette, Queen Marie, 220
Antwerp, 24, 124, 165, 167, 169, 207, 208, 216, 218
Apollo Theater, 105
Appellate Court, 235
Apsarā, 102
ARA (Alien Restriction Act), 171
Arrest, 13, 120, 131, 150, 169-171, 177-179, 187-189, 195, 196, 200, 201, 204, 227, 228, 258, 259
Art Nouveau, 11
Arthritis, 158
Article 27 (French Penal Code), 59, 238
Assassination, xiii, xiv, 121, 122
Assumptionist, 14
Astruc, Gabriel, 100, 101, 148, 252, 261
Audience, xxxiv, xxxviii, xl, 17, 25, 45, 78-80, 87-91, 97, 98, 100, 104, 105, 109, 145
Augustus, Prince Ernst, 167, 217
Austria, 100, 121
Austria-Hungary, xiii, 142
Autopsy, xxviii, xxix, 209
Aviator, 156, 175, 230
Aylmer-Cameron, Major Cecil, 130

B

Babu, 42, 50, 64

Baladi dance, 93, 105
Balkstra sisters, 52, 85
Ballet Russes, 148
Banjoe Biroe, 52, 81
Bankruptcy, xxii, xxiii, 5, 35, 60, 61, 74, 193, 242, 251
Barcelona, 178
Baret, Constant, 218, 261
Barney, Natalie Clifford, xv, xxxviii
Barrister, xxxvi, 171
Batavia, 41, 53, 56, 251
Battle of Mons, 122, 123, 127
Battle of Somme, xiv, 134, 136, 138, 139, 161, 198, 227, 234, 253, 257
Battle of the Frontiers, 122, 123, 143, 144
Battle of Verdun, 131, 134, 139, 150, 155, 159, 161, 164, 178
Beaufort, Marquis de, 148, 150, 156, 174, 194, 196, 210, 262
Belle Époque, xxxiii, xliii, 14, 16, 28, 76, 78, 90, 106-108, 111, 230
Belly dance, 96
Benedix, Clara, 169-172, 177, 207, 253, 258
Berkendael Medical Institute, 126
Bernard, Antoine, 156, 261
Bettignies, Louise de (Alice Dubios), 130, 131
Bharatanātyam, 95
Bigne, Valtesse de la, 76
Bismark, Otto von, 22, 26
Bissing, General Moritz von, 166, 258
Bizard, Dr. Leon, 201, 236
Blackmail, 246
Bloomers, 12, 17
Blume, Lisa, 210, 211
Boer War, 20
Boldini, Giovanni, 79

Bonaparte, Princess Marie, 178
Bouchardon, Pierre, 173, 183, 184, 190, 191, 193-225, 230, 231, 233, 237, 249, 259
Boulanger, Georges, 139
Bouloumie, Dr. Pierre, 158
Briand, Aristide, 135, 178, 208
British counterintelligence, 147, 149, 150, 151, 153, 160, 163, 168, 215, 227
British Empire, xxxvi, 20, 21, 167
British Expeditionary Force (BEF), 122, 123, 125, 127
British Intelligence Division - (Room 40), 173, 181
British jurisdiction, 174
British Police, 147
Brown, Sarah, 16, 89, 107
Bryce Commission Report, 125
Buddhist, 42, 77, 85, 91
Bunge, Otto David Eduard, 174, 186, 211
Buys', Miss, xvii, xix, 2, 3, 251

C

C. S. *Telconia*, 180
Cabaret, 16, 78
Café concert, xxxviii, 96
Caillaux, Joseph, 233
Caillaux, Madame Henriette, 233
Cake-Walk, 107, 108
Calve, Emma, 90
Cambodian, 17, 78, 79
Cambon, Jules, 102, 154, 185, 229, 262
Cancan dance, 16, 89
Candi-Jago, 85
Candi-Sari, 77
Cannibalism, xxix
Capellen, Edouard Willem van der, xli,

144, 145, 149, 150, 163, 166, 167, 173, 182, 186, 194, 199, 204, 205, 211, 225, 230, 231, 261
Capiau, Herman, 127, 128
Caricature, 22, 23, 27
Carnet A, 139
Carnet B (Red Book), 137, 139, 140
Carnier, Inspector, 197
Cartier, Francois, 185
Catholics, 1, 9, 14, 15, 83, 112-115, 117
Cats, Jacob, 6
Cavalieri, Lina, 90
Cavell, Miss Edith, xliii, 126-129, 131, 132, 134, 242
Cavelli, Blanche, 89
Cazeaux, Martial, 175, 176, 185, 211, 258, 259
Censorship, 56
Central Information Bureau (Cologne), 207
Ceylon, xxxv, xxxvi
Chateau de la Dorée, 218
Chemin des Dames, 135, 205
Choreography, 17, 78
Cinema, 77, 78
Cirque, 86
City of Lights, 76, 82
Clandestine, 24, 58
Clemenceau, Georges, 137, 138, 190
Cleopatra, 89
Clinching evidence, 206, 220
Clunet, Edouard, 59, 100, 192, 194, 195, 200, 201, 206, 210, 212, 215, 219, 220, 223, 228-230, 234-238, 261
Code of Manu (Manusmriti), viii
Code of Napoleon, viii, xxxii, xlii, 7-9, 111
Codename, 166, 167, 207, 227, 253, 258
Colette, Sidone-Gabrielle, 99, 108

Comptoir National d' Escompte de Paris, 168, 211
Compulsive Buying Disorder, 43, 248
Concièrgerie, 220, 228
Conservative, xlii, 9, 11, 14, 15, 33, 114, 235
Conspiracy of Optimism, 133
Consumerism, 77
Contraceptive, 40
Contrexéville, 156, 158, 159
Council for Revision, 234, 254
Counter-insurgency, xxix
Court-martial, xiv
Criminal Investigation Department, 171
Croy, Princess Marie de, 127
Cryptanalyst, 229
Cryptologist, 209
Culture Physique, 108

D

d'Alençon, Émilienne, 16, 80, 107
Danseuse, xliii, 238, 241
Davis, Richard Harding, 76, 124
Death penalty, xiv, 120
Death trap, xxxvii, 163
Debauchery, 160
Debussy, Claude, 79
Defense counsel, 229
Deguez, Mlle Suzy, 106
Delsarte method, 107
Demimondaine, vii, xiv, xxxix, xl, 16, 25, 107, 192, 203, 215, 236
Denis, Ruth, 105
Denvignes, Joseph, 181, 182, 184, 187, 200, 212, 216, 217, 226, 258, 262
Department of Interior Defense, 169
Desmond, Olga, 104

Deuxième Bureau/Second Bureau, 27, 130, 139, 150, 155, 159-161, 163, 164, 166, 184, 185, 232, 253, 262

Devadāsi, xxxvi, 93, 94

Devil's Island, 118, 120

Diabetes, xxvi, 158

Diaghilev, Sergei, 99, 148

Diplomatic Book, 199

Diplomatic channel, 216, 259

Directorate of Military Operations (MO5), 22

Divorce, xxxvii, 19, 33, 35, 52, 53, 61, 75, 76, 83, 103, 104, 143, 197, 251, 252

Dix, Otto, 75

Doctored evidence, 181, 220

DORA (Defense of the Realm Act), 171, 253

Double agent, 161, 168, 174, 209, 245

Dreyfus Affair, xliii, 14, 115, 116, 120

Dreyfus, Alfred, xiv, xv, 13-16, 56, 114-121, 181

Drumont, Edouard Adolphe, 13-15, 115

Dubail, Auguste, 205, 209, 210, 222

Duke of Cumberland, 167, 217, 219, 262

Duncan, Isadora, 16, 80, 105, 108

Dutch East Indies, xxiv, xxvi, xxvii, xxviii, xxxi, 17, 39, 44, 50, 53, 75, 77, 81, 91, 194, 251

Dutch Legation (London), 151, 152

E

École Polytechnique, 114, 115, 117, 120

Edmonds, James Edward, 22, 23

Education, xx, 2, 4, 6, 12, 24, 51, 111, 113, 115

Edwardian, 19, 20, 243

Egyptian Ballet, xl

Egyptology, 142

Eiffel Tower, 180, 184, 201, 205, 208

Electra-complex, xviii

Elysée Palace Hotel, 188

Emmich, Otto von, 125, 126

Enemy within, 190, 213, 232, 234, 236

English Channel, 152, 153, 180, 257, 258

Entrap, 162, 165, 176, 179, 192

Equestrian, 86, 92, 191

Erman, Johann Adolf, xl, 142

Eros, 35

Erotic, xxxviii, 18, 93, 94, 98, 101, 108, 165, 243

Espionitis/spyscare/spy-fever, xlii, 20, 21, 26, 27, 247

Estachy, Jean, 237

Esterhazy, Ferdinand, 118, 119

Esvres, 218

Execution, xiv, xl, xliii, xliv, 9, 21, 26, 59, 102, 113, 120, 129, 131-134, 166, 173, 229, 234, 236-238, 241, 242, 249

Expedition Cross, 63

Eye of Dawn, xxxiii, 91, 219, 238

F

Falguiere, Jean Alexandre J., 79

Falloux Law, 113

Fashion, 16, 42, 46, 48, 75, 77, 80-82, 98, 106, 111, 166, 177

Father fixation, xviii

Faure, Félix, 119, 233

February Revolution (1917), 217

Ferdinand, Archduke Francis, xiii, 121, 122

Fin de siècle, 76, 81

Fire Dance, 108

Firing squad, xiv, 233, 242
Flamenco Dance, 107, 169
Folies Bergère, 107, 108
Folkestone Bureau, 24, 130
Foreign Office (London), 171
Foreign Office (The Hague), 151, 235
Fortuny, Mariano, 80
Fourth Regiment of the Zouaves, 237
Franco-Prussian War, 26, 112, 114, 121, 124
Franco-Russian Military Convention, 122
Franz-Namur, Paul, 75
Freemasonry, 62
French Cipher Bureau, 181
French counterintelligence, 118, 138, 139, 160, 161, 173, 174, 184, 232
French Criminal Code, 59, 120, 223
French General Staff, 15, 114-116
French Intelligence Service, 115, 118, 139, 168, 218
French Law of Armed Conflict Manual, 201
French Penal Code, 223, 238
French Revolution, 113
Freudian, xviii, xxi, 35
Frida, Louise Jeanne (Tante Frida), xxx, xxxiii, 38-45, 54, 56, 57, 63, 66, 71, 72, 74, 255
Friesland, xvi, 1, 2, 87
Fröbel, Friedrich, xx, 4
Fryatt, Charles Algernon, 132, 133
Fuller, Loie, 16, 78, 87, 90, 108
Funeral, 241

G

Gambetta, Léon, 115
Gamelan music, 79

Gender-role, 2, 8, 15, 31
George, Prince of Greece, 178
German agent, 24, 31, 128, 161, 164, 165, 171, 172, 174, 187, 206, 207, 208, 210, 212, 215, 221, 229, 232, 245, 249
German Codebook, 181
German counterintelligence, 128, 129, 131-133
German Crimes Calendar, 125
German embassy (Paris), 13, 115
German embassy (The Netherlands), 24, 149, 199
German General Staff, 123, 141
German intelligence service, xlii, 128, 230, 249
German Military Code, 129
German Naval SKM Codebook, 181
German secret service, 128, 146, 199, 211, 233, 262
Germano-phobia, 21
Godmother, 30, 249
Goekoop, Cecile, 76
Goodvriend, 44, 57, 72
Goubet, Colonel, 166, 187, 188, 211, 214, 228
Grand Hotel (Paris), 84, 154-156
Grand Hotel d'Orsay, 182, 184
Grandes Horizontales, 16
Grant, George Reid and Janet, 169-171
Griebel, chief of police in Berlin, xl, 142, 194, 224, 230, 262
Groote Houtstraat, 3
Guerrilla, xxix, 124
Guillonnet, Octave, 75
Guimet, Émile, xxxiv, xxxvi, 91, 92, 95, 142, 174, 194
Gypsy, 87

H

H21, 146, 164, 188, 201, 207-212, 215, 221, 227, 253
Haanstra, Wybrandus, xx, 255
Hague Convention, 124, 125, 201
Hair Dance, 106
Hall, William Reginald, 173
Hallaure, Jean, 155, 156, 159, 214, 228, 229, 257, 258, 262
Handaye, 154, 165
Haute Couture, 80, 81
Hem, Piet van der, 75, 100
Henry, Hubert-Joseph, 115, 117
Herod, 96
Hindu, xxxiv, xxxvi, xxxviii, 15, 17, 42, 85, 92-95
Hoedemaker, Henry, 153, 154, 165, 257
Hotel Continental (Vigo), 175
Hotel de Boer, 48
Hotel Paulez, The Hague, 145
Hotel Plaza Athénée (Paris), 183
Hotel Ritz (Madrid), 169, 176, 177, 182, 199
House of Worth, 80
Household Nun, 9, 18
HVB Codebook, 181
Hydrotherapy, 157, 158

I

Imperial army maneuvers, 104
Indian, vii, viii, xxxiv, xxxvi, xxxviii, xxxix, 15, 87, 88, 90, 93-95, 97, 98, 101, 169, 229, 238, 246
Infidelity, xxxvii, 70
International woman, 203, 245
Invasion novel, 19, 20, 21
Israels, Isaac Lazarus, 75

J

Jaffna Pattanam, xxxv
Jagow, Traugott von, 224
Jaurès, Joseph Jean, 121
Javanese, xxxiii, xxxviii, 17, 43, 79, 82, 85, 91, 93, 95, 105, 107, 109
Jesuit, 15
Jihad, xxix
Jullien, Major, 210, 237
July Crisis, xiii, 142
Junoy, Emilio, 183, 259, 261
Justinian Code, 8

K

Kalle, Arnold, 177-182, 184, 187, 199-201, 205-208, 211-215, 218, 222, 225-228, 230-232, 253, 259, 262
Kāmasūtra, 101
Kell, Vernon, 150
Keyzer, Francis, 88, 97
Khan, Inayat, xxxviii, 252
Khmer tradition, 78
Kiepert, Alfred, xxxix, xl, 104, 105, 194, 203, 217, 256, 261
Kindergarten, xx, 4, 255
Kingdom of Hanover, 219
Kireevsky, Mrs., xxxiv, 88, 95
Kroemer, Karl, xli, xlii, 24-26, 146, 147, 152, 163-166, 176, 178, 205, 211, 213-216, 218, 221, 225, 226, 229, 231, 253, 258
Krohn, Hans von, 180, 226
Kruger Telegram, 20
Kruger, Paul, 20

L

La Bourboule, 158
La Croix, 14, 15, 118
La France Juive, 112
La Libre Parole, 13-15, 112
Ladoux, Captain Georges, 131, 159-168, 173, 174, 176, 178-188, 193, 198-200, 202, 204, 205, 207-213, 215, 216, 218, 219, 226, 228, 231, 245, 249, 253, 258, 259
Lady Godiva, xxxviii, 89
Lady MacLeod, 88, 89, 91, 92, 97, 252
Laferrier, Mme. A., 80
Lanvin, Jeanne-Marie, 81
Le Queux, William Tuffnell, 20-23, 124, 125
Le Roi de Lahore, 101
Leeuwarden, ix, xv-xix, xxv, 1-3, 61, 74, 85, 91, 143, 251, 255
Lefebvre, Jules Joseph, 89
Leiden, xix, xx, 255
Léonide, Sister, 228, 233, 236, 237, 239
Levillion, Mme., 80
Leyden method, xx
Liège, 122-124, 144
Lintjens, Anna, xli, 168, 199, 205, 211, 216, 230, 259
Little orchid, ix, xvii, xxi, xxii, xliv, 3, 5, 34, 59, 60, 61, 144, 239, 255
Lord Buddha, 92
Lord Subramānya, 92
Louise, Princess Victoria, 167, 217
Lovesick, 162
Lumière brothers, 77
Lyautey, Louise Hubert G., 135, 182, 187

M

M'ahesa, Sent, 105
MacLeod, Uncle Norman, 62, 69
Madrid-Berlin traffic, 179, 180, 182, 183, 205, 210, 211, 231
Malay, 43, 98
Malvy, Louis Jean, 137, 229
Mannequin, 2, 74, 98
Mantilla, 169, 170
Maple warehouse, 149, 196
Marguerie, Henry de, 84, 86-88, 148, 162, 218, 229, 258, 262
Marie, Sister, 233
Marina, xxi, 58, 156, 157, 162, 163, 187, 195, 198, 217
Massard, Emile, xiv, 15, 223, 237, 238
Massenet, Jules, 101, 102, 262
Massloff, Vladimir de (Vadime), xxi, 59, 156-159, 161-163, 165, 166, 170, 176, 183-187, 195-198, 203, 204, 216, 217, 219, 224, 226, 228, 229, 235, 253, 254, 257, 262
Mast, Elisabetha M. C. van der, xxxvii, 73
Master spy, 22, 26
Mata Hari Syndrome, xliii, 242-245, 247, 248
Mata Haridans, 243
Matrimonial, xxiv, xxxvi, 37
Maunoury, Henri, 168, 174, 187, 219
Medan, xxvii-xxix, 44, 46-50, 252
Mediterranean, 41
Ménagerie, 195
Menier, Gaston de, 90, 252, 261
Merlot-Larcheveque, Mme., 80
Mérode, Cléo de, 16, 17, 78-80, 82, 87, 89, 90, 92, 107
Messimy, Adolphe-Pierre, 229, 261

Metropol Theater, xl, 142, 143, 256
Meulen, Antje van der, xvi, xix, 6, 35, 60, 61
Meyer, Arthur, 90
MI5/E branch, 23, 25, 26, 129, 169, 170, 173, 253
Mill, John Stuart, 6, 8
Milloue, M. Leon de, 91
Ministry of War, 139, 155, 187, 205, 206, 213, 262
Miscarriage of justice, xiv, xliii, 13, 121, 129
Misogyny, vii, 11, 35, 58, 65, 111, 148, 223, 256
Modeling, xxxiii, 74, 75, 83, 89
Molier Circus, xxxiii, 86, 155, 252
Molier, Ernst, xxxiii, 86-88, 92
Moltke, Helmut von, 123, 124, 141
Money trail, 197, 217, 225
Monier, Police inspector, 155, 162, 183, 228
Monte Carlo, xxxv, 102, 252
Mornet, Andre, 222, 224-228, 230, 231, 237
Morocco, 178, 181, 185, 227
Motherhood, 2-4, 8, 10, 40, 42, 134
Moulin Rouge, xxxiv, 89
Mt Gede, 53
Mt Kloet, 52
Murder, 26, 122, 132, 232, 249
Musée Guimet, 91, 92, 96, 97, 174, 252
Music hall, xxxiv, xxxviii, 30, 89, 90, 97, 100, 107, 108, 185
Muslim, xxviii
Mutiny, xliii, 134, 136-138, 213
Mysticism, 101
Mythomania, 98, 248

N

Narcissism, xxi, xxii, 42, 60, 247
Narcissistic, xxi, xxii, 34, 38, 47, 58, 60, 159
Naṭarāja, xxxiv, 92, 93
National Exhibition of Women's Labor, 75
Nautch, 93
Naval intelligence, 173
Neuilly-sur-Seine, xxxviii, 142, 146, 147, 149
Neutral, 125, 133, 143, 177, 230, 236
New Woman, xlii, 10-13, 18, 28, 111, 113, 243
Nicholas II, Tsar of Russia, 217
Nicolai, Walter, xlii, 180, 223, 249
Nieuwe Uitleg, xli, 145, 149
Nijmegen, 83, 84
Nivelle Offensive, 135, 136, 138, 178, 205, 213
Nivelle, Robert Georges, 134-137
Nonnie (Non) Jeanne-Louise, xxvii, xxxii, 19, 44, 56, 57, 64, 67, 70, 72-74, 81, 83, 103, 144, 235, 251, 252
Norman (son), xxvii, xxix, 19, 40, 41, 44, 50, 64, 85, 156, 157, 251
Nude of art, 97
Nude of commerce, 97
Nymphomaniac, 242, 247, 248

O

Occult, 115
Odissi, 95
Office of the Military Justice, 187
Oliver, Paul, xxxviii, 262
Olympia Theater, 17, 100
Oorijzer, 1, 2

Oriental Dream, 90, 252
Orthodox, xxxiii, xxxvi, 7, 10, 18, 28, 35, 39, 42, 45, 56, 64, 111, 113, 232
OSA (Official Secrets Act), 171
Otero, Caroline la belle, 16, 94, 96, 107
Oxycyanide of mercury, 203

P

Palace Hotel (Paris), 189
Palace of Justice, 190, 220, 222
Pamphlet, 13, 14, 22, 29, 35, 112, 133
Panama Crisis, 13
Paquin, Mme. Jeanne, 80, 81
Paradigm shift, xliii, 248
Parasite, 27, 244, 245, 248
Paris World Exposition, xxxiii, 17, 77-82, 107
Parker, Edward, 171
Passport, xli, 15, 143, 169-171, 189
Patriarchal, vii, viii, 8, 11
Patriotism, 2, 21, 126, 130, 134
Pearl, Cora, 89
Penataran temple, 52
Pervert, 12, 68, 248
Pétain, Philippe, 137
Petit, Gabrielle (Miss Legrand), 131, 132
Phosgene gas, 161
Picquart, Georges, 118
Pillarization, 1
Pillow talk, 167, 243
Plantation, xxviii, 42, 52, 66, 81, 107
Poincaré, Raymond, 235, 237, 254, 227, 253, 258
Port Folkestone, 24, 130, 147, 171, 257
Port Philip Heads (Australia), 181
Pougy, Liane de (Anne Marie), 16, 75, 76, 81, 107
Prefecture of Police (Paris), 161, 168, 187
Pregnancy, xxvii, 40, 44, 59, 238
Prejudice, viii, xiv, 4, 119, 149, 190
Presidential clemency, 129, 235, 236, 254
Pre-trial, xliii, 184, 193, 219, 224, 225, 254, 259
Priem, Gerrit Hendrik, 35, 56, 62, 72, 101
Prinzip, Gavrio, xiii
Priolet, Albert, 188, 228
Prisoner-of-war, 201
Propaganda, 13, 14, 118, 121, 125, 126, 133, 134, 137, 138, 141, 198, 201, 205, 242, 243
Prostitution, xxxiii, 31, 73, 83, 90, 257, 259
Protestant, 9, 11, 15, 16, 112, 115, 189
Provisional liberty/parole, 200, 202, 204, 206, 212
Psychosis, 21
Puccini, Giacomo, 102, 262

Q

Quien, Georges Gaston, 128, 129

R

Radio traffic, 178, 182-184, 201, 202, 205-211, 215, 216, 227, 232
Radiogram, 208
Poiret, Paul, 80, 81
Police Commissariat, 157, 161
Port Falmouth, 152, 154, 168-170, 176-178, 181, 187, 207, 208, 210, 213,
Railroad, 41

Rape of Belgium, 123
Rauditz, Ernest, 80
Red Cross, 29, 88, 126, 131, 186
Red Dancer, 163
Register of Aliens, 26, 189, 253
Reutlinger, Leopold, xxxvii, 103
Revenge, xxvii, xxviii, xlii, 121, 133, 137, 138, 154, 159, 212, 234, 242
Reynal, Mr., 235
Rheumatism, xxvi, xxix
Richer, Marthe (The Lark), 174, 175, 179, 180, 226, 245
Rig Veda, 92
Rivière, Adjutant, 222, 229, 233
RMS *Lusitania*, 128, 134
Robespierre, Maximilien, 220
Roelfsema, Dr., 81
Rolland, Misrachi von, 178
Roman Catholic, 14, 83
Rothschild, Henri de, 90, 261
Rousseau, Felix Xavier, 142, 218, 261
Rousseau, Mrs., 218, 252
Royal Academy of Arts, 74
Royal Dutch Indies Army, 63
Royal Theater, The Hague, 145
Rubenstein, Ida, 16
Russian war-fleet, 180

S

S M S *Magdeburg*, 180
S M S *S119*, 181
S. S. *Arguaya*, 175, 176
S. S. *Arundel*, 147
S. S. *Brussels*, 132
S. S. *Hollandia*, 168, 169, 175, 207, 210
S. S. *Koningin Wilhelmina*, 56
S. S. *Prinses Amelia*, 41
S. S. *Zeelandia*, 152, 153, 257
Sabotage, 20, 27, 115
Sacrifice, xliv, 4, 12, 29, 84, 130, 132, 213, 245
Saint Cyrian, 120, 222
Saint Gilles prison, 129, 131, 132
Saint Lazare, 190, 192-194, 201, 220, 233, 236, 237
Saint Cyr, 15, 112, 113, 118, 119, 160, 187
Salammbo, 96
Salome, 89, 96, 107, 108
Salon, xxxviii, 16, 88, 90, 99, 156
San Sebastian, 154
Sanjaya Dynasty, 17
Sarajevo, xiii
Savarre, L., 80
Savoy Hotel (London), 175
Scapegoat, xlii, xliii, 15, 16, 117, 119, 120, 138, 150, 161, 196, 232
Schalk, van der, 144, 146, 262
Schlieffen Plan, 123, 124
Schragmüller, Fräulein Doktor, 24, 165, 167, 169, 209, 245
Scotland Yard, 149, 168, 169, 171, 175, 207, 253, 258
Scoundrel D. letter, 120
Sculpture, 92
Secession Hall, 105
Second Battle of Aisne, 135
Second Boer War, 20
Secret ink, 131, 146, 152, 185, 199, 200, 204, 212, 214, 221, 222
Secret Service Bureau, 23
Section III B, 180
Self-indulgent, xxxviii, 35
Selfless angles, 129, 133
Self-mystification, xxxvi, 58, 98, 247, 248, 256

Semprou, Albert Ernest, 222, 224, 229, 230, 233, 237
Separation, xxxiii, xxxvii, 56, 57, 64, 66, 71-73, 82, 84, 159, 163, 252
Serbia, xiii, 122, 142
Serbian Black Hand, xiii
Serimpi, 17, 93
Serpentine Dance, 108
Singasari temple, 52
Siva, xxxvi, xl, 17, 92, 93
Smith-Cumming, George M., 24, 150
Sneek, xix, 4, 37, 251
Somme Offensive, 136
Sorel, Cécile, 90
Souvenir, 182
Spa, xxiv, xxix, 158
Spirit of 1914, 141
Spy-hunting, 23, 181
Spymaster, 130, 165, 167, 229, 231, 245, 246
Spy-nest, 27
Star of Dance, xxxiv, 252
Statistical Section, 115, 118
Steinheil, Marguerite, 233
Submarine, 132, 228
Suffrage, 10, 11
Sufi, xxxviii
Sumatra, xxviii, 46, 63, 91
Surveillance, 24, 83, 139, 140, 160, 201, 214
Suylenburg, Hilda van, 76
Switzerland, xli, 143, 158, 187, 207, 232
Syndicalist, 137
Syphilis, xxvi, xxvii, xxviii, xxix, 53, 55, 64, 67, 68, 70, 201

T

Tableau, 89, 148
Taconis, Pieter W., xx, xxiv, 74
Taglioni, Marie, 98
Tank, 198, 227, 228, 234
Tarlet, Police inspector, 155, 162, 183
Telegraph cable, 180
Territorial Infantry, 191
Thanatos, 35
The Apotheosis of Ernest, 87
The Crusaders, 45, 75, 91, 97
The Dutch Law of Persons, xxxi
The Hague Convention, 124, 125, 201
The Hague School, 74
The Tower of London, 23, 179
Thermal cure, 158
Third Council of War, 183, 190, 191, 220, 222, 234, 235, 237
Third Republic, 11, 116, 232
Thomson, Basil, 169, 171-176
Tinsley, Richard, 24-26, 149
Toonel School, 75
Torpedo, 128, 181, 227
Tourbey, Jeanne, 90
Traitor, 116, 118, 119, 167, 198, 215, 235, 246
Treason, 13, 116-118, 120, 190
Tricolor, 148
Triple Alliance, 181, 200
Triple Entente, xiii, 142, 181, 200
Trocadéro, 77, 79, 90
Trottoir roulant rapide, 78
True Woman, xxx, xlii
T-service, 24
Tuberculosis, xix, 201
Tumpang, 42, 44, 46, 50, 85

U

U-boat, 132
Union Generale, 14, 115-117
University of Annals (Paris), xxxviii
Ūrvashi, xxxix, 18

V

Van Woostraat, xxxiii, 83
Vātsāyana, 101
VB Codebook, 181
Védrines, Jules, 230
Venereal disease, 30, 190
Venus, 88, 97
Verster, J. T. Z. Balbian, 37, 91
Vichy, 158
Victoria Hotel, Amsterdam, 144
Victorian morality, viii, 8, 9, 111
Vienna Electricity Exhibition, 78
Vietnamese, 78
Vigo, 152, 154, 168, 175-177, 185, 211, 258, 259
Villa Rémy, 142, 146, 160
Villany, Adoree 108
Vincennes, 237
Violent, 53, 64, 122, 124, 221
Violin, 88, 100
Virginal nudity, 108
Visser, Mr., xix, xx, 4, 36
Vital Statistics Office of Holland, xli
Vittel, 156-163, 165, 189, 197, 214, 218, 219, 224, 226, 253, 257
Voyeuristic, 88

W

Wadden Sea, 1
Wanderlust, 30, 58, 152, 256
War College, 114
War Ministry, 139, 140, 155, 187, 205, 206, 209, 213, 262
Ward, Clara (Princess of Chimay), 89
Wiesbaden, xxix, 40, 251
Wild Woman, 12
Wilhelm, Crown Prince, 164-166, 217, 219
Wilhelmina, Queen of Holland, 45, 75, 236
Willem I military base, 42, 52, 81
Willem's Cross, 63
William II, Kaiser, 20
William III, King of Holland, xvii
Wolsink, 38, 63
Womanizer, xxv, xxvi, 19, 55, 118
Worth, Charles Frederick, 80
Wurfbain, Monsieur, 146, 166

X

Xenophobia, 191

Y

Yser, 149, 262

Z

Zambeli, Carlotta la, 102
Zelle, Johannes Hendriks, 236
Zeppelin, 124, 262
Zola, Émile, xiv

About the Author

Sanusri Bhattacharya is Associate Professor of the Department of Philosophy at B.Z.S.M. Mahavidyapith in the district of Bankura, West Bengal, India. She is author of *Terrorism and Moral Questions* (2007). She has been a Nehru-Fulbright Visiting Lecturer Fellow to USA in 2013, and lives and works in India.

www.ingramcontent.com/pod-product-compliance
Lightning Source LLC
Chambersburg PA
CBHW070137100426
42743CB00013B/2728